Tradition
and
Reform

in the Teaching
of English:
a History

We teach and teach and they learn and learn: if they didn't, we wouldn't.
James N. Britton

The relationship between poet and reader is a touching of hands in the dark.
C. Day Lewis

"Classic." A book which people praise and don't read.
Mark Twain

The fact is, we are not a book-reading people. The vast majority of our ninety-odd millions of population have no literary appetites which cannot be supplied by the newspapers, the magazine, and an occasional "best seller" novel.
Bliss Perry

All the historical books which contain no lies are extremely tedious.
Anatole France

Tradition
and
Reform

in the Teaching
of English:
a History

Arthur N. Applebee

NATIONAL COUNCIL OF TEACHERS OF ENGLISH

ACKNOWLEDGMENTS: Grateful acknowledgment is made to the following authors and publishers for permission to quote from their works in this history. For passages from *How to Read a Page* by I. A. Richards: Reprinted by permission, copyright 1942 by W. W. Norton & Company, and Routledge & Kegan Paul, Ltd. Copyright renewed 1969 by I. A. Richards. / For a passage from *Understanding Poetry: An Anthology for College Students* by Cleanth Brooks and Robert Penn Warren: Reprinted by permission of Holt, Rinehart and Winston, Inc. / For passages from *High School English Textbooks: A Critical Examination* by James J. Lynch and Bertrand Evans: Reprinted by permission, © 1963 by the Council for Basic Education. / For a passage from *Slums and Suburbs* by James Bryant Conant (McGraw-Hill Book Co. and Signet Books): Reprinted by permission of the project administrator, Conant Studies of American Education, Educational Testing Service.

STAFF EDITORS: Ann Warren, Diane Allen
STAFF DESIGNER: Norma Phillips Meyers
COVER DESIGN: William May

Library of Congress Catalog Card Number 74-82650
NCTE Stock Number: 55014
ISBN 0-8141-5501-4

National Council of Teachers of English
1111 Kenyon Road, Urbana, Illinois 61801
Third Printing, April 1976

Contents

7058

Preface

Though English is a young subject, less than one hundred years old, its teachers have from the beginning been leaders in the reform of school programs. The emergence of the subject during the 1880s and 1890s was itself part of one battle between the "ancient" and the "modern" subjects for control of the college preparatory curriculum. With the position of the moderns secure by the turn of the century, English took the lead in throwing off these preparatory school functions and establishing a new pattern of common school education. This was part of the first wave of the progressive movement in education, and though teachers of English remained suspicious of the movement in its institutional form, they remained true to its spirit and moved in the same directions. As a result, the 1920s and 1930s can be seen as a grand experiment in implementing progressive education in the English classroom, an experiment that overreached itself during the 1940s and early 1950s, losing sight of its own original principles. This in turn provoked a reaction, short but intense, which brought the profession together in support of "academic" goals during the 1960s: teachers from elementary school through college recognized a unity of purpose that had sometimes been forgotten. This academic resurgence, though it began in a rejection of progressivism, in the end led to the reestablishment of the authentic parts of the progressive vision, allowing teachers in the 1970s to begin again, with new insight and new courage, the difficult task of fundamental educational reform.

The factors which have led to these changes in the teaching of English are complex. Shifts in school populations, educational philosophy, psychology, and the scholarly disciplines from which English as a secondary school subject derives have all had a more or less direct influence upon instructional patterns. How these interact with one another, with goals for English teaching, and with classroom practice are major concerns in a history such as this. Our knowledge of the history of the teaching of English is not yet definitive, but we know enough to trace the broad movements in the theory and practice of the teaching of English from its origin to the present day.

The universe of concern in such a study is large, almost limitless. It moves outward on the one hand through general trends in educational thought to patterns of social and moral philosophy, and on the other through the disciplines of English to patterns of scholarship and definitions of knowledge. And it moves inward toward the specific changes in classroom practice in the schools and classrooms of the nation. The approach taken here is a compromise between these competing demands. We will sketch enough of the general trends to understand the forces to which English was responding, and enough of the classroom practice to give a sense of what was happening in the schools; but the emphasis remains on trends and movements in the teaching of English as a whole, broad strokes rather than fine details. The universe has been simplified, too, by focussing on the aspect of the teaching of English that has, since the beginning, taken up the largest proportion of the teacher's time, energy, and enthusiasm: the teaching of literature. This focus on literature rather than on English instruction will cause little distortion in this history; the goals and emphases have moved in parallel for the major components of the course. Where there have been important developments which do not impinge upon literature directly, I have tried to point to them at least in passing.

The general pattern of the discussion is chronological, though more in a sense of "epochs" and "movements" than a year-by-year recital of events. This introduces another kind of distortion at some points in the narrative, with movements parallel in time but distant in motivation discussed at some distance from one another; this is especially true of transitional periods when one era is coming to an end and another beginning. Again, I have tried to indicate parallel developments at least in passing, pointing the reader forward or back to fuller discussions; but the real solution to this problem is to emphasize that the separate chapters are not meant to be a chronicle, and provide one only when the book is taken as a whole. For those who want it, Appendix I offers a brief chronology.

For the teacher of English, a book such as this is both an end and a beginning; it gives a sense of where his profession has been in the past, and a sense of the issues and the forces which will shape it in the future. In offering this history in the form I have chosen, looking at the past on its own terms rather than using it to provide "perspective" on contemporary issues, I am inviting others to use the material provided here for their own ends; preliminary versions of the manuscript have already been used as evidence of "clear trends" with which I do not agree. One point in particular that has arisen several times has been an analogy between developments in English and a pendulum swing between student and subject, affective response and cognitive discipline. In spite of its apparent applicability, I think this is a misleading metaphor: for all of its apparent motion, the pendulum never moves forward, never changes, never offers us something new. The teaching of English, on the contrary, has had a rapid and healthy evolution. I think it is better today than it has ever been in the past; it is certainly different.

Such disagreements are themselves healthy, and if this book can serve to generate many more of them it will have served one useful purpose. Still, I have come away from my study of the past with a number of quite specific lessons which I think it has taught me. These arise from the fabric of the history, rather than from its argument; they are certainly not theses defended in the course of the narrative. Yet I think they are important and have drawn them together in the last chapter.

There has been very little systematic exploration of the history of the teaching of English, though there are a few very useful beginnings. Much of the material is relatively inaccessible, in doctoral dissertations and out-of-print reports; this has meant, inevitably, that each discussion has had to begin without any assumptions of prior knowledge. I hope this book will change that, reducing the need for each writer to recapitulate the universe. There is much to learn: I offer the book confident that it is accurate in its general tenor and emphasis, and equally sure that it must be wrong in some of its detail.

Many people have courageously worked their way through early drafts of this manuscript, pointing me in new directions and correcting my errors. Early in the project, I asked a group of prominent members of the National Council of Teachers of English to list for me titles which they felt had "significantly influenced" the teaching of literature in American secondary schools. It was a deliberately ambiguous and difficult brief, but they responded generously and in detail. Their suggestions ranged across all fields, from literary criticism to educational philosophy, psychology, and sociology. All the references were eventually followed up, and some led me in new and unexpected directions. For these lists, then, special thanks to G. Robert Carlsen, Alfred H. Grommon, W. Wilbur Hatfield, Lou L. LaBrant, Albert H. Marckwardt, Joseph Mersand, and James R. Squire.

The manuscript itself has been read in whole or in part by many people. A few of these have influenced it deeply, forcing me to redraft and revise again and again. For asking the difficult questions, then, thanks to James R. Squire, Lou L. LaBrant, Roger K. Applebee, and Marcia Lynn Applebee. The last of these has had the dubious pleasure of reading each of the drafts in all of its versions.

My final debt of gratitude is to Robert L. Church. His comments, offered as an historian rather than a teacher of English, were the most fundamental of all. He taught me to ask a different set of questions than I had asked before, gave enough encouragement to keep me going, and enough criticism to force me to begin again, and yet again.

London, England   A.N.A.
February 1973

Above all things, let the Scriptures be the chief and most frequently used reading book, both primary and high schools and the very young should be kept in the gospels. Is it not proper and right that every human being, by the time he has reached his tenth year, should be familiar with the holy gospels, in which the very core and marrow of his life is bound?
—Martin Luther[1]

To define a uniformity and purity of language in America—to destroy the provincial prejudices that originate in the trifling differences of dialect, and produce reciprocal ridicule—to promote the interest of literature and harmony of the United States—is the most ardent wish of the author.
—Noah Webster, in the Preface to
his **Blue-Backed Speller** (1783)[2]

... familiarity with Greek and Roman writers is especially adapted to form the taste, and to discipline the mind, both in thought and diction, to relish of what is elevated, chaste, and simple.
—The Yale Report of 1828[3]

It is not what a boy learns at school that makes the man, but how he learns it. . . . If the acquisition of knowledge were the chief object in education, very useful as an acquaintance with the dead languages is, indispensable in fact to the man of letters, one might with propriety doubt the expediency of spending so large a portion of youth and early manhood in the study. But the earnest, laborious student of language develops a power which no other training could possibly give him, and in comparison with which all his acquisitions of mere knowledge sink into utter insignificance.
—Francis Gardner, Headmaster of
Boston Latin School, 1867[4]

Latin has come to be taught confessedly as a gymnastic . . . and Latin sets the pattern for English.
—Samuel Thurber, Master at Girls'
High School, Boston, 1902[5]

Chapter I

Early Traditions

Though English did not emerge as a major school subject until the 1890s, the instructional traditions which have shaped it are much older. At least three traditions were already fully intertwined in the English curriculum of 1890: an ethical tradition which placed its emphasis on moral and cultural development, a classical tradition of intellectual discipline and close textual study, and a nonacademic tradition more concerned with "enjoyment" and "appreciation." The interactions of these various traditions in the early history of the teaching of English represent less a battle between conflicting points of view than a web of accepted assumptions, all the more pervasive and far-reaching because they were never made explicit. To untangle some of this web, we will begin with the ethical tradition, and the earliest form of systematic instruction in the vernacular—the teaching of reading.

The Ethical Tradition in Elementary Instruction

The roots of elementary reading instruction as it developed in the American colonies go back at least to the Council of Mainz (813), which firmly linked religious instruction with the teaching of reading. After some seven hundred years, this tradition was carried over into the teaching of English through the translation of the Latin "Book of Hours" as the *Prymer of Salisbury Use* (ca. 1490). Though the primer and the ABC were initially separate, they were combined toward the end of the sixteenth century to lower printing costs.

1

Through this practice the beginning reading book acquired both a title, "primer," and a heritage of ethical concern.[6]

The typical early primer included an alphabet and syllabarium, a creed, a catechism, and a collection of prayers and devotional exercises. Though these materials were originally included simply because they were considered important for the child to know, during the Reformation they became caught up in the struggles between conflicting faiths. As catechisms proliferated, primers multiplied apace.

The New England Primer

In the New World the tradition of instruction through sectarian primers continued unabated. Though at first relying on British imports, the American colonists soon began to issue their own editions, culminating in *The New England Primer,* issued by Benjamin Harris, a Boston printer, sometime between 1686 and 1690. Harris had previously published a similar book in London, under the title *The Protestant Tutor for Youth* (1679). For the New England version he reduced the size of the book and gave it a new title, but the parts remained those with which the colonists were familiar: each began with the letters of the alphabet, followed by a syllabarium, the Lord's Prayer, at least one catechism, and various other religious and instructional pieces, often heavy with moral lessons. One of the most famous is the child's prayer beginning, "Now I lay me down to sleep," which appeared for the first time in a 1737 version of the *Primer;* its author is unknown.[7]

Little else in the *Primer* was as literary as this little verse. For the most part the selections were didactic, chosen for the virtue of their dogma rather than for their suitability for children learning to read. The book had one major advantage over its predecessors, however; as a result of the Westminster Assembly (1643-49), there was for the first time a single generally accepted catechism.[8] Incorporating this catechism in a familiar instructional format, and with a title pitched toward the colonists' regional pride, *The New England Primer* was an immediate success. For over a hundred years it was without serious challenge as the instrument of beginning reading instruction in America, and for another hundred years it was frequently reprinted.

The *Primer* arose out of a particular tradition of instruction to fulfill the particular needs of the American colonists. By its very success, it generated challengers and imitators, and though the first of these soon fell away, other forces eventually reshaped the American landscape, demanding new materials for use in the schools. Though the *Primer* itself attempted to reflect changing national concerns in its successive editions, the basic character of the work was inalterable. The young United States, on the other hand, was faced with problems other than those which had dominated its colonial days. Chief among these were problems of unity: how to provide the disparate colonial states with a common tradition of culture and government, a common spirit of responsible republican citizenship, a common language that would transcend the regional dialects. Religious dogma, which had determined the history of the primers and given them their internal structure, was no longer of prime importance.

Webster's Grammatical Institute

The belief in the power of the primers to achieve aims far beyond the limited goal of learning to read, however, continued. Noah Webster clearly had faith in it when as a teacher in Orange County, New York, he compiled a spelling book designed explicitly to foster the unity and common culture which he sensed that the nation lacked. Published in 1783 as *The First Part of a Grammatical Institute of the English Language*, his *Blue-Backed Speller* also filled a need for an American source of books at a time when the usual supplies from Britain were upset by the war.[9] A true descendent of the earlier texts, Webster's *Speller* combined under one cover alphabet, primer, speller, and reader, using materials which were unabashedly adult and didactic. Thus a section entitled "Precepts concerning the Social Relations" offered advice to young women:

> Be cautious in listening to the addresses of men. Is the suitor addicted to low vices? is he profane? is he a gambler? a tippler? a spendthrift? a haunter of taverns? and, above all, is he a scoffer at religion? — Banish such a man from thy presence, his heart is false, and his hand would lead thee to wretchedness and ruin.[10]

Still it was not the lessons but the spelling lists which were the most important part of the book. Webster set out consciously to reform and simplify the erratic American spelling system of his day, and to impose an order on the chaos that had previously been the rule. With his speller and, later, *The American Dictionary* (1828), he to a large extent succeeded. Like the *Primer* before it, Webster's *Speller* became a nearly universal medium for instruction; it was still in use in some areas of the country as late as 1900.

The third part of Webster's *Grammatical Institute* is also important for our purposes, for *An American Selection of Lessons in Reading and Speaking* (1795) was much closer in format to a school reader in the modern sense. In this volume, Webster continued the secularization of school materials; rather than the Catholicism or Protestantism of early books, selections were chosen for patriotic content, ethical emphasis, and usefulness in the development of the speaking voice. (Oratory and elocution had become important concerns to a nation newly constituted as a republic and destined to be governed, or so it seemed, by the constant disputations of its Congress.) Though Webster no longer defined appropriate selections in the rigid terms of the early primers, one of the major functions of school materials, as he wrote in his introduction, remained to "impress interesting truths upon youthful minds."[11] Webster's *American Selection*, together with the grammar that formed the second part of the *Grammatical Institute*, never attained the overwhelming popularity of the *Blue-Backed Speller;* nonetheless it dominated instruction for nearly fifty years, and set a pattern which most of its immediate successors followed.

A number of collections similar to Webster's were quite popular at a regional level. Most noted were those by Lindley Murray and Caleb Bingham in the 1790s, and John Pierpont a few decades later. In their editing and choice of selections, these books reflected a Protestant ethic of thrift, honesty, ownership of property, love of country and of God, and dedication to work. Though increasingly secular in content, they continued in their own way the colonial tradition of moral education as a primary function of reading instruction. The *Spectator* papers and other works of the Augustans dominated during the early part of the century, being in turn supplanted by the works of the then-contemporary Romantic writers during the 1820s. Still, it was not until the 1830s that secular began to consistently outnumber biblical selections in school readers.[12]

The texts which followed Webster gave increasing attention to the literary quality of the selections. Lindley Murray's three books (1799-1801) were devoted half to poetry, while Pierpont's series (1820-30) included, for the first time, excerpts from Shakespeare. Nonetheless there was a strong counter-movement toward "content" readers in which reading exercises were subordinated to the study of other subjects. The century produced, among others, *The Christian Reader* (made up entirely of tracts and hymns) and *The Farmer's School-Book*, with offerings on "Making and Preserving Cheese," "Raising Calves," and "The Nature of Manure." The excesses of these readers helped literature to emerge in the 1880s as the accepted vehicle for reading instruction, but only after a long and often vituperative professional debate.[13]

McGuffey's Readers

But before literature emerged as a school subject in its own right, there was one more giant in the teaching of reading. This was a six-book series by William Holmes McGuffey, the first volumes of which appeared in 1836; as with the two earlier texts, their use was virtually universal for the next fifty years.

The content of this series was again decidedly moral, though not overtly religious, advocating a stern Protestant ethic through carefully chosen selections from a wide variety of American and European authors. Patriotism was fostered and American productions given a solid place, but the readers were not as narrowly nationalistic as Webster's had been. The books were graded by level of difficulty, with selections of real literary value predominating in the fifth and sixth readers, though all of the lessons remained short—usually a page or two at most. And finally, the teaching materials surrounding the selections placed strong emphasis on the mechanics of reading aloud, presenting such topics as "Articulation," "Inflection," "Accent," "Emphasis," "Modulation," and "Poetic Pause."[14]

These three early educational giants—*The New England Primer,* Webster's *Grammatical Institute,* and the McGuffey readers—did more than just embody the changing interests and pedagogy of the nation they served. They also provided a common background of culture and allusion, a common heritage for a nation too young to have any other. The *Primer* spread a common catechism, Webster's *Institute* advanced a common system of spelling and promoted a chauvinistic nationalism, McGuffey's readers created a literary heritage, even if one based on fragments and precis. This sense of an ethical and cultural heritage has certainly remained as one of the major goals of the teaching of literature, though later generations of teachers would come to question the kind of heritage a collection of excerpts could offer.

The Classical Model in School and College

Even as the ethical tradition was developing as part of reading instruction, other pedagogical models were emerging in the secondary schools and colleges. Most of these models developed from an analogy between the study of English and the study of the classical languages, an analogy conditioned and reinforced by the prevailing doctrines of "mental discipline" and "faculty psychology." Throughout the period under discussion—roughly from 1750 to 1865—the fate of English studies in the high schools is similar to that in the colleges. Sometimes one exerts the leading influence, sometimes the other, but the difference between the two is never great.

Though the roots of English studies can be traced back at least to the Latin catalogs of John Leland and Bishop John Bale in the 1540s, it is not till the end of the nineteenth century that there was anything even approximating what we now roughly subsume under the heading "the study of English."[15] The pedagogical theory of mental discipline was at the root of the long delay; it held that the purpose of education was to exercise and train the mental faculties, in particular the faculties of "memory" and "reason."[16] The value of any given subject was directly proportional to the degree of internal structure which the subject exhibited, the apparatus of rules and "knowledge" which a student could be required to master. The complex vocabulary and rules of syntax of the classical languages had offered an obvious and fertile field for such training. Other subjects could compete for attention only as they demonstrated that they, too, had a substance that would insure the same discipline of the mind that the classical languages provided. Thus the problem which English, and in particular English literature, had to surmount was that, as far as the classicist could see, it was too easy—it had no substance, no organized body of knowledge, no rules, no theory, in short nothing to promote the rigorous mental training, the discipline, that was the justification of an education. Only by being grafted onto other disciplines with more evident justifications did literature find a place at all in the early curriculum, for it was only in such a form that it seemed to offer more than the "mere chatter about Shelley" of which so many complained.[17]

English Grammar

Grammar was the first formal study of English to become a widespread part of the curriculum, and it did so by taking up the methods and approaches which had dominated in the teaching of the classical languages. Grammar was an especially powerful model because of the various traditions in its own history—once "English grammar" had become respectable, a variety of speculative, historical, rhetorical, and textual studies that were loosely related to it were similarly legitimized; some, like rhetoric, were so revitalized that they became permanently separated from their parent subject.[18]

Grammatical studies in the classical languages had traditionally emphasized two elements: the learning of rules, and their "use" or practical application. An extensive methodology had grown up around both aspects, and this was transferred more or less intact to studies of English grammar.[19] "Parsing" and analysis of sentences, diagramming, the learning of paradigms, and the correction of "errors" in usage all entered the curriculum through this tradition, together with the rote memorization of definitions and rules for the various grammatical categories. Such studies claimed to be teaching the practical use of language, as well as to offer formal discipline in the best classical tradition.

The Prescriptive Tradition

The shift of grammatical studies from the classics to English involved a shift from a method of *teaching* a foreign language to one of *correcting* a native one. During the eighteenth century this was accentuated by an attempt to regularize the English language on the model of Latin and Greek, leading, among other results, to Bishop William Warburton's editions of Shakespeare and Richard Bentley's of Milton. Bentley's comments on the last lines of *Paradise Lost* are well known, but they are worth quoting again as an illustration of the kind of criticism that was developing, as well as of the breadth of interest of the studies that were then subsumed under the heading of "grammar." Bentley's demands for "proper" usage and his ultimately specious adherence to logical canons are typical of the approach when it was codified, though his works were repudiated by many who shared his general point of view. He concludes his "New Edition" of *Paradise Lost* (1732) with a lengthy note.

> And how can the Expression be justified, *with* wand'ring Steps and slow? Why wand'ring? Erratic Steps? Very improper; when in the Line before, they were *guided by Providence*—And why *Slow*? when even *Eve* profess'd her Readiness and Alacrity for the Journey . . . . And why *their solitary way*? All Words to represent a sorrowful Parting? When even their former Walks in Paradise were as solitary as their Way now: there being no Body besides Them Two, both here and there. Shall I therefore, after so many prior Presumptions, presume at last to offer a Distich, as close as may be to the Author's Words, and entirely agreeable to his Scheme?
> THEN hand in hand with SOCIAL steps their way
> Through EDEN took, WITH HEAV'NLY COMFORT CHEER'D.[20]

When Hugh Blair and his colleagues separated rhetorical from grammatical studies later in the century, they approached literature in a similar way.

The prescriptive tradition of language instruction became dominant between 1750 and 1800, finding its way into the schools where it has flourished ever since. Noah Webster included a school grammar in this tradition as the second part of his *Grammatical Institute* (1784) and Caleb Bingham prepared a similar volume as part of his own series (1799).[21] Though both enjoyed a moderate initial success, they were soon supplanted by *Murray's Grammar*, published in England in 1795 and soon in use in America. This text was more systematic in its approach than the others had been, and virtually dominated the field for the next several decades. By 1850 it had gone through some two hundred editions.[22] Lindley Murray has been dubbed "the father of English grammar" as a result of this text, though he is a father figure whom many generations of schoolchildren, and not a few of their teachers, would have been happy to do without.

With a ready supply of texts, an inherited methodology, and a recognizable justification in the theory of mental discipline, English grammar was offered in most American schools by 1810. This was tacitly recognized by the College of New Jersey (which later became Princeton University), when it asked its 1819 candidates for admission to be "well acquainted" with English grammar: it was the first time that competence in any aspect of the vernacular had been required for entrance to any college in America. By 1860 most colleges had introduced similar requirements.[23]

Rhetoric and Oratory

Grammar, however, was considered more or less a school subject, a prerequisite for the higher studies of the college but not, usually, a study which would be continued there. The growth of English studies at a more advanced level owes its first impetus to a group of Scottish educators who divorced the studies of rhetoric and oratory from their early roots in grammar during roughly the same period that grammar was itself becoming an important school subject. The group included, among others, Adam Smith, David Hume, Lord Kames, and Hugh Blair; they argued in the decades after 1740 that the arts of public reading and speaking deserved an important place in the education of clergy and laity alike.

Logic, under which the rules of grammar, rhetoric, and "composition" had often been subsumed, was the immediate parent, Edinburgh the birthplace. Here from 1730 on, Professor John Stevenson devoted the first hour of his two-hour-a-day logic class to rhetoric, illustrating the classical rules of composition with extracts from Dryden, Addison, Pope, and other English and French writers. Here in 1748 Adam Smith began a series of public lectures on rhetoric and belles lettres, the first time that literary criticism had been dealt with in a separate course of lectures.[24] When Smith left for the University of Glasgow in 1751, to become like Stevenson a professor of logic, the series continued under Robert Watson—who in turn left to take up a chair of logic, rhetoric, and metaphysics at St. Andrews in 1756. In 1759 Smith's mantle descended to Hugh Blair, an Edinburgh clergyman and literary figure well known in his day both for his published sermons and his championship of the spurious poems of Ossian. Under Blair, the lectures were for the first time given within the university, rather than as part of an extramural series; Blair himself became Regius Professor of Rhetoric and Belles Lettres in 1762.

Blair apparently borrowed Adam Smith's lecture notes, and certainly there was little difference in the approaches of this early series of teachers. Whereas the grammarians were concerned with syntax and morphology, the rhetoricians placed their emphasis on "expression," both written and oral (the latter eventually evolving into the separate studies of oratory). Diction, style, figurative language, the "flowers" of rhetoric—these were the concerns to which they turned their attention and which, until a new movement in the 1880s and 1890s began to argue that practice was more important than theory, constituted the teaching of composition in American secondary schools and colleges.[25] Like the grammarians who were their professional colleagues, the rhetoricians were prescriptive, filling their texts with rules to be followed, and with examples of errors of expression as well as of the successes of the best writers. The main point of reference was the Latin and Greek tradition, now translated into English. Blair made extensive use of classical illustrations in his lectures, discussing Virgil, Cicero, Aristophanes, Tasso, and many others. At the same time, however—and this is the significant departure which Blair shared with John Stevenson and Adam Smith— he wanted to argue that the principles which they followed are universal and could be applied to English and French authors as well. Favorite examples included Addison, Pope, Swift, Dryden, Milton, and Shakespeare, though the latter violated many of the rhetorical "laws." (Blair explained Shakespeare's transgressions as "blemishes" due to "the grossness of the age in which he lived.")[26] It is interesting to note that, while the "greats" of English literature were acknowledged, many of the most thoroughly discussed authors were contemporaries or near-contemporaries of the rhetoricians. Pope and Swift were still living when Professor Stevenson began his lectures in 1730; the *Tatler* (1709-11) and *Spectator* (1711-12) papers were just twenty years old. All were at a peak of popularity.

Blair published his notes as *Lectures on Rhetoric and Belles Lettres* in 1783 and retired from active lecturing the following year. The book quickly became a popular text in America as well as England. Yale adopted it in 1785, Harvard in 1788, Dartmouth as late as 1822; during the nineteenth century it also found its way into many secondary school classrooms.[27]

Though the Scottish rhetoricians made a clean theoretical separation of grammar and rhetoric, in practice both approaches were simultaneously applied to literature. Throughout the nineteenth century, "rhetoric," "analysis," and "criticism" usually indicated much the same course of study, in which a literary text would be critically examined to insure that it conformed with the prescriptive rules of grammar and rhetoric, all in the ultimate service of the student's own speaking and writing skills.[28]

The rhetorical approach of Blair and his colleagues did not require any literature to be read at all, but by the 1840s some schools were supplementing the rhetoric handbooks with individual works for parsing and analysis. This was an important shift, yet it was a change only in the material and not in the method of instruction. The texts were few in number till the end of the century, and approached with the same exhaustive line-by-line analysis that the handbooks had illustrated. *Paradise Lost* found its way into the curriculum by this route in the first half of the nineteenth century, and it is not accidental that it is also the most Latinate of our English classics. It was often joined by Pope's *Essay on Man,* another favorite illustration in the books of the rhetoricians.[29] These works provided an excellent exercise ground for the grammars and rhetorics of the time, and though they must be seen as the forerunners of the school editions of English authors that would dominate instruction at the end of the century, it is clear that any interest in literature that might emerge from such studies would arise *in spite of* rather than *through* the approach that was taken.

These studies were the first of the English studies to win acceptance at the college level, though they were generally thought of as a rather minor aspect of preparation for the clergy. It was under their umbrella that America got its first professor of English, in the person of a clergyman, Ebenezer Kinnersley. Kinnersley was the second head of the "English School" of an academy in Philadelphia, and was appointed professor of the English tongue and oratory when the academy became a college in 1755. (Still later, it became the University of Pennsylvania.) Kinnersley was also a scientist of some note and a friend of Benjamin Franklin; his successor in 1773 was a lawyer by trade. Other universities slowly followed the same pattern; Harvard, for example, established its Boylston Professorship of Rhetoric and Oratory in 1806, with John Quincy Adams as the first incumbent (1806-09). During the tenure of Edward Tyrrel Channing (1819-51), the work at Harvard was expanded to include individual texts for parsing and analysis, but, as in the high schools of the period, the literature was still well subordinated to the rhetorical studies.[30] Though Amherst experimented with a course in English and American Literature in 1827 and Dartmouth mentioned English literature in 1822, before 1860 English studies in most colleges consisted of rhetoric and oratory, and nothing more.[31]

Literary History

By the late 1840s, riding a crest of interest in historical and biographical studies, literary history had also emerged as an important aspect of English studies. This took as its model the studies of ancient civilization, which were a well-established part of the classical curriculum. Though both the classical course and its English translation began with broad and humanistic goals, an emphasis on rote memorization and on names, dates, and places, dominated virtually all applications.[32]

The first textbook in this tradition to be widely used in America was Thomas Budge Shaw's *Outlines of English Literature,* published in England in 1848 and reprinted in America the following year. The book was a simple narrative and included no selections from the authors at all, but it was very popular and went through many editions before the end of the century.[33] Charles D. Cleveland,

A Philadelphia schoolmaster, also published a history of English literature in 1849 and followed it up with a history of American literature ten years later. These were very successful. Boston English High School, having been content with Blair's *Rhetoric* for twenty years, introduced Cleveland in 1852, substituting Shaw six years later.[34]

The entry for each author in Cleveland's series was rather similar to an encyclopedia listing—all the dates, the books, the immediate and historical reactions. Though generous excerpts were also provided, the "Questions for Examination" which conclude his volumes reflect the real emphasis. Of Lady Russell they ask, "Whose wife? . . . What does Burnett say of her letters?" Of Robert Dodsley, "What was his first publication?" Of Milton, "What is his first poetical work, and what its subject? What the second? Third? Fourth? Fifth? Sixth? Seventh? Eighth? Ninth? Tenth? . . . What does Brydges say of Johnson's Life of Milton?"[35] To our eyes such books are unattractive and even unpedagogical, but they take their shape from the emphasis on formal discipline already noted. If the value of a subject lies in its structure and in the demands that it puts upon memory, then pedagogically the soundest approach is the compendium (whether of grammar, rhetoric, or history) which presents that structure and that material in the most elaborate detail.

Histories such as Cleveland's and Shaw's became very popular during the 1850s and 1860s, and with their introduction schools for the first time began to claim to be teaching "literature" rather than rhetoric, oratory, or reading.[36] Still, though literary history was a popular subject, the curriculum was very unstable; schools changed from one textbook to another, and then changed back again—presumably because none of the texts were really satisfactory. By 1870 the emphasis on information in literary studies was well established, with examination questions like those Cleveland had proposed facing students throughout the country.[37] Such studies of facts about literature remain an element in high school instruction to the present day, though their justification has changed from mental discipline to knowledge of our literary heritage.

The Nonacademic Tradition

While an ethical tradition was emerging in elementary school reading materials, and a classical one in secondary schools and colleges, a more amorphous but equally important nonacademic tradition of English for "appreciation" was developing outside of the traditional curriculum. This made no attempt to justify English as an academic study, championing it instead on other, and at the time less arguable, grounds.

The Extracurriculum

One area in which the appreciative tradition flourished was the extracurriculum of the nineteenth century colleges, in particular in the students' literary and debating societies. The debates and journals of these clubs dealt with the political and philosophical issues of the time—issues more or less ruled out of the classical curriculum of the colleges. In their societies, students could debate the topics they wished, and could and did invite controversial figures to address them. Thus Ralph Waldo Emerson, whose Divinity School Address (1838) had come too close to pantheism for conservative faculties to accept, was able to speak three times at Williams, though the college had banned him from the campus. He always appeared under the auspices of a student group, in an off-campus building.[38] The many literary magazines founded and supported by the societies during this period provided a similar forum for students to debate contemporary issues, as well as to polish their skills in English composition; their college courses were more likely to concentrate on improving their Latin and Greek.

Through their libraries, the societies also offered the literary fare which the colleges themselves ignored. Throughout the country, these libraries were the only place for the student to read contemporary fiction, poetry, biography, or drama; on most campuses the libraries of the literary societies surpassed those of the colleges themselves in both quality and number of volumes. (It would not be until the end of the century that the great research collections in the modern languages would be established.)[39] All of the evidence available suggests that these activities were greeted enthusiastically by the students of the time, forming an important part of their collegiate experience, if not of their formal curriculum. As one measure of their concern, we can tally the response of Harvard students to an edition of Shakespeare offered for sale in 1807; of 175 students, 99 subscribed.[40]

It is important to note here that these activities were usually quite happily sanctioned by the colleges. What the colleges objected to was giving English literature a place as a subject to be *taught* rather than something to be read and enjoyed on one's own. Most expected that students would read widely in contemporary literature, both in secondary school and college.[41] But as will become apparent in the next chapter, this extracurriculum of the students' creation became after 1870 a major part of the curriculum itself.

The Finishing School

In the early nineteenth century, students in preparatory schools and colleges could expect exposure to English literature only through the extracurriculum. In the finishing schools, however, which sought to offer a "practical" course for the student who would not go on to college, English studies and the other modern subjects had a somewhat better time. Benjamin Franklin, for example, in his plans for a Philadelphia academy (ca.1750), had seen a practical value in English literature as a model for writing, as a subject for declamation and oral reading, and as a moral exemplum. Though Franklin's program was never implemented,[42] it was only a few years later that his friend Ebenezer Kinnersley became America's first professor of any aspect of English, when a similar Philadelphia academy became a college.

In the years that followed, the various English studies worked their way first into the "English" course that arose in opposition to the Latin or classical program of studies. Blair's *Rhetoric*, for example, was included in the first course of study (1821) at Boston English High School; it was never used at Boston Latin School at all.[43] In the college preparatory curriculum, as in the colleges themselves, the literary interests of the student were left to the extracurriculum, where debating clubs and literary societies grew up on the college model.[44]

Girls' schools during this period were almost all finishing schools, and English studies did find an early place in some of them; the belles lettres were considered an appropriate subject for polite conversation, if nothing else. Thus it was not entirely accidental that many early English textbooks were for "Young Ladies," or prepared by schoolmasters in girls' finishing schools.[45] Lacking a rigorous academic cachet, these "appreciative" studies of English carried a certain stigma, an air of being a second-best choice for those who it was presumed could not handle the rigors of classical studies. When Oxford, for example, finally allowed English into its examinations in 1873, it was only for the pass degree; honors students did their work in Latin. And as late as 1889, the U.S. Commissioner of Education in his annual report was tallying students taking English in business schools and in schools for the blind, deaf, and feebleminded, but not in public or private secondary schools.[46]

Reprise: 1865

By 1865, schools and colleges recognized a variety of loosely related minor studies of the vernacular—rhetoric, oratory, spelling, grammar, literary history, and reading all had their places, often conflicting with one another for attention.[47] Though many of these studies made use of literary selections, literary study in its own right had yet to find a place or a justification. Rhetorical and grammatical studies often included literary texts, but instruction was designed and carried out in the service of composition, not literature. Literary history, though the schools called it the teaching of literature, was biographical in emphasis and often involved no literature at all. Only the nonacademic tradition stressed the reading of literature for its own sake—and this tradition had found no place in the classical curriculum of the colleges or preparatory schools.

There is another way of viewing the situation, however, which highlights the potential strength of the embryonic subject: this is to recognize that by 1865, English studies had become a part of all three major traditions. Though in each case the study of English was subordinate to other goals, there was for the first time the possibility that all of these traditions might be united within the teaching of a single subject. And this is in fact what happened in the following decades: English studies increasingly found ways to claim the intellectual strength of the classical tradition, the moral strength of the ethical tradition, and the utilitarian strength of the nonacademic tradition. It was a fruitful alliance, though sometimes a confusing one, and led in the end to a subject whose content and goals had no real counterpart in any of the traditions from which it arose.

CHAPTER I NOTES

1. Quoted by Nila B. Smith, *American Reading Instruction* (New York: Silver, Burdett and Co., 1934), p. 11.
2. Smith, *American Reading Instruction*, p. 38.
3. Quoted by Theodore R. Sizer, *Secondary Schools at the Turn of the Century* (New Haven: Yale University Press, 1964), p. 2.
4. In *American Journal of Education* 19 (1870): 491. Quoted in Herbert Galen Lull, *Inherited Tendencies of Secondary Instruction in the United States*, University of California Publications in Education, vol. 3, no. 3 (April 15, 1913): 199.
5. Samuel Thurber, "The English Studies," *English Leaflet* 11 (December 1, 1902). Quoted by John Muth Bernd, *Approaches to the Teaching of Literature in Secondary School, 1900-1956* (Dissertation, University of Wisconsin, 1957; University Microfilms No. 24,264).
6. The name came about because the exercises began at "prime" or sunrise, the first hour of the day. On the early history, see Rudolph R. Reeder, *The Historical Development of School Readers and of Methods in Teaching Reading* (New York: Macmillan Co., 1900); Smith, *American Reading Instruction*; and Clifton Johnson, *Old-Time Schools and School Books* (New York: Dover Publications, 1963).
7. Textual variants of the *Primer* are discussed at length in Paul Leicester Ford, *The New England Primer* (New York: Teachers College, Columbia University, 1962). Ford also reprints the 1727 edition.
8. The catechism promulgated by the Assembly had both a "Longer" and a "Shorter" version. In America it was further abridged and simplified by John Cotton as "Spiritual Milk for American Babes."
9. Webster's *Speller* had many titles in later years, including *The American Spelling-Book* and *The Elementary Spelling Book*. It got its common name because it was usually bound between oak covers pasted over with blue paper. The popularity of the spelling bee in post-revolutionary America was due in part to the impetus of this book. On its use, see Reeder, *Historical Development*; Smith, *American Reading Instruction*; Johnson, *Old-Time Schools*; and J. Stephen Sherwin, *Four Problems in Teaching English* (Scranton, Pa.: International Textbook Co. for the National Council of Teachers of English, 1969).
10. Cited in Johnson, *Old-Time Schools*.
11. Cited in Smith, *American Reading Instruction*, p. 49.
12. See Ruth M. Elson, *Guardians of Tradition: American Schoolbooks of the Nineteenth Century* (Lincoln: University of Nebraska Press, 1964). The use of the various series has been discussed by several authors: Reeder, *Historical Development*, pp. 38 ff.; Smith, *American Reading Instruction*, pp. 51 ff; Joseph Mersand, "The Teaching of Literature in American High Schools: 1865-1900," in *Perspectives on English*, ed. Robert C. Pooley (New York: Appleton-Century-Crofts, Inc., 1960), pp. 273-75; and Peter D. Witt, *The Beginnings of the Teaching of the Vernacular Literature in the Secondary Schools of Massachusetts* (Dissertation, Harvard University, 1968; University Microfilms No. 69-11,507), pp. 39 ff.
13. This debate was in large part funded by the publishers, who had obvious vested interests in the results. Speeches and articles pro and con were commmissioned and reprinted as sales pamphlets. The most vitriolic

debate seems to have been between supporters of McGuffey's and of Marcius Willson's *School and Family* series. On *The Farmer's School-Book*, see Johnson, *Old-Time Schools*, p. 294.

14. These are from the 1879 edition of the *Fifth Reader* and represent quite sophisticated studies. "Articulation," for example, included attention to the different "Vocals, Subvocals, and Aspirates" which are the "Elementary Sounds" of English, as well as substitutions which are permissible from one sound to another, and "Faults to be remedied." This text is readily available in Commager's reprint edition. The emphasis on oral reading is typical; silent reading did not become important until the 1920s. *McGuffey's Fifth Eclectic Reader*, with a foreword by Henry Steele Commager (New York: New American Library, 1962).

15. On the early studies of English, see William Riley Parker, "Where Do English Departments Come From?" *College English* 28:5 (February 1967): 339-51. Parker's unpublished research has been extensively reported in Walter Scott Achtert, *A History of English Studies to 1883 Based on the Research of William Riley Parker*, (Dissertation, New York University, 1972; University Microfilms No. 72-31,057).

16. These doctrines and their effects on school programs are discussed at length in Lull, *Inherited Tendencies*. After 1835, when a translation of Pestalozzian methods became available in English, the faculties to be trained expanded to include aspects of "sensation" as well as memory and reason.

17. The quote is from E. A. Freeman, Regius Professor of History at Oxford, talking in 1887. To him the proper stock to which literature should be grafted was language study. The lack of substance in literary studies was also a frequent theme in America. Carpenter, Baker, and Scott in their early textbook argued that the slow start for English at the secondary level lay "not so much in the lack of desire for instruction as in the general feeling that there was no general body of instruction to give." George R. Carpenter, Franklin T. Baker, and Fred N. Scott, *The Teaching of English in the Elementary and the Secondary School* (New York: Longmans, Green, and Co., 1903), p. 45. Freeman is cited in *The Rise of English Studies*, D. J. Palmer (London: Oxford University Press for the University of Hull, 1965), p. 96.

18. The scope of grammar is suggested by the various topics treated in a grammar dating from about 166 B.C. It included attention to accurate reading, explanations of figures of speech, exposition of subject matter, explanations of rare words, studies of etymology, statements of regular grammatical forms, and criticism of poetry. Paul Monroe, ed., *A Cyclopedia of Education* (New York: Macmillan Co., 1911); from the article on "Philology."

19. The grammatical categories of traditional "school grammars" also derive directly from classical models. See Sherwin, *Four Problems*; Ian Michael, *English Grammatical Categories and the Tradition to 1800* (Cambridge: The University Press, 1970); and Louis G. Kelly, *25 Centuries of Language Teaching* (Rowley, Mass.: Newbury House, 1969).

20. Quoted in Sterling Andrus Leonard, *The Doctrine of Correctness in English Usage 1700-1800*, University of Wisconsin Studies in Language and Literature no. 25 (1929), p. 107. Leonard's book is the best single source on the prescriptive tradition.

21. This was titled *The Young Lady's Accidence*, reflecting a division of grammatical studies into accidence (morphology) and syntax. That it

was for "young ladies" reflects the fact that English studies found an earlier home in schools for girls than they did elsewhere, a point to which we will return.

22. This figure includes editions derived directly from Murray. Dumas Malone, ed., *Dictionary of American Biography* (New York: Charles Scribner's Sons, 1935). Cf. Johnson, *Old-Time Schools*.

23. Edna Hays, *College Entrance Requirements in English: Their Effects on the High Schools* (New York: Teachers College, Columbia University, 1936), p. 15.

24. Smith's qualifications for the series were the same as for his work in political science: a solid grounding in philosophy and in the classics at Cambridge, and wide reading on his own. Smith's lectures, which Meikle suggests may have been given under the auspices of the Philosophical Society, were popular enough to be renewed in subsequent years. They were never published, but have recently been rediscovered in the form of a student's lecture notes. The history of the Scottish rhetoricians has been recounted by Henry W. Meikle, "The Chair of Rhetoric and Belles Lettres," *University of Edinburgh Journal* 13 (Autumn 1945): 89-103, and from a slightly different perspective in the introduction to Smith's lecture notes (Adam Smith, *Lectures on Rhetoric and Belles Lettres*, edited with an introduction and notes by John M. Lothian (Camden, N.J.: Thomas Nelson & Sons, 1963). See also Palmer, *Rise of English Studies*, 171-78; Michael, *English Grammatical Categories*, 197; and Parker, "Where Do English Departments Come From?"

25. Scott and Carpenter were active in this movement, as was Barrett Wendell at Harvard. See F. N. Scott and J. V. Denny, *Paragraph Writing* (1891), and Barrett Wendell, *English Composition* (1891). The "flowers" was J. Mennye's designation in his *English Grammar* (1785). Cf. Leonard, *Doctrine of Correctness*, p. 114.

26. Hugh Blair, *Lectures in Rhetoric and Belles Lettres*, 3 vols. (Dublin, 1783). Quotes are from vol. 1, p. 48.

27. Blair's book was eventually translated into German (1785-89), French (1796), Spanish (1798), Italian (1801), and Russian (1837); it was the most successful of many similar texts helping to spread the rhetoricians' approach. See Witt, *Beginnings of Teaching Vernacular*, p. 36; and Meikle, "Chair of Rhetoric," p. 91.

28. The course often took its title from the particular text used. Later in the century, the rhetorical forms of intensive analysis were joined by others deriving from philological studies. These will be dealt with in the next chapter.

29. For a near-contemporary account, see Anna C. Brackett, "Teaching of English Literature," *The Academy* 3 (February 1888): 14-18. See also Witt, *Beginnings of Teaching Vernacular*, pp. 27, 228.

30. Adams' *Lectures on Rhetoric and Oratory* (1810) were widely praised. Channing was also very popular; he numbered Dana, Emerson, Holmes, and Thoreau among his students. Parker, "Where Do English Departments Come From?" See also Witt, *Beginnings of Teaching Vernacular*, pp. 35, 48.

31. Grandgent has commented on this in discussing the modern languages at Harvard: "As to English, its advance has been more in the nature of peaceful penetration. Its delay in getting started seems to have been due, not to opposition, but to a general failure to see in it anything more than a minor element in preparation for the ministry. Charles H.

Grandgent, "The Modern Languages," in *The Development of Harvard University Since the Inauguration of President Eliot 1869-1929*, ed. Samuel Eliot Morison (Cambridge, Mass.: Harvard University Press, 1930). At the secondary level the situation was no better. As late as 1876, Carpenter, Baker, and Scott claim there "was scarcely to be found in the United States, any definite, well-organized system of secondary instruction in the mother-tongue." Hays echoes their findings, claiming that English was "non-existent" before 1870. Carpenter, Baker, and Scott, *Teaching of English*, p. 46; and Hays, *College Entrance Requirements*, p. 10.

32. Lull, *Inherited Tendencies*, documents both the original goals and the degenerate practice.

33. Shaw was a Cambridge graduate teaching in Russia; he prepared the book for his students there. On Shaw's life, see Sir Leslie Stephen and Sir Sidney Lees, eds., *The Dictionary of National Biography* (London: Oxford University Press, 1921-22).

34. See Witt, *Beginnings of Teaching Vernacular*, pp. 173-75; John E. Stout, *The Development of High School Curricula in the North Central States from 1860 to 1918*, Supplementary Educational Monographs, vol. 3, no. 3 (Chicago: The University of Chicago Press, June 1921), pp. 3-4. Witt found two other histories in frequent use in Massachusetts before 1870: William Spaulding's *The History of English Literature* (1853), and William Francis Collier's *A History of English Literature* (1862).

35. Charles D. Cleveland, *A Compendium of English Literature, Chronologically Arranged, from Sir John Mandeville to William Cowper* (Philadelphia: E. C. & J. Biddle, 1851. First Edition, 1849).

36. Witt found in surveying thirty-four Massachusetts secondary schools that fourteen began to teach literature between 1850 and 1867, another twelve before the end of the 1870s, and eight in the 1880s. "Literature" usually meant one of the histories.

37. Literature remained an optional subject, however; rhetoric and grammar were required. Cf. either of the reports of an 1888 survey carried out by the Massachusetts Teachers Association: *English in Secondary Schools*, Report of a Committee of the Massachusetts Teachers Association (December 1, 1888); "English in Secondary Schools," *The Academy* 3 (January 1889): 593-609. Like Witt, the Committee found that a large proportion of those teaching literature were using manuals of "facts about authors."

38. As a result of the same speech, he was banned from Harvard, his alma mater, for thirty years (Monroe, *Cyclopedia*). On his appearances at Williams, see Frederick Rudolph, *The American College and University: A History* (New York: Vintage Books, 1962), p. 142. Rudolph provides an extensive discussion of both the curriculum and the extracurriculum of the colleges during this period.

39. Cf. Rudolph, *American College and University*, p. 143; and René Wellek, "Literary Scholarship," in *American Scholarship in the Twentieth Century*, Merle Curti, ed. (Cambridge, Mass.: Harvard University Press, 1953).

40. Witt, *Beginnings of Teaching Vernacular*, pp. 4-5.

41. Thus Beers explained that Yale students were expected to have read a good deal of English literature, even as he was arguing that this knowledge should not be tested since it would not be needed "in the further pursuit of the prescribed college studies." Henry A. Beers, "En-

trance Requirements in English at Yale," *Educational Review* 3 (May 1892): 427-43.

42. Franklin's proposals have been quoted by many later writers. He continued to be an advocate of the modern subjects, in 1789 attacking the "unaccountable prejudice in favor of ancient customs and beliefs" which had led to the continuance of the classical languages "after the circumstances which formerly made them useful cease to exist." Carpenter, Baker, and Scott, *Teaching of English*, pp. 38-39.

43. "English course" in this context does not refer to the teaching of English, but to a course of study that usually emerged as a nonacademic alternative to the classical course. In spite of its title, the English course did not *necessarily* include any more attention to English studies than did the parallel classical curriculum. See Stout, *High School Curricula*, p. 4; and Carpenter, Baker, and Scott, *Teaching of English*, pp. 45-46.

44. The strength of such interests is clear, though there is no single discussion equivalent to Rudolph's history of the extracurriculum at the college level. Sizer, for example, in his discussion of the academies notes that many had flourishing literary and debating societies akin to those in the colleges. Carpenter, Baker, and Scott, *Teaching of English*, make a similar point (p. 45). Witt, *Beginnings of Teaching Vernacular*, provides somewhat more detail (pp. 21 ff.). In *The Age of the Academies*, ed. Theodore Sizer (New York: Teachers College, Columbia University, 1964).

45. The belief that a literary education was particularly appropriate for women was widespread and persistent. Palmer, *Rise of English Studies*, p. 38, notes it, and Samuel Thurber was still arguing the point in 1894. Samuel Thurber, "English Literature in Girls' Education," *School Review* 2 (June 1894): 321-36. See also Carpenter, Baker, and Scott, *Teaching of English*, p. 45; and Witt, *Beginnings of Teaching Vernacular*, p. 37.

46. *Report of the Commissioner of Education for the Year 1889-90*, vol. 2 (Washington, D.C.: U.S. Government Printing Office, 1893). This was the first attempt to survey the various components of the curriculum. The tables mentioned here are printed on pp. 1390-92, 1621-28, 1657-58, 1641-42, and 1666-69. English literature was evidently surveyed in the secondary schools but not considered important enough to report. On the Oxford pass degree, see Palmer, *Rise of English Studies*, p. 70.

47. For an illustration of the variety of offerings in 1865, see Appendix II.

[The Poet] is the rock of defence for human nature; an upholder and preserver, carrying everywhere with him relationship and love. In spite of difference of soil and climate, of language and manners, of laws and customs; in spite of things silently gone out of mind, and things violently destroyed; the Poet binds together by passion and knowledge the vast empire of human society, as it is spread over the whole earth, and over all time.
—William Wordsworth, Preface to
Lyrical Ballads, 1800[1]

The future of poetry is immense, because in poetry, where it is worthy of its high destinies, our race, as time goes on, will find an ever surer and surer stay. There is not a creed which is not shaken, not an accredited dogma which is not shown to be questionable, not a received tradition which does not threaten to dissolve. Our religion has materialised itself in the fact, the supposed fact; it has attached its emotion to the fact, and now the fact is failing it. But for poetry the idea is everything; the rest is a world of illusion, of divine illusion. Poetry attaches its emotion to the idea; the idea is the fact. The stronger part of our religion to-day is its unconscious poetry.
—Matthew Arnold, 1880[2]

One would hesitate to ask to dinner a man who confessed complete ignorance of The Canterbury Tales.
—Arlo Bates, **Talks on the Study of Literature, 1897**[3]

Not only is it impossible for a pupil, without the study of Latin, to obtain the discipline and culture pertaining to an English education, but it is vain for a teacher, without a fair acquaintance with Latin or Greek, and at least one modern foreign language, to attempt instruction in English.
—C. M. Gayley and C. B. Bradley,
Suggestions to Teachers of English in the Secondary Schools, 1894[4]

Chapter II

The Birth of a Subject

Before it could emerge as a major school study, English, and in particular English literature, had to develop a methodology rigorous enough to win academic respect. It also had to overcome the supposition that imaginative literature posed a real threat to the moral well-being of its readers. The Romantic era brought a solution to both problems: that of methodology through the new techniques of the German philologists; that of moral well-being through a redefinition of culture and of the artist's role. Together these two movements made it *possible* for English to become a major subject, but they did not insure the success of the venture. This success depended upon institutional changes in the American system of education, changes begun through the influence of the college entrance requirements, and consolidated by the report of the Committee of Ten. These institutional changes succeeded in welding the various studies of English together as a single subject and provided it with its first, albeit rather tenuous, coherence. By 1900 the questions would have shifted from *whether* to teach grammar, rhetoric, literary history, spelling, and composition, to *how* to teach English.[5]

The Cultural Value of Literature

The ethical tradition which implied that literature in school reading material could be used for moral education proved a double-edged sword for the early teacher of English: if literature had the

21

power to do good, it must also have the power to do evil. Well into the nineteenth century, imaginative literature was as likely to be attacked as a source of corruption as to be defended as a way toward salvation.

History, biography, and travel books had always had a certain moral cachet, but fiction and drama, with their appeal to imagination rather than truth, were definitely suspect. Horace Mann was typical of many influential educators when he argued that novels should not be taught because their appeal was to emotion rather than to reason.[6] When Yale's William Lyons Phelps, as a young instructor, instituted America's first course on the contemporary novel in 1895, he was forced to drop it after comments in the popular press. Opposition to drama was also strong: in 1828 a Boston teacher was dismissed for reading to his class from one of Shakespeare's plays, and even at the college level Oberlin refused to allow Shakespeare to be taught in mixed classes until the 1860s.[7] Such incidents became rarer in the second half of the century, but the convictions which led to them were strongly held; as late as 1893, after *Hamlet* had been on the college entrance lists for over a decade, the *New England Journal of Education* still took time to give editorial support to a class who had refused to read the play:

> All honor to the modest and sensible youths and maidens of the Oakland High School who revolted against studying an unexpurgated edition of *Hamlet*! The indelicacies of Shakespeare in the complete edition are brutal. They are more than indelicacies, they are indecencies. They are no part of Shakespeare's thought, have no connection with the play, and can be eliminated with as little jar as the oaths of a modern slugger.[8]

The editor was presumably following the lead of the rhetoricians in attributing these "indelicacies" to "the grossness of the age" in which Shakespeare had written.

The Romantic Tradition

The poets and critics of the Romantic period provided a new justification for literature as a reservoir of cultural values and a source of moral strength. Writing against the background of the upheavals caused by the scientific and industrial revolutions, they turned to the artist to provide, through the superior development of his faculty of Imagination, the needed corrective to the intolerable socioeconomic conditions produced by strict adherence to the "rational" laws of the marketplace.[9] The artist would have a different kind of knowledge—to the Romantics usually a "higher" kind—which was no less essential than the rationalism to which it was opposed. The cumulative products of this artistic imagination came to be identified with a nation's culture, in the process transforming "culture" from a *process* into a *state*, a body of knowledge and tradition to be consciously valued and consciously studied. (Historical studies such as those discussed in Chapter I received part of their impetus from this aspect of the movement.)

The conception of culture as a product of the arts originates with Coleridge and runs throughout the writings of the Romantics. Wordsworth relies on it in his preface to *Lyrical Ballads* (1800); so does Shelley in his *Defence of Poetry* (1821). Through these and similar writings, the status of the arts and of the artist was elevated until, in the end, a view emerged which argued that all art is in essence moral. "Poetry strengthens the faculty which is the organ of the moral nature of man," Shelley wrote, "in the same manner as exercise strengthens a limb."[10]

Culture and Education

The educational implications of the Romantic view of culture were formulated most fully by Matthew Arnold. In *Culture and Anarchy* (1867), he provided a widely read interpretation of culture as the cumulative vision of mankind, winnowed by time and sanctioned by genius. Such a culture, Arnold argued, could be the source of a new principle of authority to replace the eroding bonds of class and of religion; it was the only hope of preventing the anarchy which would otherwise surely follow. Though better remembered in America as a poet and critic, Arnold was also an inspector of schools; it was from this vantage point that he recognized that public education, if it were given culture as a primary goal, could emerge as the new unifying and civilizing agent. Classically trained himself, Arnold argued on behalf of culture broadly defined, and in no way asserted the superiority of the vernacular literature; indeed he explicitly argued the proven value of the Greeks over all who came later.[11] In the American high school, however, the classical languages would soon decline; the main benefits of his arguments accrued to the emerging studies of English literature.

Americans who embraced Arnold's interpretation of cultural education did so in the hope of stemming the erosion of traditional systems of values. In a very real sense, educational opportunities were extended because schooling with its attendant "culture" was seen as a new agent of social control. For the definitions of the culture to be transmitted through its schools, America looked to New England, in particular to Boston. It was a reassuring culture that could be found there during the late nineteenth century, a mid-Victorian culture which avoided such problems as civil war and industrialization by turning to a pastoral, detached literature.[12] As

Francis Underwood, himself the editor of a series of literature anthologies, put it in 1879:

> In this country all things are so new, and political events have such an intense significance, that we do not look at affairs as posterity will look at them. But who can doubt that, when the true perspective has been adjusted, ours will be known as the age of Emerson, Irving, and Hawthorne, of Bryant, Longfellow, and Whittier, of Lowell and Holmes?[13]

His hope and faith was that literature could gradually surpass and suppress from memory such "political events" as civil war. His catalog of authors is a catalog of the New England literary elite as well as of the American contribution to the emerging high school literary canon.

Horace Scudder

The most widely quoted American spokesman for an Arnoldian view of cultural education was Horace E. Scudder, a member of the Cambridge (Massachusetts) school committee, chief editor for Houghton Mifflin, and, later, editor of the *Atlantic Monthly*.[14] He tied his arguments for the teaching of literature to America's common-school traditions, where the place of literature "is in spiritualizing life, letting light into the mind, inspiring and feeding the higher forces of human nature." Like Arnold, whom he sometimes quoted directly, Scudder cast his concern in the context of contemporary social upheaval, of "hands which are nervously pulling at the stones of our political edifice, . . . hands that are knotted with hopeless toil." From this vantage point, he offered a comprehensive criticism of the teaching of literature at all levels of the common school. His argument hinged on the effectiveness of the "classics" in engendering "spiritual grace," on the winnowing effects of time as the arbiter of literary merit, and on the value for Americans of their own unique literary heritage. Scudder was remarkably balanced in his views: he wanted such works as *Little Red Riding Hood* in the nursery school, complained that school readers had misused literature to the point that in them "Pegasus is harnessed to a tip-cart," and recognized that the values which he hoped to foster were ultimately larger than the Americanism he also espoused.[15] His views, with their essential optimism and grand mission for the teacher of English, carried much weight in the debates of the 1880s and 1890s. The teacher who accepted them— and in the end most did—could for the first time claim the full support of the ethical tradition for all of his teaching of literature.

Philological Studies

The cultural value of literature provided a new and popular motivation for the inclusion of studies of literature in the curriculum, but it did not provide them with a methodology. This was to come from the historical and textual studies of language propounded by the German philologists and their American successors. What these scholars offered was a scientific study of language, a methodology equal in rigor and academic respect to any of the classical studies.[16]

Continuing the pattern of transposition from the classical to the modern curriculum, philology has its roots in studies of classical civilizations, transposed by the German Romantics to the study of German and later of English. The word itself dates at least to the writings of Plato; it was revived in 1777 by Frederich Wolf at the University of Göttingen. Defining his task broadly as providing the biography of a nation, Wolf included as legitimate philological study attention to the grammar, criticism, geography, political history, customs, mythology, literature, art, and ideas of a people, but like earlier philologists, he was interested in the culture of Greece and Rome. His theoretical statement, however, implied no such limitations, and was eventually extended to other cultures by his followers.

The justification of modern language study through philology involved a process of slowly shifting focuses of attention. The Germanic languages were originally studied not for their importance in German culture, but because scholars hoped to find in that culture remnants of an earlier Indo-European culture and language. Gradually, as a body of serious studies emerged, German, Anglo-Saxon, and Celtic began to be studied for their own sake; later still, studies of the Romance languages began to be approached with the same methodology. Folklore was an especially important ground for justifying modern studies, for it occupied an ambiguous historical position. It was studied originally for its presumed roots in an ancient oral culture, yet the tales studied were also very obviously a part of the contemporary culture in which they were collected. As philology became more confident in its modern studies, it moved closer and closer to contemporary literature—first the Anglo-Saxon poets, then Chaucer and medieval England, later Spenser and Shakespeare, and finally, by the end of the nineteenth century, the whole modern field.

Given the considerable disrepute into which philology has now faded, it is worth remembering the high ideals with which it began. The compilations and bibliographies, the variorum editions and collections of folklore, the lengthy textual notes and arguments over seemingly minor detail had as their original impetus the Romantic ideal of the study of a national spirit. In the hands of a few men—Jacob Grimm is the most brilliant example—such studies came close to realizing their lofty goals, but in the hands of most they quickly degenerated into the mechanical and pedantic textual criticism that has earned philology its present low esteem. In fact, philology asked more than most men could manage, requiring a systematic, analytic scholarship on the one hand and a creative, synthetic mind on the other—for one was asked both to discover and to recreate the cultural history of a nation. The more limited definition of philology as a study of language was more or less forced upon the serious student, and it is this more limited definition that has given philology its negative image.[17]

Philology in the University

However much it might degenerate, philology offered the fledgling subject of English the justification it needed in the colleges of the second half of the nineteenth century, giving it the impetus to become a major component of the emerging university system. Before philological studies began to dominate, the professor of English was a curiously ambiguous entity. As we have seen, in many institutions he was simply a clergyman whose oratorical skills gave him license to lecture on language and rhetoric. In others, English professors were trained originally in law, in logic, or in modern history. All were expected to tutor in other subjects, ranging from political science and economics to biology and mathematics. Neither English nor the other modern languages produced much in the way of indigenous American scholarship during the first half of the nineteenth century, in spite of Emerson's famous "American Scholar" address at Harvard in 1837. There were no producing scholars in the modern languages, no periodicals, and no university presses. Between 1850 and 1900, however, this changed completely, with philological scholarship transforming the study of modern languages at the same time that Germanic ideals of research were transforming graduate education in general.[18]

Francis James Child

The rise of philological studies in the United States is reflected in the career of Francis James Child, who presided over the expansion of the curriculum at Harvard to include the study of English literature. After graduating in the Harvard class of 1846, Child stayed on to tutor in math, history, and economics. Three years later he became one of a growing number of Americans studying in Germany, returning to Harvard in 1851 to succeed Channing as Boylston Professor of Rhetoric and Oratory. During the ensuing decades he emerged as one of America's leading scholars, his definitive edition of Spenser's poetry (1855) and his *English and Scottish Ballads* (1857-58) firmly establishing his reputation.[19] Still it was as a professor of rhetoric and oratory that he offered his lectures on language and literature, including three elective courses: History of the English Language; Anglo-Saxon; and Chaucer, Shakespeare, Bacon, Milton, and Dryden.[20] For twenty-five years, his responsibilities for the rhetoric course prevented him from broadening the offerings further. Finally in 1876, after a successful series of guest lectures brought him an offer of a position at the newly-established Johns Hopkins University, Harvard released Child from the rhetoric course and made him its first professor of English. In the same year Robert Grant, one of Child's students, earned the first American Ph.D. in English literature. (It is indicative of the general state of graduate education that after leaving Harvard, Grant took a Columbia law degree and went on to a lucrative Boston law practice. Though he later wrote novels, plays, verse, essays, and travel books, his graduate work was clearly not vocational.)[21]

The Spread of Philology

Johns Hopkins' contribution to English studies was not limited to forcing Harvard's hand. The ideals of specialization, of productive scholarship, and of scientific study of the modern languages were pursued there along philological lines, even without Child's influence.[22] Graduate work in English consisted of rigorous textual and linguistic study; mastery of the early languages—Old French, Old High German, Anglo-Saxon, and Middle English—was an essential part of the training. In its insistence on rigorous graduate preparation for studies of the modern languages, Johns Hopkins established the first model for the training of teachers of English; up to that point, there had been no standards of preparation at all.

With the sanction of philology, the teaching of literature spread quickly through the American college and university system. Francis Andrew March became professor of the English language and comparative philology at Lafayette College in 1857, only six years after Child took up the Boylston Professorship at Harvard.[23] By 1875 Moses Coit Tyler was teaching a course in American literature at the University of Michigan.[24] And by 1879, just three years after Child was released from the Harvard rhetoric course, elective offerings there had increased from three to seven, and other faculty members were offering literature courses of their own.[25] Though in 1883 when the Modern Language Association was organized, representatives of twenty leading colleges could tally only thirty-nine teachers of English among their several institutions, by 1900, major universities in all sections of the country were offering graduate degrees in English literature—Berkeley and Stanford in the West; Michigan, Chicago, Wisconsin, and Vanderbilt in the Midwest; Harvard, Yale, Johns Hopkins, and many others in the East. At the undergraduate level, literature had become an almost universal offering and had assumed its still-continuing place as the largest component of English instruction.[26]

In examining the role of philology in the English studies of the late nineteenth century, it is important to remember the complex traditions upon which it was superimposed. Much that was not philological went on in the early departments of English, stemming from the earlier traditions of rhetorical analysis, from the long tradition of popular, nonacademic criticism, and from oratory (itself a child of rhetoric), which placed more emphasis on sensitive reading and "interpretation." The interactions among such studies are complex and have not been documented well enough to pursue very far. It is quite clear, however, that the prestige of philology served to *justify* English studies without necessarily *limiting* them, especially at the undergraduate levels. A number of influential teachers—chief among them William Lyons Phelps at Yale, Bliss Perry at Williams, and Hiram Corson at Cornell—quite openly resisted philology. They offered instead the goal of "appreciation," but they lacked an adequate methodology to offer in place of the new-found rigor of philology. Their writings and teachings provided instead the academic roots for a dissenting tradition which would contribute in the years after 1900 to the rejection by the high schools of the collegiate model.[27]

High School Programs

When systematic, regular instruction in literature emerged in the high schools, it came under the same guises that brought it into the colleges. William James Rolfe, a prolific writer whose philological scholarship earned him considerable praise, is credited with introducing the first regular high school instruction in literature.[28] Rolfe began teaching in Day's Academy in Wrentham, Massachusetts, in 1848, during the next ten years moving on to the Dorchester and later the Lawrence high schools. His teaching of English during this period came to Child's attention and led to an honorary A.M. from Harvard in 1859 (before his philological studies or school texts had been written). After a brief interlude in Salem, Rolfe became principal of Cambridge High School, where he remained until he left teaching for a life as an author and editor, in 1868. By 1907, three years before his death, he had written or edited some 144 volumes, ranging from Latin and science texts to two forty-volume school editions of Shakespeare (1871-84, 1903-06). The breadth and diversity of his interests parallels that of the early college teachers of English.

When Rolfe arrived at Cambridge High School in 1862, literature was already a well-established if somewhat peripheral part of the curriculum; it had first been taught there in 1848, under the guidance of his predecessor as principal, Elbridge Smith. Rolfe regularized the study and legitimized it with his philological scholarship; he also placed it firmly within the classical tradition of instruction. Formal discipline was the basis of the pedagogy adopted, with considerable stress on rote learning of rules and memorization of isolated facts — Cleveland's *Compendium* was a popular text at the school. An examination in Milton given in 1866 during Rolfe's tenure at Cambridge High is indicative of the general tenor of his courses:

1. Give a sketch of Milton's life to 1638.
2. Give a brief outline of "L'Allegro."
3. Give examples of obsolete or obsolescent words from the poems studied.
4. Give examples of words used by Milton in a different sense than they are today. Illustrate.
5. Write a passage from "Il Penseroso."
6. Indicate which words in the passage are from the Anglo-Saxon, which from the Latin. How do you tell?
7. Explain all allusions in the passage.
8. What do the following illustrate?
   [Here followed a set of examples of rhetorical figures.]
9. Write a passage from "Lycidas."
10. Explain the peculiarities in the passage from "Lycidas."[29]

History and philology explain all ten.

When instruction based on this classical model was joined with the Romantic conception of culture during the last quarter of the nineteenth century, the teaching of literature for the first time met all requirements that could be put upon a subject for study: usefulness, discipline, moral value, interest, even patriotism. Many variations would be played upon these themes, and many writers would still argue pro and con; but this new-found intellectual rigor and cultural strength of English literature prepared the way for its eventual acceptance as a legitimate, even a major, course of study in the schools.

Institutionalization

The College Entrance Requirements

School programs have an inertia which can create a surprisingly large gap between educational thought, as expressed at conferences and in the professional literature, and educational practice as it actually transpires in the schools. Such a gap was undoubtedly present in English instruction in American high schools during the late nineteenth century. Because one function of the high school was preparatory, and because then as now the success of its preparatory courses was more important to a school's prestige than its finishing courses, radical change was forced upon the schools in a remarkably short time. In 1800 formal instruction in literature was unknown; by 1865 it had made its way into the curriculum as a handmaiden to other studies; by 1900 literature was almost universally offered as an important study in its own right. College entrance requirements were the moving force.

College admission presented rather a different problem for preparatory schools during the nineteenth century than it does for schools today. Instead of facing secondary school graduation requirements, candidates for admission were assessed on the basis of entrance examinations set by each college. The topics for these examinations were announced in advance and had a way of dictating the preparatory school curriculum for the year. As the requirements changed, the curriculum changed with them.[30]

Typically enough, literature gained its foothold in the requirements through the nonliterary uses to which readings could be put. We have already noted the early and quite widespread requirements in English grammar; Harvard added a requirement in "reading English aloud" in its catalog for 1865. This was expanded and clarified in 1869-70, but the real milestone was the Harvard requirement for 1873-74: literature was to be studied, not for itself or even for philology, but as a subject for composition.

> *English Composition.* Each candidate will be required to write a short English composition, correct in spelling, punctuation, grammar, and expression, the subject to be taken from such works of standard authors as shall be announced from time to time. The subject for 1874 will be taken from one of the following works: Shakespeare's *Tempest, Julius Caesar,* and *Merchant of Venice*; Goldsmith's *Vicar of Wakefield*; Scott's *Ivanhoe,* and *Lay of the Last Minstrel.*[31]

This requirement institutionalized the study of standard authors and set in motion a process which eventually forced English to consolidate its position within the schools.

Uniform Requirements

The Harvard model was quickly followed by other colleges and universities; it offered an easy way to recognize literary studies without raising difficult questions about standards and methods: the subject tested would be composition, not literature. There was, however, no agreed canon of texts on which to base the examinations, and the lists changed yearly. Each college set its own examinations, quickly confronting the high schools with a flood of titles in which they were to prepare their students.

That the schools soon raised an outcry is hardly surprising, nor is the movement for uniformity which followed. By 1879 the first attempt to set requirements at a regional level began with the organization of the Conference of New England Colleges at Trinity College; this was followed by a succession of similar organizations in both the northern and southern states.[32] Finally, in 1893, after an appeal from Wilson Farrand, principal of Newark (New Jersey) Academy, the newly formed Association of Colleges and Preparatory Schools of the Middle States and Maryland proposed a joint conference with other associations concerned about the entrance requirements in English.[33] As a direct result, the National Conference on Uniform Entrance Requirements in English met for the first time in May 1894, with representatives from the Association of Colleges and Preparatory Schools of the Middle States and Maryland, the New England Commission of Colleges on Entrance Examinations, and the New England Association of Colleges and Preparatory Schools. In later years they were joined by other powerful groups, including the North Central Association and the College Entrance Examination Board.[34] The dictums of this National Conference succeeded those of Harvard in shaping the teaching of literature.[35]

The group began by approving a list already promulgated by the New England Commission of Colleges on Entrance Examinations, in order to avoid disrupting work already underway in the secondary schools. They split the list into two parts, however, one for "wide" and the other for "deep" study. This was a practice that had already developed informally in high schools faced with a proliferation of titles and with requirements for close, analytic study which often seemed antithetical to more humanistic goals.[36] The use of two lists offered a compromise between the two conflicting points of view, the shorter list belonging firmly to the advocates of disciplined study, the longer list to the proponents of appreciation.

The final separation of the requirements in literature from those in composition was due to the influence of Yale University. Until 1894 the Yale faculty resisted the new requirements altogether, arguing that entrance examinations were designed to assess a candidate's readiness for the studies of the first year—and the first year at Yale included no English.[37] Until the 1891-92 academic year, there were no required English studies at all; at that point a prescribed half-course was added as part of the second year. During the 1892-93 academic year this was expanded again when William Lyons Phelps, newly appointed as an instructor, offered a survey of English literature to freshmen—the first time the first year students had had even an elective offering available.

The emergence of literature was part of the larger struggle over elective courses; when Yale finally did take a stand, the proponents of modern studies had won a clear victory. Rather than a subject for composition, literature would be studied in its own right; examination texts were to be selected "as well for their probable attractiveness to the preparatory student as for their instrinsic importance." The list for 1894 was chosen from "writers of the present century" and included "The Rime of the Ancient Mariner," *Ivanhoe*, "The Lady of the Lake," *The Alhambra*, "Essay on Clive," the fourth Canto of *Childe Harold*, "Essay on Byron," *The House of the Seven Gables*, *English Humorists of the Eighteenth Century*, and *The Princess*. (Though some of these are now part of the high school canon, it is interesting to note that they entered the curriculum as contemporary literature.) Yale soon found that its decision to set its own lists was raising another outcry; during the following year it accepted the uniform lists in spite of their emphasis on traditional texts. Other schools quickly picked up the new, more liberal justification that Yale had provided for literary study, however, dropping the old emphasis on composition.[38]

The Committee of Ten

The difficulties caused by a proliferation of entrance requirements were not limited to English, prompting the National Council of Education of the National Education Association to call in 1892 for the appointment of a Committee of Ten to arrange a series of subject-area conferences to consider the whole problem of secondary school studies. Charles W. Eliot, president of Harvard and long an advocate of the modern studies, was named as chairman.[39]

The committee was unique in its composition and effects. Fully half of its members were not even members of the NEA, though all were active in the field of education. They ranged from Eliot, president of Harvard, to William Torrey Harris, U.S. Commissioner of Education, and James B. Angell, president of the University of Michigan. If this group were to suggest change, it would have a good chance of implementation. The competence and experience of the committee covered the full range of American education at the time: half of its members had experience in the lower school, half were from the colleges; most were from the eastern states, but they also numbered James H. Baker of the University of Colorado and Richard H. Jesse of the University of Missouri among their members. If the representation of the professional educators, the teachers of teaching, was slight, it was simply because in 1892 these were not yet of much importance.

The committee worked through a series of commissions, each with ten members, meeting separately and submitting their reports to the main committee. The final report was a collection of these documents with a lengthy preliminary, drafted mostly by Eliot, which attempted to create a consensus out of the often conflicting recommendations of the individual conferences.

The first important decision came in November 1892, when it was decided to call conferences in just nine fields, one of which was English.[40] Ten members were appointed in each of the nine fields, together with alternates. Each conference was to meet separately and elect its own chairman and secretary. The Conference on English met at Vassar College, selecting Samuel Thurber, master at Girls' High School, Boston, as chairman and George Lyman Kittredge, Child's successor at Harvard, as secretary.[41] Its report represented a summary and a reconciliation of the contemporary points of view about the teaching of English. It began with a statement of the purpose of such studies:

> The main objects of the teaching of English in schools seem to be two: (1) to enable the pupil to understand the expressed thoughts of others and to give expression to thoughts of his own; and (2) to cultivate a taste for reading, to give the pupil some acquaintance with good literature, and to furnish him with the means of extending that acquaintance.[42]

This simple two-part statement presented the necessary unification of the many disparate studies which go beneath the rubric English. Communication and appreciation were the focal points, and if English in later years was to lose some of its vigor because of the diversity of activities which it would be forced to assimilate, in the 1890s that same breadth allowed the various minor studies to be brought together into one far more vigorous whole.

This unification of the many parts of English was one of the most important effects of the *Report* of the Committee of Ten. The other major effect was to accord the new subject a status at least as important as that of the classical subjects. The Conference on English recommended that a total of five periods a week for four years be devoted to the various aspects of English studies, and the committee as a whole went so far as to accept four a week for the four years in its general recommendations. In the suggested programs of study, however, English is contracted a bit further. Out of the four years of study described for four alternate programs, English receives a full five periods a week in only the third year of the "English" course, and is cut to three and even two at various points in all other programs. Nevertheless, English is the *only* subject recommended for definite inclusion in the program of study for every student during each of the four high school years.[43]

The actual description of the English course by the Vassar Conference is more of a summing up than a statement of consequence in the future development of the subject. The themes which were of importance in the emergence of the subject are touched upon, as well as a number of issues irrelevant to the basic problem of how and why the teaching of English literature attained a prominent place in the American school curriculum.

The discussion began by asserting that "at the beginning of the seventh school-year the reading book may be discarded, and the pupil should henceforth read literature." Literature, however, was to include "prose and narrative poetry in about equal parts"—drama was still conspicuous in its absence. Histories such as Cleveland's *Compendium* were out of favor, but philological and rhetorical studies were defended as "necessary if the pupil is to be brought into anything but the vaguest understanding of what he reads."[44] The main report pointed out the recurrent though not explicitly stated theme of the Conference on English: the study of English could become "the equal of any other studies in disciplinary or developing power."[45]

The Literary Canon

As schools and colleges increased their attention to English literature, in particular to the study of the complete texts required in the college lists, publishers began to bring out annotated school editions of popular works. These go back at least to 1867, when William Rolfe launched his career as editor and author with his American version of Craik's edition of *Julius Caesar*. His emphasis, not unexpectedly, was philological; it set the pattern that would prevail till 1900. The book contained an Introduction, The History of the Play, The Sources of the Plot, Critical Comments on the Play (26 pages), the play itself (102 pages), Notes (82 pages!), and an Index of Words and Phrases Explained.[46]

By the mid-1880s, annotated classics were in widespread use, alongside the school readers and histories such as Cleveland's and Shaw's. The college entrance requirements, with their lists of specifically prescribed texts, gave great impetus to the development of these texts; many different publishers issued their own series before 1900, generally with some reference to one or another of the college entrance lists—presumably a major selling point. Distinguished teachers and scholars were solicited to edit these editions, providing them with copious and sometimes irrelevant notes and study guides.[47] Given the suddenness with which English literature developed as a major school subject and the lack of teachers trained to teach it, some such apparatus may have been a necessity at the time;[48] eventually it was to provoke a harsh reaction.

The rise of uniform requirements as well as the appearance of many different series of annotated texts raises the interesting question of how the high school literary canon was determined. Some influences are relatively clear, chief among them the prestige of

Milton and the Augustans from the early rhetoric and grammar texts, in which they had been used as material for analysis. A strong tradition of Shakespearean criticism had also been built up, though this seems to owe more to the recognition of Shakespeare's merit than to the ease with which he could be analyzed. At the same time, the literature of the English Romantics found a place in the early lists; such literature first appeared as contemporary selections in the school readers and then worked its way into the high school.

The classical analogy which had influenced the selection of works for analysis by the rhetoricians also continued to operate; it is evident even in the term "classics" which early came to be used to describe the body of English standard authors. As the curriculum grew, the analogy became if anything stronger: *Julius Caesar* was taught during the same year as Caesar's *Commentaries;* the Latin or Greek epic was followed by Longfellow or *Paradise Lost;* British and American orators were paired with Cicero and Demosthenes. The classical tradition had both a prestige and a methodology which the early teacher of English hoped to emulate; whether conscious of it or not, he was quite successful in doing so.[49]

Another question which the emerging list of texts raised was whether the high school or the college was leading the way in shaping the requirements. Here there is no simple answer: neither the colleges nor the high schools reflected any sort of consensus about the specific works to be read. Neither, of course, have schools since, though there has always been a good measure of agreement on which books are and are not appropriate literature for the high school. Rather than the schools of the 1880s or the colleges of the 1890s, the source of the "classics" in the school curriculum seems to be the tradition of belles lettres, which has never required scholastic attention to survive.[50] These are Franklin's "best" and Harvard's "standard" texts, representing the kind of unspoken consensus to which Cleveland paid tribute as he explained the basis of his own selections:

> I have constantly endeavored to bear in mind a truth, which even those engaged in education may sometimes forget, that what is well known to us, must be new to every successive generation; and, therefore, that all books of selections designed for them should contain a portion of such pieces as all of any pretentions to taste have united to admire. Milton's "Invocation to Light," Pope's "Messiah," Goldsmith's "Village Pastor," and Gray's "Elegy" are illustrations of my meaning.[51]

The traditions on which the concept of Great Books is based, and which have made it so popular, run very deep. There have been few surprises in the various lists of texts encountered so far, and there are few in the lists which follow. The first includes all titles which were taught in more than 25 percent of the high schools of the North

Central region between 1886 and 1900; the second, titles used in from 10 to 25 percent of the same schools. Both are arranged in order of decreasing frequency.

I

1. *The Merchant of Venice*
2. *Julius Caesar*
3. *First Bunker Hill Oration*
4. *The Sketch Book, Evangeline, The Vision of Sir Launfal*
5. *Snowbound*
6. *Macbeth*
7. *The Lady of the Lake*
8. *Hamlet*
9. *The Deserted Village*
10. Gray's *Elegy, Thanatopsis, As You Like It*

II

1. *The Courtship of Miles Standish*
2. *Il Penseroso, Paradise Lost*
3. *L'Allegro, Lycidas*
4. *Ivanhoe, Sir Roger de Coverley Papers* from the *Spectator, David Copperfield, Silas Marner*
5. *In Memoriam, Behavior, Enoch Arden, Marmion, Tales of the White Hills, The Lays of Ancient Rome, A Midsummer Night's Dream, The Vicar of Wakefield, The Iliad*
6. *Henry VIII, Among the Hills, The Cotter's Saturday Night, The Chambered Nautilus, Comus,* Bryant's *Favorite Poems, The Princess, Saul, King Lear*

Another two hundred titles appeared at least once in the schools surveyed, as indicative perhaps as anything else that the springs being tapped in the formation of the literary canon are wide indeed.[52]

English at the First Plateau

With the *Report of the Committee of Ten* in 1894 and the formation of the National Conference on Uniform Entrance Requirements in English during the same year, the place of English studies within the secondary school curriculum was firmly established. In the years that followed, the question would no longer be whether but how the subject should be taught. During the next half century there would be many changes—changes in materials, changes in philosophy, changes in methods, changes even in students. But none of these changes would be as rapid or as dramatic as that which brought the teaching of literature into the curriculum in the first place.

We can get some sense of that change that had occurred if we consider offerings in English in the North Central area. Between 1860 and 1900, the proportion of schools offering courses in "grammar" dropped from 60 to 35 percent; "analysis" fell from 55 to 3 percent; "rhetoric" from 90 to 63 percent. At the same time, offerings in "English literature" rose from 30 percent in 1860 to 70 percent by 1890, "American literature" from zero to 20 percent, and "literature" from 5 to 20 percent. After that period, the separate components were gradually assimilated into English I, English II, English III, and English IV. These first appeared in the high schools between 1886 and 1890 and formed the basis for the consolidation of English studies offered by the Committee of Ten; after their report, they became universal.[53]

John E. Stout found considerable school-to-school variation in offerings in English in the North Central area before 1900, but suggests that these are due more to the size and goals of the school than to regional differences. From the beginning, English was offered more frequently in the large cities and in the nonacademic curriculum of the schools studied. Peter D. Witt echoes these findings on the basis of his research on the early teaching of literature in Massachusetts, but both of these studies focus on relatively homogeneous geographic areas. Edna Hays, studying the influence of entrance requirements on schools nationally, found some broad differences rooted in geographic distance from the eastern colleges, with their rigid examination system of entrance requirements and generally more traditional program of studies. Though she concluded that all areas of the country were eventually influenced by the entrance requirements, this influence was earliest in eastern secondary schools, and weakest in schools in the Far West.

The annual report of the U.S. Commissioner of Education for the year 1900-1901 makes it clear that there were also quite substantial differences between the various geographic regions of the United States, differences that cannot be explained on the basis of the size of the school or community. During that year, the proportion of secondary school pupils enrolled in literature courses ranged from 22 percent in Idaho and 32 percent in New York to 96 percent in Washington, D.C., 84 percent in California, and 73 percent in Massachusetts. In general, states in the North Central area had a lower percentage of their students in literature courses, and the western states a higher. Private school pupils were less likely than public school students to study literature (38 to 45 percent); girls outnumbered boys in such studies by three to two. Even at this relatively late date, however, more students were studying Latin than were studying English.[54] Since rhetoric did not make it into the list of subjects reported until 1894-95, and literature only in 1897-98, the U.S. Commissioner's reports provide a convenient turn-of-the-century benchmark but little evidence of historical trends during the early history of the subject.

The relative importance of the National Conference and the Committee of Ten in the struggle to win recognition for English studies was debated at the time and is no more certain today. A balanced view must give some credit to both—to the Ten for unifying the subject and raising its prestige, to the National Conference for adding the compulsion that insured its prosperity. Neither alone would have led to the teaching of English as we know it today.

The teaching of literature at the turn of the century was still a very new and uncertain enterprise, and most of the issues which torment the teacher of English at the present could be heard clamoring in the near distance. Several points were granted by most teachers, however, and various approaches to the subject were confined within these basic premises. One was that the value of education, of *all* education, lay in mental discipline; thus any proposal for the study of English literature had disciplinary value as part of its justification.[55] Another was that the unique value of literary studies was their guarantee of a continuing cultural tradition, an extra-historical perspective encompassing and preserving the values of Western civilization. Third, there was the conviction that all of the varied studies of language, literature, and composition which had previously had to fend for separate places within the curriculum were really only different aspects of the same central study. And finally there was the belief that this study was the one subject within the school curriculum to which all students needed a steady exposure.

CHAPTER II NOTES

1. Quoted by Raymond Williams, *Culture and Society 1780-1950* (London: Chatto and Windus, 1958), p. 41.

2. A. Dwight Culler, ed., *The Poetry and Criticism of Matthew Arnold* (Boston: Houghton Mifflin Co., 1961), p. 306.

3. Arlo Bates, *Talks on the Study of Literature* (Boston: Houghton Mifflin Co., 1897), p. 125.

4. C. M. Gayley and C. B. Bradley, *Suggestions to Teachers of English in the Secondary School* (Berkeley, Calif.: University of California, 1894). In *Some Trends in the Teaching of Literature Since 1900,* John R. Searles (Dissertation, University of Wisconsin, 1942), p. 22.

5. This chapter will discuss the main lines of argument that won a place for English. These arguments did not go unchallenged, but the counterproposals did not become important till after 1900; they will be touched on only briefly here.

6. Mann did approve of rhetoric, in spite of its use of literary examples. It offered a "scientific" rigor and discipline. When the Massachusetts Board of Education announced a plan in 1840 to provide leisure reading materials for children and adults through the district school libraries, its lists included no fiction and no poetry. Peter D. Witt, *The Beginnings of the Teaching of the Vernacular Literature in the Secondary Schools of Massachusetts* (Dissertation, Harvard University, 1968; University Microfilms No. 69-11,507), pp. 10-21; 42.

7. See William Lyons Phelps, *Autobiography with Letters* (London: Oxford University Press, 1939), p. 301; Witt, *Beginnings of Teaching Vernacular,* p. 33; William Riley Parker, "Where Do English Departments Come From?" *College English* 28:5 (February 1967): 339-51.

8. A. E. Winship, "Unexpurgated Shakespeare," *New England Journal of Education* 37:15 (1893): 4. As quoted by Witt, *Beginnings of Teaching Vernacular,* p. 340.

9. Adam Smith reenters the story here. His *The Wealth of Nations* (1776) was instrumental in creating an awareness of industry as an institution with its own rules and rationality. Raymond Williams provides detailed discussion of the interaction between the pressures of the industrial revolution and conceptions of "culture," "art," and the "artist" in his *Culture and Society.*

10. Quoted by D. J. Palmer, *The Rise of English Studies* (London: Oxford University Press for the University of Hull, 1965), p. 41.

11. Williams, *Culture and Society*, places Arnold in the tradition beginning with Coleridge; of *Culture and Anarchy* he writes: "Its impact was immediate, and it has remained more influential than any other single work in this tradition" (p. 115). Arnold was appointed to the Inspectorate in 1851; he became Chief Inspector of Schools in 1884 and retired in 1886, two years before his death. From 1857 to 1867 he was also Professor of [Classical] Poetry at Oxford. See W. F. Connell, *The Educational Thought and Influence of Matthew Arnold* (London: Routledge and Kegan Paul, 1950). On the superiority of the Greeks, see *The Poetry and Criticism of Matthew Arnold*, pp. 411, 434.

12. Witt, *Beginnings of Teaching Vernacular,* presents a concise summary of the attitudes of the literary elite, both with respect to proper subjects for literary works and with respect to the use of the schools as

instruments of social control (pp. 63ff.). Witt in turn draws on Michael B. Katz, *The Irony of Early School Reform: Educational Innovation in Mid-Nineteenth Century Massachusetts* (Cambridge, Mass.: Harvard University Press, 1968).

13. Francis H. Underwood, *English Literature, and Its Place in Popular Education* (Boston: Lee and Shepard, 1879), p. 4.

14. *The Atlantic Monthly*, founded in 1857, was the chief forum for this school of thought. It carried the word to teachers and administrators across the nation; the soft tones it championed did much to hasten public acceptance of literature in the schools. See Witt, *Beginnings of Teaching Vernacular*, p. 96; and Harry B. Krouse, "History and Evaluation of the Critical Trends, Exclusive of Fiction, in the *Atlantic Monthly*, 1857 to 1898" (Dissertation, University of Wisconsin, 1972; University Microfilms No. 72-22,101).

15. Horace E. Scudder, *Literature in Schools, An Address and Two Essays*, Riverside Literature Series (Boston: Houghton, Mifflin, and Co., 1888), p. 31.

16. The history of philological studies has been recounted by Kemp Malone in his presidential address to the Modern Humanities Research Association, "The Rise of Modern Philology," *Annual Bulletin of the Modern Humanities Research Association* 30 (November 1958): 19-31, and earlier in Paul Monroe's *Cyclopedia of Education* (New York: The Macmillan Co., 1911). See also Samuel Thurber, "Suggestions of English Study for Secondary Teachers of English," *The Academy* (January 1891): 2 ff. Thurber states that "Philology is simply science applied to language," and argues that teachers should be prepared in German, "the indispensable tool of scientific research."

17. Wellek has discussed this contrast between the goals and the practice of the early philologists. René Wellek, "Literary Scholarship," in *American Scholarship in the Twentieth Century*, ed. Merle Curti (Cambridge, Mass.: Harvard University Press, 1953).

18. Wellek, "Literary Scholarship," pp. 111-112.

19. Wellek, "Literary Scholarship," credits Child with being the only "producing scholar" in the modern languages in America at that time. See also Don Cameron Allen, *The Ph.D. in English and American Literature* (New York: Holt, Rinehart and Winston, 1968).

20. The content of the courses varied slightly from year to year. The list here is Grandgent's. Charles H. Grandgent, "The Modern Languages," in *The Development of Harvard University Since the Inauguration of President Eliot 1869-1929*, ed. Samuel Eliot Morison (Cambridge, Mass.: Harvard University Press, 1930).

21. Allen, *Ph.D. in English and American Literature*, p. 7. Grant's thesis "summarized the various theories about Shakespeare's sonnets."

22. A. S. Cook was Johns Hopkins' first instructor in English. He had a Rutgers A.B. and had also studied in Germany. On developments at Johns Hopkins, see Allen, *Ph.D. in English and American Literature*, and Parker, "Where Do English Departments Come From?"

23. March was an Amherst graduate whose interest in language studies was apparently stirred by a series of lectures given by Noah Webster. He also taught French, German, Latin, Greek, law, political economy, political science, philosophy, and botany. Dumas Malone, ed., *Dictionary of American Biography* (New York: Charles Scribner's Sons, 1935).

24. Separate courses in American literature remained the exception until 1900. Usually American literature was considered part of the English tradition and taught together with it. Evelyn Rezek Bibb, *Anthologies of American Literature, 1787-1964* (Dissertation, Columbia University, 1965; University Microfilms No. 66-1728).

25. A. S. Hill, A. S. Briggs, and Barrett Wendell were among the early instructors in English at Harvard. George Lyman Kittredge began as a graduate student in 1884, eventually succeeding Child in the English professorship. Kittredge's studies shifted more towards literature, but he was a disciple of Child and continued the philological work as well. See Grandgent, "Modern Languages," and Allen, *Ph.D. in English and American Literature.*

26. See Parker, "Where Do English Departments Come From?" p. 341, and Allen, *Ph.D. in English and American Literature,* p. 11. When Ida A. Jewett surveyed offerings in state teachers colleges in 1900, she found literature to be the most common offering in English. *English in State Teachers Colleges: A Catalogue Study,* Contributions to Education, no. 286 (New York: Teachers College, Columbia University, 1927).

27. Wellek, "Literary Scholarship," p. 117, has commented caustically on the blend that sometimes developed: "They taught graduate students bibliography and sources, 'Shakespeare on the graduate level' (that is, the distinctions of quartos and folios, sources, stage conditions), and meanwhile they read poetry to undergraduates in a trembling or unctious voice. Sentimentalism and antiquarianism are not incompatible, even philosophically." But see also Witt, *Beginnings of Teaching Vernacular,* p. 288; Searle, *Trends in Teaching Literature,* p. 21; and Allen, *Ph.D. in English and American Literature.*

28. Malone, *Dictionary of American Biography.*

29. Witt, *Beginnings of Teaching Vernacular,* p. 169.

30. This pattern was somewhat attenuated in the West and Midwest, which after 1871 began to move towards a system of accreditation. The conflict this caused reached a head after 1900. (See Chapter III.)

31. Harvard University, *Twenty Years of School and College English* (Cambridge, Mass.: Harvard University, 1896), p. 55. These quotations have been frequently reprinted. For further background, see Alfred H. Grommon, "A History of the Preparation of Teachers of English," *English Journal* 57:4 (April 1968): 484-524. The requirement for 1869-70 is of some further interest as an example of the interaction of school and college interests. It listed *Julius Caesar* as one required text, presumably the edition edited by Child's protege, James Rolfe.

32. On the uniformity movement, see James Hocker Mason, *The National Council of Teachers of English—1911-1926* (Dissertation, George Peabody College for Teachers, 1962); and Edna Hays, *College Entrance Requirements in English: Their Effects on the High Schools* (New York: Teachers College, Columbia University, 1936). Important meetings have been minuted by the New England Association of Colleges and Preparatory Schools, *Addresses and Proceedings* (1886, p. 41; 1888, pp. 53-55); and the New England Commission of Colleges, *Thirteenth Annual Report* (1899, pp. 9-10).

33. Association of Colleges and Preparatory Schools of the Middle States and Maryland, *Proceedings* (1893, p. 108). See also Hays, *College Entrance Requirements,* pp. 24 ff.

34. The formation of the College Entrance Examination Board was itself part of the movement towards uniformity. In 1899 the Association of Colleges and Preparatory Schools of the Middle States and Maryland found that conditions were still chaotic; Nicholas Murray Butler then took up a long-standing suggestion of Harvard's Eliot for a joint college admissions board that would frame questions as well as set texts. The CEEB resulted, holding its first examination in June 1901. Hays, *College Entrance Requirements*, p. 33.

35. The history of the conference has been summarized several times. The official report is Albert S. Cook's *A Brief Summary of the Proceedings of the Conference on Uniform Entrance Requirements in English, 1894-1899* (n.p.,n.d.). See also Francis H. Stoddard's "Conference on Uniform Entrance Requirements in English," *Educational Review* (1905): 375-83; and Edna Hays' broader perspective, *College Entrance Requirements*. On the success of the lists, see James Fleming Hosic, *Reorganization of English in Secondary Schools*, Bulletin 1917, no. 2, U.S. Bureau of Education (Washington, D.C.: Government Printing Office, 1917), p. 12.

36. See J. G. Wright, "First Year English in the High School," *School Review* 1 (January 1893): 15-23; Gussie Packard Dubois, "Home Reading for the Secondary Schools," *School Review* 3 (November 1895): 485-95; and John E. Stout, *The Development of High School Curricula in the North Central States from 1860 to 1918*, Supplementary Educational Monographs, vol. 3, no. 3 (June 1921), p. 140.

37. Literature was taught as an elective offering in the upper years. Beers, who defended the absence of an entrance requirement, himself taught a Shakespeare course. Yale was alone among the New England colleges in not having any entrance requirements in English. See Henry A. Beers, "Entrance Requirements in English at Yale," *Educational Review* 3 (May 1892): 427-43; George Wilson Pierson, *Yale College: An Educational History, 1871-1921* (New Haven: Yale University Press, 1952), pp. 85-86; and Allen, *Ph.D. in English and American Literature.*

38. Carpenter, Baker, and Scott point out, however, that the requirement was misinterpreted by many schools, so that "it was not for several years that a study of the content of certain English masterpieces became an essential part of the preparatory school curriculum in English." George R. Carpenter, Franklin T. Baker, and Fred N. Scott, *The Teaching of English in the Elementary and the Secondary School* (New York: Longmans, Green, and Co., 1903), p. 48. See also Stout, *High School Curricula*, p. 134, and Hays, *College Entrance Requirements*, p. 31.

39. The most thorough discussion of the background and influence of the Committee of Ten is Sizer, *Secondary Schools at the Turn of the Century*. On Eliot's views, see Edward A. Krug, *Charles W. Eliot and Popular Education* (New York: Teachers College Press, Columbia University, 1961), p. 7; and Grommon, "History of Preparation of Teachers of English."

40. The full list was: "1. Latin; 2. Greek; 3. English; 4. Other Modern Languages; 5. Mathematics; 6. Physics, Astronomy, and Chemistry; 7. Natural History (Biology, including Botany, Zoology, and Physiology); 8. History, Civil Government, and Political Economy; 9. Geography (Physical Geography, Geology, and Meteorology)." *Report of the Committee of Ten on Secondary School Studies, with the Reports of the Conferences Arranged by the Committee* (New York: American Book Company for the National Education Association, 1894), p. 5.

41. The other members of the English Conference were Edward A. Allan (University of Missouri), F. A. Barbour (Michigan State Normal School), Frank M. Blackburn (University of Chicago), Cornelius B. Bradley (University of California at Berkeley), Francis B. Gummere (Haverford College), Edward E. Hales, Jr. (University of Iowa), Charles L. Loos (Dayton, Ohio, High School), and W. H. Maxwell (Superintendent of Schools, Brooklyn).

42. *Report of the Committee*, p. 86.

43. Ibid., pp. 46-47.

44. Ibid., pp. 89-91.

45. Ibid., p. 21.

46. Joseph Mersand, "The Teaching of Literature in American High Schools: 1865-1900," in *Perspectives on English*, ed. Robert C. Pooley, (New York: Appleton-Century-Crofts, Inc., 1960), pp. 279-80.

47. Stout, *High School Curricula*, p. 134; and Mersand, "Teaching Literature: 1865-1900," pp. 290-92. Here America seems to have followed the British pattern. Palmer finds over two hundred school editions in circulation in England by 1887, exclusive of Shakespeare. *Rise of English Studies*, p. 50.

48. Carpenter, Baker, and Scott, for example, argued in 1903 that "certainly half" of high school teachers of English had had no college or university training in their subject, and were "incompetent" to teach it. *Teaching of English*, p. 33.

49. I am indebted to Lou LaBrant for pointing out these parallels after reading an early version of this chapter.

50. See, for example, Carpenter, Baker, and Scott's definition of literature: ". . . that select body of prose and poetry which the world of cultivated men and women, untroubled by educational theories, is willing to call literature" (*Teaching of English*, pp. 155-56). Whether this tradition is the proper source of school texts is another issue.

51. Charles D. Cleveland, *A Compendium of English Literature, Chronologically Arranged, from Sir John Mandeville to William Cowper* (Philadelphia: E. C. & J. Biddle, 1851; First Edition, 1849).

52. Stout, *High School Curricula*, pp. 137-40.

53. These figures are from Stout's study and are summarized in more detail in Appendix II.

54. *Report of the Commissioner of Education for the Year 1900-1901* (Washington, D.C.: Government Printing Office, 1902), pp. 1925, 1941, 1915; and Bureau of the Census, *Historical Statistics of the United States: Colonial Times to 1957* (Washington, D.C.: Government Printing Office, 1960). In 1900, 50.6 percent of public day school students in any of the four high school years were enrolled in Latin courses; 38.5 percent were enrolled in English (*Historical Statistics*, p. 210).

55. Even Carpenter, Baker, and Scott, who are often clearly in an Arnoldian tradition, also claim that "The mind grows by acquiring ideas, by the exercise of memory and judgment" (*Teaching of English*, p. 160). It was quite usual for "discipline" and "appreciation" to be expounded by the same men during this early period; after 1900 they came increasingly to be seen as incompatible.

Those of us who are working to bring a fuller life to the industrial members of the community, who are looking forward to a time when work shall not be senseless drudgery, but shall contain some self-expression of the worker, sometimes feel the hopelessness of adding evening classes and social entertainments as a mere frill to a day filled with monotonous and deadening drudgery; and we sometimes feel that we have a right to expect more help from the public schools than they now give us.

—Jane Addams to the National Education
Association, 1897[1]

... in the absence of any course of study, teachers usually elevate the college entrance requirements into the vacant place—a place for which those requirements were never designed and never adapted. ... Evidently, were it not for the influence, whether attractive or repulsive, of the college requirements, the high school teacher of English would be generally without moorings.

—Report of the Standing Committee on
Courses of Study, 1907[2]

Agitation for reform in English is not unique. It is identical in spirit with the effort to develop a better type of course in history, mathematics, science, and foreign languages and has much in common with the current demands for increased emphasis upon art, music, physical education, manual training, agriculture, and domestic science. After more than half a century of struggle, the public high school has definitely established itself as a continuation of common-school education, as a finishing school (in the good sense of that term) rather than as a fitting school, and now, recognizing its freedom and its responsibility, it has set to work in earnest to adjust itself to its main task.

—National Joint Committee on English,
1917[3]

The whole tendency of the recent movement in teaching English is away from the formal. Old divisions of subject-matter are being ignored, the interests of students are being taken more fully into account, and social demands of various sorts are beginning to function in the selection of materials.

—John E. Stout in 1921 after a survey of
the school curriculum since 1860[4]

Chapter III

A School for the People

The *Report* of the Committee of Ten (1894) and the establishment of the National Conference on Uniform Entrance Requirements in English marked the end of the battle to win recognition for English as a subject at all. The years after 1894 witnessed a gradual spreading and strengthening of English courses, and a simultaneous development of a professional literature. Articles on the teaching of English began to appear regularly in journals concerned with high school education, and the first books designed specifically for teachers of English were published. One of the first American texts was written by a former superintendent of the Cleveland Schools, now turned professor of the art and science of pedagogy at the University of Michigan. This was B. A. Hinsdale's *Teaching the Language Arts* (1896). It was followed a few years later by Percival Chubb's *The Teaching of English in the Elementary and Secondary School* (1902), and in the following year by Carpenter, Baker, and Scott's book of virtually the same title.[5] The two later books were reprinted well into the 1920s.

These books and articles helped to create a new professional consciousness and self-respect. For the first time the issues raised and discussed in detail could be methodological—not generalizations about philological or rhetorical approaches, but detailed attempts to apply these generalizations to high school programs. The dialogue which was initiated at this time was one *within* the profession, rather than one *between* advocates of English and those of other studies. Teachers of English came increasingly to feel that they had a professional identity, a competence to decide what studies to offer, and a corresponding ability to proceed without the guidance of the colleges. After 1900, groups of teachers in widely scattered parts of the country began to organize English clubs and associations to share ideas more effectively and to speak with a more powerful, collective voice. The New England Association of Teachers of English, founded in 1901, was the first; it included William Lyons Phelps and Albert S. Cook among its founding members. During the next ten years, similar groups were founded for English teachers in New York City, New York State, Chicago, Illinois, Indiana, and the North Central Association; but there was little contact among them.[6]

This growing independence marks the beginning of the second battle in which teachers of English found themselves—a battle to transform the high school, and with it the high school course in English, from a "fitting school" oriented toward college entrance, into a "common school," a school for the people, whose chief function would be preparation for life.

The pressures to create such a common school came from many directions. One was a tremendous growth in high school enrollment. In 1890 there were just over 200,000 pupils in high schools scattered across the nation; by 1900 this had more than doubled; by 1915 it had doubled again.[7] The pressures generated by these rising enrollments were enormous, even more so because they were coupled with and partly motivated by massive changes in the philosophical and psychological underpinnings of educational theory. Faculty psychology and mental discipline were to be discredited after the turn of the century, and the secondary schools to take on a host of new functions which had little to do with the demands of the colleges.

Percival Chubb, principal of the High School Department of the Ethical Culture Schools in New York City, outlined with remarkable insight the issues that would dominate the succeeding decades when he prepared his textbook on the teaching of English. "In prescribing literature that is to be read during the High School period," Chubb wrote in 1902, "two requirements must be kept in mind." The first was the "characteristics, the needs, and the interests of the adolescent mind"; the second, "the vocational needs and social demands" that were increasingly to be made upon the high school curriculum.[8] Already in Chubb's writings it is evident that the emphasis is shifting: it would no longer be the student who must adjust to the school, proving his competence to follow the prescribed, academic course, but the school that must adjust to the student, meeting his personal and social needs. "It is at this point," Chubb continued, "that there will be a clash—felt nowhere so much as in the English work—between the old ideal which emphasizes formal discipline and thoroughness in a few things, and the new which emphasizes culture-content and many-sided development."[9]

The "new ideal" which Chubb was discussing was the first wave of the progressive movement in education, a movement with complex social and political roots. Its effects on the schools in general and the teaching of English in particular were to be far reaching.[10]

New Goals for Education

Changes in Philosophy

One of the major sources of change was what came to be called Social Darwinism; this had its origins in the writings of Herbert Spencer, who argued that the history of a culture could be represented as a process of evolution. Though Spencer was convinced that social evolution took place only over a large time scale and could not be speeded up, an influential group of his followers came to believe that it could be guided and accelerated in the service of specific social goals. Albion Small, head of America's first sociology department at the University of Chicago, made the point in an address to the National Education Association (NEA) in 1896. There he placed the school at the center of social reform, arguing that there was "no means for the amelioration or reform of society more radical than those of which teachers hold the leverage."[11]

Small helped to provide a philosophical justification for crusaders who, like Jane Addams, were coming to recognize the pragmatic value of enlisting education in the cause of reform. One year after Small's address to the NEA, Addams went before the same body to talk of the problems of "Educating the Immigrant Child." Her conclusions, cast directly in terms of her experience at Hull House in Chicago, indicted the school for isolating itself from life as her immigrant children knew it. She argued that education must begin with the experience the child already has, and concluded that "the city street begins this education for him in a more natural way than does the school." Unlike earlier cultures which succeeded in glorifying the place of the workingman, Addams complained, America kept the factory worker "totally detached from that life which means culture and growth."[12] Through the active and continuing efforts of Addams and her fellows in other reform movements, the public elementary and secondary schools were gradually enlisted as agents of progressive social change. It was a major step in the separation of school and college functions.[13]

Changes in Psychology

At about the same time, the psychological underpinnings of pedagogical theory were being reformulated in response to the influence of G. Stanley Hall and, slightly later, Edward Lee Thorndike.[14] Both had studied under William James at Harvard and shared his interest in empiricism, but they developed this in quite different directions. Hall became the leading American spokesman for the child study movement, concentrating in his work on delineating the characteristics of the normal stages of growth. He believed that the life of each individual recapitulates the life of the race, and drew from that the conclusion that the curriculum should parallel and reflect these historical stages. Hall had tremendous influence on pedagogy and played an important part in shifting the pedagogical emphasis toward basing instruction on the characteristics of the student.

Thorndike placed more emphasis on the psychological laboratory, and in 1901, in a series of articles coauthored with Robert S. Woodworth, published experimental evidence attacking the theory of transfer of training. This in turn called into question the use of "mental discipline" as a justification of school studies: if training in one area was not generalizing to others, the major justification of the classical curriculum would crumble. Educators quickly drew the necessary implications, using the articles as the signal for the final abandonment of faculty psychology, already hard-pressed by the shifting concerns of the school.[15]

John Dewey

It remained for John Dewey to provide a unified perspective on the forces of change that were developing.[16] As a graduate student at Johns Hopkins University, he had been trained primarily in philosophy but had been introduced to psychology and pedagogy by G. Stanley Hall. After several moves, Dewey arrived in 1894 as chairman of the department of philosophy, psychology, and pedagogy at the University of Chicago; two years later he founded a laboratory school in which to test his pedagogical theories. Out of this school, and a series of talks with parents, came his *The School and Society* (1899). In this and his later writings, Dewey presented a provocative and timely analysis of the interrelationships among education, the community, and the nature of the child, giving strong voice to what came to be known as the progressive movement in education.

Among the many points Dewey made, three contributed directly to the emancipation of the high school from the college program in English. First was the conception of reform through education as part of an intentionally progressive society; this had no parallel at all in the classical curriculum of the colleges or in the Germanic scholarship which soon replaced it. Second was the rejection of the traditional body of literature and history as the sole purveyors of culture. As Jane Addams had pleaded, these were far from the life of most students. Though in one sense this challenged the central role which English was beginning to assume in the high school curriculum, it also provided a justification for abandoning the classical pedagogy which had come to dominate English teaching. Finally, there was Dewey's conviction that democracy demands education in the problems of living together for *all* in the community; there could be no provision for a cultural elite. To teachers who used Dewey as a major reference point, the arguments of the Committee of Ten and the dictates of the National Conference on Uniform Entrance Requirements in English could only seem antiquated. The progressives, too, would eventually claim that preparation for college and preparation for life should not be differentiated, but in the new ideology it would be the common-school rather than the college that offered the proper, undifferentiated alternative.

High School against College

The Domination of the Uniform Lists

Even as the arguments of Dewey, Hall, and Addams were offering new goals for teachers of English, institutional forces set in motion at the time of the Committee of Ten seemed to be carrying them ever further in the opposite direction. One important factor was an 1899 report from the NEA Committee on College Entrance Requirements; this reaffirmed that there should be no differentiation of the college preparatory from the terminal course, and then proceeded to outline an English program in which the lists of the National Conference on Uniform Entrance Requirements in English had a prominent place. Instruction in literature and in composition were integrated around a series of focuses taken directly from studies of rhetoric: narration, description, and exposition, for example, were each given a semester of emphasis. This was widely used as a model for high school programs, and eventually became a focus for the criticism of those resisting college domination.[17] The method of correlating instruction in literature and composition was especially provocative; in an ironic reversal of earlier emphases, the course led to a long campaign to separate composition from the teaching of literature, so that composition would receive due attention.[18]

Still it was the domination of the Uniform Lists that caused the most anger. Because individual colleges and, after 1900, the College Entrance Examination Board, used them as the basis for their entrance examinations, the schools had little choice but to accept the selections, whether they considered them appropriate or not. In 1905 the lists were broadened to include two alternates on the list of five for close study, and thirty on the list for more general reading, but even after this expansion it was a very narrow base on which to construct a curriculum. During 1907 the extent to which these lists had nevertheless come to dominate became apparent in a series of reports published by the *School Review*. Results of the first study are typical of all three. Surveying conditions in sixty-seven high schools in the Midwest, it found that the Uniform Lists were determining the curriculum and producing an unexpected degree of uniformity in the English courses offered. In order of decreasing frequency, and with the year of their first appearance in the lists added parenthetically, the ten most popular selections included:[19]

Shakespeare	*Julius Caesar*	(1874)
Shakespeare	*Macbeth*	(1878)
Eliot	*Silas Marner*	(1881)
Milton	*Minor Poems*	(1895)
Shakespeare	*The Merchant of Venice*	(1874)
Burke	*Speech on Conciliation with the Colonies*	(1897)
Lowell	*The Vision of Sir Launfal*	(1886)
Coleridge	*The Rime of the Ancient Mariner*	(1890)
Scott	*Ivanhoe*	(1874)
Macaulay	*Essay on Addison*	(1879)

These include three of the six on Harvard's list of 1874. All ten were being taught in more than 60 percent of the schools—*Julius Caesar* in over 90 percent. The second survey, originating in the Midwest but surveying conditions nationally, found that all seventy of the schools replying to its questionnaire used the Uniform Lists to shape their course.[20] And the third report, this time coming from more conservative New England, commented with some astonishment that the entrance lists were being elevated into a course of study—"a place for which those requirements were never designed and never adapted."[21]

Dissatisfaction with this situation took a different form in the East than in the rest of the country. The source of the difference was the extent to which the entrance examinations were important in college entrance. A system of high school accreditation initiated by the University of Michigan in 1871 had spread to almost two hundred other western and midwestern colleges by 1896. The difference this made was outlined by Fred Newton Scott, whose own professional career began at Michigan after this system was well established. He described the system of accreditation as an "organic" approach which recognized the natural interdependence of the various parts of the educational system, and which respected the judgment of the teachers involved at each stage. The colleges, of which he considered himself a part, were willing to give advice if called upon. "But we do not prescribe," he insisted, "we do not dictate." The eastern examination system, on the other hand, was from Scott's point of view "feudal"; with it, the colleges attempted to dictate the content of lower school programs about which they knew little.[22]

Scott's call was to abolish the lists. Teachers in the East, where entrance examinations remained the rule, sought instead to increase the freedom of the school within the general framework of the Uniform Lists. The difference was fundamental, but it was submerged in a general attack on the lists after 1905, culminating in the founding of the National Council of Teachers of English (NCTE) in 1911.[23]

The Founding of NCTE

The movement which led to the founding of NCTE began in New York City, under the prompting of Clarence Kingsley from the Manual Training High School, Brooklyn, and Theodore C. Mitchill of Jamaica High School; the former led the movement for a general reorganization of secondary education, the second the specific protests against the examinations in English. The situation in English was discussed at length at meetings of the state and local English associations in 1907, 1908, and 1909, culminating in the circulation of "An Open Letter to Teachers of English" by the Executive Committee of the New York State Association of English Teachers.[24] This embodied the sense of the resolutions passed by the association and summarized objections to the current system of examination.

Prominent members of the committee guiding the protest included Percival Chubb, still of the Ethical Culture Schools in New York City, and E. R. Clark of the East High School, Rochester, as well as Mitchill. This committee also took its case directly to the National Education Association at its 1910 meeting in Boston, asking for a formal protest against the lists. Their request was dealt with by the English Round Table of the Secondary Section of the NEA, chaired by Edwin Miller, head of English at Detroit Central High School. Miller was a long-standing foe of the entrance requirements, and under his guidance the Round Table appointed a Committee on College Entrance Requirements to investigate the New York Association's request. James Fleming Hosic was selected by Miller to head the committee, and also to succeed Miller as chairman of the Round Table for the following year.[25] Hosic was head of the English department at Chicago Normal College and an old associate of Miller's. Together they had founded the Chicago English Club in 1905, and three years later Hosic had been among the founders of the Illinois Association of Teachers of English. Fred Newton Scott, under whom Miller had studied, was quickly enlisted in the cause, as was John M. Clapp of Lake Forest College, who had been active with Hosic in the Illinois Association. These men, all from the Midwest, controlled events during the period between the New York protests and the actual founding of NCTE.

In addition to Hosic, the Round Table Committee on College Entrance Requirements included members from New York, Washington, Michigan, Kentucky, and California—Scott and Clapp advised but were not members. Hosic was the only college representative, and even he was from a two-year normal school.[26] The group began by enlisting the aid of existing associations to survey conditions in the teaching of English, paying particular attention to the effects of the entrance requirements. The difficulties encountered in coordinating this work led Hosic to secure a Round Table resolution asking for the establishment of "a national council of teachers of English";[27] this was passed at the summer 1911 meeting of the NEA in San Francisco. As Hosic described it in announcing the organizational meeting for the new association, the intention of the Round Table resolution "was to create a *representative* body, which could reflect and render effective the will of the various local associations and of individual teachers, and, by securing concert of action, greatly improve the conditions surrounding English work."[28] Out of about four hundred who received an announcement from Hosic in early November, some sixty-five gathered at the Great Northern Hotel in Chicago on December 1 and 2, 1911. Twelve states were represented, with high school teachers from the North Central area in the majority. New York sent two representatives, Clark and Mitchill from the committee which had launched the protest.

Hosic had planned the meeting carefully, even to the point of having a draft constitution and names for committees ready in advance. Fred Newton Scott was chosen as the first president, giving the new organization a spokesman of acknowledged prestige in the academic world. Scott had already been president of the Modern Language Association (1907), and later became president of the North Central Association (1913) and of the American Association of Teachers of Journalism (1917). Emma J. Breck, head of the English department at Oakland (California) High School, and Theodore Mitchill were elected first and second vice presidents, respectively—thus giving the National Council representatives on both coasts. Hosic was chosen as secretary, Harry Kendall Bassett of the University of Wisconsin as treasurer. Though the officers of the association were largely from the colleges, they were men who, like Scott and Hosic, actively supported the development of an independent high school course.

Three decisions taken during the first meetings were especially important to the later history of the young association. One was to actively sponsor local organizations, giving each affiliate the right to appoint a member to the Board of Directors which governed the Council. By the end of the first year nineteen groups had affiliated themselves, extending the Council's reach by some five thousand members. The second decision was to sponsor working committees in a variety of areas; seven were appointed during the first year alone. The reports that emanated from the more vigorous of these again served to extend the Council's influence beyond its immediate membership.[29] The third decision was to accept a proposal from Hosic to found, at his own expense, a new journal devoted to the problems of the teaching of English, which though privately owned would serve as the official organ of NCTE. With the help of Newman Miller, editor of the University of Chicago Press, the first issue of

English Journal appeared in January 1912; it has been published continuously to the present day.

Mitchill's selection as second vice president indirectly acknowledged the importance of the New York protests in the genesis of the Council; that he was only second vice president symbolized the fate of those protests in the new, largely midwestern group. Though Mitchill and Clark offered the earlier "Open Letter" for approval on the first day of meetings, the Council refused to endorse it because of its implicit acceptance of an examination system of college entrance.[30] NCTE chose instead to work through *English Journal* and its new committees to develop an English program that would not depend at all upon the guidance of the Uniform Lists. Though teachers from the East remained active in the Council, both individually and through local affiliates, they tended to be a conservative influence pressing for higher standards and more disciplined study.[31]

The Fate of the Lists

Though unwilling to endorse the New York recommendations, NCTE did view the Uniform Lists as an appropriate focus for criticism. The report of Hosic's Round Table committee was printed in the second issue of *English Journal* and distributed to all members of the National Conference on Uniform Entrance Requirements— which led the Conference to invite Hosic and three other committee members to attend their sessions in February and again in May 1912. When new lists were prepared at the May meeting, they were considerably more liberal—"doubtless," Hosic claimed, much influenced by the committee report.[32]

NCTE continued to feel, however, that its most fruitful response to the lists was to provide schools with a better alternative. This was the motivation behind the appointment of a Committee on Types of Organization of High-School English. One of its first undertakings was a questionnaire survey of current practices. Published in 1913, the report of the committee's survey of 307 schools indicated once again that the curriculum in literature was "with few exceptions" determined by the Uniform Lists; there were no separate "types" to investigate.[33]

This survey did not make much progress towards providing an alternative program, though a later report in which the committee was involved was very influential.[34] In the meantime, through an active campaign for school libraries and distribution of book lists for home reading, NCTE attempted to help schools broaden their curricula. The first book list was prepared by a committee under the chairmanship of Herbert Bates, from Kingsley's Manual Training School, Brooklyn. Published in time for the third annual meeting in 1913, the sixteen-page list sold for a nickel. It went through eighteen reprintings before being expanded to sixty-four pages in 1923. Both editions were widely distributed; more than one million copies had been sold by the time a third edition was issued in 1931.[35]

The Council also expended considerable energy on a crusade to expand and improve school libraries. Presenting statistics to show that the cost of English instruction was less than that of any other subject, the Committee on English Equipment argued in 1913 that libraries were the most important resource suffering from lack of funds. Convention resolutions called on schools to employ trained, professional librarians and to provide libraries within their own buildings rather than relying on community facilities. At the same time, *English Journal* provided information about library use and organization, and called attention to especially interesting or successful experiments.[36]

Though neither home reading lists nor the stress on school libraries originated with NCTE, the vigorous support which it offered to both gave teachers one of their first constructive alternatives to the narrowly-based literature program of the National Conference.

Faced with continuing criticism, the college entrance examination in English continued to change. By 1916, the examiners were offering two completely different examinations, of which a candidate would take only one. The first or "restricted" examination continued to be based on a small list of titles for intensive study; the second or "comprehensive" examination allowed the candidate "to show that he has read, understood, and appreciated a sufficient amount of English literature"—no lists were provided at all.[37] This in theory ended the hegemony of the National Conference: henceforth a school could choose for itself whether to use the restricted lists without jeopardizing its students' chances for college entrance. Many schools did continue to use the lists, however, and certainly the titles which had appeared on them continued to be widely taught.

The trend after 1916 was toward increased emphasis upon the comprehensive examination, until the restricted lists were finally abandoned in 1931; at that point the College Entrance Examination Board became solely responsible for the entrance examination in English. This decision, discussed in more detail in the next chapter, brought to an end the National Conference on Uniform Entrance Requirements in English, and with it the last vestiges of what Scott in 1901 had called the "feudal" system in which the colleges could directly dictate the programs of the high schools.

Toward New Methods

The revolt against college domination of the high school program had no clearly worked out principles for restructuring the program.

"A school for the people" was a good rallying cry, and as such it served its purpose well; but it was singularly vague in its implications for the teaching of English. Many varied and interesting proposals were made between 1900 and 1917, but as a set they lacked unity and direction; nevertheless, they gradually led to implementation of a progressive methodology and thus opened the way for development of a more systematic and coherent program in later years.

Almost all changes offered began out of a rejection of the earlier, analytic approach to literary studies, moving instead toward an emphasis on the work as a whole, and of the ideas or values embodied in it. Even during the period in which philological studies were at their strongest, there had been a dissenting tradition which claimed that the proper goal for the teaching of literature should be "appreciation." Henry Hudson, a contemporary of William Rolfe and also an editor of Shakespeare, was typical when he argued in 1881 that "Far more good will come, even to the mind, by foolishly enjoying Shakespeare than by learnedly parsing him."[38] In the initial enthusiasm for philology, such protests were simply brushed aside, but eventually the pedantry of the annotated texts, with their exhaustive notes and editorial apparatus, generated a reaction of its own. The first response was a new justification for analytic techniques as a means toward fuller understanding of the text— thus placing philology in the service of the appreciative tradition. Proponents of this compromise tended to feel that Hudson was wrong in thinking that students *could* "foolishly enjoy" Shakespeare without first "learnedly parsing" him. Franklin T. Baker, in his textbook with Scott and Carpenter, carefully pointed out that "to assume that intellectual effort brought to bear on a subject makes it distasteful is to hold a brief for the stupid and lazy." Percival Chubb, too, acknowledged the need to train students in careful analysis: he suggested that Burke should be studied for three recitations a week over a two-month period, though not very much literature would need to be treated in this way.[39] This tradition of subordinating philological and rhetorical analysis in the justification of studies but maintaining its place in the methodology was quite firmly established by 1900.

The Types Approach

When the search for alternative methodological procedures began in earnest, one of the first suggestions was to replace the study of language characteristic of philology with the study of genres or "types." Till the end of the eighteenth century, types had been studied as patterns to which authors conformed, but during the Romantic period this prescriptive tradition had gradually eroded; genres came to be viewed as having a history and a pattern of evolution which could be a worthy object of study in itself. Hippolyte Taine gave this point of view its fullest expression in his *History of English Literature* (1863), which in turn influenced many American men of letters. During the 1870s and 1880s, studies of types received increasing attention in departments of English, entering the undergraduate curriculum by 1886 at Yale and 1887 at Harvard.[40] The approach was then extended to the secondary school as part of the attempt to liberalize the curriculum. Allan Abbott was an especially prominent early advocate; his description of "An Experiment in High-School English" (1904), explaining the types course at the Horace Mann School, was widely cited for the next fifteen years. His argument, coming before philology had been firmly rejected, stressed the study of types as another way to help students overcome the difficulty of the selections. By studying the various genres, students would learn to solve the particular reading problems which each posed.[41]

Though the study of types was offered as an alternative to philological approaches, it carried with it no very clear methodology of its own. Like literary history, it could and often did become nothing more than a method of arranging the order of study of books to be intensively analyzed. Though there was persistent attention to types from the time of Abbott's article on, it remained as a relatively minor part of the secondary program till the 1920s.

Concern for the Child

Even as proponents of the types approach were proposing changes in the organization of course material, the child study movement was beginning to argue that the teacher should select materials that the child would find both manageable and interesting; these would replace the classic texts which seemed so difficult to teach. G. Stanley Hall addressed such problems as early as 1886 in a pamphlet entitled *How to Teach Reading, and What to Read in School*. In the program he outlined, selections were to be organized and sequenced on the basis of the interests and abilities of the student. Psychological rather than literary principles would dominate; if necessary, teachers would have to rewrite material "till it really and closely fitted the minds and hearts of the children."[42] Hall relied on his recapitulation theory to determine what materials would and would not be appropriate at a given age. Continuing the argument in his later volumes, *Adolescence* (1904), he suggested that myth and legend were the "best expression of the adolescent stage of our race." His specific suggestions, many of which were taken up by teachers of English as part of the evolving high school canon, included "the literature of the Arthuriad and the Sangrail, the stories of Parsifal, Tristram, Isolde, Galahad, Geraint, Siegfried, Brunhilde, Roland, the Cid, Orlando, Tannhauser, Beowulf, Lohengrin, Robin Hood, and Rolando."[43]

This concern with fitting the material to the child led directly to the first statistical studies of reading interests. Hall published a number of these in his own journal, *Pedagogical Seminary*, but a slightly later one in the *School Review* (1902) was more influential with English teachers. As its author, Allan Abbott, explained it, the study originated out of the belief that "It is our business as teachers to study the lines of normal growth, and to lead our pupils from one interest to the next higher, putting aside the special delights of our own libraries until our pupils also shall have reached maturity."[44] Other teachers who followed Hall's general lead proceeded to produce simplified versions of Shakespeare, and even of history, in order to allow the child "to come face to face with the masters."[45]

Rather than the disciplinary value of classical pedagogy, Hall and his followers stressed the place of literature in moral development. "Patriotism, reverence, self-respect, honesty, industry, contentment," he wrote, "these I hold to be the great ethical teachings which should be primarily sought by these selections."[46] In the reaction against philology between 1900 and 1917, such concerns finally won acceptance as the major justification for the teaching of literature in the secondary school program. This opened a number of new vistas for enterprising teachers. The Bible, though banned from the schools in some states, began to be part of the course of study in others. Sex education—or more euphemistically, social hygiene—also had some early advocates, though the suggestions were very timid. *The Lady of the Lake*, "rationalizing, dignifying, and purifying the emotions of sex," was the choice of one teacher. A somewhat bolder colleague suggested Irene McLeod's "Unborn," a poem which, it was asserted defensively, breathes "an expectancy of motherhood that is scarcely less virginal than maternal."[47]

For most teachers, an emphasis on the "content" or "values" of a book became inextricably intertwined with response to the "whole work"—all in opposition to the previous emphasis on analysis and mental discipline. This was initially a pragmatic rather than a theoretically-based linkage, but it found powerful support in Max Eastman's *The Enjoyment of Poetry* (1913). This book argued that poetry is far too complex to be adequately handled through analysis, but that it has such deep psychological roots that analysis is not needed. Children in particular could be expected to respond with enjoyment, if teachers did not kill their natural enthusiasm by handling literature improperly.[48] The book had considerable influence on secondary school teachers, helping to convince them that they were right in moving toward less analytic approaches; it was being cited in major reports on the teaching of literature as late as the 1950s (see p. 168, below).

It was partly in response to such trends that Franklin T. Baker, speaking as second president of the Council, reminded his audience

at the 1914 convention that English literature would acquire whatever status and popularity it was ever to have only when its
teachers were willing to require disciplined study.[49] His position
had changed little since 1903, and though he still had many
supporters, the situation in English had changed greatly. The
appreciative and ethical traditions in the study of literature were
merging, at least temporarily, in a rejection of the classical pedagogy on which his remarks were based.

Contemporary Literature

The concern with the child led almost inevitably to a new
emphasis on modern writings. If teachers were really to start
"where the student is," they would have to start with the dime
novel, the newspaper, and the magazine. This concern was reinforced by those who saw the magazine and newspaper as legitimate
genres replete with their own conventions and characteristics to
analyze and tabulate. Through most of the enthusiasm, however,
there ran a curiously ambiguous undercurrent: the majority of the
teachers who championed current works hoped in the end to lead
their students away from them, toward what the teachers saw as
the real riches of the literature of the past.

Fred Newton Scott set off one wave of this concern with his
second NCTE presidential address (1913). Involved at the university level in the teaching of journalism, he was appalled by the low
standards of the mass circulation papers. He was also convinced
that the root of the problem lay not in the papers themselves but in
the public which was buying them; if tastes could be raised, the
newspapers would improve in their wake. Demonstrating a flair for
publicity himself, Scott used his address to call for a "Newspaper
Week" to focus teachers' attention on the problem; it was up to
them, he argued, to close "the one gate wide enough to let in all the
serried hosts of evil." The speech generated the desired attention,
both in the public press and among teachers—so much so that it
served as the model for a "Better Speech Week" a few years later.[50]

Magazine literature was frequently coupled with the study of
newspapers, and it too was approached with a fundamental mistrust of the high school student's taste. Most teaching began with
the assumption that students would have to be led to an interest in
the "better" magazines. But if tastes could be improved, replied
the opponents of such studies, why stop there? "If it is possible—
as everyone seems to admit—to pull the boys and the girls away
from Hearst's newspapers and to interest them in the more respectable magazines, then why, according to the same logic, does it not
follow that it is possible to lift their taste to a still higher plane,
where they will naturally enjoy the best literature?" It is a logical

extension of the basic argument, but the professor presenting it lets his prejudices take over in the closing paragraphs:

> Let the [English teacher] popularize his course, if he must, so that plenty of crumbs fall to the beggars within the gates; but let him really spend himself in piling high the feast for the golden-brained, hungry-souled boys and girls, who will be able, if he does not stunt their growth, to take their places finally, after toil-worn years, at the banqueting table of life, beside the real kings and queens of the earth.[51]

Most high school teachers of English were more sincere in their support of a common-school curriculum, but most agreed that in the end the classic texts were most important. They were willing, even eager, to use contemporary materials, but only as a bridge back to the works with which the curriculum had long dealt.

Vocational Education

In the concern with the needs of the student rather than of subject matter, vocational education became an important dimension of the school program as it developed after 1900.[52] Many communities began to offer special vocational courses, sometimes as an additional track within established schools, sometimes in new buildings devoted exclusively to commercial and industrial education. These posed a special problem for the teacher of English: if the value of literature is ethical, and if the classics contain its fullest expression, then children in vocational schools would seem to have an even greater need for exposure to their literary and cultural heritage. It was only in the high school that they were likely to be exposed to it at all.

This was of course the position adopted in the *Report* of the Committee of Ten, and in 1911 Eliot defended it before the New England Association of Teachers of English. "Can anyone question," he asked, that the college entrance lists "consist exclusively of specimens of English literature which it is in the highest degree desirable that boys and girls from fourteen to eighteen . . . should be made acquainted with?"[53] It was unfortunate for the business English curriculum that Eliot put his arguments in the context of the college entrance lists; though in the New England Association he could expect considerable support, in the rest of the country such arguments were not well received. The vocational curriculum had more pressing concerns than the classics, and could take comfort in Dewey's arguments that all subjects, not just English and history, had cultural value.

The changes that followed in the teaching of English may have been more drastic than anticipated by those who originally argued for a special vocational course. The programs that were developed emphasized more businesslike skills than literature, even "vocationally oriented" literature, seemed to offer: many became basically courses in composition, with units on salesmanship, advertising, and printing added for variety and breadth. When literature did enter in, it suffered from a variety of rationalizations that attempted to force a place for it within a basically alien set of goals. "The Rape of the Lock," for example, was enthusiastically offered at the University of Nevada for its "many interesting hints as to the commerce and industry of the period." Another teacher boasted of having interested her agricultural students in the study of myths by demonstrating to them how frequently myth-names appeared in commercial advertising.[54] Such enthusiasts notwithstanding, literature yielded before the demands for practical skills. A 1918 survey of the teaching of English in schools having at least two hundred students in commercial courses did not even bother to ask about the teaching of literature—not an unexpected result when the "Ideal Course" suggested by an NCTE committee included the study of literature in but two semesters out of eight.[55]

Teaching Aids

Concern with the interests of students also developed into a concern with aids that would help in "creating" or "holding" that interest. These took two forms, one concentrating on oral presentation, the other on "visualization." The development of oral reading as a form of literary study will be discussed in the next section; the concern with visualization has roots in Sir Francis Galton's argument in *Inquiries Into Human Faculty and Its Development* (1883) that the untrained mind thinks largely in terms of pictures. Writers such as Carpenter, Baker, and Scott took from this a belief that the chief pleasure that children would get from reading would be the result of "mental pictures of scenes and actions"; they also thought that these mental pictures would be easier to remember and more directly connected with real life than "verbal formulas."[56]

Almost any kind of accompaniment to literary studies could be justified with one of these two sets of arguments. The Committee on English Equipment listed many items that Council members would find useful, among them photographs and slide-projecting "lanterns." Ingenious teachers came forward with other suggestions, ranging all the way from a hatbox model of Beowulf's mead hall to literary maps, plot diagrams, songs, and records. Always practical, the *English Journal* provided catalogs of photographs, picture postcards, and songs for the teacher to use in assembling his own collection.[57] Silent films received attention, too, especially after film versions of some of the classic texts began to appear. Nobody suggested film as a legitimate field of study—most considered it decidedly illegitimate—but it could be used for plot analysis or for work in composition.[58]

How extensive such practices were is impossible to ascertain, but a survey published in 1918 provides some clues. Although it dealt with only the better schools in Ohio, and received a rather poor return of only 33 out of 100 questionnaires (the majority of replies coming from city schools), it does indicate at least a degree of congruity between *English Journal* discussions and conditions in the schools. Of the 33 schools replying, 16 used wall maps and charts, 21 used a stereopticon and slides, 25 used pictures in teaching, 19 used a Victrola, 19 had a school library, and 5 used the city library. A slightly earlier Illinois survey found that 65 percent of the schools had a map of America, 78 percent had a map of England, 20 percent used projection lanterns, and 30 percent used a stereopticon.[59]

The Role of Drama

The methodological advances which received the greatest attention and fullest development were in the teaching of drama. Two forces converged in drama during the years before World War I, one from an academic stress on oral presentation, the other from a progressive concern with self-expression; they elevated drama to a position it has never had since.

The Academic Tradition

The central figure in the academic justification of drama was Hiram Corson of Cornell University. His works, especially *The Aims of Literary Study* (1895), were cited by virtually every writer concerned with drama in education—Carpenter, Baker, and Scott; Chubb, and Hall acknowledged their debt to him. Corson's principal concern was to free literary study from the excessive factualism which diverted attention from the ethical value of the works studied. His cure was oral reading, not as performance or entertainment but as a means to a disciplined knowledge of the text. To read well aloud, Corson argued, was to make the meaning clearer and to catch the spirit more accurately than would be possible with any amount of analytic study.[60] Other professors interested in drama gave impetus to Corson's argument, reinforcing the academic aspect of the movement. Brander Matthews, who was appointed professor of literature at Columbia in 1892 and moved to a chair of dramatic literature in 1900, similarly insisted that a play is "something written to be acted before an audience in a theatre." George Pierce Baker, another professor very active in drama, initiated a course in play-writing at Radcliffe in 1905 and was able to offer it to Harvard students the next year. His courses helped to generate interest in serious American drama; Eugene O'Neill was one of the earlier and better-known students.[61]

Hall, citing Corson and others, was convinced that drama had a major role in the development of moral values. Taking up the argument in *Adolescence* (1904), he joined it with his recapitulation theory and concluded that the study of language which the anno- tated texts embodied was out of place; it was only late in history— and thus ought to be late in the life of the child—that language was handled by the "eye which reads instead of the ear which hears." Drama, on the other hand, offered "a school of domestic, civic, and patriotic virtue" ideally suited to "the social nature of youth." Hall recalled that in ancient Greece the theater had been "a place of worship . . . paid for from the public treasury"; he clearly intended it to fill much the same function in modern schools.[62]

The work of these men helped to overcome a long-standing public ambivalence about drama. America had a tradition of stage performance and road shows, but it was heavily commercialized; melodrama, comedy, and patriotic works predominated. Though extremely popular, the theater was also disreputable. Very little drama was allowed in the nineteenth-century schools; even when Shakespeare began to appear in the college entrance lists, it was usually in carefully edited editions. After 1900 this situation began to improve, partly in response to the support drama was beginning to receive in the universities. Serious theater, sponsored by ama- teur or noncommercial companies, became quite popular, with several peaks of activity from 1906 until the beginning of the war.[63]

By 1910 the Drama League of America had been organized to coordinate the scattered companies that had sprung up and to campaign actively on behalf of serious theater; it paid special attention to activities in schools and colleges. When NCTE was founded the following year, it quickly appointed a drama committee under the chairmanship of Thatcher Guild of the University of Illinois. Guild reported that 70 percent of the freshmen at his university had taken part in amateur dramatics in high school. A national survey reported by the same committee two years later found that 86 percent of schools made provision for plays to be given "regularly" by students; another 20 percent arranged for students to attend "plays of worth."[64] Such efforts were actively supported by NCTE, which circulated prompt books, published lists of suitable plays for the high schools, and voted (at the 1918 convention) to ask all high school principals to engage at least one teacher qualified to coach plays.[65]

Oral reading of all sorts became an important mode of literary study at this time; teachers of the novel as well as of poetry were asked to remember "the subtle interpretation of emotions that the voice alone can give." Percival Chubb became especially enthusiastic about such studies, arguing in an address to the 1913 convention that "there must be a great return to the oral and the auditory" to prevent our culture from becoming "increasingly eye-minded." Allan Abbott also supported drama, placing it within the context of the study of types. He outlined a high school course for Council members, following Matthews in treating drama as a literary form meant for the stage. Play production for teachers who approached it in this way was much more than spectacle or exhibition; it was undertaken very much, as the Drama League of America put it, in the spirit of "sound literary and artistic effort on the stage"—an alternative rather than a supplement to other forms of study.[66]

The Progressive Tradition

The other, supporting stream of interest in drama came more directly out of the progressive movement, representing a blend of Dewey's concerns to democratize the classroom, to foster the growth of personality, and to promote social goals of cooperation and group work.[67] Self-control, presence, and ease of movement were among the benefits students could expect, but above all they would learn to work with one another, in the process developing class spirit and community unity. Teachers who defended drama from this point of view were less likely to see it as a means of literary study than as one of self-expression; the plays were often written by the teacher or the students themselves. Pageants were the most extreme expression of this philosophy, providing, as the secretary of the budding American Pageant Association told *English Journal* readers in 1914, unequalled opportunity to develop "joyous neighborhood spirit."[68]

The Effects on the Schools

The effects of the dramatic interests of this period on the schools were varied. From the emphasis on student activity there arose a whole series of student- and teacher-written plays and masques; these were published regularly by the *English Journal* until the mid-twenties, when they mercifully died out. The first appeared in 1912 and its footnote—"Written as a regular exercise in the Course in Children's Literature in the Chicago Teachers College"—unwittingly emphasized the degree of spontaneity and literary merit which most would offer.[69] More lasting in its effects was the little theater movement; able to justify itself both as literary exercise and as democratic effort, the school or class play became a national tradition.[70]

Emphasis on community effort in drama was itself part of a larger concern with "socialization training." This became especially prominent after Dewey published his *Democracy and Education* (1916). The underlying premise was simple enough; as a 1918 *English Journal* editorial put it, teachers had discovered that "Training in a little autocracy is poor preparation for citizenship in a democracy."[71] Students must be given a more active role in the life of the school, and that life itself needed to have more relation to the life of the "outside world." Textbook summaries of materials for study, the authoritarian stance of the classroom lecture, the recitation of memorized lessons—all came under attack in attempts to transform the school from "an intellectual court of justice" into "an epitome of typical group life." In one widely quoted experiment, "Reading Clubs" replaced literature classes so that students could more nearly direct their own reading. Another school brought the "social agencies of society" within its walls by staging a public trial of Banquo for complicity in the murder of Duncan. Still another solved "The Social Problems of Our Little Town" by staging a story-night in opposition to the local "picture show"—and winning![72] Though the more extreme versions of such activities eventually died out, one outgrowth, the project method, grew in influence during the postwar era; it will be discussed again in Chapter V.

The Reorganization Reports

The Cardinal Principles

The forces working to alter the basic assumptions of the high school program were not limited in their influence to the English course. The revolt against the college entrance requirements, the new focus upon the student, the concern that democratic values and institutions be reflected within the classroom—these were to transform almost all aspects of the curriculum. The National Education Association, working through a series of committees and commissions headed by Clarence Kingsley, took up the broad questions involved in the reorganization of subject matter and instructional procedures within the high school. The main report was issued in 1918 as the *Cardinal Principles of Secondary Education.*

This report accepted the emphases that have been discussed in connection with the teaching of English, providing them with what was to become their definitive statement and defense. The main objectives of education, as the report presented them, were seven: 1. Health. 2. Command of fundamental processes. 3. Worthy home-membership. 4. Vocation. 5. Citizenship. 6. Worthy use of leisure. 7.

Ethical character.[73] These goals are a long way from those of the Committee of Ten, and if they had many antecedents, they were brought together here by a national committee of some influence and prestige, in a concise statement that would be widely quoted and often referred to.

The Reorganization of English

The subject of English was dealt with in detail by a National Joint Committee on English, cosponsored by Kingsley's Commission on Reorganization and by NCTE. Kingsley asked Hosic to head the Joint Committee in 1911, at the same NEA convention that directed him to proceed with arrangements for the founding of NCTE. Thirty members were eventually appointed, representing (with a few changes and additions) the NEA Round Table Committee on College Entrance Requirements and the NCTE Committee on the High School Course in English. Secondary school members continued to dominate—of the thirty, only nine had college appointments at the time, and three of these were in teachers colleges. Not surprisingly, there was considerable overlap between the committee and those who were active in NCTE during the same period; many of the convention addresses and *English Journal* articles during these years could be seen as working drafts of various sections of the final report.[74] The final report, *Reorganization of English in Secondary Schools* (1917), was the culmination of the revolt of the high school teacher of English against the domination of his course by the college entrance requirements.

Little in the report was new. Like the earlier statement of the Vassar Conference on English organized by the Committee of Ten, its value lay in bringing together in one comprehensive statement points of view that its members had been developing at conferences and conventions and in the professional journals throughout the preceding decade. Gathered together in one volume, and united by a common opposition to the college entrance lists, these arguments could serve as a manifesto for reform, a convenient reference point whose principles could be endorsed and implemented as a more or less coherent whole. As such, and bearing the endorsements of NCTE and NEA, its influence was considerable.[75]

Reorganization of English in Secondary Schools began by affirming the independence of the high school and rejecting the principle that preparation for college was also the best preparation for life. However important the college entrance requirements may have been in initially securing a place for English in the curriculum, the longer-term result had been to achieve a "monotonous and unintelligent uniformity" (p.7). Picking up an argument the parent commission would use in the *Cardinal Principles* report a year later, the committee urged schools to provide "a considerable range" of course content to meet the varying backgrounds of the students, while at the same time preserving "a reasonable uniformity of aims and a body of common culture." In particular, "Skill in thinking, high ideals, right habits of conduct, healthy interests, and sensitiveness to the beautiful are attainments to be coveted for all" (p.26).

The main points discussed in the report paralleled those that had prominence in the professional literature. The justifications for literary studies fell into three categories—cultural, vocational, and social and ethical. To achieve these ends, there should be (as Hall had suggested) "Subordination of excellence of style . . . to value of content and power to arouse interest" (p. 46). Rather than a formal discipline, English was to be "social in content and social in method of acquirement." This would be achieved by structuring the course around "expressional and interpretative experiences of the greatest possible social value to the given class" (p. 27). As has already been evident in earlier discussions, however, it was the "great books," the classics, which most successfully demonstrated that they had this "social value." Or as the subcommittee on literature for the upper secondary school grades put it, "Who shall say that boys and girls of to-day will not need their [the classics'] clear note of inspiration and courage as much if not more than their fathers and mothers of yesterday" (p. 65). The subcommittee on business English waxed especially eloquent about the virtues of literature that "is in the spirit of the present, that has a commercial tang, that treats of the problems and even of the activities and processes that they will meet after leaving school." Yet even this subcommittee affirmed too the values of "standard literature . . . well chosen and sanely taught," as "a good antidote for the harmful pleasures that invite the weary workers in our cities" (p. 97).

The report was very specific about the works to be studied. It provided two lists for each grade level, one of books "for class work," the other of books "for individual reading." The distinction was that of the National Conference on Uniform Entrance Requirements in English, but it served here, presumably, to provide "common culture" and "considerable range." The grade-by-grade distribution of literary works was carefully planned to correspond to the committee's conception of pupils' emotional and intellectual stages. For the eighth and ninth grades, they urged "stirring narrative, full of movement and manly virtue. This is the place for Homer's heroic Greeks and Macaulay's noble Romans, for the elemental passions of ballad times, for Scott and Stevenson and all others of their stirring company." The tenth grade, through the use of such plays as *The Merchant of Venice* and *Julius Caesar,* would deal directly with "serious questions of right and wrong." The eleventh would be the time "frankly to discuss the relations of men and women to each other," but only in the context of the "high ideality" of *Idylls of the King* and *Silas Marner*. Finally for the twelfth grade, the Joint Committee suggested a "literary" course, organized chronologically and including both American and English literature.[76]

What the committee members did *not* do with literature is as important as the lists they provided. They did not abandon the titles used by the National Conference on Uniform Entrance Requirements in English; they did not suggest overshadowing them with modern and "relevant" works. They did not propose that class study be devoted to contemporary social commentary. While greatly shifting the goals and much of the presumed activity within the classroom, they did not shift the materials that were to be used in attaining those goals. Of the authors on the college entrance lists before 1900—the lists formulated before agitation within the profession began to force change—all but three were part of the Joint Committee's suggestions. Only Johnson, Dryden, and Burke fell completely from favor.[77] The concerns with social issues and with the productions of modern writers were generously reflected in the Reorganization report, but their place was clearly to be in the lists for individual reading. For class study, the literary canon continued virtually unchanged.

In this emphasis, the Joint Committee was not unusual. George Counts, surveying fifteen cities "representing progressive tendencies" during the spring of 1924, found that English received more emphasis than any other study. Half the time in the course was devoted to literature, the other half to a variety of language activities loosely related to composition. The most frequently taught titles were *Silas Marner*, "The Rime of the Ancient Mariner," *Macbeth*, *A Tale of Two Cities*, *Idylls of the King*, *The House of the Seven Gables*, *Ivanhoe*, *Julius Caesar*, and *The Merchant of Venice*. All were in the Reorganization report lists, and all but *Idylls of the King* had appeared in the entrance lists before 1900. Counts also found that thirty-four of forty-nine specific courses examined emphasized intensive study for at least some of the texts required.[78]

Continuations

War broke in upon the trends summarized in the Reorganization reports, accentuating some and postponing the development of others till later years. The Declaration of War in April 1917 crystallized definitions of "needs and interests" in terms of national aims, and English teachers across the nation responded with enthusiasm. The Drama League dropped its literary emphasis and provided a play on food conservation. Decatur, Illinois, appalled to discover that a quarter of its students never read the daily paper at a time of history "in the making," made newspaper study a required part of the English course. For all, literature became a way to instill a sense of national heritage and to encourage patriotism.[79]

One of the concerns generated by the war, the teaching of American literature, was among the few that achieved a more or less permanent place in the curriculum, though it took some ten more years before a uniform pattern for these studies emerged. During the postwar period the North Central Association actively supported the movement to establish such studies; its Commission on Secondary Schools, for example, distributed a questionnaire after the war to assure itself that the schools in the region were diligently pursuing "Training for Citizenship." Other NCA committees concerned with English were similarly careful to include a chronological survey of American literature in various alternate positions within their recommended courses of study in 1922 and again in 1930.[80] NCTE showed a parallel if less intense concern, holding convention sessions on "The Teaching of American Ideals" and editorializing that English should "result in a finer, truer, and larger Americanism on the part of those who study it."[81] When these recommendations were taken up by the literary anthologies of the late twenties and thirties, American literature was firmly established in the curriculum.

The real legacy of this period was inspirational rather than methodological: teachers who had set out to build morale and foster patriotic sentiments, and who had seen their goals reflected in the behavior of their students, emerged convinced of the power of literature to effect such changes. None stopped to wonder whether both the teaching and the response might have had a common origin in the wartime milieu. Teachers who sought to formulate a role for their teaching in "a new world, safe for a new democracy" were above all else enthusiastic about what they were doing: as one put the problem, "The first great aim in the literature course is a training for citizenship by a study of our national ideals embodied in the writings of American authors, our race ideals as set forth by the great writers of Anglo-Saxon origin, our universal ideals as we find them in any great work of literary art."[82]

How to translate such enthusiasm into a functioning school program was the problem for the next generation of teachers.

CHAPTER III NOTES

1. Jane Addams, "Educating the Immigrant Child," Beaver Island Reprint no. He 375; from National Educational Association *Addresses and Proceedings, 1897* (Chicago: University of Chicago Press for the NEA, 1897).

2. New England Association Standing Committee on Courses of Study, "The Course of Study in English—The Call for It, the Character of It and the Construction of It," *School Review* 15 (October 1907): 559-75.

3. James Fleming Hosic, comp. *Reorganization of English in Secondary Schools*, Bulletin 1917, no. 2 (Washington, D.C.: Bureau of Education, 1917), p. 11.

4. John Elbert Stout, *The Development of High School Curricula in the North Central States from 1860 to 1918*, Supplementary Educational Monographs, vol. 3, no. 3 (Chicago: University of Chicago Press, June 1921), p. 235.

5. *PMLA, School Review, Education, Teachers College Record*, and *The Academy* all devoted considerable attention to the teaching of English in schools either before or during this period. For an extensive bibliography of writings from all sources, see George R. Carpenter, Franklin T. Baker, and Fred N. Scott, *The Teaching of English in the Elementary and the Secondary School* (New York: Longmans, Green, and Co., 1903). See also B. A. Hinsdale, *Teaching the Language Arts: Speech, Reading, Composition* (New York: D. Appleton, 1896); and Percival Chubb, *The Teaching of English in the Elementary and Secondary School* (New York: Macmillan Co., 1902).

6. On the founding of the New England Association, see Charles Lane Hanson, "The Early Years of Our Association," *The English Leaflet* 48, no. 427 (March 1949): 33-47. Hanson had studied with Child at Harvard. On other groups in existence by 1911, see James Hocker Mason, *The National Council of Teachers of English—1911-1926* (Dissertation, George Peabody College for Teachers, 1962), pp. 51-52, 67-68. This list is of groups which cooperated in founding NCTE and is probably not complete.

7. At the same time, the percentage of those in English classes was also rising, from 38.5 in 1900 to 58.4 in 1915. See Appendix V, and Bureau of the Census, *Historical Statistics of the United States: Colonial Times to 1957* (Washington, D.C.: U.S. Government Printing Office, 1960), p. 207.

8. Chubb, *Teaching English in the Elementary and Secondary School*, p. 239.

9. Ibid., p. 241.

10. Lawrence A. Cremin in his *The Transformation of the School* (New York: Vintage Books, 1961) is the major source for the following discussion of social and intellectual changes in the period before 1917. See also Edward A. Krug, *The Shaping of the American High School* (New York: Harper & Row, 1964).

11. National Education Association, *Addresses and Proceedings, 1896*, p. 184; cited by Cremin, *Transformation of the School*, p. 99.

12. Addams, "Educating the Immigrant Child." From NEA, *Addresses and Proceedings, 1897*.

13. The colleges were moving in quite another direction, towards specialization and Germanic scholarship. See Frederick Rudolph, *The*

American College and University: A History (New York: Vintage Books, 1962).

14. On American psychology at this time, see Cremin, *Transformation of the School*, pp. 100-15; and Edwin G. Boring, *A History of Experimental Psychology* (New York: Appleton-Century-Crofts, 1929).

15. Thorndike's warnings not to generalize too far from his findings went unheeded. Educators picked them up quickly; they were cited two years later by Carpenter, Baker, and Scott, for example (*Teaching of English*, p. 76). E. L. Thorndike and R. S. Woodworth, "The Influence of Improvement in One Mental Function upon the Efficiency of Other Functions," *Psychological Review* 8 (1901): 247-61, 384-95, 553-64.

16. On Dewey, see especially Cremin, *Transformation of the School*, pp. 115-26.

17. "Report of the Committee on College-Entrance Requirements," National Education Association *Addresses and Proceedings, 1899* (Chicago: University of Chicago Press for the NEA, 1899), pp. 632-814. The group included two members of the National Conference on Uniform Entrance Requirements in English: John Tetlow and Wilson Farrand. The suggested course was based on a presentation by W. F. Webster, principal of East High School, Minneapolis. See Paul Truman Rosewell, *A Historical Survey of Recommendations and Proposals for the Literature Curricula of American Secondary Schools Since 1892* (Dissertation, University of Nebraska Teachers College; University Microfilms No. 66-2081); Joseph Mersand, "The Teaching of Literature in American Secondary Schools: 1865-1900," in *Perspectives on English*, ed. Robert C. Pooley (New York: Appleton-Century-Crofts, Inc., 1960); and Harold Rugg, "Three Decades of Mental Discipline: Curriculum Making Via National Committees," in *Curriculum Making Past and Present*, Twenty-Sixth Yearbook of the National Society for the Study of Education, Part One (Bloomington, Ill.: Public School Publishing Co., 1926).

18. This campaign was unsuccessful to the extent that separate courses in literature and composition and separate examinations from the College Entrance Examination Board were not forthcoming; the real objective of reforming the teaching of composition to make it less literary and more personal in emphasis was nonetheless accomplished. For discussions of the merits of separation, see, for example, Edwin L. Miller, "Rebuilding an English Course," NEA *Addresses and Proceedings, 1910* (Chicago: The University Press for the NEA, 1911), pp. 483-87; Editorial, "'Comprehensive' and 'Restricted'," *English Journal* 5:4 (1916): 281-82; E. H. Kemper McComb, "Separation of the Teaching of Composition from the Teaching of Literature: What It Is and How It Works," *English Journal* 6:2 (February 1917): 69-79; and Hosic, *Reorganization*.

19. George W. Tanner, "Report of the Committee Appointed by the English Conference to Inquire into the Teaching of English in the High Schools of the Middle West," *School Review* 15 (January 1907): 37-45. Hosic was involved in this survey.

20. Cyrus L. Hooper, "Existing Conditions in the Teaching of English," *School Review* 15 (April 1907): 261-74. Again, Hosic is mentioned.

21. This is quoted more fully at the beginning of this chapter. The domination of the lists has been discussed and documented by a number of authors. See Edna Hays, *College Entrance Requirements in English: Their Effects on the High Schools* (New York: Teachers College, Columbia Uni-

versity, 1936), pp. 92-107; Mersand, "Teaching Literature: 1865-1900"; Hosic, *Reorganization*, pp. 11-21; Mason, *NCTE 1911-1926*, pp. 39 ff.; Robert S. Fay, *The Reorganization Movement in English Teaching, 1910-1917* (Dissertation, Harvard University, 1967; University Microfilms No. 68-12,068), pp. 69-74; John Muth Bernd, *Approaches to the Teaching of Literature in Secondary School, 1900-1956* (Dissertation, University of Wisconsin, 1957; University Microfilms No. 24,264), pp. 50, 74.

22. Fred Newton Scott, "College-Entrance Requirements in English," *School Review* 9 (June 1901): 365-78. Scott became an instructor in English literature at Michigan in 1889; in 1903 he became head of the department of rhetoric. On accreditation, see Theodore R. Sizer, *Secondary Schools at the Turn of the Century* (New Haven: Yale University Press, 1964).

23. Mason, *NCTE 1911-1926*, and Fay, *Reorganization Movement*, provide the most detailed discussion of the events leading up to the founding of NCTE. See also the other discussions referenced in footnote 21 above, and "The National Council, 1911-36," *English Journal* 25:10 (December 1936): 805-29.

24. The letter was later reprinted in *English Journal*. (Executive Committee of the New York State Association of English Teachers, "An Open Letter to Teachers of English," *English Journal* 1:3 [March 1912] 179-80.)

25. Technically, the appointments would have been made by the president of the secondary section, but this was Principal Mackenzie of Miller's Detroit Central High School. The Round Table itself was simply an annual forum in which anyone at the convention could participate. The agenda began with prepared speeches which were then opened for discussion; several hundred teachers were often present. These developments are not mentioned in the minutes of the 1910 meeting but are referred to indirectly in the volume for the next year. See NEA *Addresses and Proceedings, 1910* (Chicago: University of Chicago Press for the NEA, 1911), "Round Table Conferences: A. English," pp. 483-93; and NEA *Addresses and Proceedings, 1911* (Chicago: University of Chicago Press for the NEA, 1911), especially James Fleming Hosic, "The Questions at Issue: Preliminary Report of a Committee on College-Entrance Requirements in English," pp. 592-98.

26. The other members of the committee were Charles Swain Thomas, head of English at Newton (Massachusetts) High School but a midwesterner by birth and education; Benjamin A. Heydrick, head of English at the High School of Commerce in New York City; Henry B. Dewey, state superintendent of schools, Washington; Edwin L. Miller, who had just been promoted to assistant principal at Central High School, Detroit; Mrs. Henry Hulst, head of English, Grand Rapids High School; Reuben Post Halleck, principal of the Male High School in Louisville; Miss Fannie W. McLean, head of English at Berkeley (California) High School. (Heydrick and Thomas had at earlier points in their careers taught in universities, and both had published textbooks on the teaching of English. B. A. Heydrick, *How to Study Literature* (1901); C. S. Thomas, *How to Teach the English Classics* (1910).

27. "Round Table Conference on English, July 12, 1911," NEA *Addresses and Proceedings, 1911*, p. 556. The minutes give a slightly different version than Hosic later recalled for *English Journal* readers. (James Fleming Hosic, "The National Council of Teachers of English," *English*

Journal 10:1 [January 1921]: 1-10.) The resolution was proposed by Walter Hunting, superintendent of public instruction in Nevada ("The National Council, 1911-36," p. 809).

28. The model of the NEA's Council on Education apparently led to the choice of "Council" instead of the more usual "Association" for the new organization; this is reflected in the emphasis on representativeness in this quotation, and in the later decision to govern NCTE through a Board of Directors whose members would be appointed individually by the affiliated organizations. "Proceedings of the First Annual Meeting," *English Journal* 1:1 (January 1912): 30-45.

29. Fay (*Reorganization Movement*, p. 119) credits the committees with being the Council's greatest source of influence. During the first decade alone, there were reports on articulation of high school and elementary school English; revision of grammatical terminology; home reading; English in country schools; plays in school and college; teacher preparation; speech; labor and cost of English teaching; freshman English; economy of time; and reorganization—often with several reports from the same or related committees. See "The National Council, 1911-36," pp. 816-17.

30. "Proceedings of the First Annual Meeting," p. 37. This was obviously an emotional issue, still being justified in retrospect in "The National Council, 1911-36." W. Wilbur Hatfield later paid tribute to Hosic's "astounding" accomplishment in keeping the local associations, with their different outlooks, within the Council. "In Memoriam: James Fleming Hosic," *English Journal* 48:3 (March 1959): 160.

31. Charles Swain Thomas, as editor of *English Leaflet* (the journal of the New England Association) from 1909-1940 and as an associate professor at Harvard, came to be the leading spokesman for the New England view, though he began teaching in his home town of Pendleton, Indiana, in 1887, and remained for the most part in the Midwest till 1908. He did not settle permanently in the East till after a spell as director of English in Cleveland (1918-20). See Council News and Comment, "Charles Swain Thomas," *English Journal* 32:7 (September 1943): 389-90; and Marion C. Sheridan, "Here We Are," *English Leaflet* 52, no. 507 (January 1953): 2-11.

32. James Fleming Hosic, "Progress in Articulating School and College English," NEA *Addresses and Proceedings, 1912* (Chicago: University of Chicago Press for the NEA, 1912), p. 762.

33. "Types of Organization of High-School English," Report of the Committee, *English Journal* 2:9 (November 1913): 575-95.

34. The committee was one of those forming part of the National Joint Committee responsible for the Reorganization report, discussed later in this chapter.

35. See "The National Council, 1911-36," pp. 817-18; *English Journal* 18:7 (September 1929): 599; and James Mason, *NCTE, 1911-1926*, who summarizes sales at various points in his chronology, e.g., pp. 91, 335, 348.

36. "English Equipment," Report of the Committee, *English Journal* 2:3 (March 1913): 178-84; and "Proceedings of the Third Annual Meeting," *English Journal* 3:1 (January 1914): 54. As examples, see Carrie E. Tucker Dracass, "An Experiment in Library Training in the High School," *English Journal* 1:4 (April 1912): 221-31; Iva M. Young, "A New England High-School Library," *English Journal* 4:9 (November 1915): 571-76; Emma J.

Breck, "The Efficient High-School Library," *English Journal* 5:1 (January 1916): 10-19; and Editorial, "Go Thou and Do Likewise," *English Journal* 6:4 (April 1917): 271.

37. Typical questions, both from 1920, asked: "List books that you like and dislike, telling why." "Describe the major or minor characters from any three novels." Hays, *College Entrance Requirements*, p. 80.

38. Henry Hudson, *English in Schools* (1881; reissued 1906); quoted by Peter D. Witt. *The Beginnings of the Teaching of the Vernacular Literature in the Secondary Schools of Massachusetts* (Dissertation, Harvard University, 1968), p. 276.

39. Carpenter, Baker, and Scott, *Teaching of English,* p. 182. On Chubb as a fusion of the older and newer approaches, see John R. Searles, *Some Trends in the Teaching of Literature Since 1900* (Dissertation, University of Wisconsin, 1942), pp. 34 ff.

40. Under E. T. McLaughlin and Barrett Wendell, respectively. For the fullest discussion of the types approach and its historical antecedents, see Irvin Ehrenpreis, *The "Types Approach" to Literature* (New York: King's Crown Press, 1945).

41. Allan Abbott, "An Experiment in High-School English," *School Review* 12 (September 1904): 550-58. On its influence, see Ehrenpreis, *Types Approach,* pp. 1-4, 85. The earlier course at Horace Mann had been described by Franklin T. Baker, "The Course in English in the Horace Mann School, Teachers College," *Teachers College Record* 1 (May 1900): 1-36. Abbott went there in 1902. Bernd, *Approaches to Teaching Literature,* pp. 82-86, also comments on the link between the types approach and the liberalization of the course; he quotes Abbott to the effect that "The familiar doctrine of interest—in its educational sense—will be seen at the bottom of this plan."

42. G. Stanley Hall, *How to Teach Reading, and What to Read in School* (Boston: D. C. Heath and Co., 1886), p. 32; similarly in G. Stanley Hall, *Adolescence: Its Psychology and Its Relation to Physiology, Anthropology, Sociology, Sex, Crime, Religion, and Education,* vol. 2 (New York and London: D. Appleton and Co., 1914; first edition, 1904), p. 444: "Excrescences must be eliminated, the gold recoined, its culture power brought out."

43. Hall, *Adolescence,* vol. 2, pp. 442-44.

44. Allan Abbott, "Reading Tastes of High-School Pupils, A Statistical Study," *School Review* 10 (October 1902): 585-600. See his earlier "'Entrance English' from the Boy's Point of View," *Education* 22 (September 1901): 78-88. Many "studies" of reading interest followed, though very few were well designed or well reported by today's standards. As examples, see Charles M. McConn, "High-School Students' Rankings of English Classics," *English Journal* 1:5 (May 1912): 257-72; and G. W. Willett, "The Reading Interests of High-School Pupils," *English Journal* 8:8 (October 1919): 474-87.

45. Caroline E. Britten, "A Loose-Leaf Textbook in English Literature," *English Journal* 2:3 (March 1913): 145-50.

46. Hall, *What to Read,* p. 36.

47. W. R. Humphreys, "The Literary Study of the *Bible* in Michigan High Schools," *English Journal* 6:4 (April 1917): 209-20; T. W. Gosling, "How the High-School Teacher of English Can Assist in the Exploitation of Pupils' Powers," *English Journal* 2:8 (October 1913): 513-17; and Sarah

J. McNary, "Sex Education: The Opportunity of the Teacher of English," *English Journal* 8:4 (April 1919): 242-47. See also *Teaching Social Hygiene through Literature* (New York: American Social Hygiene Association, 1920), which reprints two articles on sex education from the April and July 1920 issues of *Social Hygiene* 5 (pp. 263-72; 391-99).

48. Max Eastman, *The Enjoyment of Poetry* (New York: Charles Scribner's Sons, 1913). For further discussion, see Searles, *Trends in Teaching Literature*, pp. 48-51.

49. Franklin T. Baker, "High School Reading: Compulsory and Voluntary," *English Journal* 4:1 (January 1915): 1-8.

50. Fred Newton Scott, "The Undefended Gate," *English Journal* 3:1 (January 1914): 1-14. Scott is the only NCTE president to serve two terms. The first Council committee on speech was headed by Scott, and later by Claudia E. Crumpton. It was under Crumpton that the committee issued a *Guide to Better Speech Week* (1919). This was apparently highly successful but drew criticism from the organizations of teachers of speech, who thought the Council was intruding in their areas. A *Better Speech Year* (1925) was eventually produced in cooperation with the National Association of Teachers of Speech but was less successful. See "The National Council, 1911-36," pp. 820-21; and Donald P. Veilh, *An Historical Analysis of the Relations Between "English" and "Speech" since 1910* (Dissertation, Teachers College, Columbia University, 1952).

51. James Cloyd Bowman, "The Use of the Magazine in English," *English Journal* 5:5 (May 1916): 332-40. As examples of other views, see William Frederick Edgerton, "A Recent Experiment with Magazine Literature," *English Journal* 1:5 (May 1912): 278-83; Maurice W. Moe, "Magazine Poetry in the Classroom," *English Journal* 4:8 (October 1915): 523-25; and Allan Abbott, "A High-School Course in Periodical Literature," *English Journal* 2:7 (September 1913): 422-27.

52. Stout, *High School Curricula*, pp. 207 ff., details the growing effects of vocational programs on school organization as well as specific subject-area offerings.

53. Charles W. Eliot, "The Differentiation of the High-School Course in English," *English Leaflet* no. 91 (June 1911): 2. In this debate Eliot was paired with D. O. S. Lowell of Roxbury Latin School against Charles A. Prosser, Massachusetts deputy commissioner of education, and Samuel Thurber, Jr. The debate is symbolic of the fate of English studies, with Eliot from the first period and Prosser who in 1945 would launch the "life adjustment" movement. For comments on the debate, see Rosewell, *Historical Survey of Recommendations*, p. 82; James Warren Olson, *The Nature of Literature Anthologies Used in the Teaching of High School English 1917-1957* (Dissertation, University of Wisconsin, 1969; University Microfilms No. 69-22,454), pp. 26-33; and C. S. Thomas, "The English Course in the High School," *English Journal* 1:2 (February 1912): 84-94.

54. Herbert Wynfred Hill, "The Problem of Harmonizing Aesthetic Interests with the Commercial and Industrial Trend of Our Times," *English Journal* 2:10 (December 1913); 609-12; and Mabel Fleming, "The Myths of Commerce," *English Journal* 7:4 (April 1918): 270.

55. These courses were being offered in place of rather than in addition to other English work. Leverett S. Lyon, "The Business-English Situation in the Secondary School," *English Journal* 7:9 (November 1918): 576-86;

and Sherwin Cody, "The Ideal Course in English for Vocational Students," *English Journal* 3:5 and 6 (May and June 1914): 263-81, 371-80.

56. Carpenter, Baker, and Scott, *Teaching of English*, p. 169. They point out that the use of pictures in teaching can be traced at least to fifteenth century primers, and that they are used in the teaching of composition as well as literature. They include an appendix, "Dealers in Photographs and Prints."

57. See for example Mary Crawford, "The Laboratory Equipment of the Teacher of English," *English Journal* 4:5 (March 1915): 145-51; Julia Davenport Randall, "A Literary Map of London," *English Journal* 4:2 (February 1915): 125; Jeanette F. Abrams, "A List of Published Airs for Songs in *The Golden Treasury*," *English Journal* 4:6 (June 1915): 387-97; Martha E. Clay, "The Hat Box in Literature," *English Journal* 5:10 (December 1916): 680-83; and Cornelia Carhart Ward, "The Use of Pictures in the Teaching of Literature," *English Journal* 4:8 (October 1915): 526-30.

58. There were early silent films of "The Vision of Sir Launfal" and *The House of the Seven Gables*, for example. The first *English Journal* article devoted just to movies was Robert W. Neal, "Making the Devil Useful," *English Journal* 2:10 (December 1913): 658-60. For a favorable view, see Carolyn M. Gerrish, "The Relation of the Moving Pictures to English Composition," *English Journal* 4:4 (April 1915): 226-30. And for a harsh attack, see Alfred M. Hitchcock, "The Relation of the Picture Play to Literature," *English Journal* 4:5 (May 1915): 292-98.

59. Cecile B. McCrosky, "The Administration of English in the High-School Curriculum," *English Journal* 7:2 (February 1918), 108-17. The Illinois survey is cited in Hosic, *Reorganization*, pp. 150-52.

60. Corson's concern with ethics is evident even in his first teaching appointment—as professor of moral science, history, and rhetoric at Girard College in 1865. He moved from there to St. Johns in 1866, and to Cornell in 1870. On Corson's leadership and influence, see Searles, *Trends in Teaching Literature*, pp. 44-47. See also Hiram Corson, *The Aims of Literary Study* (New York: Macmillan Company, 1895).

61. Dumas Malone, ed., *Dictionary of American Biography* (New York: Charles Scribner's Sons, 1935); Kenneth Macgowan, *Footlights Across America* (New York: Harcourt, Brace and Co., 1929); and Arthur Hobson Quinn, *A History of the American Drama from the Civil War to the Present* (New York: Appleton-Century-Crofts, 1936).

62. Hall, *Adolescence*, vol. 2, pp. 416, 442.

63. The three most important peaks included 1906-07, when the New Theater, the Robertson Players, and a revitalized Hull House Theater (originating at Addams's Hull House in 1899) all were organized in Chicago; 1911-12, with the organization of Thomas Dickinson's Wisconsin Players, the Toy Theater in Boston, and the summer theater at Lake Forest, Illinois; and 1915-16, which produced the Provincetown Players, Boston's Washington Square Players, and Chicago's Little Theater. All generated publicity and interest. See Quinn, *History of American Drama*; and Macgowan, *Footlights Across America*.

64. Thatcher H. Guild, "Suggestions for the High-School Play," *English Journal* 2:10 (December 1913): 637-46; "Report of the Committee on Plays in Schools and Colleges," *English Journal* 4:1 (January 1915): 34-40.

76 Tradition and Reform

65. J. Milnor Dorey succeeded Guild as chairman of the drama committee. The library was established under his guidance (Mason, *NCTE, 1911-1926*, p. 139). "The Play Producer's Notebook" was an irregular but frequent feature in *English Journal* from 1917 on; it was written by members of the committee, often anonymously. For the first, see *English Journal* 6:3 (March 1917): 192-93. Dorey had also provided an earlier list in 1915 (pp. 406-07), and a separate publication in cooperation with the Drama League ("The National Council, 1911-36," p. 15). For the convention resolution, see "Proceedings of the Seventh Annual Meeting: Business," *English Journal* 7:1 (January 1918): 74.

66. Mary Frothingham Pritchard, "The Value of Story-Telling in the High-School Course," *English Journal* 4:3 (March 1915): 191-93; Percival Chubb, "The Blight of Literary Bookishness," *English Journal* 3:1 (January 1914): 15-27; Allan Abbott, "A High-School Course in Drama," *English Journal* 2:2 (February 1913): 93-98; and Mary Grey Peck, "The Educational Movement for the New American Drama," *English Journal* 1:3 (March 1912): 129-37. Peck was appealing for members.

67. The progressive's interest in dramatics is clear in Dorey's career: he later became executive secretary of the Progressive Education Association (1928-31).

68. Thomas Wood Stevens was one of the main organizers of this group in 1913; he edited its *Bulletin* (1913-21). Interest in pageants declined rapidly after World War I. Lotta A. Clark, "Pageantry in America," *English Journal* 3:3 (March 1914): 146-53.

69. Mary Ethel Courtenay, "Clytie: A Lyrical Play for Children," *English Journal* 1:3 (March 1912): 138-45. Over a dozen more of those had appeared in the *Journal* by 1919.

70. A similar movement developed in England at about this same time. Caldwell Cook's work at the Perse School became known in America after the publication of his *The Play Way* (1917); he was in the progressive rather than the literary tradition. "Play" in his title meant play as opposed to work, rather than "play" as "drama," though his methods involved much of that too. He and the American enthusiasts seem to have developed their methods out of similar concerns (there was an English surge of interest in serious non-commerical drama at this time), but without direct contact.

71. Editorial, "The Democratization of Method," *English Journal* 7:8 (October 1918): 53. Walter Barnes in his *The New Democracy in the Teaching of English* (Chicago: Rand McNally & Company, 1923) eventually gave this movement its fullest expression; the book was a collection of lectures.

72. Editorial, "What Is Socialization?" *English Journal* 7:2 (February 1918): 135; W. S. Hinchman, "Reading Clubs Instead of Literature Classes," *English Journal* 6:2 (February 1917): 88-95; C. C. Certain, "The Trial of Banquo," *English Journal* 4:3 (March 1915): 152-59; and Alma Allison, "The Social Problems of Our Little Town, And How We Met Them," *English Journal* 5:7 (September 1916): 477-82. Allison was from Madison, Wisconsin.

73. Commission on the Reorganization of Secondary Education of the NEA, *Cardinal Principles of Secondary Education*, U.S. Bureau of Education Bulletin 1918, no. 35 (Washington: Government Printing Office, 1918), pp. 10-11.

74. The Joint Committee had its first meeting in Chicago in November 1912, in conjuntion with the second annual NCTE convention. The members were Allan Abbott, Elizabeth G. Barbour, Mary D. Bradford, Emma J. Breck, C. C. Certain, Randolph T. Congdon, Mary E. Courtenay, Joseph V. Denny, Charles W. Evans, Mary B. Fontaine, Allison Gaw, Mary E. Hall, W. Wilbur Hatfield, Benjamin A. Heydrick, Helen Hill, Alfred M. Hitchcock, Mrs. Henry Hulst, Walter J. Hunting, William D. Lewis, Orton Lowe, E. H. Kemper McComb, May McKitrick, Edwin L. Miller, Minnie E. Porter, Edwin T. Reed, Edwin T. Shurter, Elmer W. Smith, Charles Swain Thomas, and Harriett A. Wood.

75. Rugg, "Curriculum Making Via National Committees," pp. 44-45, called the report "the most forward looking report of any national subject committee up to 1920." For documentation of the extent of its influence, see Edna Hays, *College Entrance Requirements*; Fay, *Reorganization Movement*; and Olson, *Nature of Literature Anthologies*. All three, though they come at the question from different vantage points, conclude that the point of view of the report was widely adopted.

76. Hosic, *Reorganization*, pp. 69-70.

77. The comparison here is with Hays' summary lists (see Appendix III) and the lists of specific titles included in the reports of the subcommittees on literature.

78. The cities were Trenton, Atlanta, New Orleans, St. Louis, Kansas City, Pueblo, Los Angeles, Berkeley, Salt Lake City, Lincoln, Joliet, Cleveland, Detroit, Rochester, and Newton. George S. Counts, *The Senior High School Curriculum*, Supplementary Educational Monographs, no. 29 (Chicago: University of Chicago Press, 1926).

79. See "News and Notes," *English Journal* 7:9 (November 1918): 609; J. O. Engleman, "Outside Reading," *English Journal* 6:1 (January 1917): 20-27; Clara Whitehill Hunt, "The Child and the Book in War Times," *English Journal* 7:8 (October 1918): 487-96; Allan Abbott, "The English Teacher and the World-War," *English Journal* 7:1 (January 1918): 1-6; and Dudley Parsons, "The English Teacher and Patriotism," *English Journal* 8:2 (February 1919): 154-63.

80. Olson, *Nature of Literature Anthologies*, pp. 57-58; 288-89. See "North Central Association of Colleges and Secondary Schools: Report of the Committee on English," *English Journal* 11:5 (May 1922): 307-14; and E. L. Miller, "College Entrance Requirements in English: A Committee Report," *English Journal* 20:8 and 9 (October and November 1931): 626-40, 714-29.

81. W. Wilbur Hatfield, "Summer Meeting of the Council," *English Journal* 9:6 (June 1920): 353; and Editorial, "What Is English?" *English Journal* 9:10 (December 1920): 600.

82. Horace Ainsworth Eaton, "English Problems After the War," *English Journal* 8:5 (May 1919): 308-12; and G. Eunice Meers, "Specific Aims in the Literature Course," *English Journal* 8:8 (October 1919): 488-95.

Whatever exists at all exists in some amount. To know it thoroughly involves knowing its quantity as well as its quality. Education is concerned with changes in human beings; a change is a difference between two conditions; each of these conditions is known to us only by the products produced by it—things made, words spoken, acts performed, and the like. . . . To measure a product well means so to define its amount that competent persons will know how large it is, with some precision, and that this knowledge may be recorded and used. This is the general Credo of those who, in the last decade, have been busy trying to extend and improve measurements of educational products.

—Edward L. Thorndike, "The Nature, Purposes, and General Methods of Measurements of Educational Products," 1918[1]

The standards of our day demand that our courses of study be derived from objectives which include both ideals and activities, that we should frankly accept usefulness as our aim rather than comprehensive knowledge, and that no fictitious emphasis should be placed upon the value of formal discipline.

—W. W. Charters, **Curriculum Construction,** 1923[2]

Every teacher of literature should make or adopt a satisfactory analysis of the higher skills involved in appreciative reading, and should make systematic plans for helping pupils to master these skills. Some people, it is true, are so deficient in the simple techniques of word recognition and sentence or paragraph interpretation as to be incapable of making progress on the higher levels. Professor Gates' book, among others, shows how to pick out these cases, how to discover their difficulties, and what to do for them. Most high-school teachers of English can profitably give considerable time to helping their students learn to read in the real sense.

—W. Wilbur Hatfield, "Literature Can Be Taught," 1927[3]

This day of crisis and chaos still finds the schools vociferously disclaiming responsibility for social leadership. Not until educational materials and practices are systematically tested with relation to the needs of contemporary life can there be any escape from the banalities that frequently pass for scientific contributions to education.

—John J. DeBoer, "Changing Objectives in English," 1932[4]

Chapter IV

Science and
the Teaching of English

When teachers of literature turned to the problems of defining goals and methods in the postwar period, they found themselves in a new and not entirely comfortable position. Always before they had had unity imposed essentially from without: first there had been the goal of winning a place within the curriculum, then that of redefining the subject to be free from college domination in "a school for the people." Though they carried through the task of generating a new framework for their teaching with considerable enthusiasm, the lack of a single unifying principle led to many false starts and long periods of misdirected energies.

Overview of the Progressive Era

The period between the wars was a time of pedagogical innovation on a grand scale, symbolized if not always led by the Progressive Education Association. Teachers of literature responded throughout this period to many forces that were at heart progressive; but they had to respond, too, to the demands of their own discipline. As a result the great bulk of teachers, and of their leadership within the National Council, thought of their teaching as progressive, though not of themselves as Progressives. Yet they had the rhetoric and the enthusiasm, and moved in many of the same directions.

Though at times during these years the subject of English would seem to be expanding in all directions at once, two broad movements underlay the majority of changes. One was the concern with the application of science to education, with an ultimate focus on efficiency. The other was the movement toward "experience" as the central metaphor of the educational process. In literary studies, that metaphor was realized first as simple vicarious experience through literature, then gradually broadened to literature as "exploration"—exploration of self, of society, of the past and present world. The movement toward science and that toward exploration were closely related; they shared roots in the progressive movement as a whole and were often carried forward by the same men and women in the teaching of English. Each is complex, however, and will be treated separately—science in this chapter, the movement toward literature as exploration in the next.

English in its final synthesis as "exploration" was hardly circumscribed, and the countless proposals and counterproposals that had occurred along the way only added to the insecurity of the classroom teacher. One result was a growing professional disorientation by the thirties, a serious gap between educational theory and educational practice that forced a retreat, a stepping back from the ideal vision of the curriculum at which the profession had finally arrived. This movement away from broad goals toward a narrow focus for the curriculum has its beginning in the Eight-Year Study of the Progressive Education Association, its middle phase in concern with general education and language, and its end in what has come to be known as "life adjustment." These final phases of progressivism will be dealt with in Chapter VI.

During the decade following the First World War, educators in all fields became enchanted with the virtue and promise of science, seeing in it the solution to many of the continuing problems of the schools. The areas to which science was to be applied were virtually limitless: they included the determination of educational goals, the validation of procedures, the lowering of costs, and the justification of programs to the public. The teacher, the philosopher, the administrator—each imitated the scientist; and though in fact their science was sharply limited by their training and the primitive state of the disciplines to which they turned for guidance, their conclusions shaped—and continue to shape—much educational practice.

The Movement in Education

The Concern with Efficiency

The application of science to educational problems took place against the background of a widespread but loosely formulated identification of "scientific" with "efficient," largely as a result of the adoption of principles of "scientific management" by American business. Gradually, scientific business methods had come to seem the solution to all of the nation's ills; and schools, ever a drain on the taxpayer's pocketbook, were always a tempting target for reform. After 1910 the critics became especially vocal, charging in the popular press that schools were costing too much and producing too little.[5]

The office of the superintendent, the "front office" of the school system, bore the brunt of the attack and was responsible for the brunt of the professional response. Though the exact steps taken varied from city to city, the net result was a shift in the nature of the superintendency away from that of providing philosophical guidance toward that of educational management. This was to some extent a necessary shift; the rising enrollments were creating school systems of a size and complexity previously unknown, and bringing with them problems of budget, staff, and organization that only managerial skills could handle. Still, the response to the pressures for efficiency was too extreme, carrying with it the seeds of damage to the teaching profession as a whole. In many school systems, "efficient" education came to be identified too closely with "good" education, and broader perspectives to be submerged in the concern with budgets and short-term "results."

Objective Measurement

Closely allied with the movement for scientific management was a new concern with scientific measurement, led largely by E. L. Thorndike. His motives are evident in the quotation at the opening of this chapter: to effect rational change in education, it would first be necessary to have accurate measures of the educational "products." He and his students concentrated on objective paper-and-pencil measures of "achievement" in the major school subjects. Though the first of these tests did not appear till 1908, they were taken up enthusiastically as the concern with efficiency mounted.[6]

Measurement got its real impetus, however, from a related focus on the "resources" or "abilities" which the students brought with them. Intelligence tests had played a part in psychological investigations at least since Galton's work in the 1870s and 1880s, but it was the Binet scales (1905-08) and Lewis M. Terman's Stanford revision (1916) that brought the concept of "IQ" into widespread currency. By the beginning of World War I, the American Psychological Association was convinced enough of the value of such measures to offer to prepare a series of group intelligence tests for the army. The offer was accepted, leading eventually to the famous Scale Alpha (for recruits who could read English) and Scale Beta (for recruits who could not). The army's success in using these two tests to sort out their recruits provided educators with an object lesson whose import was quickly realized. Whatever other issues the data may have raised, it was clear the tests were successful in their original purpose of classification. Teachers realized that if the systematic use of tests could predict performance in one or another position within the army, it should also be able to predict performance in response to one or another mode of instruction in the schools. By using the tests to form groups of "similar" students, the school would be able to provide instruction geared more closely to their particular abilities. And this—as English teachers and their more scientific colleagues all recognized—would be more efficient.[7]

Rebuilding the Curriculum

Given a concern with scientific management, inventories of abilities (the resources), and measures of achievement (the products), there remained the problem of deciding what should be taught (the demand). This task was begun by the Committee on Economy of Time in Education. Appointed, fittingly enough, by the Department of Superintendence of the National Education Association, it published four major reports between 1915 and 1919.[8] The reports found three ways in which efficiency could be promoted within the curriculum: by the elimination of nonessentials, by the improvement of teaching methods, and by the organization of subject matter to correspond more closely to the realities of child development. The approach to defining the "minimum essentials" of the school curriculum was rigidly empirical: studies of life in the school and in society would show what was needed and appropriate. Though there was some shifting of emphasis away from what *is* towards what *should be* in the later volumes of the series, the overall effect of the committee was certainly to focus educational philosophy on the empirical rather than the speculative, and to focus curriculum on functional skills rather than conceptual or ethical goals. Existing school procedures and knowledge that was obvious, functional, and easily measured both received a new and important emphasis, not because committee members felt this was a proper shift in priorities—many explicitly argued otherwise—but because these were the aspects of education which the developing scientific methodology was best able to handle.

Franklin Bobbitt, professor of educational administration at the University of Chicago and a former student of G. Stanley Hall, carried the functionalism of the Committee on Economy of Time to its logical, if extreme, conclusion. His primary concern was the specification of objectives through careful analysis of life-needs. As he put it in 1924,[9] the first task "is to discover the activities which ought to make up the lives of men and women; and along with these, the abilities and personal qualities necessary for their proper performance. These are the educational objectives" (p. 9). He had little tolerance for the traditional goals upon which educators had relied, pointing out that "culture," "character building," or other such "vague high-sounding hopes and aspirations" (p. 32) would not do. His own list of objectives—included as an illustration of the kind of statement needed rather than as a complete set—was nothing if not specific. It included 821 consecutive, numbered points, and a final category of "occupational activities" which were too numerous to be presented in detail. The points he did include ranged from "1. Ability to use language in all ways required for proper and effective participation in the community life" (p. 11) to a series that ran:

129.   Ability to care for the hair and scalp.
130.   Ability to care for the nails.
131.   Ability to care properly for the feet.
132.   Ability to control sex-functions in the interests of physi-cal and social well-being (p. 14).

Though Bobbitt's specific procedures for curriculum develop-ment have an inherent tendency to stress goals which can be easily formulated, rather than those which are most significant, his own discussions of general education placed a singular emphasis on exactly the subjects which were least amenable to the "scientific" analysis of life activities he proposed. Of the nine "lines of training" he thought important for all students to receive, the first three had long been special concerns of the teacher of English:

(1)   English language: reading, oral and written expression.
(2)   Citizenship attitudes, judgments and activities. Social Studies.
(3)   Literature: English and general (p. 69).

And Bobbitt stated, too, that of the list of 821 specific objectives of education, "it seems that general reading, including literature, can serve in some measure in the case of most of them" (p. 90).

How literature and reading were functional in the general com-munity life needed some consideration, and Bobbitt detailed seven services they performed. The points were rather redundant, having in common an emphasis on the value of experience *through* litera-ture. Literature takes the reader "out of what would otherwise be his little world"; he "relives the human experience" of other times and other men; his thoughts are broadened and elevated; his responses tuned to those "who have seen most clearly, and . . . felt most deeply"; he gains new interests; he *lives*: "Life is action and reading is one mode of action."[10] Such a broadening of life through the vicarious experience of literature was as close an approximation to a functional goal for literary studies as anyone would be able to provide.

Studying the Curriculum in English

The teacher of English was well protected as pressures for scientific efficiency came to bear upon the schools: of the various school subjects, English was one of the cheapest to provide. Its cost per recitation was low, so that other subjects (the hapless classical languages among them) would bear the brunt of the economic assault on the schools.[11] When Bobbitt and others turned to scientific analysis of curriculum goals, English again came off well: language in its variety of uses inevitably surfaced high on any list of "universal needs." Even literary studies, much harder to justify in terms of concrete life-activities, were protected by the widespread belief in the importance of literature in character development and ethics. Finally, English studies as they had been brought together by the Committee of Ten were broad enough to allow an exceedingly wide array of functional activities to be provided within one class, with the teacher making very few changes in classroom procedures for any one of them. The net effect of the many minor adjustments, however, was sometimes of major importance.

Minimum Essentials

Attempts to formulate minimum essentials for literature withered from the beginning. Hosic was a member of the NEA Committee on Economy of Time and prepared the English sections of their reports. He managed a long and detailed analysis of "The Essentials of Grammar and Composition," but his discussion of literature was short and "confessedly inadequate."[12] Only with respect to the actual act of reading did the NEA committee have much to say about the efficiency of literary studies; here the concern was with size of books, length of lines, and color of paper.[13] NCTE had its own Committee on Economy of Time in English, contemporaneous with that of the NEA; its efforts to deal with literature were no more successful. Of five general points in its final report, only one dealt with literature at all. That one was hardly radical, calling simply for "The teaching of literature suitable to the age and development of pupils, and the elimination of those classics beyond their emotional and intellectual reach. The introduction into our courses of such contemporary material as will give pupils a better appreciation of present-day ideals."[14] This offered little challenge to the teacher of literature, and was in line with reforms already proposed in the Reorganization report (1917).

The real effects of the movement toward essentials came in language studies. After the reports on economy of time in English, a new committee on "essentials" was appointed under Sterling A. Leonard of the University of Wisconsin. Though the committee never published a formal report, it had much influence through the writings and speeches of the individuals involved. Leonard himself was led into a study of *Current English Usage*, published by the Council in 1932. This gathered opinion on a variety of constructions usually condemned in language texts, and found that many were judged acceptable in actual use. Followed by Albert H. Marckwardt and Fred Walcott's *Facts about Current English Usage* (1938) and Charles C. Fries' *American English Grammar* (1941), this aspect of the movement toward essentials eventually reshaped the teaching of language and composition in American schools.[15]

The Functional Emphasis

Though the movement for minimum essentials raised few problems for the teacher of literature, pressures from other subjects seeking to expand their place within the curriculum eventually forced English to defend itself as a functional study. The social studies offered the most direct competition and under the leadership of Charles H. Judd launched a vigorous campaign to improve their status. W. Wilbur Hatfield, who had succeeded Hosic as *English Journal* editor and NCTE secretary-treasurer, outlined the challenge in 1922: "Unless it can be made clear, even to the practical mind," that composition and literature achieve results "commensurate with the time allotment," he wrote, "they will surely be replaced by subjects more obviously useful."[16]

The provision of such proof was the task of the NCTE Committee on the Place and Function of English in American Life. Essie Chamberlain from Oak Park (Illinois) High School gave the 1924 convention address which led to the appointment of the committee. Her approach to curriculum construction was essentially Bobbitt's: a careful analysis of the social demands on English, and the meeting of those demands through methodology tested by classroom experiments.[17] Under the direction of John M. Clapp of Lake Forest College, the committee conducted an extensive survey of the uses to which skills learned in English class were being put by 22,000 people in a range of social positions. The statistical tables of the final report (1926) provided a profile for the English curriculum to follow—but it was a profile in which literature had very little place. It was simply not a part of English instruction about which questions related to "practical" aspects of life could be easily formulated, and consequently little data could be collected about it with this sort of approach. Reading was easier to deal with (one had to read newspapers and magazines, business letters and grocery lists), but still only one-sixth of the interview form was devoted to reading. Of that, only two of twenty-six specific questions dealt with literary or cultural pursuits.[18]

The Clapp committee considered its task to be one of "defining the content, scope, aims, etc. of 'English' work in schools." In their lists of specific recommendations, the first made clear the commitment to functionalism:

> The schools might well devote more attention to a number of the language activities which according to the returns are widely used by persons of the many callings and social groups reporting, and which are reported as giving much difficulty. These activities in particular are: Interviewing: word of mouth inquiries; reports to a superior; instructions for subordinates; conferences. Conversation: with casual acquaintances; at social gatherings; over the telephone. Public Speaking: informal discussion; preparing addresses. Writing: informal notes and memos for one's self; formal notes of invitation, introduction, etc. Reading: legal documents. Listening: to an interview, a conference, or a public meeting (p. 46).

All of these concerns were taken up by the English program, eventually being fused with language studies deriving from Leonard and his successors as part of a "functional," usage-based program in language and composition.

By its very failure to deal with literature, the Clapp committee helped to insulate literature from the extreme forms of functionalism that developed in other areas of the English curriculum. While non-literary activities increasingly followed the outline provided by the charts of the "Place and Function of English in American Life," the teaching of literature continued, at least through the 1930s, to follow a different path. Indeed in furnishing objective proof of the value of English instruction, the Clapp report played a role much like that of the early college entrance requirements: it gave English a solid place in the curriculum by casting the subject in terms acceptable to its opponents, while in the process virtually ignoring that aspect of instruction which has taken up the largest amount of the teacher's time, and usually of his interest.

The functional emphasis of the Clapp report was characteristic of the concerns at the time it appeared. Of the other attempts to define objectives in English, the best known was Charles S. Pendleton's analysis of *The Social Objectives of School English* (1924). This was an extensive survey of the goals for English study, using a procedure suggested by Bobbitt. In the final list of 1,581 separate "social goals" ranked in order of the frequency with which they had been cited, the highest ranking went to correct spelling, the second to the ability to speak in complete sentences. Number eight was the first objective not related to the mechanics of language use: "The habit of reading for enjoyment literature of the better sort." Pendleton's results illustrate a major difficulty in any attempt to derive a value ordering from a consensus of judgments—the top ranking did not result because spelling was the first objective of most adults, but because it appeared consistently as a minor objective. A program structured around such surveys could easily become preoccupied with relatively trivial concerns which in themselves were not highly valued by anyone; few would argue that accurate spelling was *not* useful, but few would want to elevate it to the central position it carried in Pendleton's results.[19]

Media Study

The emphasis upon functional activities eventually helped to bring studies of motion pictures and radio more firmly into the English curriculum. One of the most important influences was a series of studies sponsored by the Payne Fund between 1929 and 1932, just after the introduction of sound had radically altered the motion picture experience. The studies, reported in nine volumes, were conceived and carried through as a related set of investigations of the effects and importance of motion pictures, focussing especially on their influence on children. W. W. Charters of Ohio State was chairman of the research committee; other members came from six other eastern and midwestern universities. Their reports, though not specifically concerned with motion pictures in education, clearly demonstrated the important role which they played in the lives of children.[20] As Edgar Dale, also of Ohio State, put it in summarizing his contribution to the series, "The effect of motion pictures . . . is universal and this fact must be faced in a statesmanlike manner by exhibitors and producers, by teachers, and by parents."[21]

NCTE watched with interest as motion pictures became increasingly popular, citing reports on the size of the national audience, and later of the Payne Fund volumes, in *English Journal.*[22] Throughout the thirties, though there were a few attempts to deal with the movie as a literary experience comparable to any other, the emphasis was upon raising standards of taste, much as it had been in earlier discussions of newspaper and magazine studies. The Council's efforts were guided mainly by Newark's William Lewin, who owed his own interest in film studies to his supervisor of English, Max Herzberg. In 1932, Lewin persuaded NCTE to establish a Committee on Photoplay Appreciation and then proceeded to give it vigorous leadership. Lists of classic films were developed, standards of appreciation outlined, and finally a nationwide evaluation of the effectiveness of class study in influencing taste carried out.[23] The latter was more a demonstration than an experiment, but it showed that methods used in other English studies could be adapted for films. The name assigned to motion pictures—that of "photoplay"—was characteristic of the way in which the subject was approached; presumably it also reassured the teacher first venturing onto unfamiliar ground. By 1934 the work of the NCTE photoplay committee was well-enough known that Lewin could report that "major producers" were "consulting us as to forthcoming, projected, and suggested pictures," offering scripts to the committee for examination *before* production decisions were made.[24] Most of this collaboration centered on producing motion pictures based on the classic texts of the high school canon, for which Lewin's committee then produced study guides.

Studies of other media generated comparatively little enthusiasm among English teachers during the decades between the wars. Newspaper and magazine studies continued much as they had been before, though with increased emphasis on their "functionalism" after their high standing in the Clapp report. Methods changed little, focussing either on improving taste or on the conventions of journalism (what is the difference between an editorial and a lead article, and so on).[25] Radio broadcasting also received some attention, though again without much enthusiasm until just prior to World War II. At that point interest rose sharply, but it was focussed on the effects of propaganda rather than with radio as a medium of interest in its own right.[26] Max Herzberg, in a report from the NCTE Radio Committee, reflected the prevailing attitude when he commented that "censorship, except of a very discreet sort, is much less valuable than the establishment of a critical attitude, in which the good will be properly praised and the bad perceived and—perhaps—avoided."[27]

Evaluating the Selections for Study

The relatively minor changes resulting from the attempt to specify minimum essentials and functional activities for the teaching of literature did not mean that it would not feel the pressure for efficiency; it simply meant that efficiency in literary studies would come to focus on the proper grade placement for the selections chosen for study. One approach developed out of studies of reading comprehension and will be discussed in the next section. The other sought to treat inventories of existing attitudes as providing an authoritative "consensus."

The first of these studies were mentioned in the previous chapter; they derived from the interest in child study and helped to challenge the appropriateness of the collegiate model of instruction for the high school course in literature. They were not thought of as providing a basis for organizing the English course, though they did have some influence on the selections suggested for outside reading. Under the influence of Bobbitt, however, this changed; student interests were elevated into a criterion for the selection and placement of the works studied. Charles Sumner Crow's doctoral project (1924) at Teachers College, Columbia, was one of the first in this tradition. Crow stated explicitly that he was attempting "to test and arrange the subject-matter in a given field, English literature in the high school, in accordance with the pupils' judgement of its values given in terms of ends that are generally recognized as socially valuable."[28] He asked 1,999 seniors to rate seventy-four classics on five scales measuring whether the books were (1) interesting, (2) inspiring, (3) artistic, (4) desirable to own or recommend to others, and (5) easy to read and understand. Crow's conclusion was that only seven of the seventy-four frequently used books could be called "very effective" in meeting the goals summarized in the five scales; many titles were not rated as effective on *any* of them. (Students ranked only books they had studied intensively in class.) His findings, though frequently cited by later investigators, were hardly surprising to teachers familiar with studies of reading interests. What was new, however, was the shift in emphasis away from discovering where children were (so that their level could be raised), and toward taking the judgment of the pupil as a valid criterion for the end point of the process (the level at which instruction should be geared).

Other investigators sought their consensus of opinion from other sources—high school teachers, courses of study, literary critics, and college professors all had their advocates.[29] The college entrance lists can be recognized as an underlying influence on many of the results that emerged. In a 1930 survey of 44 "representative" courses of study from different parts of the country, for example, all but seven of the 25 most frequent selections were from the lists of the National Conference on Uniform Entrance Requirements in English. (All seven exceptions were from the junior high school grades, where the demands of the colleges seem more distant.) Of the same 25 selections, grade placements for 10 ranged all the way from the seventh to the twelfth year; none of the titles had a range of less than three years.[30] High school teachers remained for the most part undisturbed by this lack of uniformity, agreeing with John Haney of Philadelphia when he asked, "Why should our insistent standardizers demand that all sorts and conditions of teachers should instruct in a prescribed manner all sorts and conditions of pupils?"[31]

What teachers did suggest in the name of interests was the adaptation of the classic texts to make them more palatable. Again, this movement began in response to Hall's urgings during the prewar period. After the war it became more frequent, reinforced by an assumption that there were "essential" and "nonessential" parts to literary works. Thus a teacher from a Hackensack (New Jersey) high school could urge unblushingly that the "Solution of Burke" was to "Reduce the speech from seventy-eight to forty-two pages. Burke should have done that himself." And another from South Philadelphia could make *Comus* "somewhat less of a bore and an affliction" by reducing "the plot to its elements—stripped of its philosophy, its ethical note, its poetry. What is *Comus* but the baldest and crudest of melodramas?"[32] Everyone knew that children enjoyed melodrama. The startling thing in such bowdlerizations was the great enthusiasm with which they were carried out; nobody questioned whether the skeleton remaining was really the great work of literature that demanded a place in the curriculum in the first place. Discussions of such radical adaptations were published throughout the twenties and thirties as practical teaching suggestions.

Reading Skills

One aspect of the study of literature which lent itself well to scientific study was the analysis of the functional skills involved in reading. As part of the general testing movement, the measurement of reading achievement actually began rather late; Courtis' standardized silent reading test in 1915 was the first to appear. The many investigations which followed were especially important because they suggested that silent reading was more efficient than oral reading in both speed and comprehension. This was at variance with the emphasis which English teachers had been placing on oral reading and oral expression, but they adapted to the new concerns quickly. Judd and Buswell's *Silent Reading: A Study of Its Various Types* (1922) was especially influential, focussing attention on the variety of different skills which a mature reader uses—the difference between skimming newspaper headlines, reading a light poem, and appreciating a complex novel, for example.[33] Dovetailing neatly with the arguments that Allan Abbott and others had been advancing about genre studies, the book also helped to propel the types approach into a new prominence.

Finally studies of reading turned their attention toward the level of comprehension which could be expected from students reading the currently popular selections. Two studies, one from Teachers College, Columbia, and the other from Clark University, used similar procedures and arrived at similar results. Short "representative" passages were taken from literary works popular in the high school; comprehension questions were constructed for each passage; and the tests were administered to a sample of students. T. W. H. Irion completed his Teachers College study first (1925). Using selections from *The Spy*, "The Destruction of Sennacherib," *Julius Caesar*, and *The Origin of Species* in order to be able to compare results from different literary genres, he tested the comprehension of ninth graders and concluded: "The average reading comprehension as compared with the total comprehension possibilities of the selections used is so mediocre that it is very hazardous to proceed on the assumption that students in the ninth grade can read well enough to comprehend and appreciate literature merely by reading."[34] His results also suggested that there were real differences in the difficulties generated by the different genres, again provid-evidence in support of the types approach.

Mary C. Burch, in a slightly later but more extensive study (1928), recorded the responses of students in grades 7 to 12 on a similar test. She also concluded that the existing placement of texts was appropriate for only 25 percent of each grade level, but found that the differences *within* each grade were greater than the differences *between* it and the five others studied. Following Crow's lead, she used the voluntary reading preferences of the students to determine the proper range for school teaching.[35]

Though the results of these and other, less extensive examinations of the correspondence between the abilities of students and the difficulty of conventional materials were hardly encouraging, the result was paradoxically to give teachers of literature a new confidence that they did indeed have an objective, quantifiable subject matter, just like the rest of the teaching world. This attitude is apparent, for example, in the quotation from Hatfield's 1927 editorial at the beginning of this chapter; there the teaching of literature was directly equated with the teaching of "the higher skills" of reading, and both placed within the tradition of scientific study.

NCTE concern with practical reading skills continued, but except for occasional and short-lived flirtations, it soon became a separate concern from the teaching of literature. By the early thirties, with attention in reading studies shifting toward physiological defects in disabled readers and that in literature toward the provision of "experience," the teaching of reading in the high school had come to mean almost exclusively remedial work.[36]

The Focus on the Individual

Ability Groups

Demands for efficiency and economy, "objective" measures of achievement and intelligence, and a burgeoning, heterogeneous school population combined during the twenties to create a new awareness of individual differences. Ability grouping was one of the first and most lasting responses. This spread quickly after the war, with an original conception that was perfectly blameless: teachers thought it would be easier to provide individualized instruction if their classes were homogeneous.

From the beginning, however, the concern with grouping students into "inferior" and "superior" classes carried with it the danger of poor teaching. The earlier development of business English curricula had at least begun with the premise that the students in them were interested in *other* work than that in the regular English class; the new division placed the emphasis on their *inability* to do the *same* work. Thus a trend quickly developed in which the gifted classes were given an enriched curriculum, the "slow" groups a strong dose of drill and "minimum essentials." This downgrading of activities for the low group and the shift of teacher interest is apparent even in the earliest articles on ability grouping in English; by the 1930s, partly in response to studies of gifted students by Terman and others, it was deeply ingrained.[37] Superior classes clearly became the prerogative of the superior teacher. As the head of the English department in one New York City high school put it, "Gifted students thrive under the leadership of distinguished minds." Slow students, even to a New Jersey teacher obviously devoted to them, "[call] forth everything that the teacher has to offer in tact, sympathy, and understanding."[38] The point to note is that they do not call forth interest or excitement.

The Dalton Plan

Teachers of English treated ability groups as a means to greater efficiency; they also thought of them as a compromise with the ideal provision of a completely differentiated program for each student. "The highest social efficiency," wrote Hatfield in 1925, "is evidently to be attained only by giving each individual with all his peculiarities the training he most needs. So we have ability grouping, which carried through to its extreme becomes individual instruction."[39] The "Dalton" or "contract" plan represented one attempt to carry through to that desirable extreme. In essence, the plan involved each student meeting with his teachers and making a "contract" to do certain work within a given period of time, usually a week. The terms of the contract could be varied to meet the needs of the pupil, but its value was specified in advance so that each student would know whether he was working for an A, a B, or a C, and would have some measure of choice in the matter. Although the plan was really an offshoot of work done before the war at San Francisco State Normal College, it was first systematically put into practice by Helen Parkhurst in Dalton, Massachusetts. Both Parkhurst and Evelyn Dewey used the name of the latter town in popularizing the approach, though the precise formulation varied almost from school to school.[40]

With its focus on individual effort, the Dalton plan was criticized by some teachers as violating "the social nature of English instruction"—being particularly detrimental in the teaching of literature.[41] This objection was circumvented by including some contracted group work, allowing students to discuss what they had read with one another as well as with the teacher. By the late twenties, the

Dalton plan was running smoothly enough to produce some rhapsodic evaluations, like that of a teacher from the South Philadelphia High School for Girls:

> The recitation has truly, but unobtrusively passed. Group work, supervised study, socialized study, and projects both individual and cooperative have become automatically the means by which the learning process is carried on. Learning to do by doing; learning that learning is a slow process; learning that mastery is possible and that nothing else is acceptable—the goals of education have come within the conscious grasp of both teachers and students.[42]

In the end, the critics rather than the proponents of the contract method triumphed. The early concern that the individually-specified contracts put undue emphasis on individual work at the expense of group activities had been easy enough to overcome. By the early thirties, however, teachers were beginning to recognize that the goals inherent in the Dalton plan were out of harmony with the general goals of literature instruction. The interest of a student working to fulfill a contract in literature would be an interest engendered by desire to fulfill the contract; it would not be an interest in the story itself. Teachers began to find that the contract could even serve to stifle rather than arouse interest; once the contract was fulfilled, the student would simply stop reading. Finally, the contract had from the beginning placed too much emphasis upon quantitative rather than qualitative differences in the work required. The difference between an A and a B usually lay simply in the amount of work done, so that an A-student would do all of the work of the B-students, and then some. It was not enough that he do the same work better. Proper individualization of instruction, on the other hand, needed to emphasize qualitative differences in students and the work they should be doing. Hatfield rang the death knell in a 1932 editorial, though he continued to print defenses of the method for some years following: "Let the teacher, if he will, work out the contract as his idea of what he wants the pupils to do. But let him find some more social and humane method of dealing with impressionable, plastic human beings."[43]

Unit Work

The "mastery unit" was another approach to the problem of individualizing instruction that in the end developed in a rather different direction. Henry C. Morrison popularized the term in his book, *The Practice of Teaching in the Secondary School* (1926). A "unit" to him consisted essentially of all of the activities and materials necessary to bring about a given change in pupil behavior, to "inculcate the 'understanding,' " for example, "that the

colon is a signpost pointing to an enumeration." Each student
would proceed through a unit at his own speed, moving on to the
next only after he had demonstrated mastery. It was an approach
which dovetailed neatly with the concern for minimal essentials,
but it also suffered from the problems of that approach when
applied to English: literature was not easily broken down into
"units" for mastery, at least not in the sense that Morrison was
using those terms. Hatfield, though initially pleased with the
implication of purposefulness in all of the activities introduced into
the unit, quickly decided that though "such notions are decidedly
comfortable," the underlying conception of growth was inadequate.
People do not grow by the accumulation of the separate, completed
units of skill that Morrison's analysis implied. The production
model from industry could not be so directly applied to teaching.[44]

The mastery unit, like the Dalton plan, enjoyed a brief vogue
and then dropped from view. "Units," however, became ingrained
in the educational vocabulary, where they remain to this day with a
meaning quite different from that which they originally bore.
Instead of a discrete set of materials with a limited, specific
behavioral goal toward which the individual student could progress
at his own pace, "unit" came to be used to describe virtually any
set of activities centered around one common focus. Talk of mastery in Morrison's sense had very little meaning with activities of
this sort.

Leonard V. Koos, associate director of the National Survey of
Secondary Education carried out by the Office of Education, discussed some of the findings of the survey before the 1932 NCTE
convention. He pointed out that 71 percent of the nation's secondary schools were using homogeneous grouping for English classes,
a higher percent than for any other subject in the curriculum. IQ
was the most frequent criterion for forming the groups. He noted,
too, that "unit-assignments" were among the most frequent provisions for individual differences, though both the Dalton plan and
the Morrison plan "in schools reporting to use them with unusual
success" deviated widely from the plans described by the origi-
nators. Most such teaching, though it continued to go under a
variety of names, had by 1932 come to represent simply a sequence
of related activities, usually with a definite beginning and definite
end, which could be used with a single student or, more usually, with
a class.[45]

Objective Testing

In addition to using intelligence and achievement scales to divide
students into homogeneous groups, teachers of English gave increasing attention to the use of "new type" or "objective" examinations for diagnosis and evaluation. Though they had difficulty in
adapting such tests for the teaching of literature, teachers were
soon won over by arguments about the reliability, fairness, and

economy (they were easy to correct) of the objective tests.[46] As
with many aspects of the movement for efficiency and scientific
methods, however, it was the "minimum essentials" and "functional" reading skills that ultimately received the most attention.

The history of objective testing in English during this period—
both in literature and in other areas of the curriculum—is somewhat
unusual in that both liberal and conservative views of teaching
could unite, though for different reasons, in support of tests. To the
conservatives, testing was a way to keep up standards and insure
the place of discipline and memory work.[47] To the liberals, it
provided the teacher with a way to diagnose pupils' weaknesses and
thus to better meet their needs. That Hatfield undertook to edit a
series of "Practice Tests" which were commercially published and
advertised in the *English Journal* is as clear an indication as
anything of his point of view. Equally significant is a series of
"diagnostic" tests of reading ability put together by John J.
DeBoer, the *Journal*'s assistant editor and resident radical. His
rationale was explicit: "Teachers of English and instructors responsible for the educational guidance of high-school youth cannot
provide competent counsel without a fairly comprehensive knowledge of the mental and educational characteristics of the pupils
placed in their charge."[48]

The more conservative view of testing was represented by the
College Entrance Examination Board, which in the spring of 1929
appointed a Commission on English to undertake a major study of
the English examination. Charles Swain Thomas of the Harvard
Graduate School of Education was named chairman; his relatively
conservative eastern college view dominates the report (though
Hatfield was also a member of the commission). The final report,
published in 1931 as *Examining the Examination in English,* is a
fascinating portrait of attitudes both toward testing and toward
scientific method in general.

The report began by dedicating itself to scientific method. The
commission members decided that, although they could have made
pronouncements "ex cathedra," that would be "wholly unsatisfactory." Indeed, they felt they were in a unique position to avoid
"subjective conclusions." Not only did they have available for
study the accumulated data of twenty-eight years of testing by the
CEEB, but also a mass of data from other agencies. And most
important of all, "There were readily at hand methods of objective
investigation which the recent years have refined and validated."[49]

Most of the report, however, was hardly scientific. There was an
historical study of the form of the Restricted and Comprehensive
examinations over the years, and tables of the topics and options
that had been provided; old examination booklets were informally
reviewed to ascertain that both kinds of exams had been fairly
scored; one chapter devoted itself to aims of English study; another
dealt with the conditions of administering and the details of scoring

the essays. The science in the study consisted of questionnaire surveys of students and teachers about various aspects of the testing program and their English classes, and of a correlational study of the predictive value of the Scholastic Aptitude Test (SAT), the Restricted and Comprehensive examinations in English, and school grades. These scientific analyses were all relegated to an appendix and largely ignored; many of the results are not mentioned anywhere in the report. Still, they were the commission's claim to science and objectivity, and they were published in full.

Much to the chagrin of the commission, the results of their correlational analyses consistently indicated that the best predictor of college achievement was the SAT, next, the school record, then the Comprehensive, and finally the Restricted examination in English. The problem with this in the commission's view was that the SAT was a mechanical examination which did not "test the candidate's ability to paraphrase or to make a précis, or to interpret the subtler qualities of a poem read at sight." Faced with the evidence that the SAT was a better predictor of college performance in English, the commission finally rested on its humanism: "The question is not so much a result reducible to statistics as it is a determination to retain in American education certain factors contributing to civilization and culture rather than to the mechanical efficiency of the American college student."[50] In the end their recommendations suggested abandoning the restricted examination, but asked only minor changes in the cherished comprehensive essay test.[51]

While rejecting the objective examination for their own purposes, the commission managed also to conclude that teachers of English "cannot afford to ignore the value of these tests in classroom work." Indeed the report devotes a whole chapter (written primarily by Thomas) to the educational value of examinations in the classroom.[52] The purposes of such a testing program (to be a "recurrent" practice throughout the year) were several: it would give the teacher diagnostic information; it would help "systematize" instruction; and it would serve to motivate students by giving them an impartial record of achievement. There was an inherent faith that all students would achieve, and thus be able to bask in their own reflected glory; the effects of such objective proof of their own *inability* on students who might continually fail were hardly considered.

Experimental Method

Studies of reading interests and of comprehension skills were essentially static: they could say something about present conditions but were at best only suggestive about how to make things better. Indeed they could even help perpetuate the status quo: Burch, for example, explicitly used her discoveries about what the students *were* reading on their own as a criterion for determining what they *should be* reading in the school. Experimental studies of alternative teaching methods, on the other hand, did offer a way toward progressive improvement of methodology through the objective determination of the most effective procedures.

The path toward sound experimental study in the teaching of English was not an easy one, however; indeed, a cynic might even wonder if the number of false starts from pseudoscientific, improperly designed "studies" may not have done more harm than all the good from better projects. Teachers quickly picked up the terminology of science; every change in curriculum became an "experiment"; every fluctuation in student behavior became "significant"; all procedures were "evaluated." Yet only a few made even an attempt to use an experimental design, and the best of those had serious flaws.

The first experimental study of importance in the teaching of literature was Nancy Coryell's doctoral project (1927) at Teachers College, Columbia.[53] It was set in the context of a growing debate about the most successful way to approach literary works in class. Two different philosophies had long been evident: on the one hand there were teachers who lauded the benefits of allowing students to read extensively on their own with only minimal discussion of the works and no close textual analysis; this approach had become especially prevalent among teachers concerned with socializing class procedures and with insuring student interest. On the other hand there were those who felt appreciation was an *earned* achievement, the result of careful study and thoughtful analysis; here the emphasis was on extended study of a few books, with at least several weeks of class discussion devoted to the details of each. Intensive study had of course been the approach at the end of the nineteenth century, where the emphasis had been philological and rhetorical; though the form of the analysis had been much modified over the years, the value of some sort of careful class study was not usually questioned. NCTE had focussed so much attention on extensive (or "home" or "independent") reading to bring it into wider use as an adjunct to, not as a replacement for, class study. The two approaches were considered to be complementary, and both had had their place in the Reorganization report.[54]

As extensive reading became more and more accepted, however, and as the goals of instruction turned toward breadth of experience, voices began to be heard arguing that extensive reading should *replace*, not supplement, intensive study. It was this question that Coryell addressed in a year-long experimental comparison of the two procedures. As she summarized it, her extensive reading classes involved "the rapid reading of a comparatively large amount of literature with general comments and discussion in class"; the intensive reading class concentrated on "the detailed, analytical study of the minimum of literature required by the syllabus" (p. 1). The reading for the extensive group was set up to parallel but exceed the work done in the other classes; if the one read four of the *Idylls of the King*, the other read eleven, and five thousand more lines of Elizabethan poetry—and so on through the syllabus. The experiment involved nine eleventh grade classes in one school, including one extensive reading, one intensive reading, and one control group at each of three ability levels. Testing included a fairly extensive battery of standardized tests of reading and comprehension, but the major focus was on a final examination which Coryell constructed to cover only the books studied by the intensive readers. Finding at the end of the year that the two groups had progressed equally, Coryell drew the conclusion that the extensive readers "probably learned five times as much again, which they had no chance to use on the examinations."[55]

Coryell's study is of considerable importance as one of the earliest examples of relatively careful application of experimental procedures to the study of the teaching of literature. The results could hardly be ignored and prompted considerable debate between proponents of the two approaches, a debate that by the end of the 1930s ended up at about the point where Coryell had begun: a situation of uneasy coexistence.[56]

It is indicative of the general level of pedagogical science that the study was never questioned on its merits; throughout the debates the proponents of intensive study tended to ignore rather than challenge her results.[57] The study certainly could have been faulted at a number of points: only a few teachers and a few classes were involved, and these were obviously more enthusiastic about the "experimental" extensive reading approach; the measuring instrument, though testing only content from the books all had studied, was clearly weighted in its emphasis toward the goals which had governed the studies of the extensive readers; and the results after all simply indicated that there was no difference, not that the extensive readers had done better. Later studies tended to substantiate these results, but Coryell's work by itself was not that conclusive.[58]

Literature was certainly the most difficult area of English instruction to investigate with experimental methods; it was simply too difficult to measure objectively results that were framed in terms of "appreciation," "attitudes," or lifelong habits. Yet the situation in language and composition seems to have been little better: there were few true experimental studies, and those tended to have serious faults. In 1961, an NCTE committee began a review of the entire field of research in written composition; they found only five studies out of the hundreds reported that met most of their criteria for sound investigation.[59] The situation in the teaching of literature was certainly worse.[60]

Settling Down

The twenties began with a burst of enthusiasm about benefits that would derive from the application of science to the problems of English, but the proffered benefits were slow in coming, and not all to the liking of teachers. Many studies, firmly under the control of those carrying them out, did tend to support and reinforce tendencies underway in English; Coryell's project falls into this category to the extent that the measuring instrument was weighted towards the procedures in her experimental group. Yet it was not too long before English teachers began to learn that studies affecting their field would not always be under their control. Perhaps the most effective agent in educating teachers to the dangers of poorly conducted research was a series of studies of class size, in English as well as other subjects. Comparing pupil achievement on a few easily measured variables, these studies seemed to indicate that small classes had no distinct advantages over large; in some cases the students in them did not even do as well. Administrators, always under pressure to cut costs, quickly used these studies as justification for large-scale jumps in the number of pupils per teacher.[61]

Such studies eventually made NCTE leaders aware that teachers of English might not make the world's best scientists, and scientists might not know how to make the world's best teacher of English. Rewey Belle Inglis emphasized this point in delivering her presidential address to the 1929 NCTE convention: "Say over to yourselves the names of the really great teachers of history or your personal experience. Did they spend hours humped over correlations? Many of the antagonisms between the two fields could be saved if each were given due place and recognition, and persons fitted by nature and disposition for the one were not forced into the other."[62] A year later Hatfield, spurred by administrators' reactions to the studies of class size, was less sure that the current set of "scientists" deserved such "due place and recognition." He granted that scientific investigation is "obviously necessary":

> Necessary—but more difficult than educational "scientists" have usually realized. A few loosely-conducted, slightly supervised experiments with large and small classes seemed to show no great advantage in the small classes. Immediately the majority of administrators and, we suppose, of professors of education, leaped to the conclusion that classes everywhere, under all sorts of teachers, might safely be made

> larger. . . . we do not realize the complexity of the teaching-learning situation. The number of "variables" to be controlled in the experiment of the familiar "parallel groups" type is dangerously large. . . . we are credulous, unduly credulous. Scientific experiment is a new magic which sounds logical. It has not yet been used enough to produce contradictory results.[63]

His conclusion that class size could not be studied apart from other issues of curriculum and instruction represents the balance of opinion today.[64]

Still the scientific orientation had been deeply ingrained; the skepticism that developed was really a sign of the increasing sophistication of teachers and their leaders about such approaches. They did not reject science, but they did begin to move to control it. A Committee on Research was organized; annual summaries of research in English studies were prepared for the *English Journal*; and reviews of new studies began to point out the faults and limitations as well as the conclusions reached.[65] By the mid-thirties science was clearly no longer viewed as the solution to all the ills of the teaching of English, but it was just as clearly seen as one of the tools that would be put to use in the search for solutions to those ills.

CHAPTER IV NOTES

1. Edward L. Thorndike, "The Nature, Purposes, and General Methods of Measurements of Educational Products," in National Society for the Study of Education, *Seventeenth Yearbook* (Bloomington: NSSE, 1918). Cited by Lawrence A. Cremin in *The Transformation of the School* (New York: Vintage Books, 1961). p. 185.

2. W. W. Charters, *Curriculum Construction* (New York: Macmillan Co., 1923), p. 4.

3. W. W. H[atfield], "Literature Can Be Taught," *English Journal* 16:8 (October 1927): 648-49. The reference is to Arthur I. Gates' *The Improvement of Reading* (New York: Macmillan Co., 1927).

4. John J. DeBoer, "Changing Objectives in English," *English Journal* 21:5 (May 1932): 403-04.

5. On the efficiency movement, see especially Raymond E. Callahan, *Education and the Cult of Efficiency* (Chicago: University of Chicago Press, 1962).

6. National Society for the Study of Education, *Thirty-Seventh Yearbook: Part II, The Scientific Movement in Education* (Bloomington: NSSE, 1938), p. 57.

7. The army program is summarized by Cremin, *Transformation of the School*, pp. 186-87. On ability grouping in the general context of providing for individual differences, see Roy O. Billett in *Provisions for Individual Differences, Marking, and Promotion*, Monograph 13 of the National Survey of Secondary Education, Bureau of Education Bulletin 1932, no. 17 (Washington: Government Printing Office, 1933).

8. All four were distributed as yearbooks of the National Society for the Study of Education: *Minimum Essentials in Elementary-School Subjects*, Fourteenth Yearbook, Part I (1915); *Second Report of the Committee on Minimal Essentials in Elementary-School Subjects*, Sixteenth Yearbook, Part I (1917); *Third Report of the Committee on Economy of Time in Education*, Seventeenth Yearbook, Part I (1918); and *Fourth Report of the Committee on Economy of Time in Education*, Eighteenth Yearbook, Part II (1919).

9. Franklin Bobbitt, *How To Make a Curriculum* (New York: Houghton Mifflin Company, 1924). This book and his earlier *The Curriculum* (1918) were frequently cited by teachers attempting to formulate a curriculum for literature throughout the twenties and thirties.

10. Ibid., pp. 76-79.

11. English was cheaper than the other languages because, as a required course, more students took it and class sizes were larger.

12. NSSE, Fourteenth Yearbook, I; p. 147.

13. NSSE, Eighteenth Yearbook, II; the section was by W. S. Gray.

14. "Report of the Committee on Economy of Time in English," *English Journal* 9:1 (January 1920): 32-34.

15. For a chronicle of changing attitudes toward language, see Raven I. McDavid, Jr., ed., *An Examination of the Attitudes of the NCTE Toward Language*, Research Report no. 4 (Urbana, Ill.: NCTE, 1965). This provides very little interpretation or reference beyond NCTE journals. On Leonard's committee, see "The National Council, 1911-36," *English Journal* 25:10 (December 1936): 805-29.

16. "Challenged!" Editorial, *English Journal* 11:9 (November 1922): 584-85. See also "Social Studies as the Core," News and Notes, *English Journal* 9:5 (May 1920): 295-96. During 1922 considerable attention was devoted to increasing required English from three to four years. Statements in support were even obtained from Vice President Marshall. (Max J. Herzberg, "Four Years of English in Secondary Schools," *English Journal* 11:4 [April 1922]: 236-39.)

17. Essie Chamberlain, "Curriculum Building in English," *English Journal* 14:1 (January 1925): 1-12. "Fourteenth Annual Meeting of the National Council of Teachers of English," *English Journal* 14:1 (January 1925): 47-76. On her earlier interests, see her "The Possibilities of Classroom Experiment," *English Journal* 10:8 (October 1921): 427-38.

18. John Mantle Clapp, *The Place of English in American Life*, Report of an Investigation by a Committee of the National Council of Teachers of English (Chicago, Ill.: NCTE, 1926). Summarized as "Report of Committee on Place and Function of English in American Life," *English Journal* 15:2 (February 1926): 110-34.

19. Charles S. Pendleton, *The Social Objectives of School English* (Nashville: By the author, 1924). Other investigations with goals similar to those of the Clapp report included J. W. Searson, "Meeting the Public Demand," *English Journal* 10:6 (June 1921): 327-31; and a report from the Chicago English Club, "Out of School Uses of English," *English Journal* 22:6 (June 1933): 466-71.

20. The summary volume was W. W. Charters, *Motion Pictures and Youth* (New York: Macmillan Company, 1933). Two of the studies have recently been reprinted as part of the Literature of the Cinema series. Edgar Dale, *Children's Attendance at Motion Pictures*, and Wendell S. Dysinger and Christian A. Ruckmick, *The Emotional Responses of Children to the Motion Picture Situation* (New York: Arno Press and the *New York Times*, 1970). These originally appeared in 1935 and 1933, respectively.

21. Dale, *Children's Attendance at Motion Pictures*, p. 73.

22. See "Movie Madness," *English Journal* 21:9 (November 1932): 773-74. The early history is reviewed in a 1935 editorial, "How Much Analysis of Photoplays?" *English Journal* 24:3 (March 1935): 241-42. The pioneering work was done by Max Herzberg and Edgar Dale.

23. William Lewin, *Photoplay Appreciation in American High Schools* (New York: D. Appleton-Century Co., 1934). The study was later criticized on the grounds that the teachers were not competent to conduct film studies, judging from the preferences they reported. See W. W. H[atfield], "Teachers' Literary Judgment," *English Journal* 23:9 (November 1934): 775.

24. William Lewin, "New Photoplays," *English Journal* 23:6 (June 1934): 509. There was also some interest in student-made films. See Hardy R. Finch, "Film Production in the School—A Survey," *English Journal* 28:5 (May 1939): 365-71.

25. See Mabel A. Bessey, *Report of a Committee of the NCTE on the Use of the Magazine in the High School English Classroom* (Chicago: NCTE, 1935); Eleanor Tourison, "The Newspaper of Today," *English Journal* 16:3 (March 1927): 192-99; and William W. Wattenberg, "Getting Truth from Your Newspaper," *English Journal* 26:5 (May 1937): 363-68.

26. This was partly because radio was treated as part of the speech curriculum. The early work of the Radio Committee focussed on arranging broadcasts of literary works, including a series of Shakespeare's plays between 1936 and 1938, in conjunction with the American School of the Air.

See Max J. Herzberg, "Listen In!" *English Journal* 25:9 (November 1936): 775; and 26:10 (December 1937): 827-28. On radio and speech, see F. H. Lumley, "The English Teacher and Radio Broadcasts," *English Journal* 33:6 (June 1934): 478-85.

27. Max J. Herzberg, *Radio and the English Teacher* (Chicago: NCTE, 1937), p. 2. See also I. Keith Tyler, "The Listening Habits of Oakland (California) Pupils," *English Journal* 25:3 (March 1936): 206-15; and I. Keith Tyler, "What Can We Do About the Radio?" *English Journal* 27:7 (September 1938): 556-66.

28. Charles Sumner Crow, *Evaluation of English Literature in the High School*, Contributions to Education no. 141 (New York: Teachers College, Columbia University, 1924), p. 1.

29. See for example Earl Hudelson, "Our Courses of Study in Litera-ture," *English Journal* 12:7 (September 1923): 481-87; Frances Mary Hughes, "What Do High-School Teachers Say About the Classics at Present Used?" *English Journal* 13:5 (May 1924): 331-35; Stuart Noble, "A Graded Sequence in High-School Literature," *English Journal* 13:5 (May 1924): 350-52; and John M. Stalkner and Fred Eggan, "American Novelists Ranked: A Psychological Study," *English Journal* 18:4 (April 1929): 295-307. One survey was used as the basis of a basal reading series: Herbert Bruner, "Determining Basic Reading Materials Through a Study of Chil-dren's Interests and Adult Judgments," *Teachers College Record* 30:4 (January 1929): 285-309.

30. Erna B. Conrad and Katherine Hickok, "Placement of Literary Selections for Junior and Senior High Schools," *English Journal* 19:5 (May 1930): 377-84.

31. John L. Haney, "Standardization in English," *English Journal* 11:4 (April 1922): 214-21.

32. Hubert A. Wright, "The Solution of Burke," *English Journal* 12:5 (May 1923): 317-21; and Abner A. Miller, "Streamlining *Comus*," *English Journal* 24:7 (September 1935): 580-82.

33. See Nila Banton Smith, *American Reading Instruction* (New York: Silver, Burdett and Company, 1934), pp. 155-58; National Society for the Study of Education, *Twentieth Yearbook*, II (1921); and Charles H. Judd and Guy T. Buswell, *Silent Reading: A Study of Its Various Types*, Supplementary Educational Monographs (Chicago: University of Chicago Press, 1922).

34. Theo. W. H. Irion, *Comprehension Difficulties of Ninth Grade Students in the Study of Literature*, Contributions to Education no. 189 (New York: Teachers College, Columbia University, 1925), pp. 71-72. He summarized his results in "Economy in the Teaching of High-School Literature," *English Journal* 16:2 (February 1927): 114-19.

35. Mary Crowell Burch, "Determination of a Content in the Course in Literature of a Suitable Difficulty for Junior and Senior High School Students," *Genetic Psychology Monographs* 4 (Nos. 2 and 3): 1928.

36. One major burst of interest came in the late 1930s, after the conclusion of a federal study of silent reading in New York City. This was reported by Stella S. Center and Gladys L. Persons in *Teaching High School Pupils to Read* (Chicago, Ill.: NCTE, 1937).

37. See Louise Anderson, "English for the Inferior Section of the Ninth Grade," *English Journal* 12:9 (November 1923): 611-16; Cora Lehr, "En-glish with a High I.Q. Class," *English Journal* 14:10 (December 1925): 742-53; Mabel C. Hermans, "Experiments with Gifted Children," *English Journal* 20:7 (September 1931): 540-47; Prudence T. Lanphean, "What

Cleveland Is Doing for Superior Students," *English Journal* 26:9 (November 1937): 723-28.

38. Helen Louise Cohen, "English for the Gifted," *English Journal* 24:3 (March 1935): 208-11; Ruth Axford Stewart, "Dedicated to the Low IQ," *English Journal* 24:3 (March 1935): 204-07. Stewart was admittedly talking about an extreme case; her class had an average IQ of 76. The same attitudes were evident in teachers of students in the 90 to 100 range, however. See Lou L. LaBrant, "Differentiated Teaching of Literature," *English Journal* 20:7 (September 1931): 548-56.

39. "The Social Conception," *English Journal* 14:5 (May 1925): 414-15.

40. On the early work, see Cremin, *Transformation of the School*, p. 296. It was popularized in Evelyn Dewey, *The Dalton Laboratory Plan* (New York: E. P. Dutton, 1922), and in Helen Parkhurst's *Education on the Dalton Plan* (1922). Dewey's description was based on observations in Dalton and in two British schools that had adopted the approach.

41. Marion C. Sheridan, "An Evaluation of the Dalton Plan," *English Journal* 15:7 (September 1926): 507-13.

42. Olive Ely Hart, "The Dalton Plan vs. Individualized Instruction," *English Journal* 18:2 (February 1929): 168-70.

43. Clyde Hissong and Mary Champe Hissong, "English under the Dalton Plan," *English Journal* 19:10 (December 1930): 822-24. "Contracts," Editorial, *English Journal* 21:10 (December 1932): 842-43.

44. "What Should a 'Unit' in English Be?" *English Journal* 22:10 (December 1933): 844-45. Morrison himself addressed the 1930 NCTE convention ("The Cleveland Meeting," *English Journal* 20:1 [January 1931]: 56). For an earlier and more favorable reaction, see " 'Units' in Learning," *English Journal* 16:10 (December 1927): 816-17.

45. Leonard V. Koos, "The National Survey of Secondary Education," *English Journal* 22:4 (April 1933): 303-13. The full report of this aspect of the survey is in Billett, *Provisions for Differences*.

46. See J. C. Tressler, "The New Type of Examination," *English Journal* 9:10 (December 1924): 709-15.

47. Thus Mabel S. Satterfield and Salibelle Royster argued that pupils would gain "mental discipline" and learn "to know the events of *Silas Marner*" by being given objective tests. "The New-Type Examination in English," *English Journal* 20:6 (June 1931): 490-95.

48. John J. DeBoer, "A College Qualifications Test in Reading," *English Journal* 21:8 (October 1932): 629-41. He was given editorial support for the project in the same issue.

49. Commission on English, *Examining the Examination in English*, Harvard Studies in English, vol. 17 (Cambridge, Mass.: Harvard University Press, 1931), p. xii.

50. Ibid., pp. 153-54.

51. This is one of the indications of Hatfield's lack of influence on the report. He complained editorially that the commission should have heeded its own findings and abandoned *any* special exam in English. "College Entrance Examinations," *English Journal* 20:9 (November 1931): 770-71.

52. See "Report on College Entrance English Exam," News and Notes, *English Journal* 20:9 (November 1931): 774-75. This notes Thomas' chapter with special approval.

53. Nancy Gillmore Coryell, *An Evaluation of Extensive and Intensive Teaching of Literature*, Contributions to Education no. 275 (New York: Teachers College, Columbia University, 1927).

54. One reflection of the Joint Committee's attitude was the fact that "Extensive Reading" was dealt with in a chapter of its own, separate from the chapters on the teaching of literature. On the Reorganization report, see Chapter III.

55. This was in a report to the 1927 NCTE convention. "The 1927 Council." *English Journal* 17:1 (January 1928): 57-81.

56. The extremes of the two points of view were illustrated by the debating positions at one convention. John Gelman, "The Values of Required Reading," *English Journal* 19:8 (October 1930): 663-42; and Mary E. Lowe, "Required Reading Versus Free Reading," *English Journal* 19:8 (October 1930): 642-51. The editor suggested they be read as "a joint contribution."

57. The Commission on English (*Examining the Examination in English*, p. 26) was typically dismissive: "Miss Coryell's study reveals certain advantages of extensive reading, but this does not imply that a real appreciation of literature can be secured without very close and detailed work upon selected masterpieces."

58. Other studies supporting free reading are summarized by James R. Squire in "English Literature," in the *Encyclopedia of Educational Research*, 4th ed., ed. Robert L. Ebel (New York: Macmillan Company, 1969), pp. 461-73.

59. Richard Braddock et al. *Research in Written Composition* (Urbana, Ill.: NCTE, 1963). When Purves and Beach carried out a similar survey of investigations in the teaching of literature, they found flaws in virtually all the studies examined. Alan C. Purves and Richard Beach, *Literature and the Reader: Research in Response to Literature, Reading Interests, and the Teaching of Literature* (Urbana, Ill.: NCTE, 1972).

60. It is indicative of the state of affairs in literature that when the National Society for the Study of Education devoted its *Thirty-Seventh Yearbook* to the scientific movement in education, it included chapters on the teaching of handwriting, spelling, English usage, and reading—but none on literature.

61. Important early (pre-1925) studies were conducted by Calvin O. Davis in the North Central Association and Paul R. Stevenson at the University of Illinois. See Callahan, *Education and the Cult of Efficiency*, pp. 232-39.

62. Rewey Belle Inglis, "Retrospect and Prospect," *English Journal* 19:1 (January 1930): 11-21.

63. Editorial, "Pedagogical Research," *English Journal* 19:8 (October 1931): 665-66.

64. See William S. Vincent, "Class Size," in Ebel, *Encyclopedia of Educational Research*, pp. 141-46.

65. See Walter Barnes, "English Research and the National Council," *English Journal* 23:1 (January 1934): 9-18; Committee on Research, "The Contributions of Research to Teaching and Curriculum-Making in English, January, 1933, through June, 1934," *English Journal* 23:9 (November 1934): 718-31; and Dudley Miles, "Class Size in High-School English," Book Review, *English Journal* 21:1 (January 1932): 77-78. The Miles article was a review of a study by Dora V. Smith (soon to be NCTE president) in which her results were attributed to the "intelligence, vigorous personality, and profound enthusiasm" of Smith—and hence could not be generalized.

The aim of teaching literature is the utmost possible broadening and enrichment of young people's experience, and their better appreciation or valuing of all experience, rather than of books alone.

—Sterling Andrus Leonard, **Essential Principles of Teaching Reading and Literature**, 1922[1]

In the common schools, at least, the social basis of literature will become established by the importunities of a civilization on trial. . . . The introduction of democracy into industry; the use of wealth for the welfare of the people; the protection of womanhood and childhood against the rapacity of individualism gone mad; the final eradication of mob rule and lynch law; the elimination of brutality and injustice in our courts and penal institutions; the growth of a world state in which war will be as extinct as the private duel—children are not only to understand these movements, they are to learn to desire them with studied intensity.

—John J. DeBoer, "The Materials of the English Curriculum," 1932[2]

. . . Our major task in the ordinary school is to teach all our pupils to read ordinary matters with ordinary intelligence and to express ordinary thoughts with reasonable clarity. This emphasis upon the practical enforces very directly our responsibility as teachers of a tool subject. . . . Our English course should embody experiences . . . analogous to the expected general experiences of life.

—Charles Swain Thomas, Presidential Address to the NCTE, 1935[3]

The state course of study in English is liberal in tendency. . . . Handicaps to the practical use of the couse in schools throughout the state are chiefly a paucity of book supply, local insistence upon more formal elements of instruction, lack of preparation on the part of teachers in point of view and in knowledge of the kind of materials sponsored by the course, and fear that the Regents' examinations or college entrance requirements will differ in emphases from the state course of study.

—Dora V. Smith, after surveying instruction in New York State, 1941[4]

Chapter V

A Framework for Teaching

During the decades between the First and Second World Wars, teachers of English were searching for a new and coherent framework around which to structure their teaching. The concern with scientific method was one aspect of that search, but, as in the progressive movement in education as a whole, it was never the only one. In the teaching of literature in particular, the answers which science offered were slow in coming and unsatisfactory when they arrived. The writings and speeches of William Heard Kilpatrick of Teachers College, Columbia, provide the best single example of the problems toward which teachers of English soon turned their attention. Many cited Kilpatrick directly as they sought to rationalize and defend their own approaches; others less overtly but no less obviously reflected his emphases and concerns, and sometimes even his solutions. As a disciple of Dewey and student of Thorndike, Kilpatrick was himself a blend of the forces that led to the redefinition of English instruction: his concerns were scientific, philosophical, psychological, reformist. And if that blend were improbable, so would be the blend within the teaching of English.

In this chapter, the discussion will focus on the elaboration of a metaphor of experience and later of exploration as the heart of the educational process. Important contributing topics will include the project method, the redefinition of the value of literature in terms of "vicarious" and later of "ordered" experience, the emergence of radical social goals in response to the Depression, and the synthesis of all these elements in a series of "pattern curriculums" offered in the late 1930s. Other important movements which began during the twenties or thirties—in particular the Eight-Year Study of the Progressive Education Association, a new interest in semantics, and the New Criticism—culminated somewhat later and will be discussed in the next chapter.

The Project Method

The Method Proposed

The project method was Kilpatrick's methodological solution to the many demands on the progressive teacher. He outlined it briefly in *Teachers College Record* in September 1918, and elaborated it in more detail in a later book, *Foundations of Method* (1925). Accepting the progressives' rejection of mental discipline and their concern with moral and ethical development, he also pointed out that the method of teaching could itself convey important lessons to the student, lessons which have nothing to do with overt subject matter. Since in a democratic society "the typical unit of the worthy life" is "the purposeful act," Kilpatrick argued that this should also be the "typical unit of school procedure."[5]

Though in many ways this view of education was philosophically rather than psychologically derived, Kilpatrick carefully justified it in psychological terms. Here his analysis followed Thorndike in stressing that learning results from the Law of Effect: "any movement of mind or body that succeeds (or brings satisfaction) has for that reason a better chance of being used again." The virtue of the purposeful act as the basis of education is that it insures the working of the Law of Effect; the fulfillment of "purpose" brings satisfaction and thus forges the necessary bonds between stimulus and response.[6]

The project method was Kilpatrick's way of institutionalizing the purposeful act, and he described four kinds that could claim a legitimate place in the curriculum. One was the project to embody an idea in external form, as in writing a letter; the second, the project whose goal was simply to enjoy something, as in hearing a story; the third, to solve a problem, as in deciding why New York City has outgrown Philadelphia; the last, the project to attain a skill, as to bring one's handwriting up to grade 14 on the Thorndike scale.[7] The project that quickly came to dominate the literature did not really correspond to any of Kilpatrick's four categories; it might best be called the project to complete a task, as to make posters for a local show, to publish a school newspaper, or to build a model of the Globe theater.

Even Bobbitt in his functionalism had paid tribute to the value of "experience" in describing the uses of literature and reading; Kilpatrick, by placing the "purposeful act" at the heart of the educational process, made experience and education virtually synonymous. As he put it, the "psychological order is the order of experience, of democracy, and consequently of learning." And it was experience which would bridge the sometimes awesome gap between subject matter and child, between the world of the sophisticated adult and that of the naive schoolboy:

The subject-matter of the curriculum is race experience, the picked winnings of the race, the best ways mankind has yet devised of meeting its problems. . . . The child has experience, the race has experience. The child's experience is, of course, childish; but it is merely small, the beginning, the germ; the fuller form we see in the race experience.

Thus the project method, and education itself, could ultimately be seen as the broadening of experience, opening up the child's view until it could encompass the full "race experience": "The best way in which I can now conceive the curriculum itself is as a series of experiences in which by guided induction the child makes his own formulations. Then they are his to use."[8]

The Response

English teachers were in general quite receptive to Kilpatrick's exposition of method. Hosic provided an outline of the "Problem-Project Method" in the November 1918 issue of *English Journal* (only two months after Kilpatrick's *Record* article),[9] and the *Journal* followed up with many examples of the successful use of the approach during the next several years. W. Wilbur Hatfield, a colleague of Hosic's at Chicago Normal School and his successor at NCTE, also undertook to explain and illustrate the method; he considered it most appropriate for the teaching of writing, however, and did not deal with literature at all.[10]

By the end of the 1920s, the project method, the problem method, unit instruction, and the Dalton plan had become, in application, virtually indistinguishable. Yet each of the approaches had, in its original formulation, made a unique contribution to the rapidly evolving methodology. What the project method did for the teaching of literature was to bring experience within the curriculum. Though the activities would eventually bear little relationship to those Kilpatrick had envisioned, they would be planned and carried out to broaden and extend the student's range of experiences in the way that Kilpatrick had argued.

Toward Experience

Literature and Experience

Teachers' first response to the emphasis on experience was to treat literature as a "vicarious" experience of the events described. As Hosic described it in his doctoral dissertation (1921), in this view literature "enlarges and enriches the experience of the reader and extends his knowledge of life."[11] The roots of this emphasis are complex—those whom Hosic cited as in essential agreement included Arnold, St. Beuve, Corson, Hudson, Baker, Bobbitt, and Charters. The change during the twenties was to shift the focus from the past cultural experience Arnold had defended toward the present experience of the child himself. Sterling A. Leonard, in a textbook published a year after Hosic's study, gave the concern with vicarious experience its fullest statement. Throughout, he emphasized the life embodied in the books studied, rather than their "literary" characteristics. As he wrote in his preface, the "fundamental and central idea" of his discussion was that "children's reading of literature should be always an achievement of realized, true, and significant experience." He explained further on, however, that he meant "true in the largest sense, of giving a right idea of relations between people in actual life, and between thoughts and acts and their consequences according to natural law and social order." He meant that the vicarious experience offered must be a traditionally moral experience —an assertion soon to cause trouble for the progressive teacher of English.[12]

What Leonard was doing was fusing the emphasis on values that had been so important during the reorganization period with the emerging focus on experience. The underlying argument was simple enough: if literature is moral and also provides a vicarious experience, then the morality of the literature must come from the vicarious experience itself. Teachers fresh from the propaganda campaigns of the war had little doubt that literature's effects were quite direct. Secure in this belief, an NCTE committee on international relations attacked the "far reaching and pernicious influence" of Tennyson's "Charge of the Light Brigade"; they thought that the unquestioning obedience of the soldiers was the wrong kind of experience for schoolchildren to have.[13] A similar acceptance of the power of vicarious experience led to an interest in biographical studies. As Martha Shackford of Wellesley College put it in arguing for teaching the life of Goldsmith: "He gives balance and sanity; he saves us from dangerous complacence. His life was touched with pain and loneliness, but he was not dismayed. By living his life over with him our hearts ought to be softened and purified."[14]

Yet by the middle of the decade the ethical approach to literary experience was raising as many problems as it had solved. The early twentieth century had produced a host of new writers who challenged the very foundations of literary taste as well as the conventions of society. With the ethical orientation in literary studies, the orientation which said in effect that the morally good was the aesthetically beautiful, there was really only one verdict which could be reached about these writers. Harry T. Baker of Goucher College pronounced it in 1923:

If we know anything worth knowing about past literature, we can say something sensible and often helpful about that much over-praised novel, *Main Street*, or about the blatant productions of the Vulgarian School of versifiying, headed by Vachel Lindsay, Carl Sandburg, and a few nondescript immigrants, and sponsored by strong-minded ladies like Harriet Monroe and Amy Lowell. . . . The most noticeable feature of their curious volumes is that they need the services of a delousing station. If there is one especially prominent "note" in American minor poetry at present—and all of it is minor poetry—it is the note of complacent vulgarity.[15]

Baker's arguments illustrate the predicament in which the progressives in English found themselves. Concern with modern authors was a basic tenet; so was an emphasis on the system of values implicit in the work. The immediate response was to postpone judgment, studying the new authors without attempting to introduce them into the high school curriculum. *English Journal*, for example, began to be more systematic in its attempts to inform teachers about developments in the general field of literature. Percy Boynton of the University of Chicago was commissioned to provide a series of scholarly articles on "American Authors of Today"; the first appeared in September 1922. Though the *Journal* had published earlier articles by literary critics, the Boynton series was the formal beginning of a practice which continued unbroken for nearly forty years; it eventually brought such distinguished names as Louis Untermeyer, Ezra Pound, Theodore Dreiser, Vachel Lindsay, Mark Van Doren, Zona Gale, and J. B. Priestley to the *Journal*'s pages[16] During the Depression especially, when many literary magazines went bankrupt, these were often original studies of some import rather than simply overviews of current opinion for teachers.

Gradually the need for new techniques of criticism began to be clear. Llewellyn Jones, editor of the literary review of the *Chicago Evening Post*, provided a lengthy reformulation in a two-part article on aesthetics in October and November of 1925. Acknowledging his debt to Ogden and Richards, and to Ainslie's translation of Croce,[17] he defined art as "a complete and successful expression of a part of life—perhaps a very small part—experienced as one experience in which all the factors hang together." It is this coherence which distinguishes art, not any "parochial" moralism or didacticism. Jones proposed two standards for judging art. The first was the extent to which the artist was "sincerely giving us experience"—and not "trying to prove a point, put over a thesis or generalization: in short indulging in propaganda." Notice that what Jones has done here is to continue the emphasis on experience while purging it of a direct relationship with values. His second criterion was whether the work had achieved *form:* "that is, whether all that is not essential to the experience, all the accidentals that surround it in real life, have been purged away, so that the work has unity and affects us as a single organic whole." Again, this continues the concern with experience but makes it dependent upon form rather than content. Such an analysis destroyed the basis on which literature had been justifying its place in the curriculum, but Jones presented a new function which it might serve: ". . . although we repudiate the heresy that art must teach us moral lessons, we must admit that major art does have an educative function: it reconciles us to existence by presenting existence in an ideal (not a morally ideal but an intellectually ideal) light: as something that hangs together, that is not anarchic."[18]

This analysis provided teachers with the ideal solution to the problem of twentieth century literature. Its emphasis on experience continued the easy link with the methodological and philosophical proposals of Kilpatrick and Dewey. At the same time, by substituting intellectual order for moral value it justified the approaches of the new authors. The process of assimilation was not easy, especially for teachers in whom the previous approaches were thoroughly ingrained, but the direction was at least clear. Increasingly during the twenties and throughout the thirties, discussions of literature were phrased in terms of the experience which the work under study would provide.

One should not conclude, however, that "experience" was in any sense to become a developed critical approach; rather it was the underlying goal toward which the various approaches were oriented. The study of types, for example, was stressed by many of those who wanted to treat literature as experience. Leonard used it to structure a high school course that would group together experiences presenting similar sorts of difficulties in reading and interpretation.[19] After Mabel Irene Rich provided teachers with an anthology organized by types in 1921, complete with a laudatory introduction by James Fleming Hosic, the study of types emerged as the first widely accepted alternative to the study of single classics from the college entrance lists.[20] Historical studies received support from teachers who argued that in order to experience fully a work of literature, it was necessary to understand fully the social and cultural milieu in which it originated.[21] Teachers whose concerns were more directly pedagogical turned to the instructional unit as the major way to insure that students would achieve a proper "experience." Some suggested units focussed on a central reading, the experience of which would be enhanced by a plethora of other activities organized around it. Others focussed the experience instead on a single concept (e.g., liberty, patriotism), often in the process revealing a continuing concern with the inculcation of a very particular set of values.

Countercurrents

The movement toward literature as experience remained a movement away from the formal study of literature, even after the structured nature of the experience became central to its justification. Throughout the period of concern with experience, however, there were strong countercurrents urging other emphases. One such voice was raised by Joseph M. Thomas of the University of Minnesota, seventh president of NCTE. In his address to the 1919 convention, he paid full tribute to the criticism that had been directed toward early forms of literary study; but he went on to argue that the abuses of the past were no cause to abandon the great tradition. He had only caustic comments for English teachers who

> . . . have given up trying to interest the student in what they think he ought to be interested in, and are experimenting in a vain effort to find what he will like. They have not foresworn English, but have definitely abandoned literature. Instead of the *Spectator*, they read the *Literary Digest*; the local newspaper has replaced Lincoln and Franklin. Milton and Tennyson have been given up for something "peppy" in the way of new poetry. And I even hear of schools in which the *Saturday Evening Post* is studied in English. They have sold their birthright for a mess of Potash and Perlmutter.[22]

The major point that Thomas and others who sounded the same call were making was that while the goals of those seeking to reconstitute the literature curriculum were laudable, the direction that had been taken in search of those goals was doomed to fail. Martha Shackford, another unconvinced college professor, made her point in the process of describing the properly educated "freeman" in another article. In her view it was necessary to enforce a discipline and concentration that the high school lacked: ". . . until a child learns intellectual courage, the necessity of hard work, the fundamental significance of attacking and overcoming difficulties, he will never progress from the amoeba stage of intelligence."

This was an argument for mental discipline, dressed up in the new vocabulary of "intellectual courage," "responsibility," and progressive social orientation. It is thus especially interesting to note that tribute is paid to the experience approach in its manifestation as cultural history: the discipline Shackford advocated was to come from viewing literary works as "products of a very comprehensible social and political condition in each age, interpreted by individuals with imaginative insight, yet deriving much from the tendencies of the previous age."[23]

Another major voice of reaction was that of Harvard's Irving Babbitt, chief proponent of the American humanists. His emphasis was much the same as Matthew Arnold's, placing in literature functions previously assumed by religion, family, and social class. Pointing out that "the old education was partly humanistic, partly religious; the new education is humanitarian, concerned, that is, less with making wise individuals than with improving society as a whole," he asserted that teachers must decide whether "our education, especially our higher education, is to be qualitative and intensive or quantitative and extensive." Babbitt opted for the former alternative, asking teachers to "ignore certain equalitarian fallacies that are now being preached in the name of democracy."[24] This social conservatism, coupled with a lack of interest in modern studies, prevented Babbitt and the humanists from being widely accepted in the schools or the universities; but they kept alive a tradition of attention to great books and great ideas that eventually reemerged in the writings of Mortimer Adler and others in the 1940s.

Concern with student interest also continued as an element of the experience approach, though Kilpatrick found it necessary to draw a distinction between "a state of interest" in which children would "be always and merely" amused, and "active interest" which would be conducive to growth on the part of the child. A similar distinction prompted Lou L. LaBrant to protest against "the practice, much more common than our publications would indicate, of using the carving of little toy boats and castles, the dressing of quaint dolls, the pasting of advertising pictures, and the manipulation of clay and soap as the *teaching of English literature*." If such devices were really necessary to insure interest, "The remedy would seem to be in changing the reading material rather than in turning the literature course into a class in handicraft." Hatfield followed LaBrant's article with an editor's note suggesting that there were "two modern points of view," and pointed to another article in the same issue supporting such activities.[25] It would be a long time before teachers would willingly give up the "aids" they had developed.

Another part of the experience philosophy that provoked reactions was a concern with "guidance" through literature which some teachers, especially in the junior high schools, used to replace their earlier concern with ethics. This was already evident in articles on sex education at the end of the reorganization period, but reached its height in the late twenties. It was put into perspective by Howard Mumford Jones in 1929:

> I meet Susie and Willie seriously debating with all the earnestness of their naive young souls the question of whether a nice girl can afford to stay away from a petting party; and I wonder whether the experiences of Maggie Tulliver in *The Mill on the Floss* will guide them in their solution: I do not recall that she petted, though she seems to have gotten herself even more seriously involved than do modern girls who pet; and my mind goes back to the *Manual of Courses of Study* which declares in all seriousness that the study of the classics will help Susie

and Willie in the interpretation of problems of thinking and conduct
that meet the individual in his daily life. . . . And with Susie and Willie
before my mind, I am tempted to murmur, in the language of Al Smith,
"Bologny!"[26]

Jones argued instead for starting with the child, not with the
literature, choosing Kipling and Sherlock Holmes, if that would
interest them, rather than Milton and Jefferson.

The Social Perspective

As the forces of fascism began to stir in Europe, and the pangs of
Depression began to be felt even in America, literature again found a
didactic function. One strong influence was the vigorous school of
Marxist and left-wing writing and criticism which flourished inter-
nationally, and which was led in America by such men as John Dos
Passos, Michael Gold, and Joshua Kunitz. For many of these men,
content, rather than form, again became the only criterion of
excellence. In the words of V. F. Calverton, editor of *Modern
Quarterly* and a leading spokesman of the left, the goal was to build
"a new society which will embody, like Soviet Russia today, a social,
instead of an individualistic, ideal." *English Journal,* in keeping
with its policy of informing teachers of all aspects of the current
literary scene, assiduously brought these men to its pages — carefully
counterposed with editorial comment and more conservative points
of view, but there nonetheless for all to read and ponder.[27]
    Most teachers of English were ready to heed the implicit social
orientation that these writers were offering. In a time when established institutions did seem to be faltering, and just distant enough
from the previous world war for the disillusionment it had generated
to have faded, the original progressive concern with social progress
could reemerge, if anything more radical for its long suppression.
One focal point for the social theorists was Teachers College,
Columbia. There a group of educators under the leadership of W. H.
Kilpatrick eventually forged an unusual measure of intellectual
cohesion. The fullest statement of their creed was *The Educational
Frontier* (1933), a yearbook produced for the National Society of
College Teachers of Education by a committee dominated by the
Teachers College group. The task of education as it was presented
there was "to prepare individuals to take part intelligently in the
management of conditions under which they live, to bring them to an
understanding of the forces which are moving, to equip them with
the intellectual and practical tools by which they can themselves
enter into direction of these forces."[28] In such a program the focus of
study would be upon current social issues and problems; in many
ways it was a return to Dewey's earliest concerns.

The social perspective so evident in *The Educational Frontier* was not limited to the Teachers College group, even though it is usually identified with them. Indeed, the basis was quite broad, reflecting a strong national movement towards socialism in the late twenties and early thirties. The President's Committee on Social Trends, set up by Herbert Hoover in 1929, placed a similar stress on the need to reconstruct society's value system:

> The clarification of human values and their reaffirmation in order to give expression to them in terms of today's life and opportunities is a major task of social thinking. The progressive confusion created in men's minds by the bewildering sweep of events revealed in our recent social trends must find its counterpart in the progressive clarification of men's thinking and feeling, in the reorientation to the meaning of the new trends.

To the American Historical Society's Commission on the Social Studies in the Schools (1934), it was the public schools which should ease the birth pangs of socialized society, educating its students for the end of the "age of individualism and *laissez-faire.*" Even the NEA was willing, as it viewed the national situation in 1932, to endorse a commitment to social reconstruction through education.[29]

The reconstructionist point of view took as its starting point Dewey's observation that "education is the fundamental method of social progress and reform"; its end point was radicalism. George S. Counts challenged the Progressive Education Association in a 1932 address, "Dare Progressive Education Be Progressive?" in which he argued the need for education to emancipate itself from the middle class, reaching for political power to lead the nation to socialism. He argued, too, that indoctrination of students would be a necessary part of the struggle toward the desired goals. *The Social Frontier,* the major journal of the reconstructionists (with Kilpatrick as chairman and Counts as editor), dealt squarely with the ideological issues raised by such approaches. Founded in October 1934 to give more effective voice to the group, its pages chronicle the increasingly radical rhetoric that eventually split the movement and helped to plunge progressivism as well as the reconstructionists into disfavor. By February 1936, the journal had turned to the rhetoric of class warfare as the means to the collectivism which was the major social goal. In so doing it lost many of its supporters; this was further than even most of the Teachers College group were willing to go.[30]

The social reconstructionists, whether laying out basic tenets in *The Educational Frontier* or arguing on the pages of *The Social Frontier,* had a strong sense of mission and a fervent belief in the power of education as an instrument for good. Though the group to a large extent centered around Kilpatrick, they gave little attention to the specifics of curriculum and method that would have been needed to directly influence current practice. Their accomplishment was instead indirect: they reawakened the social consciousness of the progressive teacher, the belief in reform and progress that had originally given progressive education its name. Certainly the rhetoric of the social reconstructionists was accepted by teachers of English during the early 1930s. Stella Center, of John Adams High School in New York City, assessed "The Responsibility of Teachers of English in Contemporary American Life" in her presidential address to the 1932 NCTE convention. The responsibilities were broad:

> If tariff walls mount to incredible heights and our political leaders pursue a policy of eighteenth century isolation, it lies especially in the province of English instruction, by a program of reading and discussion, to develop a feeling of world solidarity and to create better international understanding.[31]

Why this was "especially the province of English instruction" was not quite clear; presumably the answer lay at least in part in the long ethical tradition which had most recently been reflected in the work of E. Estelle Downing's NCTE Committee on International Understanding. This committee was reorganized at the same convention and the cause of peace was taken up with renewed zeal. The Council announced that together with the NEA it was "officially sponsoring the peace movement in the schools." Journal articles, convention sessions, and—a major first for the Council—official resolutions were enlisted in the crusade on which "the future of the world depends."[32]

Yet at the same time teachers of English rejected the call for indoctrination. When George S. Counts challenged the schools to build a new social order, Hatfield agreed editorially that there would indeed be great changes in society during the lives of the students; the proper way to prepare them, however, was by training them to think—not by imposing thoughts upon them. And when a few years later a language workbook included an advertisement for a telephone company, John J. DeBoer, assistant editor of the *English Journal* and long a backer of the peace movement, editorialized on the dangers of propaganda in the schools: "This propaganda in behalf of a private utility is so obvious it would not be alarming were it not typical of other influences more insidious. Pressure groups of various kinds constantly besiege the school and frequently invade the classrooms with viewpoints inimical to public welfare." His answer, like Hatfield's to Counts, was to point out that "Not suppression but exposition should be the guiding principle of American education."[33]

Ultimately, teachers of English rejected the plea of the social reconstructionists because they saw other values implicit in their subject matter. Thus Oscar J. Campbell warned in his 1934 NCTE presidential address that "The greatest danger in such a time as ours is that one's mind may be completely captured by the immediate and pressing. Values which are not obvious are in danger of becoming obscured or lost. Our duties in a rapidly changing world can best be discharged if we remain cognizant of the nature of our subject and of those deeper regions of personality to which it brings life and energy." And two years later Dora V. Smith, addressing the same body in the same capacity, felt it necessary to ask, "Are we willing to give boys and girls a share of the attention we have devoted to English as a subject and to the indisputable claims of the social order?"[34] It was time, in other words, to return attention to the children who had been somewhat out of view since the Depression had begun.

Patterns for the Curriculum

An Experience Curriculum

In November 1929, at the instigation of the new president, Ruth Mary Weeks, the Executive Committee of NCTE appointed a Curriculum Commission to develop a "pattern curriculum" that would illustrate the best current practice and thus provide a stable reference point in the midst of the rapidly shifting instructional concerns. Over one hundred Council leaders served on the commission's fourteen subcommittees, together with representatives from the NEA, the American Association of Teachers Colleges, the National Association of Teachers of Speech, the National Association of Journalism Advisers, the North Central Association of Colleges and Secondary Schools, and the Southern Association of Colleges and Secondary Schools.

The undertaking was in many ways more ambitious than any of the earlier efforts to define the scope of English instruction, for what the commission had in effect to attempt was a new synthesis. The earlier reports on English—from the Vassar Conference of the Committee of Ten and from the National Joint Committee on English—had gathered together a consensus of contemporary opinion; the new commission had to forge such a consensus where none existed, to plan a new and largely untested shape for the teaching of English.

The task was carried through with enthusiasm and a certain measure of success. Responsive to the many different forces that had been reshaping instruction, and aware that there had been few systematic attempts to embody the emerging principles into coherent practice, the Curriculum Commission made no pretense that the result was in any sense a national prescription for English instruction; indeed the Commission thought it abundantly clear that any "attempt to create a single curriculum suited to pupils in environments so different as are to be found in the United States would be folly."[35] The final report, *An Experience Curriculum in English* (1935), was rather intended as a pattern that other groups could take as a starting point in developing a curriculum to fit their own particular circumstances.

The report began with the premise that "Experience is the best of all schools. . . . *The ideal curriculum consists of well-selected experiences.*" The process of selecting those experiences was the process Bobbitt had outlined and the Committee on the Place and Function of English in American Life had illustrated: it was to "survey life, noting what experiences most people have." And it was one step more: it was necessary to look, in these same surveys of life, for the "desirable possible experiences they miss" (p. 3). In deriving this no longer strictly empirical display, the commission was breaking no new ground; their unique contribution was an attempt to weave the selected experiences into a coherent curriculum stretching from kindergarten to college.

The "radical progressive unit" was taken as the basic element around which to structure the curriculum. This was the commission's attempt to revitalize and focus the somewhat nebulous unit that had emerged from the blend of Morrison units, projects, and contracts. As they put it, a unit "means an *organic whole* which is at the same time both a *structural and a functional* part of a larger organic whole" (p. vii, fn. 1).[36] Units lasted anywhere from five to fifteen days, and were themselves organized into what the commission termed "experience strands," each of which was a series of similar types of experience "arranged like broad easy stair steps in a reasonably steady progression of intellectual difficulty and social maturity" (p. viii).

The final report divided the various experience strands into several sets, including Literature Experiences, Reading Experiences, Creative Expression Experiences, Speech Experiences, Writing Experiences, Instrumental Grammar Experiences, Corrective Teaching, and Electives. These were in general the work of different subcommittees working under different chairmen, and were quite varied in the extent and direction of the changes they embodied. Probably the most progressive—and most widely attacked—stand taken in *An Experience Curriculum* was the abandonment of formal grammar in favor of functional instruction. The point was made bluntly: "There is no scientific evidence of the value of grammar which warrants its appearance as a prominent or even a distinct feature of the course of study." The only concession made at all was the inclusion of the study of grammar as a formal system among the suggested electives for high school seniors (pp. 228, 289).[37]

The curriculum in literature was equally liberal in conception, placing its emphasis upon pupils' experiences, upon informal discussion, upon broadening horizons and refining perception. Experiences which might be "harmful" were to be carefully excluded, including "such horror or sex experiences as the immature cannot sustain without shock and warping of their natures," as well as "sentimentality, glamorous presentation of evil-doing, inconsistent characterization, misrepresentation of moral cause and effects, and contravention of natural laws." With these exceptions, individual experience would be enlarged in as many directions as possible, allowing no one concern, however ardent its advocates, to circumscribe the literature curriculum: "the inculcation of knowledge or ethical ideals, the posing of social problems, the cultivation of the power to perceive beauty, or the mere provision of an escape from trying actuality are, all of them, too narrow objectives" (pp. 19-20).

Yet when faced with the task of providing a pattern curriculum in literature, the commission found itself subverted by the very conventions it had established for the final report. The chief reforms it was advocating for literary studies (unlike those in grammar) lay in the way each work was to be studied; they did not involve the sequence or, to any large extent, the works that would be used in the first place. The ideal classroom approach was seen as one of wide reading and little discussion—much like the method Coryell had used with the "experimental" group in her recent and controversial dissertation. Faced with the need to provide a sequence and organization (and little else), the report showed no clear preference for any of the various methods of organizing materials, and no clear conception of how the "experience units" differed from any other approach. Thus the major experience strands were an astonishingly traditional blend of currently popular approaches:

A. Enjoying Action
B. Exploring the Physical World
C. Exploring the Social World
D. Studying Human Nature
E. Sharing Lyric Emotion
F. Giving Fancy Rein
G. Solving Puzzles (e.g., mystery stories)
H. Listening to Radio Broadcasts
I. Enjoying Photoplays

Within these strands there are sample units on animals, heroes, and humor; on allegory, epic, and myth; on the origin of man, the effect of inventions, and industrial expansion; on rhythm, figurative expression, and characterization; on patriotism and brotherhood; and many, many more.

In spite of the rhetoric, the units do not in any significant way lead to—and were not meant to lead to—important experiences through literature. What they do attempt is to provide the functional skills that were considered prerequisite to the actual experience of

literature. The experiences that are offered, on the kindest judgment, are better than the earliest philological approaches; but they
are artificial and lifeless in their own way. Thus the final unit in the
strand Enjoying Action has as the Primary Objective (the "ultimate
goal" of such study), "To enjoy adventures which are more interesting because their backgrounds are so different from our own environ-
ment." For Enabling Objectives, it offers "To visualize clothing,
weapons, houses, and other details of the background. To note
peculiarities of speech and social customs, if there are any. To catch
some of the attitudes and ways of thinking which are different from
ours" (p. 44). Even the list of Typical Materials is traditional,
including among others novels by Scott, Cooper, Dickens, and
Stevenson that had been on the college lists at the turn of the
century. Or again, we can take a unit that sounds more promising,
Number 6 in the strand Exploring the Social World. This offers as its
Primary Objective, "To observe the effects of widening trade
horizons on our daily lives"; for Enabling Objectives: "To see how
new frontiers and new customs were the direct result of the desire of
man to increase his trading area; to catch some idea of the need for
invention, investigation, and discovery; to note the organization of
big business and the resulting efficiency and economy which it
implies" (p. 49). Here the materials are less traditional, including
Whitman's "I Hear America Singing," *Andrew Carnegie's Own
Story,* and Norris' *The Octopus.* Yet even in this unit, among the
best in the series, the concept of experience seems completely
unrealized. The student will, if the objectives are successfully
pursued, gain a certain measure of knowledge; he will not, however,
have been given any inkling of the peculiar virtues of literature in
conveying that experience. (One might question whether, given
these particular objectives, literature really has any peculiar virtues.)

Conducting Experiences in English

Even as the final report was being presented to the November
1935 convention, some of the problems were recognized. Dora V.
Smith, not herself a member of the Curriculum Commission, noted
that method and content had not been clearly synthesized in the
literature sections. Two years later, the Council saw fit to organize a
new committee under the chairmanship of Angela M. Broening to
provide illustrations of how the materials in the first report could be
translated into action. The focus of the problem was clear in the title
chosen for the second volume, published in 1939 as *Conducting
Experiences in English.*[38]

By the time *Conducting Experiences* was published, *An Experience Curriculum* had been widely emulated. Textbooks were already

purporting to embody the approach, and courses of study across the country had been modified in keeping with its principles.[39] In the new publication teachers were shown how to put the materials to work. In literature, the connection between method and content was tightened by recognizing the centrality of the reader's response: "He takes as much of the book as he can, rewriting it, as it were, in the imagery of his own experience." The goal of the teacher in this process would be to foster a "natural, vital discussion of the experience shared by the author."[40]

The heart of the book, however, was again the specific illustrations of "conducting experiences." These were, as in the earlier report, a mixture of approaches ranging from the excellent to the banal. One of the best of the literature units was the first offered: it outlined a sequence of lessons following a heavy storm, during which eighth grade students discussed their reactions, read poetry, and eventually wrote their own poems. But most of the literature activities, like those in *An Experience Curriculum*, failed to make clear how experience *with* was leading to the desired experience *through* the literature being studied.

A Correlated Curriculum

The Curriculum Commission attempted to formulate a program for English that could function within schools as they were presently organized. It lauded experiments designed to end "the artificial separation of one subject from another,"[41] but left the full exposition of such a program to a subcommittee which became virtually independent. This committee produced a separate report, *A Correlated Curriculum*, in 1936.

Rather than presenting *a* curriculum, the committee analyzed a spectrum of programs ranging from partial to total correlation. The general approach was cautious: faults as well as virtues were noted at each stage of the continuum. Unlike *An Experience Curriculum*, which was presented as a successful pattern to be emulated, *A Correlated Curriculum* was seen as describing an experiment—one deserving widespread testing to answer the questions it raised, but one whose generalizability still needed to be evaluated. The committee was especially careful to preserve the traditional virtues of English instruction; indeed, among its lists of criteria for evaluating attempts at correlation was one that asked if the tested values of any subject would be lost, and another that asked if the degree of subject-area competence brought about by departmentalization would be reduced in the new program.[42]

The movement toward correlation gained its support from the most progressive schools and will be dealt with in more detail in the next chapter. Among its many roots, one of the most important was the growing influence of the Gestalt psychologists. These emphasized the importance of the total pattern or "gestalt" in psychological processes, a concern which teachers generalized into a concern with "world pattern" and "unified experience." To provide this total perspective, teachers argued, it would be necessary for the curriculum itself to be unified through integration or correlation of the traditionally disparate subject areas. The NCTE committee gave another reason for correlation in its discussion. The exigencies of the Depression economy had forced cuts in school budgets: it was hoped that "curricular consolidation" through correlation would circumvent "curricular curtailment" (p. 11).

Initial reactions to the report were not favorable. Franklin Bobbitt, in a review for *English Journal*, attacked *A Correlated Curriculum* for a "dislocation in the order of investigation." "We believe," Bobbitt wrote, "that the department of English must take care of matters more fundamental than correlation before it can be ready to prepare anything more than a merely descriptive account of relatively unevaluated practices, such as the present investigation." It was the "basic assumptions of the department, as ably represented by the committee," that needed "re-examination, reorientation, and careful reformulation." Perhaps surprised by Bobbitt's reaction, the *English Journal* solicited a second evaluation, this one from L. T. Hopkins of Teachers College, Columbia. The second review, though considerably more favorable, found the same problems with the report that Bobbitt had delineated: the starting point remained English, and correlation remained a device to aid in the learning of that subject. There would be no fundamental change in the educational process. Indeed, Hopkins questioned the basic assumption that "synthesizing parts or elements into a complex whole will satisfy the needs of pupils for wholeness or unity in their experience."[43] And if that assumption could be soundly questioned, the approach would have little left to recommend it.

Literature as Exploration: The Final Synthesis

The many different forces which had been shaping the teaching of literature were in the end successfully synthesized not by NCTE, but by Louise M. Rosenblatt writing for the Commission on Human Relations of the Progressive Education Association. In contact with leaders of the Council but drawing more heavily on leading social scientists, her magnum opus, *Literature as Exploration* (1938), dealt at length with the proper role of and approach to literary studies.[44]
Like the Council's Curriculum Commission, Rosenblatt recognized a distinction between experience through and experience of or with literature—and like them also she considered the experience through literature to be of central importance. But she did not accept the premise, stated explicitly in *An Experience Curriculum*, that the teacher's attention would focus primarily on the experiences *with*

literature, since these could be manipulated in a way that the others could not. Indeed, Rosenblatt concluded that none of the currently popular ways of *using* literature—whether to increase social awareness, broaden the range of information, or develop sensitivity to literary form—were likely to lead to an "intimate personal response" (p. 70). Rosenblatt had no illusions that such a response could be easily aroused; it would require an approach infinitely more complex than any of the approaches teachers were accustomed to taking. The complexity, in her view, stemmed directly from the fact that "There is no such thing as a generic reader or a generic literary work; . . . there are only unnumberable separate responses to individual works of art" (pp. 32-33).

Thus it is the response of the student rather than the content of the work of literature which becomes the object of the teacher's attention. It is this response which must be challenged, refined, enlarged—by the process of reflection upon the response and upon the elements in the work which provoked it. In the end it is not important that a student be able to distinguish among the various literary forms; it is important that he learn to respond maturely to progressively more complex writings. *Literature as Exploration* is not a pattern curriculum in the sense of the Council publications, and in many ways the approach outlined does not lend itself to formulation in those terms. What emerges, finally, is the picture of quiet discussion, "a friendly group, come together to exchange ideas" (p. 83). This group, much more than the materials they use, is the heart of the educational process.

The importance of such an exchange of ideas was also dealt with at length by Rosenblatt. Though discussed from a number of different perspectives, the goals offered were essentially those of acculturation, the development of socially accepted and socially valuable modes of thought and patterns of reaction. "Any individual born into a society must somehow . . . learn not only its language, its gestures, its mechanics," she wrote, "but also the various superstructures of ideas, emotions, modes of behavior, moral values, that that particular society has built up around the basic human relationships" (p. 223). A pluralistic, democratic society such as the United States can offer, of course, no one simple pattern, but neither does literature. Indeed one function of literature would be to illustrate the many different ways of life open to any individual.

Rosenblatt was careful to point out that what she proposed was not simply a continuation of "the old notion of 'character building through literature' "—a tradition to which her concerns are obviously related. That older tradition, however, had been prescriptive, providing "a series of models of human behavior to imitate" (p. 294). The new view of the teaching of literature would help the student to experience many models, good and bad, and to learn to deal critically and intellectually with the emotional reactions they would necessarily arouse. It was truly to be, in the terms of her title, an *exploration* of the reader's own nature, during which he would gradually "become aware of potentialities for thought and feeling within himself, acquire clearer perspective, develop aims and a sense of direction." Viewed in this way, literature had a "very real, and even central" role in the "social and cultural life of a democracy"; it was to engender the cultural patterns and modes of behavior that would control that society's future.[45]

The Effect on the Schools

The Course of Study

For some direct evidence of the extent to which classroom procedures were changing in response to these new concerns, we can turn to Dora V. Smith's monograph *Instruction in English* (1933), prepared as part of the National Survey of Secondary Education.[46] Smith analyzed 156 courses of study from 127 cities in 35 states, and visited 70 schools that presented "unique features of content or method." Her findings indicate that while some of the changes in educational theory were carrying over into the schools, others certainly were not.

Methods of instruction at the time of this survey reflected a mix of traditional and progressive approaches. Smith noted with approval a widespread provision for individual differences, either through providing for separate tracks or by varying the work around some central core. The unit method of instruction had also become widespread, and seemed to have furthered progressive teaching. Smith claimed that it had been "exceedingly beneficial" in helping teachers concentrate on the literary work as a whole, leading to "broader discussion, to less emphasis upon meticulous detail, and to the seeking of wider relationships both in literature and with other forms of expression" (pp. 59-60). Though lengthy philological analysis of texts was no longer common, too much time continued to be devoted to single works. As much as nine weeks was given over to the study of a single text in some classes, with a mode of four weeks for such selections as *Julius Caesar, Macbeth,* and *As You Like It.* While noting a general policy of promoting wider individual reading and a definite trend toward so-called "Free-reading" programs in the western states, Smith offered little evidence that such programs were in widespread use.

More positively, the time had clearly passed when the yearly lists of college entrance texts could dominate the course. Rather than the uniformity of earlier surveys, Smith found only eight texts common to the courses of study of even one-fifth of the schools. The use of literature anthologies, which will be discussed in more detail in the next section of this chapter, had also become common, forming the basis of the required course in 50 percent of the junior high schools. At the senior high school level they more often served as supplements to the study of separately bound classics. This reflected the continuing legacy of the examination syllabus: 50 percent of the schools had found no other organization for their course, continuing to present "mere lists of classics for study" (pp. 47-49). Of the thirty most frequently used texts, none were contemporary. Comparing her results with an earlier survey of conditions before 1900, Smith found that only the *Bunker Hill Oration* had vanished from the course: "Otherwise the lapse of 25 to 40 years has made little change in the requirements except to add a few more titles in kind plus the nineteenth century novel" (pp. 50-52). Yet this lack of change should not have been surprising, given the conservatism in this respect of the recommendations of the National Joint Committee on English. The only other major change was the appearance of American literature courses as part of the eleventh grade program in the majority of schools.

The main alternative to the organization by lists of classics was the study of types or genres. With its roots in "appreciation" and new impetus from studies of reading, this had been adopted by 47 percent of the high schools and 22 percent of the junior high schools. While Smith noted optimistically that there was "evidence in classroom practice that some teachers are able to follow a course of study organized by types without undue stress on form and technique," it was clear from her comments that such stress was a very real danger (pp. 47-49).

Finally, Smith found that the real or imagined strictures of the college continued to have a pervasive influence upon the literature curriculum. Though preparation for college was at the very bottom of the list of objectives presented in the courses of study, in practice teachers were conditioning their teaching to the college demands: "No impression remains more vivid after conference with hundreds of teachers throughout the country than the fear under which they labor because of the requirements (real or imagined) of the institution higher up" (p. 74). One must wonder, however, about the extent to which this "fear" gained impetus from the comfort of teaching the old and familiar. The process of change is never easy, and the demands upon the teacher during these decades were many and complex.

Just a few years later, Dr. Smith again had the opportunity for intensive assessment of the program in English, this time as part of the Regents' Inquiry Into the Cost and Character of Public Education in New York State.[47] A representative sampling of fifty-one of the state's communities was selected for extensive achievement testing in the spring of 1936; schools in slightly more than half of these communities were then visited during 1937. This investigation, relying less upon courses of study and more upon the results of actual testing and classroom visitations, was even less encouraging. Although New York had a recent and liberal statewide course of study, some 60 percent of the teachers reported that it was the textbooks available, not the course of study, that determined what went on in the classroom. And the book supply, though varying considerably from school to school, was in general quite limited; most programs made use of a single literary anthology for each year's course. Indeed, the movement toward wide or extensive reading (one of the hopeful "trends" in the earlier study) was one of the major casualties of the intervening years of depression. Schools with curtailed instructional programs could not afford the investment in new materials that any substantial broadening of the literature program would have implied.

Smith did find a "wholesome emphasis upon the reading of literature selections themselves and not upon facts about books, their authors, and the literary periods from which they come." New instructional approaches—the project method, socialized class procedures, small group work—had not fared well, however. Intensive reading of a single selection by the whole class was the usual situation, and the approach hardly progressive: "Question and answer procedures with the teacher in command, and recitation around the room of sentences written out at home the night before represent by far the most common activities of the average high school English class in New York" (pp. 251-53). Indeed, the study raised serious questions about the individualization of instruction. Attention given to individual differences had become "largely administrative," with materials and activities tending to differ "in amount rather than kind." "Attention to individual need had very little place in the classrooms visited," Smith complained. "General regimentation of pupils was the rule; individualization, the exception" (pp. 154-57).

The study pinpointed teacher training and teacher load, in addition to inadequate book supplies, as the most important obstacles to implementation of an effective English program. Though the majority of teachers in New York schools had completed at least a B.A., the programs they had gone through seemed in many ways inadequate. Most had emphasized "academic English," with little of the breadth necessary to implement a progressive program. Anglo-Saxon and Middle English, rather than contemporary literature, speech, library training, or literature for adolescents, were the sorts of college requirements the teachers had had to fulfill.

The extracurricular programs presented another real obstacle in some schools, absorbing so much of the teacher's time that formal classes were devoted to "deadly and uninteresting routine." With some understatement, Smith pointed out that such a situation "suggests the need of reconsidering the areas in which it is desirable for teachers to spend their best energies," especially since the "ideal" fusion of extracurricular and curricular activities was "far from realized." Though many schools visited had flourishing programs in drama, journalism, and debate, these were carried on for the most part in isolation from the English class, even when run by the same teacher (p. 227).

The Literature Anthologies

Smith's studies suggest that by the end of the 1930s, the teaching of literature was to a large extent dominated by the literature anthology rather than by statements of goals or courses of study. Anthologies produced for the general reading public rather than for the schools date from the first days of the republic but reached a peak after improvements in printing methods in the nineteenth century. These were often "gift books," elaborately bound and illustrated, and presenting quite extensive—sometimes exhaustive —collections of complete works. Almost all forms of organization for modern school anthologies had their forerunners in these early commerical books—some were organized chronologically, others by types or themes; still others presented the works of a single nation, region, period, genre, or author.[48]

As long as the college entrance lists dominated the teaching of English, however, there was little room for a school anthology. The carefully annotated editions of the set texts reflected the demands on the English course more adequately, and they were also more economical: with the lists changing regularly, these editions allowed the school to buy just the newly-appearing selections and to continue to use texts held over from previous years. About 1920, however, this situation began to change. The progressive emphasis on wider reading made it more important to increase the number of selections, while the gradual adoption of the comprehensive examination of the College Board freed the schools from the domination of the Uniform Lists. Classics continued to be taught, but instead of changing the titles each year, a school could add an anthology to supplement and broaden the course. The leaders of the progressive movement in English supported this emphasis; for example, Walter Barnes, twenty-first president of NCTE, defended the "book of selections" as an economical way of offering many satisfying experiences close together. At least thirteen of the twenty-two Council presidents between 1917 and 1938 helped to edit the anthologies of one or another major American publisher; so did Hatfield, never NCTE president but secretary-treasurer for most of this period.[49] In involving themselves in these projects, they were giving tacit support to the use of these books in the schools. Finally, the restrictions on budgets brought about by the Depression propelled the anthology from an increasingly important supplement to the separately-bound classics into the very center of the literature program—with whatever classics were to be studied bound within the anthology covers. In this way a single purchase could provide materials for the whole course, materials that could be used over and over again with new groups of students.

These collections were at least a moderately progressive force throughout the twenties and thirties. They were responsive to the broader movements for reform and provided teachers, in the absence of any other widely accepted formulation, with a set of materials arranged in a coherent order for use with their classes. Publishers began by experimenting with a variety of formats for their collections. The L. W. Singer series (1927-31) was at the conservative end of the spectrum, offering essentially the College Board texts conveniently bound in one volume; Scribner's *Literature and Living* series (1925) was at the other extreme, giving a prominent place to modern writers and social values. Most, however, tried to strike a commercially more profitable balance between these extremes, so that teachers with a variety of views could comfortably use them. One Houghton Mifflin text went so far as to include selections and study aids for two completely separate courses, one "general" and progressive in orientation, the other "college entrance" and decidedly academic.[50]

The most successful collection was the Scott, Foresman *Literature and Life* series (1922-1924), which managed to synthesize these two points of view. It carefully included all the required college entrance texts, but "woven into the great Book of Literature itself" was "abundant material for the study of contemporary literature and for the study of prose reflecting current thoughts and problems." Two devices were used to foster the synthesis. One was the rather obvious expedient of including both "academic" and experience-oriented questions for each selection (without dividing them as such). The other was to organize the selections in order of increasing difficulty and sophistication. The net effect was to increase the traditional emphases in the last two books, the functional or socially oriented selections in the first two.[51]

Most of the early anthologies emphasized the study of types or chronology, but this began to change as teachers became more concerned with "experience." One of the corollaries of the experience approach had been the need for greater breadth and variety in the selections presented, and as the scope of the anthology increased, the use of types as a method of organization offered a less and less coherent focus. By the mid-thirties, thematic units organized around important personal or social goals dominated the seventh to tenth grade anthologies, while formal and historical studies continued to be the rule for the last two years. It was common, however, to find

the various approaches nested within one another—a thematic unit
in which the materials were all of one type, or a genre study in which
the selections were presented chronologically.[52] (Many of the
illustrative units in *An Experience Curriculum* represented exactly
such a blend.)

In addition to the shift toward thematic units, the anthologies
clearly did respond to pressures for more and more modern literature, even eroding the dominance of the CEEB selections. Of the ten
most frequently anthologized authors in the period from 1917 to
1934, for example, all had been represented on the CEEB lists
between 1917 and 1934; but between 1935 and 1945 the CEEB
authors yielded four of the top ten positions. The newcomers—Walt
Whitman, Carl Sandburg, Robert Frost, and Emily Dickinson—reflected the growing interest in American literature and its institu-
tionalization as the eleventh grade course.[53]

More important than the slight changes in emphasis in the
selections was the major shift in breadth. The highly conservative
Singer series provides a dramatic illustration of the anthologies'
response in this respect: the first edition of the tenth grade volume in
1928 had contained only eight selections; the 1935 edition of the
same volume offered seventy-nine. Though few others shifted quite
so rapidly, most series did increase both the number of selections and
the number of authors represented. However these works were being
handled by the classroom teacher, their mere presence in
the course represented a significant change in the program in literature.[54]

Perspective: The Years between the Wars

The decades that fell between the two world wars were a time of
change and experiment within the teaching of English. The period
began with the liberation of the subject from overt control by the
colleges; but that very liberation, as the leaders of the profession
came to realize, raised problems of even greater magnitude than the
ones it solved. When the teaching of literature had first come into the
schools, it had had a coherent—if somewhat circumscribed—function, and it had had a methodology, albeit a borrowed one, that had
given it the aura of a systematic study. Indeed, without this
demonstrable function and method it is doubtful it could have won a
place as more than an ancillary part of the curriculum.

But the function was artificial and the method was borrowed, and
both were cast off when the teaching of literature began to assert its
role as a high school subject. The search for a new function and a new
method was begun in the rhetoric and enthusiasm that marked the
Progressive Era in education, and if the leaders of NCTE were only

occasionally themselves comfortable in the company of the leaders of the progressive movement, preferring in general a more moderate and subject-oriented position, they were buoyed by the optimism and sense of mission that pervaded the movement as a whole.[55] Whether arguing the values of science or elaborating the details of the experience curriculum, they rarely questioned the intimacy of the relationship between educational theory and educational practice.

Yet it was in the very nature of the task they had set themselves that a gap should develop. The teaching of English had become a national enterprise, involving a multitude of teachers, each of whom, if change were to be effective, would have to be not only convinced that the change was workable, but also taught how to implement it. But the leaders in the teaching of English had no panacea to offer to the teacher of literature; they were themselves engaged in the often painful process of reformulating goals and methods, and trying to reestablish meaningful limits to the universe of English instruction. As often as not, the limits proposed broadened rather than circumscribed that universe, moving the boundary ever outward through socialization to social understanding and finally to acculturation. As Robert C. Pooley put it in 1939:

> Within twenty years we have had to meet, study, and assimilate several new psychologies, at least one new sociology, and a score of isms. We have had to grapple with such concepts as "the child centered school," the activity program, the socialized recitation, the project method, integration, correlation, two- and three-track plans, and the unit plan. The progressive movement has waxed fat in the last two decades. All these movements and schemes have added immeasurably to the science and art of teaching. But they have also bred doubts, fears, and insecurity where once there was confidence.[56]

The insecurity expressed itself in many ways, only one of which was the reliance upon the argument that "the colleges require it" to justify continuing with old methods of teaching. Indeed, as the *English Journal* and the CEEB did their best to point out, the colleges did *not* require the kind of preparation that was being justified in their name, in general accommodating their requirements to the changing philosophy of secondary instruction. Still, reaction set in as the thirties waned: Dora V. Smith's 1936 presidential address to the Council was even challenged by an Ohio teacher protesting against "the forcing of the liberal methods on entire city school systems."[57]

By the end of the thirties such protests, coupled with the sobering findings of empirical studies of current practice, brought a new and more realistic perspective on the problems of teaching literature. Rosenblatt's study helped too, for it presented the coherent and systematic explanation of the place and function of literature in American life that had been lacking: and the expertise and knowledge that would be required to carry out her program were all the more evident for the competence with which she had treated the issues.[58] As early as 1936, Dora V. Smith, writing for the Ninth Yearbook of the Department of Supervisors and Directors of Instruction of the NEA, provided one description of the task that lay ahead.[59] "The fundamental question," she noted, is "what are the chances of success in the schools of our country today" limited by "narrow prescriptions in the curricula, with methods conditioned by desks nailed to the floor, and with an examination system which takes cognizance chiefly of facts and skills?"

> . . . we can begin by determining to approach literature as it is approached by intelligent, cultured people in everyday life. We can put pleasure in reading first; we can aim constantly at enjoyment and the development of hunger for more. We can test the success of our program by the desire of boys and girls to continue more reading of the same sort under their own direction. We can associate books with ever-widening interests and increased understanding of human nature and experience. . . . we can at least begin to break with the traditional program of literary chronology and technique . . . and relate literature to the limitless interests of life itself (pp. 165-69).

Even at that, the task that remained was large.

CHAPTER V NOTES

1. Sterling Andrus Leonard, *Essential Principles of Teaching Reading and Literature in the Intermediate Grades and the High School* (Philadelphia: J. B. Lippincott Co., 1922), p. 335.

2. John J. DeBoer, "The Materials of the English Curriculum," Editorial, *English Journal* 21:1 (January 1932): 68-69.

3. Charles Swain Thomas, "Variables and Constants," *English Journal* 25:2 (February 1936): 101-13.

4. Dora V. Smith, *Evaluating Instruction in Secondary School English*, A Report of a Division of the New York Regents' Inquiry into the Character and Cost of Public Education in New York State (Chicago: NCTE, 1941), p. 120.

5. William Heard Kilpatrick, "The Project Method," *Teachers College Record* 19 (September 1918): 319-35.

6. William Heard Kilpatrick, *Foundations of Method: Informal Talks on Teaching* (New York: Macmillan Co., 1925), p. 69. This book was dogmatically connectionist in its psychology, a position which Kilpatrick later abandoned. See his introduction to Hilda Taba's *The Dynamics of Education* (London: Kegan Paul, Trench, Trubner, 1932). Apparently Kilpatrick never revised his own book because he rejected the psychology on which it was based. See James R. Squire, ed., *A New Look at Progressive Education*, 1972 Yearbook of the Association for Supervision and Curriculum Development (Washington, D.C.: ASCD, 1972), p. 145, fn. 10.

7. Kilpatrick, "The Project Method."

8. Kilpatrick, *Foundations of Method*, pp. 302, 274, 310.

9. James Fleming Hosic, "An Outline of the Problem-Project Method," *English Journal* 7:9 (November 1918). There is some evidence that Hosic rather than Kilpatrick first presented the method (Squire, *A New Look at Progressive Education*, p. 142, fn. 9). The term had been used in *English Journal* as early as February 1918, in an editorial which found "much promise in the so-called project method." Editorial, "What Is Socialization?" *English Journal* 7:2 (February 1918): 135.

10. Hatfield saw in it the "fundamental unifying principle of method" that American education had always lacked, and called for articles illustrating its successful application. "Speaking of Platforms," *English Journal* 9:7 (September 1920): 420-21; "Saving the Project," *English Journal* 9:8 (October 1920): 476-77; and "An Exposition of Method," *English Journal* 11:6 (June 1922): 370. As examples, see Mariette Hyde, "Projects in Literature," *English Journal* 9:7 (September 1920): 401-06; Charles Robert Gaston, "Pegasus and Kit," *English Journal* 12:2 (February 1923): 83; Helen L. Reets, "The Project of a Journey," *English Journal* 13:2 (February 1924): 133-36; May R. Pringle, "Comparison in Method," *English Journal* 14:4 (April 1925): 303-10.

11. James Fleming Hosic, *Empirical Studies of School Reading*, Contributions to Education no. 114 (New York: Teachers College, Columbia University, 1921).

12. Leonard, *Essential Principles*, pp. 5, 31.

13. E. Estelle Downing, "What English Teachers Can Do to Promote World-Peace," *English Journal* 14:3 (March 1925): 183-92. The committee was very active, providing *Journal* readers with lists of materials and examples of teaching as well as offering programs at the annual convention.

Until the early thirties, when a reformist attitude again became popular, they provoked little response from teachers not on the committee itself.

14. Martha Hale Shackford, "Deserted Goldsmith," *English Journal* 9:2 (February 1920): 103-08.

15. Harry T. Baker, "The Criticism and Teaching of Contemporary Literature," *English Journal* 12:7 (September 1923): 459-63.

16. Editorial, "Our Own Reading," *English Journal* 11:6 (June 1922): 369. Percy H. Boynton, "American Authors of Today," *English Journal* 11:7 (September 1922): 383-91. The first was about Edwin Arlington Robinson. Boynton eventually collected the articles into a book which was itself well received ("Our Own Horn," *English Journal* 13:7 [September 1924]: 501). Council pride in his and later contributions is reflected in "The National Council, 1911-36," *English Journal* 25:10 (December 1936).

17. Grant D. D. Ainslie translated many of Croce's works, including *The Essence of Aesthetic* (1921) and *Aesthetic as Science of Expression and General Linguistic*. Ogden and Richards's *The Meaning of Meaning* appeared in 1923. Richards, Ogden, and Wood's *The Foundations of Aesthetic* was in its second edition by 1925.

18. Llewellyn Jones, "Aesthetics and Contemporary Literature," *English Journal* 14:8 and 9 (October and November 1925): 583-91, 665-75.

19. Leonard, *Essential Principles*, pp. 394-95. Wilbur Hatfield also used it, with his college freshmen. "Instead of the Survey," *English Journal* 20:10 (December 1931): 840.

20. Mabel Irene Rich, Study of the Types of Literature (New York: Century Co., 1921). On the influence of Rich's anthology and its sequel, *Classified Types of Literature* (New York: Century Co., 1926), see Irvin Ehrenpreis, The *"Types Approach"* to Literature (New York: King's Crown Press, 1945), pp. 89 ff. Similar comments are in John Muth Bernd's *Approaches to the Teaching of Literature in Secondary Schools, 1900-1956* (Dissertation, University of Wisconsin, 1957; University Microfilms No. 24,264), pp. 140 ff.

21. See Henry Seidel Canby, "The State of American Criticism," *English Journal* 13:10 (December 1924): 705-09; Grant Overton, "On Morality and Decency in Fiction," *English Journal* 18:1 (January 1929): 14-23. Both were concerned with the relationship between literature and culture. (Canby was editor of the *Saturday Review of Literature*, Overton of *Collier's*.) Teachers used the approach most frequently with Shakespeare. E.g., Winifred Smith, "Teaching Shakespeare in School," *English Journal* 11:6 (June 1922): 361-64; Emily Fanning Barry, "Avenues to Shakspeare" (sic), *English Journal* 28:7 (September 1939): 556-64.

22. Joseph M. Thomas, "The Inhibiting Instincts," *English Journal* 9:1 (January 1920): 1-21. He should not be confused with Charles Swain Thomas, who though very active did not become NCTE president till 1935.

23. Martha Hale Shackford, "Shall We Change Entrance English?" *English Journal* 14:2 (February 1925): 98-107.

24. Irving Babbitt, "English and the Discipline of Ideas," *English Journal* 9:2 (February 1920): 61-70. On the humanist movement in general, see René Wellek, "Literary Scholarship," in *American Scholarship in the Twentieth Century*, ed. Merle Curti (Cambridge: Harvard University Press, 1953), pp. 117-18.

25. Lou L. LaBrant, "Masquerading," *English Journal* 20:3 (March 1931): 244-46; Gertrude M. Woodcock, "Stagecraft as Motivation in Ivan-

hoe," *English Journal* 20:3 (March 1931): 246-49; and Kilpatrick, *Foundations of Method*, pp. 138-40.

26. Howard Mumford Jones, "The Fetish of the Classics," *English Journal* 18:3 (March 1929): 221-39. For the opposing view, see Mabel C. Hermans, "Directed Reading in Social Adjustment," *English Journal* 17:3 (March 1928): 219-28.

27. After an article of Robert Morss Lovett and a second by Michael Gold, Hatfield received so many reader reactions that he had to protest that personally he did not like Hemingway (the subject of Lovett's article) or Gold's variety of criticism, but published them "primarily as information, and secondarily as a stimulus to fundamental, catholic thinking." Editorial, "Hemingway and Gold," *English Journal* 22:3 (March 1933): 340-41; Robert Morss Lovett, "Ernest Hemingway," *English Journal* 21:8 (October 1932): 609-17; Michael Gold, "The Education of John Dos Passos," *English Journal* 22:2 (February 1933): 87-97; V. F. Calverton, "Left-Wing Literature in America," *English Journal* 20:10 (December 1931): 789-98.

28. See Lawrence A. Cremin, *The Transformation of the School* (New York: Vintage Books, 1961), pp. 229-30.

29. Cited in *The Progressive Educator and the Depression*, C. A. Bowers (New York: Random House, 1969), pp. 23-34.

30. *English Journal* noted the magazine's debut and provided information on subscriptions. "The Periodicals," *English Journal* 23:10 (December 1934): 857. See Cremin, *Transformation of the School*, pp. 230-31; and Bowers, *Progressive Educator and the Depression*, pp. 15, 44, 108.

31. Stella S. Center, "The Responsibilities of Teachers of English in Contemporary American Life," *English Journal* 22:2 (February 1933): 97-108. She received a standing ovation. "The Memphis Council Meeting," *English Journal* 22:2 (February 1933): 143-59.

32. Stella S. Center, "President's Message," *English Journal* 21:3 (March 1932): 240-41; John J. DeBoer, "The Technique of Teaching Peace," *English Journal* 22:4 (April 1933): 325-26; "The Boston Convention," *English Journal* 26:2 (February 1937): 131-39; and Essie Chamberlain, "International Mindedness Through Books," *English Journal* 22:5 (May 1933): 282-91. The resolution asserted that teachers of English "have the serious responsibility of explaining realistically to their pupils that war is not a glamorous and romantic experience, but rather an ugly, cruel, costly, and barbarous method of attempting to settle national and international disputes." Council efforts on behalf of the peace movement continued till the brink of the war. The International Relations Committee even published an anthology of peace-oriented stories and articles by contemporary figures such as Hemingway, Roosevelt, Lindbergh, and Van Loon. Ida T. Jacobs, ed., *War and Peace: An Anthology*, Bulletin 3 of the International Relations Committee of the NCTE (Chicago: NCTE, 1937).

33. Editorial, "Dare We?" *English Journal* 22:1 (January 1933): 67; and John J. DeBoer, "Propaganda in the Schools," *English Journal* 25:4 (April 1936): 325. Propaganda analysis became an increasing concern toward the end of the decade.

34. Oscar J. Campbell, "English: Its Domestic and Foreign Policies," *English Journal* 24:2 (February 1935): 100-10; and Dora V. Smith, "American Youth and English," *English Journal* 26:2 (February 1937): 99-113.

35. W. Wilbur Hatfield, chairman, *An Experience Curriculum in English*, A Report of the Curriculum Commission of the National Council of

Teachers of English (New York: D. Appleton-Century Co., 1935), p. v.

36. The "radical-progressive unit" had been discussed earlier. "Units in Learning," *English Journal* 16:10 (December 1927): 816-17.

37. For a discussion of the reaction to these aspects of the report, see Raven I. McDavid, Jr., ed., *An Examination of the Attitudes of the NCTE toward Language*, Research Report no. 4 (Urbana, Ill.: NCTE, 1965).

38. "Comments on the Curriculum Report," *English Journal* 25:4 (April, 1936): 321-24. Angela M. Broening, chairman, *Conducting Experiences in English*, A Publication of the National Council of Teachers of English (New York: D. Appleton-Century Co., 1939).

39. An appendix to the report listed eighty-three courses of study from all parts of the country which embodied the experience approach; some, however, had been issued prior to *An Experience Curriculum*. For other reactions, see, for example, Annette Mann, "Does the Experience Curriculum Idea Work?" *English Journal* 27:2 (February 1938): 173; and "An Experience Curriculum in Action," *English Journal* 27:8 (October 1938): 693.

40. Broening, *Conducting Experiences*, pp. 4-6.

41. Hatfield, *An Experience Curriculum*, p. 11.

42. Ruth Mary Weeks, chairman, *A Correlated Curriculum* (New York: D. Appleton-Century Co., 1936), pp. 6-9, 285.

43. "A Correlated Curriculum Evaluated," Books, *English Journal* 26:5 (May 1937): 417-20. Hopkins's review was printed first, Bobbitt's second.

44. Louise M. Rosenblatt, *Literature as Exploration*, For the Commission on Human Relations of the Progressive Education Association (New York: D. Appleton-Century Co., 1938).

45. Ibid., pp. v-vi. This point of view was not limited to the PEA. A Joint Committee of Twenty-Four of the MLA and NCTE endorsed a statement on the aims of literary study drafted by Louise Rosenblatt, Howard Mumford Jones, and Oscar James Campbell. It saw literature as a way to "self-reliant and well-rounded personalities." Though the committee asked for the "widest possible distribution," little notice was taken of the statement. Later statements from the MLA Commission on Trends in Education, however, did continue to affirm its basic principles. Statement of the Committee of Twenty-Four, "The Aims of Literary Study," *PMLA* 53 (1938): 1367-71.

46. Dora V. Smith, *Instruction in English*, Office of Education Bulletin 1932, no. 17. National Survey of Secondary Education Monograph no. 20 (Washington, D.C.: Government Printing Office, 1933).

47. Smith, *Evaluating Instruction in Secondary School English*. See also Dora V. Smith, "Implications of the New York Regents' Inquiry for the Teaching of English," *English Journal* 28:3 (March 1939): 177.

48. The best discussion of the early traditions is in Bibb's dissertation, though her concern is with those devoted to American selections. Among the very early texts, she cites Matthew Carey's *Select Poems, Chiefly American* (1791). Evelyn Rezek Bibb, *Anthologies of American Literature, 1787-1964* (Dissertation, Columbia University, 1965; University Microfilms No. 66-1728).

49. The comparison here is with the lists provided by James Olson of editors of the anthologies he studied. Other Council presidents during this period also produced teaching materials, but concentrated their efforts in language and compositon rather than literature. James Warren Olson, *The*

Nature of Literature Anthologies Used in the Teaching of High School English 1917-1957 (Dissertation, University of Wisconsin, 1969; University Microfilms No. 69-22,454). Walter Barnes, "The Book of Selections: Its Value in Teaching High-School Literature," *English Journal* 8:4 (April 1919): 248-53.

50. Olson, *Nature of Literature Anthologies*, pp. 87-108.

51. Olson, *Nature of Literature Anthologies*, pp. 91-105; Bernd, in *Approaches to Teaching Literature*, comments similarly on this series.

52. Olson, *Nature of Literature Anthologies*, pp. 109-15. Rich's 1921 anthology, for example, was chronologically organized within each genre.

53. Olson, *Nature of Literature Anthologies*, pp. 91, 180.

54. In Olson's study, for example, the number of authors not on the CEEB lists doubled, the number of selections rose from 3,132 to 5,865, and the number of selections appearing in only one anthology almost tripled from the first (1917-1934) to the second (1935-1945) period (pp. 174-79).

55. James Fleming Hosic, the Council's first secretary and founder of *English Journal*, illustrated the moderate position in a retrospective article published in 1932. He accused the progressives of "having lived by faith, not by sight," yet acknowledged that teachers owed them "Such real advances as education is now making." "In the long run," he concluded, "the moderate position is most likely to prove tenable—and safe." The Council always had some members who were very much a part of the progressive movement—J. Milnor Dorey and John DeBoer, for example, each went on to head the Progressive Education Association after periods of active service to NCTE—but, as Hosic put it, the Council was "an organization of collective thinking" and always had equally active conservative members balancing the most liberal view. It would be fair to say, however, that Hosic, Hatfield, and the Council as a whole were more progressive than they cared to admit. James Fleming Hosic, "The National Council after Twenty Years," *English Journal* 21:2 (February 1932): 107-13.

56. Robert C. Pooley, "Varied Patterns of Approach in the Teaching of Literature," *English Journal* 28:5 (May 1939): 242-53.

57. Myriam Page, "The Other Side," *English Journal* 26:6 (June 1937): 440-44.

58. The importance of Rosenblatt's book—and of its implications—were recognized immediately. Thus Hatfield reviewed it himself as soon as it appeared, beginning with the sentence, "*Literature as Exploration* fills the thoughtful college or secondary-school teacher of English with shame, fear, and resolution." Malcolm S. MacLear made a similar point in "What's Wrong with Us English Teachers?" *English Journal* 28:8 (October 1939): 655-63. (W. Wilbur Hatfield, "A Fresh View of Literature Teaching," Books, *English Journal* 27:7 [September 1938]: 618-19.)

59. Marquis E. Shattuck, chairman, *The Development of a Modern Program in English*, Ninth Yearbook (Washington, D.C.: Department of Supervisors and Directors of Instruction of the NEA, 1936).

No one present at that first conference [of the Eight-Year Study] will ever forget the honest confession of one principal when she said, "My teachers and I do not know what to do with this freedom. It challenges and frightens us. I fear that we have come to <u>love our chains</u>." . . . No one of the group could possibly foresee all the developments ahead, nor were all of one mind as to what should be done.

—The Story of the Eight-Year Study,
1942[1]

Neither this book nor any other can say how a page <u>should be read</u>—if by that we mean that it can give a recipe for discovering what the page really says. All it could do—and that would be much—would be to help us to understand some of the difficulties in the way of such discoveries.

—I. A. Richards, How to Read a Page,
1942[2]

Communication is one of the five or six most crucial services of war. It is one with which a half-dozen major agencies in Washington are now urgently concerned, for home front and battle front alike, following the first imperative concern with military mobilization and war production. It is plainly the one in which our seventy-five thousand teachers of English can make the special war contribution we have been looking, hoping, waiting for.

—Lennox Grey, NCTE second vice
president, 1943[3]

The field of literature past and present is a vast one, almost as large in scope as occupational, health, and community living areas. The basic-course teacher would have to become familiar with this material in order to weave the reading (poetry, plays, novels, biographies, essays, etc.) into the current areas of concentration.

—English Journal review of Education
for All American Youth, 1945[4]

One of the joys of teaching is the opportunity to influence the development and growth of the young student. There are few experiences that evoke the glow the teacher feels in seeing a young person mature in language power, in human relations, in the personal satisfactions which may be derived from increased good taste in reading and listening, and in the power to use words orally and in writing so as to achieve adequate adjustment for himself and his teen-age friends.

—Commission on the English Curriculum,
1956[5]

Chapter VI

Narrowed Goals

The expansion of the English curriculum around the metaphors of experience and exploration was followed by a conscious narrowing of the scope and goals of instruction during the ensuing decades. Much of this occurred within the context of a movement toward "general education" that came to prominence simultaneously in the colleges and secondary schools of the late thirties.[6] In part because the Depression left them with little else to do, students who would previously have dropped out early were remaining through the high school and even into the college years. This created a new band of students for whom neither vocational nor college-preparatory training would be appropriate; for these "general" students a new kind of education was needed. As the Progressive Education Association's Commission on Secondary School Curriculum put it, this would be "general education" —

> education of post-elementary grade intended to foster good living. It rules out conventional planes of professional preparation and scholarship for its own sake when these prove extraneous to the single purpose of helping the student achieve a socially adequate and personally satisfying life in a democracy.[7]

How to educate for this "socially adequate and personally satisfying life in a democracy" was the major problem faced by the progressives during the 1940s and 1950s. Two major, complementary responses developed. The first involved a narrowing of the initial progressive concern with the social needs of the student into a concern with adolescent problems, in particular the problem of adjusting to the demands of the adult world. This narrowing will be the subject of the first part of the present chapter.

The second and complementary response was to focus on language and communication skills. This also developed as part of the general education movement, but it had deeper roots in academic traditions of language study, in particular in the general semantics movement and the work of the New Critics. Both of these—the one originating in response to the use of propaganda in the First World War, the other in the complexities of twentieth century poetry— emphasized the difficulties inherent in skillful use of language, with a concomitant need for close, analytic study if the reader or listener were not to be misled. The entry of the United States into World War II brought the functional aspects of such language studies once again into the foreground, relating all of them to a central concern with "communication skills." As a War Department spokesman explained the army view over NBC radio,

> By English, the Army means skill in reading, writing, speaking, and listening, and above all, understanding what is read, written, spoken, and heard. Army men and women must be able to communicate clearly and accurately by any media; they must be able to understand the orders they give as well as the orders they receive.[8]

Under the pressures of war, such a drastic reduction in the scope of instruction generated little rebuttal. Even the American Association of Colleges agreed that "educators are not prepared to assert to military authorities that the 'intangible values' of a liberal arts education would make soldiers better fighters."[9] Under such pressures, spelling lists and vocabulary exercises proliferated, and reading skills became again an important concern of the secondary school teacher of literature.

Even as the new and narrower focus of instruction was developing, it generated a reaction among those who favored the traditional educational emphasis on intellectual training and cultural heritage. Critics of the progressives provided a discordant undercurrent from 1940 on, laying a foundation for an academic revival which eventually wrested the initiative in educational reform away from the progressives and returned it to college faculties of liberal arts. This academic revival will be discussed in Chapter VII.

Progressivism as the Conventional Wisdom

The Eight-Year Study

During the 1940s and 1950s, the educational policies of progressive education were widely accepted by American educators. The most highly publicized working out of these principles within the context of general education was the so-called "life adjustment movement"; during this time the center of educational innovation shifted from the Progressive Education Association (PEA) itself to the National Education Association (NEA) and the U.S. Office of Education (USOE). Still the origins of the movement can be traced directly to the experiences of the thirty schools involved in the Eight-Year Study of the PEA. It was in these schools that the educational experience was gradually redefined in the terminology of mental hygiene and personality development.

The genesis of the study was the 1930 convention of the PEA, during which it became apparent that the major impediment to wider experimentation with school curriculum was fear that graduating students would not be able to fulfill college entrance requirements. In response to this concern, the association appointed a Committee on College Entrance and Secondary Schools, later renamed the Commission on the Relation of School and College. It was this commission, under the chairmanship of Wilford M. Aikin, director of the John Burroughs School (Clayton, Missouri), which proposed that students in a group of leading secondary schools be exempted from the normal entrance requirements, so that the schools would be free to reformulate their programs. Over three hundred colleges, including many of the nation's most prestigious, accepted the proposal; supporting funds were provided by the General Education Board and the Carnegie Foundation.[10]

Thirty schools were eventually invited to participate. Though they included a disproportionate number of private and laboratory schools, such large city systems as Denver and Los Angeles were also part of the group. The study began in 1932 and ran till 1940, with the commission from the beginning providing counsel and comfort but conscientiously avoiding prescribing specific curricula. Indeed until 1936, when a staff of three curriculum consultants was appointed, the schools had to rely entirely on their individual and pooled resources in developing new approaches. A series of five reports issued in 1942 presented the results of a major follow-up study of college performance as well as extensive descriptions of the problems that had arisen and the attempts that had been made to solve them. Perhaps in part because, as one of the reports described it, "the problems of mastering and using this new freedom straightway turned out to be so difficult, complex, and engrossing that the original problem of college entrance requirements was almost lost sight of and forgotten," the reports provide a detailed picture of the evolution of the courses of study in the schools.[11]

Though the individual schools began and ended their curriculum reform at very different points, there were certain common threads of considerable interest. The most important for English involved experiments with "fused" or "core" or "correlated" courses—the kind toward which NCTE had turned its attention in its 1936 volume (discussed in the previous chapter). Almost all of the thirty schools experimented with a combined social studies-English course, almost always organized chronologically, and all abandoned the attempt after a few years of experimentation. The initial fused course at most of the schools attempted to juggle and reorder traditional content in the two subjects, bringing the topics covered into line with one another. Social studies tended to dominate, and many of the values of both subjects as traditionally taught seemed —as the NCTE committee had worried—to be lost. Rather than returning to the traditional organization, however, most schools reorganized the core sequence around topical focuses. This "core" tended to be somewhat eclectic: at one of the schools it embraced such diverse topics as Vocational Guidance, War and Peace, and International Literature. This mixture served as a transitional stage in which the old and new concerns stood side by side; it moved from there to what became in a great many of the schools the final focus of the core: the life problems of the adolescent.[12]

The transition to adolescent "needs" as the organizing principle was aided by the work of two derivative PEA commissions: the Commission on Secondary School Curriculum, organized as an offshoot of the Commission on the Relation of School and College in 1932, and the Commission on Human Relations, itself a 1935 outgrowth of the Commission on Secondary School Curriculum. The individual reports of the Thirty Schools make clear that the work of these commissions provided the impetus for the jump from a focus on *important themes* to a focus on themes *important to adolescents*. One influential document was a summary of "Typical Points of Focus of Concerns of Adolescents" prepared by the Commission on Human Relations and reprinted in the final reports of the study. Six main topics were outlined: Establishing Personal Relationships, Establishing Independence, Understanding Human Behavior, Establishing Self in Society, Normality, and Understanding the Universe. All but the last (which was usually ignored as programs evolved) dealt with very specific adolescent problems; typical topics included "Longing for more friends of own age"; "How late to stay out"; "Shame over lowly origins"; and "Bullying." Altogether there were over 40 topics and 140 subtopics in the outline—and these were presented only as a typical, not as an exhaustive list.[13]

The Commission on Secondary School Curriculum translated these concerns into specific programs in a series of publications between 1938 and 1941. The first, *Science in General Education* (1938), was important in the transition from "fused" to "core" courses. Offering a broader base than English and social studies alone, the science report generated courses such as "Everyday Problems" as the last stage of the evolution. The sophomore course in the Altoona (Pennsylvania) schools was typical of the sequence that evolved; it included Orientation to the New School, Family

Relationships, Consumer Problems, Communication, and Conservation of Human and Natural Resources. By this stage of their evolution, very few of the core courses in the more experimental schools showed any concern with the personal and social reform that had been so important in earlier stages of progressivism.[14]

The reports of the Eight-Year Study were published in the middle of the war and were largely ignored. That is not to say, however, that the study itself was without impact on teachers of English. It was simply that that influence came from the separate writings of the teachers in the various schools, working on committees and writing for journals throughout the period of the study. Most of the concern that had prompted the NCTE report on correlation, much of the emerging focus on adolescent needs—these first appeared in articles noting authors' affiliations with one or another of the schools of the Eight-Year Study. (It is an interesting aspect of the general distrust of the progressives in the Council leadership that, while other projects were often noted, the participation of these schools in the Eight-Year Study was rarely acknowledged.)[15]

Life Adjustment

The view of education that was emerging from the Thirty Schools and from the various commissions of the Progressive Education Association became during the 1940s the conventional wisdom of the professional educators—of the "educationists" as they would be called by their critics in the early 1950s. The Educational Policies Commission of the National Education Association, created in 1936 to speak with an authoritative voice on important educational issues, fell firmly in line with the PEA's focus upon the adolescent in a series of reports in the mid-forties: *Education for All American Youth* (1944), *Educational Services for Children* (1945), and *Education for All American Children* (1948). The first of these became the chief statement of the life adjustment movement.[16]

The commission used the device of sketching the educational programs in the mythical communities of American City and Farmville to present their proposals. They foresaw a much closer integration of school and community than has ever been attained, with national, state, and local programs supplementing one another to provide a full panoply of educational and health services. The curriculum itself centered on a "common learnings" course running throughout the secondary school program, and even somewhat beyond, providing a core of general education that followed the pattern that had emerged from the Eight-Year Study. Rather than a simple fused or correlated course, "common learnings" represented a complete restructuring of subject matter to focus (mostly through science and social studies) on topics such as choice of vocation and problems of family living.

The dominant concern with adolescent problems was finally taken up by the U.S. Office of Education and given the ill-chosen name by which it has since been known: "life adjustment." The USOE became involved in January 1944 when the Vocational Division began a study entitled "Vocational Education in the Years Ahead." The 150 vocationalists who carried out the study recognized a fundamental unity of purpose with the general education movement, as it had been working itself out in terms of the life experiences of the adolescent student. Charles Prosser used the final conference of the USOE study to offer a resolution that read in part:

> It is the belief of this conference that . . . the vocational school of the community will be better able to prepare 20 percent of the youth of secondary school age for entrance upon desirable skilled occupations; and that the high school will continue to prepare another 20 percent for entrance to college. We do not believe that the remaining 60 percent of our youth of secondary school age will receive the life adjustment training they need and to which they are entitled as American citizens.[17]

This led to a series of conferences between representatives of general and of vocational education, to formulate an approach to the problem of educating the neglected 60 percent. Eventually a Commission on Life Adjustment Education for Youth was established to carry out a vigorous "action program." Its focus remained on what the earlier conferences had called "functional experiences in the areas of practical arts, home and family life, health and physical fitness, and civic competence." In spite of occasional disclaimers, the emphasis in both name and activities was on "adjustment," "conformity," and a stable system of values. The traditional concern of progressive education with the continuing improvement of both the individual and his society was submerged and ultimately lost in this formulation.

The Rejection of Correlation

The response of English teachers to the "life adjustment" movement was a paradoxical resistance to the outward form and capitulation, at least by a broad segment of teachers, to the underlying emphases. The genuine distrust of the core curriculum so evident in the report of the NCTE Committee on Correlation in 1936 was maintained from the first experiments with a fused social studies-English course to the final "common learnings" of the Educational Policies Commission. Again and again, when the teacher of English attempted to go that route he found the peculiar virtues of his subject matter being quietly subverted—and it hardly mattered whether he defined those virtues as "practical English skills," "liberal education," or "exploration of self and society." Though an occasional teacher of English reflected the enthusiasm of the thirties, no one during the decade of the forties managed a convincing description of a working program that circumvented the problems that the Committee on Correlation had foreseen.[18]

The objections to the core course were succinctly summarized in a 1946 response to *Education for All American Youth* (1944) prepared by Mark Neville, second vice president of the Council. Neville was English department chairman at the John Burroughs School in Clayton, Missouri—the school which had provided the initial impetus for the Eight-Year Study as well as its director, Wilford Aikin. Neville's review, presented as a sharing of experiences with Farmville, outlined the evolution of experiments with fused and core courses at the Burroughs School. The major experiments had involved a fused course and a second series called the "Core Course and Broad Fields" in which the broad fields were English, social studies, science, math, foreign languages, and the fine and practical arts. In the end it was the relatively traditional broad fields that came to dominate the curriculum; the core was gradually rejected by teachers, students, and parents alike. The most important objections involved some large gaps between the theory of correlation and its actual working out in practice. English skills, the responsibility of all teachers in the core curriculum, were hard to emphasize as they developed during the content work; teachers found that rather than achieving the integrated and comprehensive view that was sought, the program became stilted and artifical. Students in the course rejected it as "too broad in scope and too shallow in depth"; they preferred the broad field courses and eventually the core was reduced to an elective. Looking back on the whole experience, Neville concluded that the real accomplishment of the years of experiment had been to revitalize the individual subject areas. Though there were many cases in which English could be improved through discussion of content from other fields, the goal of developing "pupil personality, thinking processes, group adjustments, and concepts of living" could not be reached simply by correlating.[19]

Other reactions of English teachers to *Education for All American Youth* were equally firm in their rejection of its major curriculum implications. They attacked the lack of explicit provision for literature (as Marion Sheridan noted, depending on one's predisposition, literature could either be read into the report or out of the course); the neglect of subject matter (that is, language skills and knowledge of literature); and the reliance on the artificial unity of subject matter instead of the real unity of the teacher who has successfully integrated his own knowledge. In general such attacks on the core were successful; a study at the end of the decade by a USOE worker quite sympathetic to the movement found that nationally only 3.5 percent of the course offerings in the junior and senior high school represented even the least ambitious forms of correlation, and these were concentrated in a few geographic areas. Over 90 percent of the core courses she did find, however, involved some blend of English and social studies.[20]

English as Adjustment

Meeting Adolescent Needs

Even as they were vigorously resisting the curriculum proposals of the "life adjustment" movement, teachers of English were embracing rather indiscriminately the new focus on meeting the personal and social needs of adolescence. Teachers were already well conditioned to the implied empiricism, the inventory of activities now redefined as psychological conflicts or needed "competencies." They were ready too for the reestablishment of boundaries for their subject; the almost universal perspective of the previous decade no longer seemed feasible. Finally, by accepting adolescent needs as the focus of the curriculum, teachers were continuing their tradition of concern that the school serve the child, not the subject-oriented demands of the college.

"Needs" as they came to be defined by teachers of English covered a wide spectrum that began with problems of family life and ended in international relations. The characteristic concern at all points of the spectrum, however, was with the solution of practical problems of living. When the focus of instruction was shifted in this way, English at the personal end of the spectrum of needs became guidance. This had antecedents in programs suggested at the end of the reorganization period, and again in the late 1920s, but those early attempts had failed to win many converts. Teachers had recognized that the early proponents were naive in their choices of materials, and too limited in their goals for an age in which "experience" and "exploration" were central. By the late 1930s, however, the limited, antiprogressive goals of adjustment were very much in keeping with the emerging spirit in education, while the materials and methods could claim—not always accurately—support from neo-Freudian psychology.

Sarah Roody, department chairman at Nyack High School, New York, was a leading advocate of this approach. Describing it in 1947, she began by asserting that the "lessons" to be taught through "true-to-life" literature were very simple and could be expressed "chiefly in nontechnical terms"—implying, of course, that there was a more esoteric body of knowledge behind her suggestions. The lessons she had in mind were really a catalog of psychoanalytic explanations of behavior: students would learn about the "fundamental motives from which the actions of all human beings spring," about the "ways in which many people try to evade reality," about "life-problems," normality, and maturity. And finally, of course, they would learn "how to develop the kind of personality one would like to have."[21] If such a program sounded more like a course in psychology or guidance than one in English, that was the intent. Article after article proclaimed the special need for the teacher of English, particularly the teacher of literature, to provide guidance through the emotional conflicts of the adolescent years. As a librarian from Baltimore described it, the job of the teacher or librarian was one of suggesting stories "very much as physicians prescribe sulfa drugs, by familiarizing herself with old and new productions in the field, by prescribing as best she can, and by keeping a sharp lookout for reactions."[22]

Human Relations

The social end of the spectrum of needs was dealt with under the general rubric of "human relations." The common thread in such studies was a concern with the smooth functioning of the various groups which make up the world; the focus of any given discussion ranged anywhere from the adolescent clique to international relations. This movement, too, had antecedents, all loosely related to the early progressive concern with education as an instrument of social reform. This concern had been carried through the years between the wars in the work of groups such as the NCTE Committee on International Relations and, later, in the arguments of the social reconstructionists. But it was Hilda Taba who gave the movement a focus and brought it to its fullest expression during the mid-forties. To understand the sorts of activities that emerged, it is useful to look first at her *Dynamics of Education* (1932), which can be seen as the revision of *Foundations of Method* (1925) that Kilpatrick never undertook. Taba based her arguments on the Gestalt psychologists' explorations of the structured nature of perception and cognition, abandoning Thorndike's behavioral approach. This, as Kilpatrick noted in an introduction to Taba's book, allowed the purposeful act to be joined in the service of "an all pervasive structure building." This structure building was crucial; it enabled Taba to conclude that education should be concerned with these grander structures rather than with the sorts of behavioral units that Bobbitt, among others, had attempted to detail. Instead, education would "endeavor to reach, through the specific, and by the immediate qualitative context of the specific, the general, and the fundamental." In a sense, it was "the great idea" which she stressed, the idea which would provide a superordinate structure capable of subsuming ever-wider ranges of concrete experience.[23]

Racial strife, which produced the Detroit riots in July 1943, provided the immediate context for the application of Taba's general ideas to a major project in human relations. The National Conference of Christians and Jews, concerned by the increasing evidence of intolerance and the lack of coordination among existing groups, provided funds to the American Council on Education to support a Project on Intergroup Relations, with Taba as director. The project staff—which for the first months consisted of Taba alone but later grew to eight—were clearly in the tradition of Kilpatrick and the social reconstructionists, though milder in their rhetoric and more temperate in their goals. (Taba herself had worked with Counts as well as Kilpatrick during the thirties.) As Taba and her staff described it in the summary volume (1952), their project offered a model for the development of educational solutions to social ills.[24]   When the project began, the lack of methods and materials for dealing with problems of human relations made schools reluctant to undertake such studies even when they were convinced of the need. Much of the effort during the two and a half years of the main project was therefore directed toward filling this gap, with cooperating schools deliberately chosen to provide a heterogeneous sample of local and regional problems in intergroup understanding. In all, some 250 projects were undertaken in 72 individual schools in 18 school systems. In keeping with Taba's concern with conceptual structures, however, problems in human relations were approached preventively, by attempting to develop general attitudes that would subsume and prevent more particular problems of intergroup relations. Rather than studying minority groups, for example, the project staff decided to focus on what they called "common areas of living"—family, community, American culture, and interpersonal relations. Within these familiar areas, more powerful concepts could be generated through studying such recurring phenomena as "acceptance and rejection, inclusion and segregation, prejudice and discrimination" (p. 72). Taba consistently emphasized the importance of *process* in learning, in particular that the natural progression in discussion or other learning activities should be from the concrete and specific toward the abstract and general.[25]

The Project on Intergroup Relations did not develop a specific curriculum in human relations. Its focus was instead on "action projects" organized at a local level, with the project staff helping schools to devise materials and activities related to their own particular social problems. To train as many teachers as possible in the techniques necessary to develop and test their own materials, a series of summer institutes was organized; one was held in 1945, three in 1946, and one each in 1947 and 1948. Some 260 people were involved in these summer sessions where, as the project staff summarized it, they "prepared instructional units, worked out methods of studying children and communities, drew up plans for student guidance and for school activities, and prepared strategies for community action" (p. 3). The work of these institutes, of the project staff, and of the cooperating schools led to a long series of publications on human relations and intergroup education; these presented teachers throughout the country with practical, school-based approaches for all age levels and in many different curriculum areas.[26]

Nevertheless there were major difficulties in the approach Taba and her staff advocated. The fundamental problem was naivete—a national naivete, not Taba's alone—which saw racial problems in the limited context of attitudes and dispositions rather than as manifestations of deeper institutional and economic forces. The concern was real enough, but the methods and assumptions were but a mild prelude to the civil rights movement which began almost as Taba's project finished its work. Simply to make people aware of the problem, to bring it out into the open as an issue to be dealt with rather than ignored, helped create an atmosphere in which the real roots could eventually be discovered and attacked. More immediately, there was too much similarity between the project's list of "common areas of living" and the lists of adolescent needs that were simultaneously emerging in "life adjustment." While this correspondence certainly made it easier for human relations studies to be taken up by the schools, it also made it easier for Taba's underlying concern with social reform to be short-circuited; the broader concepts she sought were often submerged in the specifics of present needs.

The pressures to preserve a limited and detached perspective were real and strong. George H. Henry, a Delaware English teacher turned principal, illustrated both the inherent reformist tendencies in human relations and the contravening community pressures in a 1947 article describing "Our Best English Unit." Students in his school, prompted to reveal their real areas of interest and "need," had turned to "the colored question" as a problem of considerable magnitude in their lives. The teacher and Henry had supported that interest, allowing the students to begin for the first time to explore the implications of racial attitudes and policies in their community. They never finished the unit; it was brought to an end by the school board after a torrent of public resistance.[27] That there were not more such conflicts was due simply to the reluctance of teachers to deal at all with ethical questions, especially in the atmosphere of suppression and censorship that developed as the Cold War began to capture the national imagination.

Organizing a Curriculum around Immediate Needs

The rejection of the core curriculum left teachers of English with the question of how to organize a curriculum designed to meet the new demands. One of the earliest attempts to solve the problem was that of the Stanford Language Arts Investigation, (1937-40), carried out under the guidance of the Stanford University education faculty with financial support from the General Education Board. H. D. Roberts, 1937 president of NCTE, was senior author of one of the reports, *English for Social Living* (1943). As he put it in the overview, "In the approach and throughout the work emphasis was given to teaching the language arts as a vital part of human living, and to the consequent replacement of routine and traditional teaching programs with those designed and tested to meet specific personal and social needs."[28]

The report suffered from the faults that would plague virtually all attempts at curriculum reformulation during this period. The guiding philosophy of meeting needs was so oriented toward the immediate school situation that it provided no guidelines for sequence or scope in the curriculum. Rather than an outline of a program, *English for Social Living* was primarily a collection of activities undertaken in different schools by different teachers, grouped together under such general areas of concern as "democratization of the classroom," "building of personality," and the need to "study and serve the community." Ultimately this focus on general problems ran the danger of ignoring the particular strengths of the subject area which it was attempting to revitalize. *English for Social Living*, like *Education for All American Youth*, gave precious little attention to literature.

Lacking any external principles by which to determine scope and sequence, the accepted practice gradually deteriorated into a "multiple approach" in which the only criterion was that students be kept interested. Though virtually any method might be of use, the materials themselves were determined on the basis of the particular needs manifested by the class. These were to be determined by a process that represented an unsystematic revival of the child study movement, usually involving a simple report from the class to the teacher. Dwight Burton, for example, in an early article presented the results of asking his students to write about the problems they were having. Like most of the products of the life adjustment movement, his inventory of needs was both specific and lacking in emphasis on the moral and spiritual side of life. He ended up with six major categories: relations with parents, relations with other adolescents, problems of personality, school problems, relations with brothers and sisters, and "miscellaneous." The first of these was illustrated in detail, with examples ranging from "1. Father 'horns in' when friends gather at the house," to "30. Home responsibility with father dead causes unhappiness." The "second step" in curriculum construction, as Burton presented it, was the selection of a "basic list" of novels "closely attuned to real adolescent problems."[29]

Though Burton's article was one of the first by a teacher of English presenting such an inventory of needs as an explicit basis for selecting the themes to be studied in the literature program, it was by no means a lone example. During the next ten years English teachers would be offered many similar inventories, from other teachers as well as from such professionals as the chief of children's service at the University of Michigan Neuropsychiatric Institute.[30] Implicit in these surveys was a new stress on the use of themes instead of chronology or genres to organize the course of study. Thematic organization did not originate during "life adjustment"; it had been a minor part of the experience approach throughout the previous twenty years. Under the pressure of meeting adolescent needs, however, themes shifted from a convenient organizational device leading to units providing similar experiences (about boats, say, or animals or regional literature) and became instead the focus of instruction: students needed to learn about family problems, the generation gap, or brotherhood. Thematic organization in practice differed little from earlier approaches, but it became the favorite method of organization in "life adjustment" classes and produced a few methodological variants of its own. Bertha Handlin, head of English at the laboratory school at the University of Minnesota, wrote in 1943 of themes as a way to allow members of a class to read different books and yet all be able to contribute to the same class discussions. Dwight Burton's suggestions, based on his teaching at the same school, were similarly focussed on selecting books whose themes were clearly related to important issues in the lives of teenage students. Although organization by chronology and by types dominated the high school course in the late 1930s, by the 1950s organization by themes or topics (which in practice became indistinguishable) had relegated both to a less important role.[31]

Selecting Materials

In a curriculum based on immediate needs, the teacher served as a resource center, providing the book to meet the need of the moment. One way to accomplish this was to redefine the values of the traditional works in the jargon of "life adjustment," just as earlier they had been redefined in terms of experience. As usual, there was no end to the flexibility of any given work: *Macbeth* was to be taught as an example of what happens when we are "willing to get our desires at all costs"; the object lesson provided would help students "begin to achieve self-control and self-direction." *Up from*

Slavery was presented as a good way "to understand how people with handicaps feel and [to] stimulate us to face our own handicaps be they large or small." "The Ransom of Red Chief" was paired with *Tom Sawyer* in a unit to help students "understand themselves and the younger members of their family better." "Love" became "a natural subject for discussion" after a class had read "The Courtship of Miles Standish." *Silas Marner* offered a "storehouse of information necessary for understanding friends, family, and one's self."[32]

Teachers more fully committed to general education and "life adjustment" provided bibliographies organized around the major focuses of adolescent needs; *The Reader's Guide to Prose Fiction* (1940) was the earliest and most comprehensive. Produced for the Committee on the Function of English in General Education of the PEA Commission on Secondary School Curriculum by Elbert Lenrow, head of the English Department at the Fieldston School, New York City, the book was a topically arranged bibliography with a lengthy introduction setting forth the author's view of literature in the secondary school. Lenrow's emphasis was very close to Rosenblatt's, and he abbreviated his own discussion somewhat by referring the reader to *Literature as Exploration* (1938). He was, however, more concerned with classroom procedures—with the question of which books to use with whom, and to what end. Accepting the general principle that literature was a means by which the student could explore both himself and his society, Lenrow noted that "the novel is par excellence the medium for the artist who would portray with amplitude both the macrocosm and microcosm of modern life." He accordingly limited the selections in his bibliography to prose fiction, quite a common approach throughout the period of "life adjustment."[33]

Lenrow assumed that students would "identify" with literary characters, manipulating their identifications "in such a way as to derive unconscious satisfactions, either of deprivations and inhibitions, or of goals, aspirations, ideals, and the like." It was only through such identifications that adolescents could "carry on those attendant and subsequent processes—exploration of self and formulation of attitudes and goals and outlook on life." To facilitate identification, Lenrow suggested books corresponding to the student's own situation. Contemporary works were more likely to show such a correspondence, but classic texts were allowed some place if taught by a skillful teacher.[34] His concern with presenting realistic life situations led Lenrow to confront "the troublesome question of how much frankness in books is appropriate for adolescents." Here he presented three major arguments against censorship. First, if the reader is really unsophisticated, he will not react to the implications of the "realistic elements." Second, if he does understand, it is better that his questions be answered "through serious literary

works rather than through devious and possibly distorted sources."
Finally, adults usually underestimate the amount of knowledge
adolescents already possess: "Those whom sentimental people are
anxious to 'shield' could often turn about and give instruction."
Lenrow was well aware, however, that many teachers and schools
would reject his argument that adolescents should have free or
nearly free access to mature books. Even one of the librarians who
worked with advance copies of the bibliography had been obliged to
note that many of the titles listed were prohibited in her library
because of "Frankness or 'obscenity' " (pp. 47-48).

The bibliography itself was an effective working out of the
principles laid out in the introduction. Some fifteen hundred novels
were included, with annotations designed to give a student or
teacher a quick idea of whether a book would be interesting or
appropriate. Only 17 percent of the titles had been published before
1900; a third were classic texts "which have stood or are standing
the test of time." There was a great range in number of titles listed
under the categories; some such as "Birth Control" had none;
others like "Family Life" had fifty to sixty. Adhering to his belief
that the books included should be appropriate and worthwhile, even
if not classic, Lenrow made no attempt to "fill in" under-repre-
sented categories; indeed, the entire list of books was chosen before
the topical arrangement was begun.

The resulting bibliography was a valuable reference work for
teachers who accepted its general principles. Like no other source
that grew out of "life adjustment," it offered an extensive list of
materials organized according to specific topics of instruction. All it
lacked was sequence, but that was deliberate since sequence was to
come from the problems of each student at a given point in time. In
spite of its thoroughness the book was not widely used by high
school teachers, largely because its annotations and classifications
were frank and direct, dealing with questions that were usually
edited out of school editions. The seemingly safe topic, "Adolescence," for example, included Gide's *The Counterfeiters* (annotated
as an examination of "the young Olivier and his delicate lover
Edouard") as well as Tarkington's innocuous *Seventeen* (p. 119).
More dangerous topics such as "Psychology of Sex" were not less
explicit.[35]

Of considerably more influence was a later bibliography, *Reading
Ladders for Human Relations* (1947).[36] This was a product of a
committee of school librarians working under the general direction
of Margaret Heaton, one of Taba's staff members. In retrospect,
and in comparison with *The Reader's Guide to Prose Fiction* (1940),
the original editions of this pamphlet seem slender and unimpres-
sive; but it represented a coherent application of Taba's general
principles, as the introduction pointed out. Three points about the
book are important. First, the books chosen for inclusion, though

few in number, were standard school texts; hence they were acceptable and accessible to a majority of teachers. Second, the topics under which they were organized were related to the general topics that the Intergroup Relations Project had chosen to emphasize, so that though not particularly impressive on their own they could be seen in the perspective of that larger framework; typical lists were based around Patterns of Family Life, Differences between Generations, and Rural-Urban Contrasts. Third, and probably most important, the selections were organized in "ladders" of ascending difficulty. Though strongly reminiscent of the "broad easy stair steps" of *An Experience Curriculum* (1935), these ladders were derived directly from Taba's theoretical concerns. She had argued earlier (1932) that education should be a continuing process of reconstruction of experience,[37] a principle that found expression in a stress on the importance of a cumulative program achieving its purpose through reconstructing experience at ever more advanced levels, rather than through a concentrated but short-term effort. The reading ladders, though they involved relatively few selections and even fewer levels of maturity, did imply that a curriculum could be constructed out of familiar materials that would be relevant to the new demands *and* still be coherent and sequential. It was this implication of sequence that virtually all other attempts to place personal or social needs at the center of the curriculum had lacked, and which teachers of English took from *Reading Ladders*. The success of this pamphlet, which has continued to be revised and expanded to the present day, is perhaps the best testimony to the wisdom of Taba's approach to curriculum reform.

Studies of reading interest, with their roots in the child study movement, also continued to be used to select teaching materials. This approach was more tolerated than motivated by life adjustment theory, but it culminated in George Norvell's definitive survey, published in 1950 as *The Reading Interests of Young People.*[38] As supervisor of English for New York State, Norvell systematically collected students' responses to works studied in class. Over a twelve-year period he gathered data on 1,700 selections taught to over 50,000 students by 625 teachers. Each book was rated on a three-point interest scale; 1,590,000 such reports were gathered, tabulated, and used to calculate "interest scores."

The tabulated data, in addition to providing an authoritative reference about the interest level of individual titles, allowed a number of generalizations about taste in literature. There was very little shift in interest levels between grades eight and eleven, only two percentage points for most selections. One of the most important—but neglected—discoveries was that there were few differences between the reading interests of superior, average, and weak pupils. Content, rather than reading difficulty, seemed to be the major determinant of interest; neither age nor IQ made a marked difference, though sex was an important factor. Norvell described the content factors he found:

> The special factors which arouse boys' interest in reading materials, as revealed by the current study, are: adventure (outdoor adventure, war, scouting), outdoor games, school life, mystery (including activities of detectives), obvious humor, animals, patriotism, and male rather than female characters. Unfavorable factors for boys are: love, other sentiments, home and family life, didacticism, religion, the reflective or philosophical, extended description, "nature" (flowers, trees, birds, bees), form or technique as a dominant factor, female characters (p. 6).

A similar list was provided for girls, together with the suggestion that the points of overlap be used to restructure the program of common reading around topics that would be of interest to both. Norvell himself used the results to compile a series of anthologies for D. C. Heath.[39]

Literature for the Adolescent

It was almost inevitable that the focus on narrowly defined adolescent needs would soon prompt and cultivate an extensive body of literature dealing thematically with the specific problems toward which teachers were turning their attention. The first serious professional attention to "adolescent" or "transitional" literature stemmed from Dora V. Smith's concern that the literary preparation of teachers gave too little attention to the literary interests of high school students.[40] By 1930 she had organized one of the nation's first courses in literature for adolescents as part of the teacher training program at the University of Minnesota. Her program generated only moderate interest, however, till adolescent needs began to emerge as a focal point of the curriculum during the 1940s. Though Smith's original emphasis had been on good books suitable for children, the forties saw the development of a new literary genre with its own authors and highly specialized audience of "adolescents" as defined by the "life adjustment" educators. Dwight Burton was one of Smith's students and became a leader in the movement to legitimize these works as part of the program in literature. Beginning to write about them in the late forties, he continued his interest after moving to Florida State University and assuming the editorship of *English Journal* in 1953. Under his guidance, the *Journal* devoted considerable attention to such works. Bibliographies were offered on "Books to Promote Insights Into Family-Life Problems"; the lead article of literary criticism was replaced once or twice a year with an article dealing specifically with adolescent literature; reviews of new titles were included as a regular feature of the "Books" section.[41]

The results of this attention were decidedly mixed. On the one hand a number of good books did begin to receive serious attention from teachers, especially in the junior high schools. *The Yearling* (1938), *The Diary of Anne Frank* (1950), and *The Catcher in the Rye* (1951) are among the better examples of what came to be considered appropriate adolescent literature. The problem in the movement was the rigid definition of books that would be interesting to adolescents as books that dealt with the specific (and often rather superficial) life problems reported when students were asked, "Now, what is bothering you today?" As Richard Alm of the University of Hawaii noted in a sympathetic review of the movement, "The last twenty years have seen not only the coming of age of the novel for the adolescent but also a flood of slick, patterned, rather inconsequential stories written to capitalize on a rapidly expanding market."[42] Since the interest in such literature was formulated exclusively in terms of the problems dealt with, there was nothing to caution the teacher against bringing such formula novels into the curriculum along with others of some independent merit. Indeed, because justifications were formulated in terms of the *problem* rather than its *solution*, there was little attention to how the popular adolescent novels solved the problems they posed. As a much later analysis pointed out, the formula-plots had a number of common implications:

(1) Immaturity . . . is somehow to be equated with isolation from the group.
(2) All problems can be solved and will be solved successfully.
(3) Adults cannot help you much. . . .
(4) Solutions to problems are . . . either brought about by others or discovered by chance.
(5) Maturity entails conformity.[43]

Such implications, which were shared by many other activities suggested at this time, eventually engendered the violent and effective reaction against the "life adjustment" philosophy which is discussed in Chapter VII.

Developing Competence in Language

Language and Communication

If one aspect of the general education movement was a concern with adjustment, a second sought to insure that the general student would have the "competence" necessary to meet the varied demands of life. As this emphasis was worked out in the teaching of literature, it merged with studies of semantics and, ultimately, with the principles of the New Criticism to provide a broader definition of reading skills. Carried to their logical conclusion, the principles of this movement implied the study of literature as form quite divorced from experience or adjustment, but at least until the mid-fifties such broader implications were carefully ignored.

Most discussions of the experience approach to literature had assumed that students, if given the appropriate book, would in fact be able to understand what they were reading. Rosenblatt's discussion in *Literature as Exploration* (1938) had questioned that assumption by posing the task of the teacher in terms of helping the student reflect upon and thus refine his responses. The discussion she provided, however, had few examples of how this would be done; what she did offer—the example of sophisticated adult conversation about books—implied quite a high level of initial response.

The twenties and thirties, however, also saw the beginnings of a new body of scholarship concerned with language as a vehicle for conveying meaning. Originally prompted by the use of propaganda during World War I, the work of I. A. Richards, C. K. Ogden, and Alfred Korzybski sought to explicate how systems of meaning operate and, as a corollary, how meaning can be distorted.[44] In the late 1930s, with war drawing near, Americans became especially interested in such studies, especially as they related to newspapers, radio, and film. An Institute for Propaganda Analysis was set up which took an active interest in school programs; later a Harvard Committee on Communication provided more sophisticated suggestions for school work. I. A. Richards, both through his writings and through his work with teachers (he was involved in the Harvard Committee, for example) had by far the greatest influence on school programs, but other forces also contributed to the methods that evolved. S. I. Hayakawa's *Language in Action* (1941) was especially influential in bringing the term "semantics" into popular parlance; through his work semantics became a topic in its own right in the English curriculum, often as part of the analysis of propaganda or advertising.[45]

The earliest full exploration of the implications of these new language studies for the teaching of literature was provided by the same PEA commission that had sponsored *Science in General Education* (1938) and *Literature as Exploration* (1938). Its Committee on the Function of English in General Education understood its charge to refer to the nonliterary aspects of language studies, putting its work in the traditions of grammar, rhetoric, and composition rather than of literature. The final report, *Language in General Education* (1940), was nonetheless to share the fate of earlier studies in these traditions: though conceived and presented as a separate discipline, it was taken up by many teachers as a useful technique for the study of literature.[46]

The report began fully in harmony with the concerns of "life adjustment." It talked of achieving "optimum development of personality"; of helping the student "find his place and his direction"; of providing the general education "that alone could be justified in the schools of a democracy." For this committee, however, such a charge implied that all children must be given the necessary tools for successful living; and the prime tool, that without which all others would be useless, was language. As the opening paragraph put it, the committee centered its work "around a concept of language as an indispensable, potent, but highly fluid set of symbols by which human beings mentally put their feelings and experiences in order, get and keep in touch with other human beings, and build up new and clearer understanding of the world around them" (p. 3). This would be studied as a system of oral and written communication, requiring the techniques of "critical thinking": "classifying, sorting, ordering, clarifying experience" (pp. 61-63).

The sorts of activities which the committee envisioned were illustrated at a number of points, though no attempt was made to offer a pattern curriculum in the various semantic concepts. Though there were some inconsistencies in the report, the committee clearly did not think that the techniques of reading could be developed incidentally. At one point they even described the language "textbook of the future" as a series of graded exercises (p. 156). A few pages later it was suggested that such teaching could instead arise naturally in the course of other studies. One suggestion pointed out that when a class "runs across the sentences: 'His whole life was devoted to one *cause*. . . . His devotion ultimately proved to be the *cause* of his death,' " the shift in meaning would be easily recognized (p. 161). Though one would be hard pressed to defend such an example as improving the students' reading of that particular passage, it does illustrate one way in which semantic studies were absorbed into the curriculum.

Richards himself provided more convincing illustrations of the usefulness of close and rigorous scrutiny of the semantics of a text. He was careful to put the emphasis on the act of reading, however, rather than on such generalizations as "meaning shifts"; as he pointed out two years after the report of the PEA committee, "The belief that knowledge of linguistic theory will make a man a better reader comes itself from . . . a misunderstanding." In *How to Read a Page* (1942),[47] he illustrated at length the techniques involved. One example came from R. G. Collingwood's *Metaphysics,* the first line of which read "Among the characteristic features of a pseudo-science are the following." Richards' reading began:

Line 1. The unpleasant flavor of *pseudo* spreads to make *characteristic features* and *among* reek with the same scorn. *Characteristic* is very

ready to take it. Nine times out of ten when we say "characteristic of
her, isn't it?" we are *not* admiring. *Features* when they cease to be
portions of the face or of a landscape, and become abstract, tend to
suggest a sort of nondescript, what-you-may-call-'em character. If we
were favorably inclined we would be more likely to say *characters,
qualities, attributes,* or *marks. Among,* of course, reflects the implication that there are any number of other nasty features (pp. 59-60).

After carefully dissecting the rest of Collingwood's argument,
Richards concluded that in fact it did not hold together.

Teachers of literature immediately grasped the implication that
reading is hard work, full of obstacles to be overcome on the way to
appreciation and enjoyment. As the head of the English department at Metamora (Illinois) Township High School put it in 1944,
"The act of reading occurs when the reader surmounts the obstacles
in his way"; his solution was to use a reading program to replace
that in literature "which the majority of the students could not
read." Most teachers were not so ready to abandon literature
altogether, preferring instead to replace talk of "experience" and
"breadth" with "small, intensive studies . . . that can operate to
make all reading more meaningful"—the justification, incidentally,
that Richards used for the exaggerated detail of *How to Read a
Page.*

Such an approach to the teaching of English won immediate
favor for the same reasons that the principles of "life adjustment"
were so quickly adopted: the goals were precise and limited; the
content was clear; and the philosophy indicated a continuing concern with the needs of the student. These reasons alone would have
insured that some such attention to language became important
after 1940; the exigencies of war speeded up the process. When an
NCTE committee working in the months just before American
entry into World War II prepared a list of "Basic Aims for English
Instruction in American Schools," its first point was that language
"is a basic instrument in the maintenance of the democratic way of
life." Though it also included attention to other goals, the NCTE
committee followed the lead of *Language in General Education*
(1940) in placing the emphasis on the "four fundamental language
arts: reading, writing, speaking, and listening."[48]

This emphasis on the unity of the language arts was furthered by
programs set up in some colleges to meet the problem of illiteracy
in the armed services. These programs usually united departments
of speech and of English under the blanket term "communications."
Lennox Grey of Teachers College, Columbia, helped to popularize
this term among secondary school English teachers. Outlining the
background in "An Urgent Letter" (1943) published while he was
second vice president of NCTE, Grey found antecedents for communication studies in prewar concern with propaganda, in studies of
the mass media, in the work of Edward Sapir and of George Herbert

Mead, and in courses in communication that had appeared in experiments with a core curriculum. But the real impetus came from the importance of communication in a nation at war. Grey successfully focussed NCTE's efforts around communication, even securing a Board of Directors resolution to that effect at the 1942 convention. When the USOE (with NCTE prompting) later called a two-day conference on English in the Victory Corps, the list of goals that emerged placed effective communication ahead of all other concerns.[49]

After the war, the concern with communication and with the "four fundamental language arts" continued as a separate, though not a conflicting, emphasis from the concern with adjustment. Both movements could and did point to *Literature as Exploration* as providing the fullest expression of their philosophy; the difference was in which chapters they chose to stress—the goals of acculturation or the techniques of careful refinement of response. The rapprochement between English and speech, however, was less successful, though NCTE continued to emphasize speaking and listening as part of the English program. After a 1947 meeting about communications programs in the freshman college course was jointly sponsored by NCTE and the Speech Association of America, the two organizations again went their separate ways. The Speech Association founded a National Society for the Study of Communication during the following year, and NCTE countered in 1949 with a permanent Conference on College Composition and Communication as part of its own organizational structure.

Reading

During the 1940s, teachers of English as well as of reading began to take a new interest in the problems of the relatively mature reader. Propelled in part by the new evidence of how difficult accurate reading could be, this concern led eventually to the inclusion of "developmental reading programs" in many secondary schools.

The methods adopted in these programs were strongly influenced by the remarkably successful training units set up during World War II to teach illiterate inductees to read.[50] In these programs, instructional materials were based primarily on the adventures of "Private Pete" and his friends, who were introduced in carefully graded films, comics, and basic texts which kept as closely as possible to the experiences and vocabulary of army life. Postwar schools attempted the same sort of match by selecting materials to meet life needs (sometimes reconceptualized in Robert Havighurst's terms as "developmental tasks") and by grading the selections using statistical measures of "readability." These measures derived from studies by William S. Gray and Bernice E. Leary (1935) and seemed to offer a scientific precision of the highest order.[51]

Even before the wartime programs, *Reader's Digest* encouraged a similar approach. To many secondary school teachers it seemed to provide contemporary writing on topics of general interest while insuring that the materials were of an appropriate level of difficulty. Though for adults habitual reading of *Reader's Digest* might be a rather limiting experience, for children in developmental programs it offered just enough challenge and diversity to insure continued growth of skills. In 1941 the *Digest* issued a school edition with a supplement of suggested questions and activities prepared by Stella Center and Gladys Persons, both of whom had been very active in NCTE. Initial experiments comparing classes using these materials with others not using them seemed to bear out the claims which had been made for the program and certainly helped to bring the materials into wider use.[52]

The *Digest* edited its materials to a standard format, simplifying and clarifying as it thought necessary to "get the message across." A similar motivation led to a revival of interest in simplified editions of popular novels. As one summary described them, "Long expository passages, tedious descriptions, and turgid narrative sections have been telescoped. The impatient reader may now get on with the tale." The "scientific" readability indices were of considerable importance here, the object being to produce texts appropriate for a given grade level. Still, the list of books that were eventually offered teachers in "simplified" editions is rather astonishing: *Black Beauty* and *Pinocchio* stand with *Ivanhoe* and *Les Miserables* among those submitted to the editor's blue pencil.[53]

The other aspect of the army programs which had considerable influence on schools was the concern with careful specification and orderly sequencing of component skills. Reading was broken down into such factors as "word attack," "sentence comprehension," "reading speed," "phonics," and "vocabulary," each of which could be separately drilled through workbooks and study exercises. Dean William S. Gray of the University of Chicago, long a leading figure in the field of reading, was coeditor of *Basic Reading Skills for High School Use,* a workbook covering such topics as phonics, vocabulary, and dictionary use. Many other publishers offered materials following a similar format. At a somewhat less mechanical level, *Reader's Digest* extended the editorial approach of its magazine to a series of texts, *Reading Skill Builders* and *Secrets of Successful Living.* Science Research Associates later used the same concept of controlled level of difficulty and accompanying comprehension questions to structure its Reading Laboratory, a kit of individualized reading lessons. Such materials found quite wide acceptance, especially in the junior high school and with lower track students.[54]

In spite of their popularity, such approaches failed to recognize certain limitations in the "science" which supported them. In particular they tended to ignore two important lessons that earlier experience should have taught them: (1) the range of ability within a given grade level is as wide as the range between the high school years, so that a difficulty index of, say, "grade 6" has very little meaning, and (2) interest level is of more importance than the linguistic and syntactic elements that were used in arriving at measures of "readability."

The New Critics

Changes in Literary Theory

The concern with language and meaning which led the high schools to emphasize communication was part of the development of a new school of literary criticism with many of the same antecedents. The "new criticism" (as John Crowe Ransom called it in 1941) was a general reaction against the impressionistic and sentimental criticism that prevailed during the early twentieth century. It was simultaneously a movement that attempted to provide techniques and a rationale for discussing the modern poets— Eliot, Auden, Yeats, and Pound, among many others—who seemed to violate the now traditional Romantic and Victorian literary precepts.[55]

To deal with the new poets and to escape from the impressionistic focus on "message," the New Critics turned to studies of the language and form of literary works, especially of poetry. *How* a poem means, rather than *what* a poem means, became the first question to be answered; questions of meaning were held to be inextricably intertwined with questions of form. These critics simultaneously excluded from the area of primary concern questions of history, biography, or ethics; their special task was to explore the structure (and hence meaning) and the success (and hence worth) of a given piece of literature, with the success itself being judged on the basis of structural principles.

The men who can be grouped together as the New Critics range from I. A. Richards and T. S. Eliot to Allen Tate, Cleanth Brooks, and Robert Penn Warren; they differed markedly in the details of their approaches and in the general evolution of their points of view. Nonetheless they shared the initial focus on the work itself and owed allegiance to the same intellectual and critical traditions. T. S. Eliot is generally viewed as the forefather of the New Critics, and his was the first strong voice urging that attention be turned back upon the poem itself. I. A. Richards, with his semantic and psychological interests, is primarily responsible for the methods that were taken up to carry out Eliot's concerns. His *Principles of Literary Criticism* (1924) and *Practical Criticism* (1929) tied the evolving critical theory into the broad stream of concern with semantics and language studies, a natural and fruitful union.[56]

The twenties and thirties, however, were years of development in which the New Critics were evolving techniques and experimenting with approaches; academic scholarship remained dominated by other approaches. The late thirties and forties saw the flood of influential books that eventually moved the New Critics into the dominant position which they have held since. Cleanth Brooks' *Modern Poetry and the Tradition* (1939), John Crowe Ransom's *The New Criticism* (1941), René Wellek and Austin Warren's *Theory of Literature* (1949), and Brooks' *The Well Wrought Urn* (1947) provided a theory and technique which gradually replaced the earlier emphases. Though Brooks could write in 1943 that the New Critics "have next to no influence in the universities," by 1953 Wellek was observing that such interests completely dominated the younger staff members and would inevitably come to dominate graduate training.[57]

The single most important influence in transforming such critical theory into classroom practice was *Understanding Poetry* (1938), an introductory anthology for college students compiled by Cleanth Brooks and Robert Penn Warren. The book was a thorough illustration of the implications of the New Criticism for instruction in literature, and was carefully designed to insure that its purposes could not be subverted. The opening "Letter to a Teacher" directly attacked previous methods of teaching:

> This book has been conceived on the assumption that if poetry is worth teaching at all it is worth teaching as poetry. The temptation to make a substitute for the poem as the object of study is usually overpowering. The substitutes are various, but the most common are:
> 1. Paraphrase of logical and narrative content;
> 2. Study of biographical and historical materials;
> 3. Inspirational and didactic interpretation.

In place of the three "substitutes" for a poem, the editors offered their own list of principles that "a satisfactory method of teaching poetry should embody":

> 1. Emphasis should be kept on the poem as a poem.
> 2. The treatment should be concrete and inductive.
> 3. A poem should always be treated as an organic system of relationships, and the poetic quality should never be understood as inhering in one or more factors taken in isolation.[58]

Brooks and Warren were well aware that such an approach was not common in the colleges, and hence gave their anthology a highly unusual form. Instead of a collection of poems with perhaps an introduction and "questions for study," they presented elaborate, illustrative analyses of the way a poem should be read. One might say that the book provided both the materials for study and the lectures on them—lectures which would have the effect of educating the teachers as well as the students (a fact which Brooks and Warren were diplomatic enough *not* to point out). Selections were arranged in a rough scale of complexity that began with simple narrative and ended with complex studies in metaphor and ambiguity. The analyses focussed on each poem as a whole, however, taking into consideration all of the various elements that together made up the structure. Brooks and Warren explicitly rejected earlier attempts to concentrate on literary form through such studies as "figures of speech" or "metrics," arguing that the effect of a work "can only be given accurately by a study of the relations existing among all of the factors" (p. xiv). The book was widely used, and was soon followed by companion volumes, *Understanding Fiction* (1943) and *Understanding Drama* (1946).

The New Critics and School Programs

The first use which high school teachers would make of the New Criticism was foreshadowed by Allen Tate in a 1940 review of *Modern Poetry and the Tradition* (1939). One of the major conclusions which he drew was that "modern poetry is difficult because we have lost the art of reading any poetry that will not read itself to us."[59] The implication that literature offered special problems of reading, that indeed it required close study before one can expect to appreciate it, was of course directly parallel to the conclusions that were being derived from studies of semantics, and served to reinforce them.

This concern with reading techniques was not in conflict with the concurrent stress on adolescent needs, but by the end of the forties it was gradually becoming clear that there was a fundamental antagonism between the basic principles of the two movements. As long as teachers responded only to the concern with the full range of meaning, they could apply the techniques of the New Critics with little problem. When they also took up the criteria of value based on formal coherence, the doctrine of needs (with its stress on content) and that of the New Critics were in serious conflict. Even here, however, the full extent of the incompatibility was somewhat ameliorated by the fact that one was primarily interested in prose, the other in poetry.

If there was any doubt in teachers' minds about the true import of the concern with form, it must have been thoroughly dispelled when the Bollingen Prize "for the highest achievement in American poetry in 1948" was awarded to Ezra Pound for his *Pisan Cantos;* the resulting controversy was covered in detail in the *English Journal.* The Bollingen Prize was awarded by the Fellows of the Library of Congress in American Letters, with money provided by the Bollingen Foundation. In 1948 the Fellows included Leonie Adams, Conrad Aiken, W. H. Auden, Louise Bogan, T. S. Eliot, Paul Green, Katherine Anne Porter, Karl Shapiro, Allen Tate, and Robert Penn Warren—a highly respected group dominated by proponents of the New Critics. Although Pound was an expatriate American under indictment for treason, the jury concluded that

> . . . to permit other considerations than that of poetic achievement would destroy the significance of the award and would in principle deny the validity of that objective perception of value on which any civilized society must rest.

Such a statement was a clear and direct challenge to any theory of literature which granted a place to *what* was said as well as *how* it was said in establishing a hierarchy of literary values. It provoked an angry, even savage, reaction led by the Pulitzer Prize-winning poet Robert Hillyer; his first articles—"Treason's Strange Fruits" and "Poetry's New Priesthood"—were published with editorial endorsements in the *Saturday Review of Literature.*

Hillyer's attack charged the New Critics with "sterile pedantry" and a "blurring of judgment both aesthetic and moral"; he prophesied that the award had "rung down the curtain on the inglorious Age of Eliot with all its coteries and pressure groups."[60]

Rather than the end of an era, however, the award of the Bollingen Prize to Pound marked the emergence of the New Criticism as the established and conventional wisdom. Hillyer's vilification, though initially tapping a current of uneasiness about the award, was soon criticized by such varied sources as the *New York Times*, the *New Republic*, the *Hudson Review*, and the *Nation*. The men he had been attacking were now the grand old men of letters: Eliot, Pound, and Ransom, for example, were all in their sixties. "Modern poetry," concluded a December 1948 article in *Poetry*, "is in fact in secure possession of the field, and its heroes are aged men with a long public career behind them."[61]

Though the New Critics were beginning to dominate scholarship and criticism during the 1950s, the rhetoric of "life adjustment" dominated the high schools. Though younger teachers trained in the New Criticism in their college programs were beginning to come into the schools, the much earlier report on *Language in General Education* (1940) represented the most extreme statement of their views that received anything like widespread support. Critical theory which emphasized form as the essence of literature, and which derived standards of value from the coherence of that form, had no place. It would not be until the early sixties, when the life adjustment movement had been thoroughly discredited and a new generation of teachers had assumed control of the English program, that the implications of the critical theory as well as the reading techniques of the New Critics would begin to affect high school programs.[62]

The Changing Curriculum

The NCTE Curriculum Studies

The most elaborate attempt to outline the form and substance of an English curriculum to reflect postwar concerns was that of the NCTE's Commission on the English Curriculum. Organized in 1945 under the general direction of Dora V. Smith, the thirty-one-member commission worked through a series of subcommittees involving some 150 other teachers and scholars to produce a series of five reports. These illustrate both the implications of "life adjustment" for instruction in English and the striking inability of the movement to provide a coherent set of principles to give order and structure to the curriculum.[63]

The first report of the commission, issued in 1952, presented an overview of the curriculum from preschool through graduate school, as well as an outline of the general approach to curriculum study which had been adopted. The commission's description of *how* to make a curriculum is interesting for what it says about the functioning of the commission itself: most of the emphasis is on insuring a wide representation of the various interest groups in the community, and of having them arrive together at a mutually acceptable consensus. It is interesting to note in this description how much the process has changed from its earlier formulations. Though the Clapp report is mentioned briefly, there is no serious attention given to empirical specification of life demands. Indeed, the "desired outcomes" of the program have become part of the process of consensus in the first stage—part of the "platform" of the Curriculum Commission itself. It is probably inevitable with such an approach that the goals arrived at will be both global and unsystematic. And as Bobbitt had pointed out many years before, imprecise formulations of what the schools were trying to accomplish would be of little value in organizing a curriculum. Even the illustration of the process provided by the commission shows these problems. A goal such as "Personal Values" is given such "specific" subtopics as "1. Development of personality—a sense of belonging and of being accepted," and "6. Establishment of enduring and worthwhile personal interests."[64]

The empiricism which in earlier curriculum discussions had focussed on the list of goals was now turned toward the description of
characteristics of the students. Such an approach was essentially
static: it provided a description of a given point in time, and very
little else. If such a description were the most that could be
available, then the teacher would have to be constantly and individually making similar assessments—learning the characteristics
of each student so that he could define the "needs" toward which
instruction should be directed.

The activities suggested as relevant "experiences" to be included
in the curriculum would then be those which could be seen as
reflecting the specified goals at a level of difficulty suitable to the
outlined characteristics of the student. Given the global nature of
the goals and the static nature of the description of the students,
virtually any kind of activity could find its place as a valid
"experience" in the curriculum, and the experiences themselves
could in turn serve as the setting for any number of practical
English skills. Thus, for example, "Correct usage" and "Forms of
Introduction" were both listed as incidental learnings derived from
the outcome "Development of personality" (p. 62).

The task given Volume I was global; later volumes were to give
practical guidance at each curriculum level. Angela M. Broening,
who had edited the earlier report, *Conducting Experiences in English* (1939), was head of the Production Committee for Volume III,
the secondary school report. This volume (1956) had the benefit of
several more years of life adjustment theory, and is even more
explicit in its acceptance of the general philosophy. The Production
Committee for Volume III saw students as shaped by two sets of
forces. The first was external, and embodied the demands that a
complex and rapidly moving modern world made upon its citizens;
the second was internal, reflecting the changing physiological and
psychological nature of the organism. These were explicated with a
detailed list of characteristics, subdivided into one section of Physical, Mental, and Emotional Characteristics and another section of
Language Characteristics. Physical characteristics reflected recent
attention to growth curves and physiological influences on behavior.
Twelve- to fifteen-year-olds, the committee noted, "undergo internal
changes involving the heart, gland, and bone structure; the heart
grows faster than do the arteries, thus causing strain on the heart
and often conflicts and emotional upsets." The list of "language
characteristics" treated language as an incidental activity: the first
characteristic listed, for example, is "Desire to have fun, a fact
which manifests itself in language expression related to sports,
amusements, and humorous situations."[65]

When the committee turned to the problem of appropriate activities for the curriculum, it became clear that incidental teaching of

the language arts really justified virtually any activity with which the teacher might feel comfortable. The committee emphasized unit teaching as the best approach to building up a curriculum, but their definition of unit was rather all-encompassing: "All that is meant by the term here is that varied activities in the language arts are developed around a central theme or purpose, clear and significant to the student" (p. 69). The Production Committee and the Curriculum Commission itself, because they stressed needs narrowly defined as immediate problems and left the language arts as incidental, never did attempt to limit what would be "clear and significant."

Literature was dealt with in two sections whose differing titles emphasize the twin strands of psychological needs and essential skills that were part of general education. One section was called "Meeting Youth's Needs through Literature," the other, "Developing Competence in Reading." Neither section offered much more than a series of echoes of the fuller discussions in *Literature as Exploration, An Experience Curriculum,* and the professional literature during the ensuing two decades. Literature was to be taught for "discovery and imaginative insight"; it would "meet the needs of youth and promote growth"; "general traits as well as individual characteristics must be taken into consideration"; "students differ"; literature can provide "broadened thinking and experience"; it is a "source of pleasure" and can aid in forming "moral values."[66] The phrases are glib and are offered with little elaboration or defense.

The section on reading skills is striking in its disregard of the kinds of skills which the New Critics were stressing. The important skills it did list for reading literature were "Evaluating truth to human experience"; "Discovering theme or central purpose"; "Relating detail to central theme or purpose of the selection"; and "Following different types of plot structure." Points of importance in the reading of poetry included rhythm, rhyme, "word color," figures of speech, and "mechanics." The general level of instruction is indicated by the final sentence: "Practice and group reading and discussion of poetry will make the inverted sentence pattern familiar."[67] It is indicative of the general emphases that Max Eastman is cited in the bibliography for the literature section; W. S. Gray (extensively) in the bibliography for reading; Richards, Brooks, and the other New Critics in neither.

The ultimate difficulty was that the curriculum specified by the commission lacked a set of structuring principles. The members found their metaphor for education in the concept of "growth," which involved "a definite sequential pattern" whose dimensions were clear enough: "The normal child grows constantly more complex, more effective, and more mature in each of his patterns" (p. 31). Yet they had no theory of cognitive or moral development which would allow them to state any more specifically the nature of the "growing complexity," the changes involved, or even the natural next stage of development. Instead, all they could offer was the static delineation of what the child is like at a given point in time so that activities could be structured to change him. Any number of activities, unfortunately, could be justified as "more difficult," "more complex," or "meeting a need," and all kinds of activities were offered.[68]

The Course of Study

In 1959 Arno Jewett, English specialist at the U.S. Office of Education, published a survey of 285 courses of study from 44 states, the District of Columbia, the Canal Zone, and Hawaii. His findings suggest that such guides reflected the emphases evidenced in the work of the Commission on the English Curriculum, though he felt that the guides described programs that were "less traditional, more flexible, and more closely geared to local needs" than those of schools not engaged in curriculum work.[69]

Jewett found that "almost all" of the courses included in the survey provided a definite sequence for the curriculum, with topical or thematic units almost totally replacing lists of classics as the method of organizing the work. Units often cut across the language arts, attempting to provide (as the Curriculum Commission had suggested) a wide base for incidental teaching of language and communications skills. Topics varied greatly, but "the importance of student interest as a means of facilitating and strengthening learning" had been "generally accepted." The junior high years tended to stress thematic units organized around the interests and needs which various traditions of research on adolescents had delineated—animal stories, adventure, and mystery from reading interest studies, for example, and family life, growing up, and making friends. About half of the junior high curricula included developmental reading programs.[70]

In the upper grades, Jewett found a much more traditional pattern, but most programs had been modified to include several different approaches. The most common pattern in grade 10 was the study of types; but in grade 11, with its now-traditional course in American literature, a wide variety of units were being taught: "Chronological, thematic, regional, literary, works of famous authors, American ideals and principles, and various others" (pp. 65-66). In the twelfth grade program the traditional course in English literature had begun to lose ground and was being replaced by a variety of electives. The most frequent substitute, however, was a course in world literature in which English literature played a substantial and usually predominant role. Some 13 percent of the courses of study included a required world literature course in grade

12, and another 10 percent offered it as an elective. Smith in 1932 had found virtually no attention to such studies.

Jewett also found that schools were incorporating the concern for language and communication that had developed during World War II. Over half of the courses of study that he examined included such studies, those published earlier focussed on propaganda analysis and critical thinking while later courses emphasized semantics and the nature of language.

The Anthologies

Jewett's findings indicate that those in charge of the courses of study—in general the more active and dedicated teachers in a given community—were responding to the emphases in the professional literature. Courses of study, however, are only one of the factors influencing what actually happens in the classroom; in this period as in the previous one, the literary anthology is at least as important. Two detailed studies of anthologies are available, one in general sympathetic and the other part of the reaction against the program of secondary education that developed during the postwar period. Together they provide quite a complete picture of the program in literature which the anthologies represented.

The more sympathetic discussion is James Olson's summary of trends between 1946 and 1957. He found a gentle evolution rather than a major shift from the pattern that had been developed during the 1930s. Those series that had not yet reorganized their ninth and tenth grade texts around thematic or topical units did so; and the topics themselves were shifted toward the more immediate needs and interests of adolescents. In the eleventh and twelfth grade volumes, the major change was the introduction of a thematic unit in contemporary literature at the beginning of the volume before returning to the standard chronological presentation for the rest of the text.[71]

The increasing concern with practical problems of living was evident in both the organizing themes and the editorial apparatus provided. The 1950 Singer anthology dropped its opening unit on "The Short Story," replacing it with one titled "Understanding Ourselves and Others"; a subtopic covered "Family Portraits and Problems." The parallel Scott, Foresman text introduced a unit titled "Families Are Like That" in an edition issued the following year. Even the anthology titles began to reflect the new orientation: Harcourt, Brace and Co. started a *Living Literature* series in 1949; Holt followed in 1952 with one more explicitly titled *Read Up On Life*.[72]

Responding to the concern with human relations, the anthologies also began to give attention to world literature. Some combined it with the study of English literature in the twelfth grade; others issued separate volumes. An ungraded Harper and Brothers text, *World Neighbors,* illustrates even in its title the limitations on the goals for such studies. The preface emphasized world peace and domestic harmony, and the selections themselves were surrounded with "practical" study questions. After reading Bernier's "The Divided Horsecloth," for example, students were asked: "Besides teaching married couples how to treat their parents, what does the story teach parents concerning their money?" Synge's *Riders to the Sea* demonstrated the "comfort" of religious faith but also illustrated "stupid beasts who allow a malignant nature to dominate their lives."[73]

As in previous periods, there was considerable difference in emphasis from series to series, with those collections designed most specifically for upper-track and college-bound students maintaining the most traditional focuses, and those for vocational students or the lowest tracks going furthest in the direction of "life adjustment."

One can conclude from Olson's survey that "life adjustment" brought no major change in the organization or content of high school anthologies. They continued to exert a moderately progressive influence on the curriculum through both their increasing attention to modern literature and their continuing de-emphasis of studies of form and technique. There is no indication that the anthologies—any more than the Commission on the English Curriculum of the NCTE or the state courses of study—had responded to the implications of the New Criticism; even the conservative editions for college-bound and upper-track students emphasized older methods of scholarship: biographical and historical studies, the characteristics of genre, and rhetorical devices predominated.

A trenchant and detailed critique of the anthologies by James Lynch and Bertrand Evans documents exactly what was happening to literary values. As a status study rather than a history, it treats the form of the anthology as a given in need of change, rather than as an evolving set of materials. To choose texts for study, the authors solicited information on state adoptions, surveyed practices in two hundred cities, corresponded with publishers, and checked their results with practicing teachers. They concluded that their final list of seventy-two texts represented all of those in major use. The sample overlaps Olson's but includes only five from the forties and some fourteen editions published between 1958 and 1962; most of these were minor revisions of earlier texts, however, so that the Lynch and Evans statistics probably provide an accurate picture of the texts Olson surveyed.[74]

Their report, *High School English Textbooks* (1963), is a good illustration of the fundamental antipathy between the emphases that had been developing in the secondary schools and the emphases of the New Critics. The task of the English teacher as Lynch and Evans saw it was "the teaching of the reading of literature" (p.5). Their emphasis was firmly on literature as literature; anthologies "should be the repositories of the very best ever thought and written in the spirit of the humanistic tradition and the Anglo-American heritage; whatever does not fulfill these criteria has no place in an anthology, regardless of grade level or the kind of reader to whom it might be directed" (p. 409). Given the professional emphases over the preceding fifty years, it was inevitable that the anthologies would not fare well in their eyes. Literary values had not been the primary emphasis in the selection of materials; much of the "very best ever thought and written" had been deemed inappropriate; the second best had often been found useful.

Lynch and Evans made a number of major criticisms of the anthologies, documenting each point somewhat repetitively as they took up each genre in turn. Their major charge was that the selections were inadequate and "second-rate," placing too much emphasis on such "currently popular topics as the space age, electronics, travel, and communication"; attention to "information, 'real-life' adventure, and social behavior"; selection for "sociological or historical reasons." To these considerations Lynch and Evans counterposed "ideas and the exercise of thinking logically and critically," "literary quality," and "promise of permanence" (pp. 64-73).

In the anthologies' treatment of each genre Lynch and Evans found a core of "respectable quality" which filled out the lists of "most frequently printed selections." These, however, were a very small percentage of the total; the frequently anthologized short stories, for example, made up only 4 percent of all short story selections. Observations of the remainder led Lynch and Evans to conclude that "the short story is not commonly regarded as a serious literary genre, but rather as an attractive short piece easily handled by the teacher and 'appreciated' by students with a minimum of teaching." The most frequent sources of the stories were, in descending order, *The Saturday Evening Post, Collier's, The New Yorker, Scholastic Magazine, The Atlantic Monthly, Esquire, Cosmopolitan, This Week, Story, Boy's Life, Seventeen, Harper's, American Girl,* and *Ladies' Home Journal.* Seventy-three percent of the selections appeared in only one anthology and were "commercial" or "formulary." To Lynch and Evans the results were a disaster:

> . . . the principal criticism to be made is not that such stories are not worth reading but that as entertainment they do not deserve a place in the textbooks prepared at considerable expense for high school classrooms. To give such stories as much space as more enduring works of genuine literature is at once to blur distinctions between the great and the mediocre (thereby frustrating the development of taste). (pp. 38-39).

Their parenthetical note is of particular interest, since it is a direct contradiction of the assertions of the experience approach. The question of the processes involved in the development of taste is the central pedagogical issue, but it has never been successfully addressed by proponents of either point of view.

Their second set of criticisms dealt with alteration of selections, a practice that had reached such proportions that nearly half of the selections in some texts were not presented in their original form. Many of the alterations represented unacknowledged "silent editings"; others involved major omissions noted with a simple ellipsis or misleading footnote (p. 442). Such changes were a source of continuing irritation to Lynch and Evans, who contended that they violated the duty of the anthology to present "the work as the author wrote it"—a necessary first step, of course, if the techniques of the New Critics were to be applied in teaching.

Another general point of criticism was the domination which the system of organization seemed to have over the selections included. As many as three-fourths of the volumes seemed to have been organized before the selections were picked. Topical (thematic) and chronological patterns of organization were the chief villains here, because both imposed a set of extraliterary considerations on the materials to be used. The study found too that such topical and chronological anthologies were the dominant forms, the first in grades 9 and 10, the second in grades 11 and 12. Lynch and Evans blamed the overemphasis on "miscellaneous nonfiction" directly on the use of topical units, which led to collections "that are more accurately described as socially therapeutic than personally and humanely educative" (pp. 79-80, 410). Again, of course, what they find offensive is a result of the success of the anthologies in responding to the concerns of the secondary school.

Lynch and Evans also criticized the fact that over half of the selections were from the twentieth century; literature written before 1800 was hardly represented at all. Looking for a reason, they found that the "correlation between the topical organization and proportion of recent literature is obviously very high," from their point of view providing another bit of damning evidence against this approach. Their worry about the displacement of "major authors in the Anglo-American tradition" also led them to object to the emphasis upon world literature in some collections: "It is at least questionable whether a high school student inadequately read in the poetry of his own culture is prepared to undertake the study of another" (pp. 113, 150-58).

The last general criticism that Lynch and Evans had to offer dealt with the tone adopted by the anthologists: in particular the "fear of difficulty" and the "deliberate catering to the adolescent mind even to the point of embarrassment."

Pieces are chosen because they lie within the narrow boundaries of the teen-age world, and their heroes and heroines are Dick and Jane just a few years older, now dating instead of playing, going to a dance instead of the local fire station, saying "round, round, jump the rut, round, round, round, jump the rut, round, round—" instead of "Jump, Spot, jump," but otherwise hardly different. The "image" of the American Boy that emerges is of a clean-cut, socially poised extrovert, an incurious observer of life rather than a participant, a willing conformer, more eager to get than to give, a bit of a hypocrite but a rather dull companion—a well-adjusted youth not much above a moron. And the "image" of the American Girl? She is the one who likes the American Boy (pp. 412-13).

It was to end the catering to that moron, to restore the anthologies to the state of "textbooks, *to be studied in and taught from,*" that the criticisms of *High School English Textbooks* were ultimately offered.

It should be clear that what Lynch and Evans were challenging was not the anthologies' success at the task undertaken, but the definition of the task itself. In a sense the fact that their study needed to be conducted at all is the strongest testimony to the domination that had been achieved by the progressive movement.

Summing Up: Literature in the Progressive Era

Lynch and Evans conducted their study in the early sixties, safely in the midst of a vigorous collegiate reaction against such trends; they were professors at Berkeley themselves. The attacks were on "life adjustment" and the narrow focus on adolescent needs, but since these were the final stages of progressivism it was the movement as a whole that was eventually discredited. The loss of the impetus toward reform and progress, with its concomitant de-emphasis of academic achievement, provided the rallying point for a variety of forces to unite against the unfortunate image of a brave new world filled with legions of school children in gray flannel suits, an image which "life adjustment" managed—not without justification—to bring upon itself.

The attack on "life adjustment" would simultaneously end John Dewey as the basic reference point for educational thought; he and his followers became the villains instead of the heroes in the new educational rhetoric. Yet though the name was discredited, the progressives made many solid and continuing contributions to the teaching of literature in American schools. Any list will of necessity be limited and thus misleading, but the following points give some sense of their accomplishment.

(1) They effectively ended the limitation of the literature curriculum to the nineteenth century canon of classic texts, opening the way for the inclusion of more, and more modern
selections as well as for important examples of world literature.

(2) They documented the wide range of individual differences
in ability and achievement that could be expected within
any high school classroom, and experimented with ways to
provide a meaningful program in literature for all students.

(3) They recognized the importance of student interest in any
successful program in literature; they developed a wide
variety of techniques to insure that interest would be present; and they described patterns of interests in children and
adolescents that remain valid today.

(4) They began the debate about the nature of the development
of taste and discrimination, recognizing that it is the essential question which should shape the curriculum in literature.

(5) They gave English a place at the heart of the curriculum
and defended literary studies as a part of English even when
unable to define their values precisely or well in the face of
demands for social relevance, efficiency, or adjustment to
life.

The failure of the progressives were also major and contributed
to the rapid rate at which their views of the curriculum would fall
from favor.

(1) In turning from literary scholarship toward the relationship
between the student and literature as the basis for the curriculum, they abandoned the old pattern before they had
developed a new set of practical criteria for determining the
relative value and the proper order for classroom studies.
They sought growth in response without a useful philosophy of what growth entailed.

(2) In part because of their lack of structuring principles, they
allowed the program in literature to be dominated by peripheral activities often having little to do with "literary
values"; in the end the rhetoric, at least, gave literature a
function which other activities could and did fulfill as well.

(3) In their concern with general education for the general student, they adopted a condescending position that removed
virtually all "striving" and challenge from the activities
suggested, especially for the noncollege-bound students.
They allowed their empiricism and pragmatism to narrow
their definitions of needs to the point that they were trivial
and dull.

(4) In their fear of college domination they lost touch with scholarship in their field, thus setting the stage for confrontation with the New Critics, rather than the reconciliation and accommodation that might have revitalized the movement.

CHAPTER VI NOTES

1. Wilford M. Aikin, *The Story of the Eight-Year Study* (New York: Harper and Bros., 1942), p. 16.

2. I. A. Richards, *How to Read a Page: A Course in Efficient Reading with an Introduction to a Hundred Great Words* (New York: W. W. Norton & Company, 1942), p. 10.

3. Lennox Grey, "Communication and War: An Urgent Letter to English Teachers," *English Journal* 32:1 (January 1943): 12-19.

4. Frances Broehl, "The Teacher of English and *Education for All American Youth,*" *English Journal* 34:7 (September 1945): 403-06.

5. Commission on the English Curriculum, *The English Language Arts in the Secondary School* (New York: Appleton-Century-Crofts, 1956), p. 15.

6. "General education" is a term that has been used to cover a multitude of sins; almost all approaches to education have been encompassed under the term by one writer or another. Discussion here will follow the Fifty-first Yearbook of the NSSE in denoting by general education the concern with the nonspecialized student with specific personal needs to be met through the schools, and in considering it an alternative to "liberal education," by which will be denoted a more subject- and culture-oriented program. See also the discussion of the Harvard report at the beginning of the next chapter. National Society for the Study of Education, *General Education*, Fifty-first Yearbook, Part I (Chicago: University of Chicago Press, 1952). See also NSSE, *General Education in the American College*, Thirty-eighth Yearbook (Chicago: University of Chicago Press, 1939).

7. Cited by Elbert Lenrow, *Reader's Guide to Prose Fiction: An Introductory Essay, with Bibliographies of 1500 Novels Selected, Topically Classified, and Annotated for Use in Meeting the Needs of Individuals in General Education*, For the Commission on Secondary School Curriculum (New York: D. Appleton-Century Co., 1940), p. 3.

8. "Summary and Report," *English Journal* 33:1 (January 1944): 49-52. The speaker was Brigadier General Joe N. Dalton.

9. "Summary and Report," *English Journal* 32:5 (May 1943): 285-87. The statement originated in a committee of the American Council on Education and was later accepted by the American Association of Colleges. For statements of the relationship between general education and English before the war, see Lou LaBrant, "The Place of English in General Education," *English Journal* 39:5 (May 1940): 356-65; and Dora V. Smith, "General Education and the Teaching of English," *English Journal* 29:9 (November 1940): 707-19.

10. On these developments, see C. A. Bowers, *The Progressive Educator and the Depression* (New York: Random House, 1969), pp. 216 ff., and Lawrence A. Cremin, *The Transformation of the School* (New York: Vintage Books, 1961), pp. 251 ff.

11. The series was titled *Adventure in American Education* and published by Harper and Bros. (New York) during 1942. It included Wilford M. Aikin, *The Story of the Eight-Year Study;* H. H. Giles et al., *Exploring the Curriculum;* Eugene R. Smith et al., *Appraising and Recording Student Progress;* Dean Chamberlain et al., *Did They Succeed in College?* and *Thirty Schools Tell Their Story.* The quotation is from Chamberlain, p. xviii.

12. See Giles, *Exploring the Curriculum*, and Chamberlain, *Thirty Schools*, for more detailed discussions of this evolution, the first from the point of view of the curriculum consultants, the second from that of the individual schools.

13. Giles, *Exploring the Curriculum*, pp. 315 ff.

14. Ibid., especially pages 4 and 44. See also Chamberlain, *Thirty Schools*, pp. 6 ff.

15. The Curriculum Commission which produced *An Experience Curriculum* (1935), for example, included at least nine members who were involved in the Eight-Year Study, though the PEA was not among the organizations asked to name an official representative.

16. At the time of the release of the first of these reports, the commission included, among others, the presidents of Harvard and Cornell; the U.S. Commissioner of Education served as an advisory member. Cremin, *Transformation of the School*, p. 329; Bowers, *Progressive Educator and the Depression*, p. 220.

17. Cited by Cremin, *Transformation of the School*, p. 334. See also *Life Adjustment Education for Every Youth*, U.S. Office of Education Bulletin 1951, no. 22 (Washington, D.C.: Government Printing Office, 1951; first ed., 1948).

18. *English Journal* carried many articles arguing the pros and cons of integration from the mid-thirties till the mid-forties. The largest concentration of conflicting points of view was gathered together in two 1945 series: "Our Readers Think: About Integration," *English Journal* 34 (November 1945): 496-502; "Our Readers Think: More About Integration," *English Journal* 34:10 (December 1945): 555-59. The tide of opinion was clearly against the concept.

19. Mark Neville, "Sharing Experiences with Farmville," *English Journal* 34:7 (September 1945): 368-72.

20. Marion C. Sheridan, "Life Without Literature," *English Journal* 37:6 (June 1948): 291-97; Grace S. Wright, *Core Curriculum in Public High Schools: An Inquiry Into Practices, 1949*, U.S. Office of Education, Bulletin 1950, no. 5 (Washington, D.C.: Government Printing Office, 1950). See also Grace S. Wright, *Core Curriculum Development: Problems and Practices*, U.S. Office of Education Bulletin 1952, no. 5 (Washington, D.C.: Government Printing Office, 1952).

21. Sarah I. Roody, "Developing Personality through Literature," *English Journal* 36:6 (June 1947): 299-304. She referred her readers to Schaffer's *Psychology of Adjustment*, Howard and Patry's *Mental Health*, and *Mental Hygiene News*. One of the most frequently cited early articles in this tradition was Mitchell E. Rappaport's posthumously published "Literature as an Approach to Maturity," *English Journal* 26:9 (November 1937): 705-14.

22. Margaret Edwards, "How Do I Love Thee?" *English Journal* 41:7 (September 1952): 335-40.

23. Hilda Taba, *The Dynamics of Education: A Methodology of Progressive Educational Thought* (London: Kegan Paul, Trench, Trubner and Co., 1932). See especially pages xvi and 257.

24. Hilda Taba, Elizabeth Hall Brady, and John T. Robinson, *Intergroup Education in Public Schools* (Washington, D.C.: American Council on Education, 1952).

25. The strategies which Taba developed continue to be an important model of the process of discussion. See Robert L. Trezise, "The Hilda Taba Teaching Strategies in English and Reading Classes," *English Journal* 61:4 (April 1972): 577-80.

26. Publications up to 1952 are summarized in a lengthy bibliography in the final report. The only one to be widely cited by English teachers was *Reading Ladders for Human Relations* (1947), which will be discussed on pages 153-54. An NCTE Committee on Intercultural Relations was active from 1943 till late in the decade. Its major accomplishment was a special issue of *English Journal* (June 1946) on racial and religious tolerance, with Louise Rosenblatt as guest editor. The most impressive part of the volume was the names of the contributors; they included Thomas Mann, Edna Ferber, Horace Kallen, Ruth Benedict, and Ernst Kris.

27. George H. Henry, "Our Best English Unit," *English Journal* 36:7 (September 1947): 356-62.

28. Holland D. Roberts, Walter V. Kaulfers, and Grayson N. Kefauver, eds., *English for Social Living* (New York: McGraw-Hill Book Co., 1943), pp. 11-12.

29. Dwight L. Burton, "Books to Meet Students' Personal Needs," *English Journal* 36:9 (November 1947): 469-73.

30. Ralph D. Rabinovitch, "Our Adolescents and Their World," *English Journal* 44:5 (May 1955): 261-67. The director of the Child Guidance Clinic of the Catholic University of America had talked of "bibliotherapy" as early as the 1944 convention ("The Columbus Meeting," *English Journal* 34:2 [February 1945]: 102-06). See also George Robert Carlsen, "Literature and Emotional Maturity," *English Journal* 38:3 (March 1949): 130-38; G. R. Carlsen, "Deep Down Beneath, Where I Live," *English Journal* 43:5 (May 1954): 235-39; Don M. Wolfe, "Students' Problems: A New Survey Made Especially for Teachers of English," *English Journal* 44:4 (April 1955): 218-25.

31. Bertha Handlin, "Group Discussion of Individual Reading," *English Journal* 32:2 (February 1943): 67-73; Dwight Burton, "There's Always a Book for You," *English Journal* 38:7 (September 1949): 371-75; Robert C. McKean, "Students Like Thematic Units," *English Journal* 45:2 (February 1956): 82-83; William G. Fidone, "The Theme's the Thing," *English Journal* 48:9 (December 1959): 518-23. On the status of themes by the 1950s, see the discussion of Jewett's survey later in this chapter.

32. Verona F. Rothenbush, "Developing Active, Thinking Citizens," *English Journal* 32:4 (April 1943): 188-95; Nellie Mae Lombard, "American Literature for Life and Living," *English Journal* 33:7 (September 1944): 383-84; "Report and Summary," *English Journal* 39:5 (May 1950): 280-83. Lombard's course was inspired by H. D. Roberts and *English for Social Living*.

33. Lenrow, *Reader's Guide to Prose Fiction*, p. 15. His school was one of the thirty in the Eight-Year Study.

34. Ibid., pp. 10-24.

35. This section included, among others, Huxley's *Point Counter-Point*, Anderson's *Winesburg, Ohio*, Lawrence's *The Rainbow*, and Dreiser's *Sister Carrie*—books of merit but a far cry from the standard high school canon.

36. Hilda Taba et al., *Reading Ladders for Human Relations* (Washington, D.C.: American Council on Education, 1947). This was prepared during the summer of 1946. A revised and enlarged edition followed almost immediately, published by ACE in 1949. Recent editions have been cosponsored by NCTE. A companion volume explained the rationale and teaching procedures in more detail: Hilda Taba, *Literature for Human Understanding* (Washington, D.C.: American Council on Education, 1947).

37. Taba, *Dynamics of Education*, p. 223. She summarized the goal of her method as "a continuous reconstruction of the total social and individual experience through self-directed activities."

38. George W. Norvell, *The Reading Interests of Young People* (New York: D. C. Heath and Co., 1950). See also his *What Boys and Girls Like to Read* (Norristown, N.J.: Silver Burdett Co., 1958), and an earlier summary report, "Some Results of a Twelve-Year Study of Children's Reading Interests," *English Journal* 35:10 (December 1946): 331-36.

39. James Warren Olson, *The Nature of Literature Anthologies Used in the Teaching of High School English 1917-1957* (Dissertation, University of Wisconsin, 1969; University Microfilms No. 69-22,454), p. 259.

40. Smith explains the origins of her program in "Extensive Reading in Junior High School: A Survey of Teacher Preparation," *English Journal* 19:6 (June 1930): 449-62. Surveys of teachers in two summer sessions indicated they were unfamiliar with such materials; the course on "juvenile literature" followed. Courses on children's literature date back much further.

41. See Richard S. Alm, "The Development of Literature for Adolescents," *School Review* 64 (April 1956): 172-77; Jean DeSales Bertram, "Books to Promote Insights into Family-Life Problems," *English Journal* 45:8 (November 1956): 477-82; Learned T. Bulman, "Biographies for Teen-Agers," *English Journal* 47:8 (November 1958); Emma L. Patterson, "The Junior Novels and How They Grew," *English Journal* 45:7 (October 1956): 381-87. Earlier, see Isabel V. Eno, "Books for Children from Broken Homes," *English Journal* 38:8 (October 1949): 457-58.

42. Richard S. Alm, "The Glitter and the Gold," *English Journal* 44:6 (September 1955): 315-22.

43. Barbara Martinec, "Popular—But Not Just a Part of the Crowd: Implications of Formula Fiction for Teenagers," *English Journal* 60:3 (March 1971): 339-44.

44. See W. H. N. Hotopf, *Language, Thought and Comprehension: A Case Study of the Writings of I. A. Richards* (London: Routledge and Kegan Paul, 1965); Douglas Waples, Bernard Berelson, and Franklyn R. Bradshaw, *What Reading Does to People* (Chicago: University of Chicago Press, 1940).

45. The Educational Director of the Institute for Propaganda Analysis addressed the 1939 NCTE convention (Violet Edwards, "Developing Critical Thinking through Motion Pictures and Newspapers," *English Journal* 29:4 [April 1940]: 301-07). Paul Diederich reviewed *Language in General Education* for the Harvard Committee ("The Meaning of *The Meaning of Meaning*," *English Journal* 30:1 [January 1941]: 31-36. S. I. Hayakawa spoke on propaganda analysis at the 1938 convention ("The St. Louis Convention," *English Journal* 28:2 [February 1939]: 143-50). See *Language in Action* (New York: Harcourt, Brace, and Co., 1941).

46. Commission on Secondary School Curriculum, *Language in General Education*, A Report of the Committee on the Function of English in General Education (New York: D. Appleton-Century Co., 1940). The committee stated that its primary debt was to I. A. Richards, who had advised it and read drafts of the report. Rosenblatt's book was endorsed as the proper approach to literature (p. vi, fn. 2); she was not on this committee but also acted as an advisor. Lou LaBrant, who was a member of the committee, has emphasized to me that the committee's language studies were seen as separate from literary work, though completely compatible; they were not meant to supplant it. Cf., however, Edward Gordon's comments ten years later: "Interpretation of poetry is a further extension of the general language work; it is another, complex and concentrated, example of emotional communication" ("Teaching Students to Read Verse," *English Journal* 39:3 [March 1950]: 149-54).

47. I. A. Richards, *How to Read a Page*, p. 19.

48. Charles B. Huelsman, Jr., "A High-School Program," *English Journal* 33:1 (January 1944): 35-40; Edward J. Rutan, "Meaning in Literature Study," *English Journal* 33:9 (November 1944): 505-07; and Basic Aims Committee, "Basic Aims for English Instruction in American Schools," *English Journal* 31:1 (January 1942): 40-55.

49. Lennox Grey, "Communication and War: An Urgent Letter to English Teachers," *English Journal* 22:1 (January 1943): 12-19; "The Council Meets in Wartime," *English Journal* 32:2 (February 1943): 104-05; and "English in the Victory Corps," *English Journal* 32:6 (June 1943): 303-09. See also Planning Commission, "English Instruction and the War," *English Journal* 31:2 (February 1942): 87-91.

50. Paul Witty was especially frank about the influence of these on his own thinking: *Reading in Modern Education* (Boston: D. C. Heath, 1949), pp. 10-11, 194-201. Another important presentation of the developmental approach was Constance M. McCullough, Ruth M. Strang, and Arthur E. Traxler's *Problems in the Improvement of Reading* (New York: McGraw-Hill Book Co., 1946). This discussed reading skills all the way from "Prereading Experiences in Preschool Years" through "Higher Levels of Graduate Study."

51. Robert J. Havighurst, "Characteristics, Interests, and Needs of Pupils That Aid in Defining the Nature and Scope of the Reading Program," in *Adjusting Reading Programs to Individuals*, Supplementary Educational Monographs no. 52, ed. W. S. Gray (Chicago: University of Chicago Press, 1941), pp. 53-59. These tasks were cited by Witty, *Reading in Modern Education*, p. 13. William S. Gray and Bernice E. Leary, *What Makes a Book Readable?* (Chicago: University of Chicago Press, 1935).

52. See Samuel Beckoff, "The Rainbow," *English Journal* 32:6 (June 1943): 325-30; Herbert A. Landry, "Teaching Reading with the *Reader's Digest*," *English Journal* 32:6 (June 1943): 320-24.

53. Olive Eckerson, "Give Them What They Want," *English Journal* 36:9 (December 1947): 523-27; Daniel J. Assuma, "A List of Simplified Classics," *English Journal* 42:2 (February 1953): 94 ff.; John R. Kinzer and Nataïie R. Cohan, "How Hard Are the Simplified Classics?" *English Journal* 40:4 (April 1951): 210-11.

54. M. Agnella Gunn et al., *What We Know about High School Reading* (Urbana, Ill.: NCTE, 1958). See especially Helen Hanlon's article,

"What Does Research Reveal—About Materials for Teaching Reading?"

55. See René Wellek, "Literary Scholarship," in *American Scholarship in the Twentieth Century,* ed. Merle Curti (Cambridge: Harvard University Press, 1953); Clarence D. Thorpe and Norman E. Nelson, "Criticism in the Twentieth Century," *English Journal* 36:4 (April 1947): 165-73; William Van O'Connor, "A Short View of the New Criticism," *English Journal* 38:9 (November 1949): 489-97; David Daiches, "The New Criticism," *English Journal* 39:2 (February 1950): 64-72. Wellek's discussion is the fullest; the others are interesting as examples of contemporary reactions to the growing importance of the New Critics. Daiches is particularly perceptive about the weaknesses as well as the strengths of the approach, and foreshadows later disillusionment.

56. These books had the curious fate of being virtually ignored by high school teachers for some twenty-five years, and then becoming basic points of reference at a time when their approach was already somewhat dated. Richards's *Practical Criticism* in particular became a common reference during the period of academic reform discussed in the next chapter. *Principles of Literary Criticism* (London: Kegan Paul, Trench, Trubner and Co., 1945; first published 1924); *Practical Criticism: A Study of Literary Judgment* (London: Kegan Paul, Trench, Trubner and Co., 1946; first published 1929).

57. Wellek, "Literary Scholarship," p. 123. Wellek refers to Brooks's comment in the course of his own observations.

58. Cleanth Brooks and Robert Penn Warren, *Understanding Poetry: An Anthology for College Students,* rev. ed. (New York: Henry Holt and Co., 1950; first published 1938), pp. xi-xv.

59. Allen Tate, "Understanding Modern Poetry," *English Journal* 29:4 (April 1940): 263-74. Brooks dedicated *Modern Poetry and the Tradition* to Tate.

60. "Report and Summary," *English Journal* 38:7 (September 1949): 405-07 (jury quotation, p. 406); 39:3 (March 1950): 170-71; and 39:5 (May 1950): 282.

61. "Report and Summary," *English Journal* 39:3 (March 1950): 170-71.

62. For a good example of the assimilation of the "skills" defined by the New Critics (in fact citing the 1950 edition of *Understanding Poetry*), see Rosemary S. Donahue, "A Problem in Developmental Reading," *English Journal* 42:3 (March 1953): 142-47. For an early example accepting their principles more fully, see Herman O. Makey, "Why?" *English Journal* 38:10 (December 1949): 554 ff.; and "In the Literature Class," *English Journal* 39:7 (September 1950): 360-66. As examples of programs during the period of transition, see Elizabeth Williams, "Teaching Judgment of Prose Fiction," *English Journal* 47:8 (November 1958): 495-99; David M. Litsey, "Comparative Study of Novels," *English Journal* 48:3 (March 1959): 149-51.

63. Volumes I to V were titled, respectively, *The English Language Arts* (1952), *Language Arts for Today's Children* (1954), *The English Language Arts in the Secondary School* (1956), *The College Teaching of English* (1965), *The Education of Teachers of English for American Schools and Colleges* (1963). All were published by Appleton-Century-Crofts, New York. The much-delayed Volumes IV and V are of a different period and emphasis.

64. *The English Language Arts*, pp. 62-67.
65. *The English Language Arts in The Secondary School*, pp. 16-20.
66. Ibid., 123-29.
67. Ibid., 180-87.
68. In spite of their shortcomings, the books were in step with educational thought at the time they appeared. Volume I was named one of the "Outstanding Educational Books of the Year" on the Pratt Library List, and Volume III in general provoked favorable comment, e.g., "Report and Summary," *English Journal* 42:7 (October 1953): 400; "The Significance of *The English Language Arts in the Secondary School*," *English Journal* 46:5 (May 1957): 286-93.

The advocacy of a "multiple approach" without clear standards for including or excluding activities was also typical. See J. N. Hook, "The Multiple Approach," *English Journal* 37:4 (April 1948): 188-92; and Walter Loban, "Teaching Literature: A Multiple Approach," *English Journal* 45:2 (February 1956): 75-78 +.

69. Arno Jewett, *English Language Arts in American High Schools*, U.S. Department of Health, Education and Welfare, Office of Education Bulletin 1958, no. 13 (Washington, D.C.: Government Printing Office, 1959), p. 5.
70. Ibid., pp. 31-39, 50 ff.
71. Olson, *Nature of Literature Anthologies*, pp. 246-47.
72. Ibid., pp. 246-49.
73. Ibid., pp. 258, 273-77.
74. James J. Lynch and Bertrand Evans, *High School English Textbooks: A Critical Examination* (Boston: Little, Brown and Company, 1963).

In their false liberalism, the progressive educators confused discipline with regimentation, and forgot that true freedom is impossible without minds made free by discipline.

—Mortimer Adler, **How to Read a Book,** 1940[1]

The issue in American education today is not drawn between those who believe in scholarship but are indifferent to good teaching, and those who believe in good teaching but are indifferent to scholarship. The issue is drawn between those who believe that good teaching should be directed to sound intellectual ends, and those who are content to dethrone educational values and cultivate the techniques of teaching for their own sake, in an intellectual and cultural vacuum.

—Arthur E. Bestor, **Educational Wastelands,** 1953[2]

The ultimate result of these pressures—the greater heterogeneity of pupils, the increasing complexity of our society, the development of modern media of communication, the proliferation of responsibilities of the English teacher—is that English as a subject is in danger of losing still more its central focus. In too many locales English has become all things to all students. The lines of the discipline have blurred, and the proper path for preparing its teachers has faded.

—NCTE Committee on National Interest, 1961[3]

It is obvious that random patching of the existing curricula, though it may have a practical look, is no longer practical. The only thing that is practical now is to gain a new theoretical conception of literature. Most of our difficulties in the teaching of English result from an immature scholarship that has not properly worked out its own teaching principles.

—Northrup Frye, in an address to the Modern Language Association, 1963[4]

... the primary motivation for this curriculum lies in the fact that the English program in most Nebraska schools lacks a planned, sequential, developmental pattern. Too frequently one teacher has no notion of what her students have done in English in previous years or what they will be expected to do in succeeding years. Consequently, each teacher feels that she must educate her students in every area of English at once. ... She cannot possibly do so.

—Nebraska Curriculum Development Center, 1965[5]

Chapter VII

An Academic Model for English

The excesses of the "life adjustment" movement eventually provoked a reaction which questioned the most basic principles of progressivism in education. If concern for the child led to school programs with no clear purpose or structuring principles, then perhaps these principles could be reestablished by returning attention to the subject matter. This was the underlying premise of the academic resurgence which dominated secondary school instruction from the late fifties till the late sixties. This resurgence, though limited in its own way and relatively short-lived, forced both progressives and their opponents to formulate their goals and methodologies with a rigor and precision that had been lacking throughout much of the "life adjustment" period. As one result, the study of education became once again a respectable endeavor, one in which academics as well as educationists were willing to engage themselves.

Critics of the Schools

The Academic Critics

Fundamental criticism of the progressive movement was beginning even as the movement hit its zenith in the late 1930s; the sources were primarily university scholars concerned about what they saw as a lack of intellectual rigor and historical perspective in the evolving school programs. Maintaining the distinction made in the previous chapter, these critics were the proponents of "liberal" as opposed to "general" education. One of the earliest influential critics was Robert M. Hutchins, inaugurated as president of the University of Chicago in 1929. In a series of lectures at Yale in

1936, later published as *The Higher Learning in America* (1936), Hutchins outlined a program which placed its emphasis on discipline and culture as a prescribed body of knowledge, summed up as the "Great Books."[6] This was in turn popularized by Mortimer Adler in his somewhat polemical *How to Read a Book* (1940). A professor of law rather than of literature, Adler first taught with Mark Van Doren at Columbia and later with Hutchins at Chicago. Blaming the progressives in general and John Dewey in particular for what he saw as "the almost total neglect of intelligent reading throughout the school system," Adler is interesting for his fundamental unity of purpose with most of the progressive movement. To him, too, reading was "a basic tool of good living," one "intimately related to the art of thinking well—clearly, critically, freely." Education in general and reading in particular were "a means toward living a decent human life." Even the list of questions that Adler thought should be asked by a reader were basically compatible with progressive doctrines: "What in general is being said? . . . How in particular is it being said? . . . Is it true? . . . What of it?"[7]

Adler in the end differed from the progressives he was criticizing on only one important point: *what* should be read to achieve these goals. And his answer was simple: the Great Books, and only the Great Books, were worth spending time on. They alone would teach the reader to read well, and until he could read well there would be no sense in reading widely. Adler was well aware that the Great Books (he included a lengthy list in an appendix) were considerably more difficult than the standard school fare, but he defended this difficulty as providing the necessary discipline without which true freedom of the mind could never be achieved.

Van Doren, whom Adler acknowledged as a shaping force in his own education, was himself commissioned by the Association of American Colleges to prepare a discussion of liberal education during the midst of World War II. His book, far more scholarly and reasoned than Adler's popularization, recognized the fundamental unity in goals with the progressive educators, but like Adler split with them on what it was that should be studied. As Van Doren put it, progressive education failed at being "perfect" precollege education by neglecting two things: "The deep resemblances between human beings, calling for a fixed program of learning which no child may evade, and the importance of the past." And like Adler, Van Doren pointed to the Great Books program as a good model to follow.[8]

Two Harvard committees appointed by president James B. Conant provided similar discussions of secondary school programs: first *The Training of Secondary School Teachers Especially with Reference to English* (1942), and later *General Education in a Free Society* (1945). Both reflected an awareness of conditions in Amer-

ican secondary schools and a healthy appreciation of the progressive efforts at reform; both, however, came down squarely in favor
of a more academic and intellectually rigorous curriculum than
seemed to be emerging. The NCTE in particular was castigated by
the Committee on the Training of Secondary School Teachers for
having "ended whatever monopoly the classics still enjoyed"
through a series of reports that exhibited "a decreasing power of
discriminating between books of permanent worth and books of an
ephemeral nature." Rather than a leisure time or recreational
activity, the committee saw reading as a difficult and disciplined
subject, one that would "challenge" the mind and thus make it
"grow."[9]

Both Harvard committees traced the ills of education to the
expanding school enrollments of the early twentieth century, enrollments that had grown so fast that the liberal arts faculties had
gladly relinquished their traditional responsibility for teacher training. The result, inevitably, had been a widening chasm between
school and college people, the one poorly trained in subject matter,
underpaid, and without time to pursue their own continuing education, the other isolated from the schools, unconcerned with methodology, and (until much later in the century) safely protected from
the problems of "mass" or "general" education. As a result of this
split, education lost touch with its earlier humanistic roots, though
these continued to flourish (the Harvard committees hoped) in the
university liberal arts faculties. The goals of secondary education,
in this view, were now too oriented toward practical and vocational
ends; there was a need to re-emphasize the ethical and cultural
heritage through a return to "great authors" and "great books."[10]

The implicit and explicit criticism of progressive education offered in the early forties by proponents of liberal education set the
stage for the later and more volatile criticism that would in a
remarkably short time make progressive education a term of deri-
sion, and John Dewey a scapegoat. Lack of intellectual rigor,
neglect of common culture, avoidance of questions of values, and
the control of the schools by an isolated and ingrown school of
education—these would be the rallying points for critics who would
fail to recognize any fundamental unity of purpose with progressive
education. Much of their criticism simply missed the point, continuing a long tradition of talking past one another that had grown up
between the schools of education and the liberal arts faculties.[11] The
Great Books course is itself the best single example of this: critics
of progressive education claimed that such books were being neglected, while in fact the progressive theorists could claim self-
righteously that they had already learned that the way to full
appreciation of these classic texts was indirect, through the lesser
and more ephemeral works that they had been assiduously bringing
into the curriculum. In fact the progressives may have been in

danger of losing sight of their ultimate goal, concentrating on the ephemeral as an end in itself, but since the issue was put not pedagogically but on the basic principles, neither side benefited from the wisdom of the other.

A Crisis of Confidence

As "life adjustment" became more popular, such criticism intensified. Some hint of the changing tone is evident in the titles chosen—they progressed from Van Doren's simple *Liberal Education* (1943) to Bernard Idding Bell's *Crisis in Education* (1949) and, in the same year, Mortimer Smith's *And Madly Teach*. By 1953 the transition from criticism which acknowledged many points of contact with the progressive movement to outright confrontation was nearly complete; that year produced Albert Lynd's *Quackery in the Public Schools*, Arthur Bestor's *Educational Wastelands*, Robert Hutchins's *The Conflict in Education*, and Paul Woodring's *Let's Talk Sense about Our Schools*. Rudolf Flesch's *Why Johnny Can't Read* with its subtle linking of progressivism and communism followed soon thereafter. Such efforts were eventually institutionalized through the Council on Basic Education, founded in 1956 with Bestor and Smith among the directors.[12]

The major charge which the critics brought against the progressive movement was anti-intellectualism; all of the other points they would make could eventually be brought back to the fear that the progressively-educated child would not be the intellectual equal of his forebears, his mind weakened by "lollipops" instead of "learning," the "discipline" of content replaced by the triviality of "life adjustment." Here was the heart of the loud protests that would be made about the "educationists," who progressed in the rhetoric from an innocent (if unfortunate) product of the rapid expansion of the schools to an interlocking and self-serving directorate with a stranglehold on the system of public education.[13]

The harsh rhetoric of the academic critics opened the way for a varied and unlikely coalition of forces. Conservatives seeking ways to reduce school budgets, superpatriots outraged by the social reconstructionists and fanned by McCarthy, parents disturbed by the implications of "life adjustment," old-line teachers who had never embraced progressive doctrines in the first place, and young teachers to whom progressivism meant resistance to new modes of scholarship—all came together in their criticism of the schools. The sins of the progressives had been many, and as the attack gained in intensity the tendency to look at their virtues grew weaker and weaker.

The final blow was Sputnik. Launched in the fall of 1957, it became a symbol of the failure of the schools and a milestone marking the end of one era and the beginning of another.[14] It also provoked its own period of national soul-searching, summed up in Vice-Admiral H. G. Rickover's *Education and Freedom* (1958). "Life adjustment" and John Dewey were his scapegoats, engineers and "talented youth" his Chosen People, and high academic standards the road to salvation. "Only massive upgrading of the scholastic standards of our schools," Rickover wrote, "will guarantee the future prosperity and freedom of the Republic."[15] Congress followed with a new infusion of federal funds through the National Defense Education Act of 1958—an act which carried in its title an ever-present reminder of just exactly what it was that had prompted federal concern.

With the passage of the NDEA, English found itself taking a definite second place to math and science, the new "core" curriculum for producing Rickover's nation of engineers. It was a sobering experience, but one that gave the many factions within the teaching of English a common cause.

In their attempts to reassert the values of English, however, teachers of English did have some powerful allies. One of the most important was Harvard's James B. Conant, who returned from a sojourn as ambassador to Britain to provide a series of trenchant critiques of the schools. The first of these, *The American High School Today* (1959), examined the comprehensive high school, an institution which Conant viewed as the proper embodiment of the American commitments to excellence and to democracy. After visits to a selected sample of schools, Conant offered twenty-one "Recommendations for the Improvement of American High Schools." These were designed in large part to improve the preparation of the academically talented students by substituting a more rigorous program in the basic subjects, including English. He asked, among other things, for subject-by-subject ability grouping (instead of the across-the-board tracking that then predominated), the use of an academic honors list, advanced courses with specified prerequisites, special classes for the highly gifted, more emphasis on composition, and four years of English for every student. The general implications of Conant's recommendations for English were clear: an important place in the curriculum, but one requiring some substantial changes in approach.[16]

English as a Discipline

Concern for the Talented

Though Sputnik in 1957 crystallized public opinion and thus serves as a convenient benchmark for the beginning of reform, in fact the underlying reemphasis of academic achievement was al-

ready well underway. One of the early forces was a revival of
interest in special programs for "academically talented" students in
reaction against the preoccupations of the progressives with the
"general" courses and "life adjustment." Concern for the academically talented was given considerable impetus by experiments
sponsored by the Ford Fund for the Advancement of Education.

Established in 1951, the Fund for the Advancement of Education
experimented with two approaches to break the lockstep progression through the secondary school grades. The first, early admissions, received considerable publicity during 1951 and 1952 but
never became very popular: high schools protested that they were
being stripped of student leaders, and colleges worried about the
social maturity of the early admittees. The second experiment,
advanced placement, was initiated in 1952; it became popular with
Ivy League schools and their prep school feeders, insuring steady if
not spectacular growth. By 1955 it was well enough established to
be taken over by the College Entrance Examination Board, with
the first exams under CEEB auspices being given in the following
year.[17]

The Advanced Placement program was simply a series of examinations; there was no syllabus or prescribed course of study.
Nonetheless, like all examinations, it developed an established form
and series of emphases that could not help but shape high school
teaching. Indeed, its influence often extended far beyond the limited number of students directly involved, leading to changes in
methods and materials at all levels of the curriculum.[18] From the
beginning English was one of the most popular advanced placement
subjects, and the emphases in its examination were those that
characterized the next wave of reform. Textual analysis and literary
criticism on the model of the New Critics was the most important
aspect of the exam; very little attention was given to the philosophical or ethical dimensions of literature.

The advanced placement model of special attention to intellectually gifted students offered the public schools one relatively direct
way to respond to the growing criticism of progressive education.
Arno Jewett, USOE specialist in language arts, told the NCTE
convention in 1952 that neglect of the fast learner was "the basis
for much of the honest criticism of our educational efforts." To
demonstrate a lowering of the average instructional level, he used
statistics on the increasing proportion of children of high school age
remaining in school until graduation.[19] Jewett was tapping such a
general concern that the Council's Executive Committee voted a
few months later to establish a Committee on English Programs for
High School Students of Superior Ability to help teachers provide
for these "neglected" students. The final report of the committee
did not appear until 1960, when it was brought out as a joint

publication of NCTE and the NEA's Project on the Academically Talented Student, but its emphases are those of the mid-fifties when the committee was most active.[20] The report makes it clear that the teacher of the academically talented should have a special status within the high school faculty. The arguments parallel those that had arisen during the initial enthusiasm for ability grouping during the twenties: the students are brighter than the average; therefore the teacher must be brighter than the average, with a better preparation in literature and a broader cultural background. As a corollary, he would need a lighter teaching load and extra financial support for advanced preparation.

The special competence of academically talented students was generalized to all aspects of school life. In addition to advanced placement exams, accelerated or "enriched" classes, and early admissions, they would be encouraged to make reports to the class, to serve as chairmen of student committees, to conduct book fairs, to do creative writing—to do, in fact, virtually anything out of the ordinary. It is very difficult, however, to understand the peculiar qualifications of the academically talented to read announcements over the loudspeaker system, or why families of superior students—and not of all students—were to be given advice on activities to broaden a student's interests (visits to places of historical or cultural interest, trips to museums, or evenings at the theater). Most of the activities suggested for these students were exactly the kinds of undertakings that the progressives had urged for everyone.

The third point that emerges from the report is a direct consequence of the extent to which the concern for the academically talented pupil was motivated by criticism of their academic preparation: the model for academic work was the college curriculum, so the proposed changes in high school programs followed very closely what went on—or was thought to go on—in college classrooms. "Advanced work" was the single answer to the problem of what to offer the academically talented, and this meant intensive reading, the Great Books, and literary rather than personal focuses for the curriculum. Often the courses simply adopted one of the introductory college anthologies.

A New Curriculum Model

The programs which began to appear for academically talented students differed fundamentally from those developed by the "life adjustment" movement. Where the progressives had come to stress immediate needs and the characteristics of the student, the new programs placed their emphasis on long-term goals and the nature of the subject. At the same time, liberal arts faculties became involved in curriculum reform in a way unparalleled since the late nineteenth century, when the college had also served as the model for the high school program. As early as 1951, the University of Illinois Committee on School Math set the pattern that later efforts would follow: scholars working to develop new programs that would stress concepts fundamental to the subject area—or the "discipline" as it came to be called. Though educators were usually involved at various stages of curriculum development, it was subject area rather than educational principles which determined the scope and sequence of the new curriculum. The University of Illinois project was followed by the Physical Sciences Study Committee (1956), the School Maths Study Group (1958), and by various other efforts in science and math.[21] At the same time, the National Science Foundation (NSF) developed a model for inservice education based on summer institutes. Founded by act of Congress in 1950 as an independent body to oversee research and training in scientific and mathematical areas, the NSF funded a series of institutes for college teachers during the summer of 1953. These were extended to the secondary school level the following year, again directly involving liberal arts departments in problems of teacher training and curriculum development.

Interest in academic reform in English—aside from the initial response to the problems of the academically talented—began more slowly. On a regional level, a series of annual conferences on the teaching of English grew out of the Yale Master of Arts in Teaching program during 1955. Under the direction of Edward Gordon and Edward S. Noyes, these conferences offered an academic view of English and stressed three separate components: language, literature, and composition. This "tripod" became the major metaphor for English during the ensuing period of academic reform. Literature at the Yale conferences was dealt with using the approaches of the New Critics, with Cleanth Brooks and other distinguished faculty members helping teachers assimilate the new point of view.[22] Of more significance nationally, the Modern Language Association (MLA) became involved in secondary education for the first time since the turn of the century, as a result of the Foreign Language Program (1952-58) funded by the Rockefeller Foundation. Under the direction of MLA Executive Secretary William Riley Parker, this program led to many reforms in foreign language teaching and culminated with the inclusion of funds for foreign languages in the National Defense Education Act of 1958. Parker's successor at MLA, George Winchester Stone, Jr., turned MLA efforts toward the teaching of English at about the same time that the leadership of NCTE, with J. N. Hook of the University of Illinois serving as its first full-time executive secretary, began to reassess the principles on which English programs were based.

The Basic Issues Conferences

The first important manifestation of renewed scholarly interest in secondary school English was a series of "Basic Issues" conferences held during 1958 with funds from the Ford Foundation. In the atmosphere of mistrust and suspicion that had developed between academic and education departments, MLA initially proposed to sponsor such a series without directly involving other professional organizations who might have been presumed to have an interest. After NCTE protested that MLA, with its college orientation, lacked the competence to deal adequately with secondary school teaching, the conferences were eventually funded under the joint sponsorship of the American Studies Association, the College English Association, MLA, and NCTE; the series brought together twenty-eight teachers of English for three three-day and a final one-day meeting to consider and define the basic issues in the teaching of English. The conferences reduced the initial mistrust among the leaders of the organizations involved and produced two short but important reports that were widely distributed: "The Basic Issues in the Teaching of English" (1959), and "An Articulated English Program: An Hypothesis to Test" (1959).[23]

The first of these reports was presented as a "sharpening" of points of disagreement within the profession, but a clear point of view radically different from that of the progressives emerges from the leaflet as a whole. The most important assertion was that English must be regarded as a "fundamental liberal discipline," a body of specific knowledge to be preserved and transmitted rather than a set of skills or an opportunity for guidance and individual adjustment. As such, the importance of specific works, of the technical vocabulary of the literary critic, and of sequence determined by the logic of the subject matter could be opened for debate in a way that was impossible when the subject was defined in terms of the needs or interests of the student. College professors of English rather than of education or psychology became the body of expert opinion of most importance in curriculum development, and national leadership through the professional organizations became the natural way to bring such scholars into the process of curriculum development. Because the basis of the curriculum was felt to lie in the subject matter, such experts could provide guidance of a nearly universally applicable sort—in contrast with the dictum of the NCTE Commission on the English Curriculum that the curriculum must emanate from the needs of the student in his particular local community.

The Basic Issues conferences, not surprisingly, turned to the programs for the academically talented to sharpen some of the issues they presented. To the extent that there was any evident concern for individual differences, the paradigm usually followed was quite consistent: "What can we do with the best students? If such an approach is good for them it must be good for everyone. How should we modify it so we can use it with the less gifted also?"[24] It was a very handy model for the academics to follow, since with it pedagogical issues could for the most part be ignored. Whatever sequence and manner of presentation were chosen, the academically talented student would be able to handle it; thus the construction of a functioning model of the academic curriculum was not an insurmountable problem. When it came time to modify the curriculum for the less able, however—a process that was really neglected for most of the sixties—it would take radical reform rather than simple modification to produce a viable structure.

The most important issue in the minds of the conferees was that of providing a curriculum that would be "sequential and cumulative from the kindergarten through the graduate school." Such structure would be the key to insuring that English-the-school-subject in fact remained English-the-discipline. Without the structure, there would be nothing to prevent a return of "the present curricular disorder" with its ad hoc activities and, even after the advent of "life adjustment," its virtually unlimited scope.[25] The conferees were uncertain about the proper basis for the sequence they hoped to develop, presenting their own conception in the second leaflet, "An Articulated English Program: An Hypothesis to Test." Echoing the Yale Report of 1828, they portrayed the literature component of the English program as "a continuous furnishing of the mind." The skeleton course they provided was distinctly traditional, beginning with the simple literary forms of folklore, legend, and fairy tales in the early elementary years, progressing through myth and legend in the upper elementary grades, and the backgrounds of the Western cultural heritage (through, for example, selections from Homer and from the Bible) in junior high school. The high school would be the place for an emphasis on intellectual development and "mastery of certain blocks of knowledge" important to the literary heritage. Though the conferees stopped short of proposing a return to set books (calling it "probably inadvisable"), they proposed that the curriculum introduce all students to certain specific varieties of literary experience. Thus for the novel, they deemed it "necessary and practicable to insist that novels of the following kinds must be read":

Simple narrative (e.g., *Robinson Crusoe*)
Picaresque novel (*Lazarillo de Tormes*)
Historical novel (*A Tale of Two Cities; The Great Meadow*)
Novel of manners (*Pride and Prejudice*)
Bildungsroman (*David Copperfield; Jane Eyre*)
Novel of ideas (*The Scarlet Letter; Arrowsmith*)
Psychological novel (*The Red Badge of Courage*)

The same years would also be used to introduce the student to Plato, Lucretius, Cicero, Augustine, Dante, and Montaigne. "What a foundation for students entering college!" the conference exclaimed, "And what a challenge to those who are not."[26] The enthusiasm was high, and only time would temper it with reality.

The Spiral Curriculum

The most influential discussion of sequence again came from the sciences, this time from a ten-day conference called at Woods Hole by the National Academy of Sciences. Under the chairmanship of Harvard's Jerome Bruner, the conference brought together physicists, biologists, mathematicians, psychologists, educators, and historians "to consider anew the nature of the learning process, its relevance to education, and points at which current curricular efforts have raised new questions about our conceptions of learning and teaching."

Bruner's final report as chairman, *The Process of Education* (1960), presented a detailed and lucid argument for a curriculum that concentrated on providing a sense of the structure of the discipline (that is, subject) under study; it also developed a concept of sequence through a "spiral" curriculum. As envisioned by Bruner, the curriculum would be based around the central ideas of the discipline, ideas which would be returned to again and again at successively higher levels of complexity. In such a program, the student would progress from an initial intuitive knowledge to an eventual explicit formalization of basic principles. In keeping with the academic and intellectual nature of the reaction of which Woods Hole was a part, the emphasis at all levels was on "scrupulous intellectual honesty," which as developed by Bruner implied a discovery or inductive approach to learning. The child would learn physics by doing the kinds of things a physicist does, being faced with the same sorts of choices and learning to make those choices by the rules of inquiry that govern physics, at ever more complex levels. "We begin," Bruner wrote in the most-quoted line from his book, "with the hypothesis that any subject can be taught effectively in some intellectually honest form to any child at any stage of development" (p. 13). Though the Woods Hole Conference began as a project in science teaching, it attempted to deal with the full range of human learning; Bruner carefully interspersed examples from the study of English in his final report. He talked explicitly of building "an ever more complex and mature understanding of the literature of tragedy," for example, and of "the great themes." Many of the later attempts to build an academic curriculum in English would try to implement Bruner's ideas.[27]

The Commission on English

The first major formulation of an academic curriculum in English was provided by the College Entrance Examination Board, which in the fall of 1959 appointed a Commission on English to "propose standards of achievement" and "to suggest ways of meeting them." The commission—which like the Basic Issues conferences was dominated by college teachers—was active over approximately a five-year period and set the tone of reform during the first half of the decade. With only sixteen members and two full-time executive staff, it was a small enough group to deliberate effectively; with James R. Squire from NCTE, George Winchester Stone from MLA, and the prestige of the College Board behind it, it was also destined to be heeded.

The fullest expression of the commission's point of view was its final report, *Freedom and Discipline in English* (1965). This indicated very little development since the Basic Issues conferences. The commission continued to use the tripod of language, literature, and composition as the basic image of the English curriculum, and though the legs of the tripod were weakened by attention to oral language activities, the discussions and recommendations in the final report were presented separately for each of the three original "legs." The discussion showed the same lack of clear structuring principles that had weakened the earlier conferences' attempt to outline a sequence for English, indeed bearing a striking though certainly unintentional resemblance to the earlier NCTE curriculum commission in its reliance upon a "consensus" curriculum.[28]

Given that the report was the work of sixteen people, the striking of some sort of consensus was probably inevitable. Still it stands in rather disturbing contrast to the emphasis on an intellectual and academic approach to English as a *discipline*—and thus presumably a study governed by more rigorous principles than consensus implied. The commission was in fact able to formulate language studies in somewhat more rigorous terms, but literature as a "liberal discipline" lacked an organizing theory. Here the commission proposed no more than reliance upon the teacher as a "professional"—that is, as one who had himself through long exposure come to "know" literature, and thus who, because of the depth and rigor of his training, would be able to select appropriate works and discuss them in appropriate ways. (Here lay one of the motives behind the choice of title: the teacher would be free to choose what to teach, but his choices would be governed by disciplined training.)

Though the commission was not able to deal with the problem of *what* to read, it had little doubt *how* that reading should be carried out. The New Critics were fully and uncompromisingly adopted in the commission's discussion, which included an outline of "fundamental questions the teacher must face as he prepares for class and then must teach his students to face as they study the work with him":

I. Questions about the text itself
  A. Questions of form
    1. What is its kind?
    2. What are its parts?
    3. How are the parts related?
  B. Questions of rhetoric
    1. Who is speaking?
    2. What is the occasion?
    3. Who is the audience?
  C. Questions about meaning
    1. What meaning has each word in its particular context?
    2. What do the diction and grammar of the text tell us about its purpose?
    3. What is the paraphrasable content of the work, its "statement"?
    4. What intention—high seriousness, irony, comedy, and the like—is apparent and how is it made apparent?
    5. What part of the meaning is sacrificed by paraphrase, by substitution of words other than those used by the author?
II. Questions of value
  A. Questions about personal response
  B. Questions of excellence (p. 58)

The majority of the questions hinge around close, analytic attention to the text; only one topic deals with personal response, and it shares the general heading of "Questions of value" with a second point, "Questions of excellence," which before the writings of the New Critics had rarely been seen in the school syllabus.

Because it had to place such a heavy emphasis on the professionalism and training of the individual teacher, the Commission on English devoted a considerable part of its endeavor to improving the training and working conditions of teachers of English. Of the fourteen specific recommendations in the first chapter of the report, for example, all but three dealt with certification requirements and teaching conditions; most were quite specific, urging that the teacher "be assigned no more than four classes a day" or that his preparation include as a minimum "one course in the psychology of learning" (p. 11).[29]

The commission's greatest success, however, came not from its recommendations in *Freedom and Discipline,* but from a series of institutes during the summer of 1962. The twenty institutes followed the model of Taba's human relations work and of similar institutes in other disciplines, providing 868 secondary school English teachers with a six- to eight-week program of graduate work in language, literature, and composition. The quality of the institutes was, as the commission itself noted, inevitably uneven, but they did succeed in involving a number of distinguished university faculty members directly in the problems of school curriculum, as well as in reinvigorating the teaching of many of the participants. The model set by the institutes was widely followed, with many of the original host institutions continuing the program on their own in later years, and others beginning them. Finally, the model they provided was taken up by the U.S. Office of Education when government funds became available three years later.[30]

Recognizing that the institutes could at best reach a small minority of practicing teachers, the commission found other ways to attempt to reeducate more substantial numbers. *Freedom and Discipline* was of course one such effort, and it was unusual as a curriculum statement in that well over a third of its pages were devoted to "Examples of Criticism" that would demonstrate directly how useful the suggested critical approach could be. A somewhat earlier report (1963) had taken much the same tack by providing a set of sample questions for end-of-year examinations in English, together with carefully graded student responses. Teachers were invited to focus attention on the questions as illustrations of "the skills and understandings" that ought to be required, and on the annotated compositions as a way to improve their own theme grading. Like all of the work of the commission, the questions and answers emphasized close analytical reading and writing. Finally, the commission prepared a series of kinescopes which were circulated free to interested schools and professional groups, illustrating "tested classroom procedures."[31]

Federal Support for English

The Struggle for Funds

The Commission on English began its efforts at a time when national curriculum reform had largely neglected English. (The commission was appointed just as the earlier College Board Commission on Mathematics was *completing* its work.) By the time its work was done, a massive infusion of federal funds was in the process of effecting reform on a broader basis than even the College Board could have managed. The funds did not begin spontaneously, however; they were the result of a vigorous and sustained effort by a number of national organizations.

Most of the battle involved the simple need for publicity. Though NCTE had had a Committee on Public Relations since immediately after the First World War, during the ensuing decades the major

Council efforts had been directed toward other members of the English teaching profession; very few of its publications were meant for the general public, or even for the rest of the educational community. Under J. N. Hook (appointed in 1952), the Council began to explore more direct means of generating publicity and improving the professional standing of the teacher of English.[32] One of the most obvious publicly-oriented programs was the Achievement Awards, begun in the 1958-59 academic year. This sought to identify outstanding high school English students, honoring both the student and his school with publicity in local papers and announcements to college admissions and scholarship offices. The Council also began a drive to increase the size of its membership, taking public stands on issues such as teaching load. It documented its position with studies which seemed to prove with scientific rigor that it was physically impossible for the English teacher adequately to teach the number of pupils he could ordinarily expect to be assigned.[33] Yet such activities were lost in the tide of national reaction to Sputnik, a point painfully demonstrated when Congress approved the National Defense Education Act of 1958 without including any funds for English. A dramatic presentation was clearly needed, and two years later it was offered by an NCTE Committee on National Interest chaired by Hook's successor as executive secretary, James R. Squire.[34] Produced in a record-breaking twelve months, *The National Interest and the Teaching of English* (1961) was a direct and shrewd presentation of the importance of English to the national welfare, coupled with a startling documentation of instructional inadequacies. The report made no attempt to discuss the sometimes subtle issues of concern to the profession; it was enough to define English as "language, literature, and composition" and to delineate the twin issues of articulation and teacher preparation as "so important and so large that they can be undertaken only by a nationally supported program."

The committee defended its assertions with a carefully prepared array of facts, some previously available and others gathered specifically for the report. The important position of English in high school programs was easy enough to demonstrate; over 90 percent of all pupils were enrolled in one or another English course, and graduation requirements in the majority of states demanded four years of study. At the same time the demand for teachers was outrunning supply by some 27 percent, with school populations expanding while the number of prospective English teachers graduating each year was holding at a level below that of the early fifties.[35]

How well were teachers being prepared to carry out the task set them? The committee's surveys found that between 40 and 60 percent of teachers in junior and senior high schools lacked even the minimum level of preparation required for a college major. Nearly half the college programs did not require a course in methods of teaching English; only one-fifth specified a course in contemporary literature or in literary criticism. One-fourth of all elementary school teachers—the first and perhaps most important teachers of English—were not even college graduates. Other sections of the report concentrated upon such crucial problems as workload, book supply, and the high cost of the remedial instruction which colleges were forced to provide. (The committee's estimate: $10,114,736.62 a year.)[36]

This first National Interest report generated widespread national attention; *Look* magazine for one commented approvingly and called it "a rallying cry for reform." It was distributed—together with a strategically brief overview—to all members of Congress and to other influential government figures. Still, Congress continued to resist placing English on an equal footing with the "defense" subjects of the earlier bill, though during 1961 it did open up some sources of funds for research and curriculum development in English under an amendment to another act.[37] Thus the Committee on National Interest was forced to continue its work, producing another major report, *The National Interest and the Continuing Education of Teachers of English*, in 1964.

This second National Interest report followed the same general format as the first, with data organized and presented to generate support for reform. While the first study had concentrated upon preservice training, the second emphasized continuing education; again the findings were startling. Only 50 percent of the English teachers surveyed in a national sampling had majored in English; a third had not majored in a subject even related to English. Over 45 percent were required to teach at least one other subject; one-fourth met 150 or more students each day. Only half the teachers felt comfortable with their own preparation to teach literature, a third with their preparation to teach composition, and 10 percent with their preparation to teach reading. Yet 30 percent had not taken a course in English in the last ten years; over half worked in school districts that required no evidence of professional growth in their subject area; most had never had the opportunity to confer about their programs with a college specialist in English or English education, with a trained local supervisor, or even with a fellow teacher. Only 800 English teachers a year were receiving any form of financial assistance for graduate study, whereas during 1962 the National Science Foundation alone had supported institutes for 40,800 teachers of science and mathematics, 90 percent of them from the elementary and secondary school. To combat these deficiencies, the Committee on National Interest again called for a massive program of federal aid, coupled with supporting activities at state and local levels.[38]

With strong support from the U.S. Office of Education, the Commission on English, the Modern Language Association, and other professional groups, the National Defense Education Act was finally broadened in October 1964 to provide funds for English and reading, as well as for many other previously excluded subject areas. In recognition of NCTE's long and active campaign for such legislation, both Squire and Council president Albert Kitzhaber were invited to witness the signing of the amended legislation into law. In one sense the ultimate expansion of federal support to other subjects—or its withdrawal from those already being funded—was probably inevitable. Education, even in a defense-minded Congress, could not long be defined primarily in terms of technology and science, and when the trauma of Sputnik began to recede in the national consciousness, the limited view of education implicit in the original NDEA was bound to be challenged. In the end the greatest benefit of the battle for federal funds was probably not the funds themselves but the spirit of professional unity which the fight itself produced. Teachers from school and college, specialists in education as well as the liberal arts, worked together toward a common goal in a way they had not done for many years; it produced at least within the national organizations a sense of profession and of the ability to bring about change that was sorely needed and that would help them maintain control over the massive influx of funds that would soon be forthcoming.[39]

The First Programs

In September 1961 Congress authorized the expansion of the Cooperative Research Program of 1954 to include limited funding of projects in English, thus initiating the flow of federal funds. A conference called by the USOE the following February outlined the scope of activities of the new program, which became known as Project English; J. N. Hook was named as first coordinator. The initial efforts followed closely the suggestions of the Basic Issues conferences and of the National Interest reports—Hook acknowledged both of them as shaping forces on his own thinking. Activities fell into three somewhat different categories: basic and applied research (over thirty projects were funded in the first year alone); curriculum study centers to produce new materials for classroom use; and conferences and professional meetings designed in general to increase professional involvement and in particular to outline needed areas of research to guide future funding. During its first year of operation, Project English expended some $400,000 of federal funds, and the figure grew spectacularly thereafter.[40]

Though a number of highly significant research studies were supported by Project English, none during the early years concerned themselves more than peripherally with literature. Composition, reading, and language skills were the primary focuses—partly because of congressional restriction, but more importantly because response to literature remained a difficult and intractable area of research.[41] The curriculum study centers, however, were a different matter. Virtually all gave at least passing attention to literature; many based their major efforts around it. The over two dozen centers that were eventually funded operated independently and with diverse emphases; there are certain generalizations, however, which can safely be made about most of them, with the realization that there were important exceptions.[42]

The majority of the centers epitomized the "academic" approach to curriculum construction outlined at the Basic Issues conferences and again in *Freedom and Discipline in English*. They were staffed with a combination of liberal arts and education specialists; subject matter rather than methodological concerns predominated. Most of the centers did not attempt to develop a radically new curriculum, instead elaborating established conceptions of English into fully developed curriculum structures. The main issues which each center had to confront were thus organization (or "focus") and sequence.

The question of the organization of the course of study was substituted at most centers for the first of the basic issues from the 1958 meetings: "What is English?" became in practice "What structure can best hold the legs of the tripod together?" As in the contemporaneous *Freedom and Discipline* report, language, literature, and composition were the major elements of the programs developed at most centers, though the interrelationships might be stressed in the "overview" and other dimensions of English studies given some passing attention. A few centers moved one or another of the studies to the center and treated the remaining "legs" as concentric, related studies, but whatever focus was chosen, the unvarying point of view was that such studies were carried on for their own sake, not for any presumed utilitarian values. Viewing the subject as a set of basic principles with their own inherent logic and sequence, it followed that the curriculum in English would have the same form and structure for all students. As G. Robert Carlsen put it in a review of some of the materials produced, the work of the centers reflected "The original meaning of the word *curriculum* as a race track having a single beginning point, a single course to run for all racers, and a single outcome."[43]

For answers to the problem of sequence, the centers turned preeminently to the work of Harvard psychologist Jerome Bruner and Canadian literary scholar Northrup Frye. Bruner's work offered both the pedagogical justification for building a curriculum around one or another conceptualization of English as a discipline, and an answer (in the "spiral curriculum") of how to address the questions of sequence. What Frye offered was the conceptualization of English needed to fit it into Bruner's mold: a series of basic structuring principles that could be discussed at increasingly complex levels. Frye's own attempt at a synoptic theory of criticism, outlined in most detail in *The Anatomy of Criticism* (1957), stressed an analysis of conventions and archetypes; in particular he presented a theory of "pre-generic modes" within which, he argued, all works of literature took their place. His four modes—Comedy, Romance, Tragedy, and Irony—were taken as important structuring elements by many of the curriculum study centers, often serving as umbrellas to justify thematic units. None of the centers heeded Frye's own suggestion that if our "immature scholarship" worked out its own "elementary teaching principles," the proper sequence would involve a shift in the center of gravity from one school of criticism to another as the child progresses. Frye postulated that the insights of the linguists would be most useful in creating kindergarten and first grade programs; the New Critics would dominate the upper high school and lower college years; and his own concern with myth and archetype would gravitate toward the junior high school grades.[44]

Frye recognized much more fully than those who turned to his writings for guidance that English lacked the kind of comprehensive theory required for an effective use of Bruner's principles, and that any attempt to base a curriculum on one of the less comprehensive bodies of theory that did exist would be too narrow for a kindergarten through college program. The curriculum study center at Florida State was one of the few that came to such a realization early in its work, abandoning Bruner as "too hazy"; most simply used the haziness to find support for their own particular positions, thus delaying till the late sixties serious attempts to redefine the structuring principles of the discipline.[45]

Anyone looking at the final products of the two dozen centers in the hope of finding in each a new conception of English would be disappointed; but such an expectation would be unfair as well as ill-founded. Federal funds were approved in September 1961; by April 1962 the first six centers had been funded; the rest followed quickly. All were conceived of as three- to five-year projects. Coming into existence so rapidly, the centers inevitably were established at universities where interest was already high and, often, where programs were already underway. What the new funds did in most centers was allow them to more thoroughly and more quickly develop curriculum models that had already been formulated. There was no time for the fundamental rethinking or even the basic research that might have generated radical change. Yet what the centers did accomplish was important enough—they produced the first sets of academically oriented material for the high school course, involving university professors of the liberal arts once again in the process of curriculum development in English.

The process of developing the courses of study was in the end probably more important than the materials themselves. A few centers—Nebraska was the prime example—planned their work as part of statewide curriculum revision, so that some programs functioned on a wider basis within circumscribed geographic areas. Still, many centers simply closed their offices at the completion of their work, filing the requisite reports with the U.S. Office of Education. Others offered their materials to commercial publishers, from whom they gradually became available. By the time they became available, however, the academic course in English was well established and the focus of professional concern was moving in other directions. The specific approaches developed by the various centers were no longer needed because the general point of view had already been assimilated by most teachers. (The two centers whose work was an exception to the general academic approach are discussed in the next chapter.)

Changing Programs

Literary Values and the Threat of Censorship

One of the major shifts brought about by the first wave of academic reform in English involved the basis for selecting materials. Literary values were to prevail over all other considerations, leading to the use of selections far more sophisticated than the usual high school fare. This in turn created new pressures for censorship of school materials.

Censorship in programs in literature usually focussed on one of two issues: political ideology or sex. The first became a problem during the late 1940s, when the first major gaps were opening up between the values of society and those of the progressive educators. The threat of communism, exaggerated by the tactics of Senator Joseph McCarthy and the House Committee on Un-American Activities, became the excuse for a widespread wave of restriction of instructional materials. Mark Van Doren, a Roman Catholic, found his books banned as communistic from the library of Jersey City Junior College; some NCTE members lost jobs in California for refusing to sign a loyalty oath; *Senior Scholastic* was banned from Birmingham, Alabama, *The Nation* from the schools of New York City; and the American Medical Association attacked the schools for having "conducted an active, aggressive campaign to indoctrinate their students . . . with the insidious and destructive tenets of the welfare state." Such pressure prompted reactions from many professional teaching organizations; NCTE went on record as early as its 1948 convention with a resolution urging that "the principles found in the Constitution of the United States should be *completely* practiced in every classroom in America." It set up its first committee on censorship at the same meeting.[46]

As the wording of the 1948 resolution suggested, initial reactions to censorship relied simply on the extra-professional considerations of the constitutionally protected freedom to dissent. This was because until the late fifties and early sixties, English teachers used very little that could be found objectionable. When they did, they were rebuffed by their seniors in the teaching profession before the public had much chance to object. As late as 1936 a student of Charles Swain Thomas at Harvard offered an article on literature and sex in which he urged the teaching of such "advanced" novels as *The Scarlet Letter* and *Women in Love,* only to meet a stiff wave of rebuttal from professional leaders across the nation.[47] And even the 1956 report of the NCTE Commission on the English Curriculum carried a cautious note about book selection, urging teachers to avoid works that might disturb youthful minds.[48] Elbert Lenrow's arguments in *The Reader's Guide to Prose Fiction* some fifteen years before had obviously made little impression.

Attitudes did change, however, stimulated in part by the landmark 1933 Supreme Court decision in the *Ulysses* case, the rising sales of "pocket" books with their often explicit stories, and the stream of "frank" war novels that emerged from World War II. As the New Critics became the acknowledged literary authorities, and as the writers of the early twentieth century gained too much age and respectability to be ignored, professional leaders began to urge the inclusion of more and more works that could be expected to provoke unhappy reactions from some elements of the community. Teachers as insecure in their own professional preparation as those surveyed by the Committee on National Interest were hardly prepared to resist the direct personal attack which often followed; the first reaction of many teachers and librarians was simply to remove a challenged book as quickly as possible.

Yet capitulation to the censors could only go so far, and some dedicated teachers resisted the pressures from the beginning— though they sometimes lost the battle anyway. A 1963 survey of the schools of Wisconsin found that the list of censored books—with a few exceptions—"would make a relatively good [reading list] to recommend to high school juniors and seniors." Specific titles brought under attack during a two-and-a-half-year period included the Bible, *The Canterbury Tales, The Catcher in the Rye, A Dictionary of American Slang, Fail-Safe,* and *A Tree Grows in Brooklyn*—seventy-eight titles in all from 606 returned questionnaires. During the same period, seventeen magazines were the subject of censorship attacks, and in eight cases—including *Life* and *The Atlantic Monthly*—the magazines were removed from circulation.[49]

Such pressures led the professional organizations most directly involved (in particular the NCTE and the American Library Association) to take steps to protect and educate their members. In addition to a continuing series of resolutions on freedom-to-teach and freedom-to-read, NCTE committees prepared a number of more extensive discussions, including procedures for English departments to follow to guard against such attacks, case studies of specific incidents, and lengthy discussions of the values of some of the particularly vulnerable works.[50] Defenses against censorship during the sixties still cited the issues of liberty and freedom of thought that had marked the first reaction, but two new arguments were added out of the changing professional orientation. One focussed on literary values and principles of criticism, the other on the professional nature of the judgment of whether a book should or should not be used with a given child at a given time.

The literary arguments were based on the importance of context in evaluating any given phrase or incident; according to the New Critics, a literary work was an entity unto itself, one that could not be legitimately fragmented nor its pieces individually examined. Thus Holden might visit a prostitute in *The Catcher in the Rye,* but the incident was moral rather than immoral because of the part it played in the total meaning of the work. A second part of the literary argument focussed upon the place of each work within the literary tradition. Thus the NCTE Committee on the Right to Read could protest indignantly that

> Because of outside pressures many English teachers cannot carry out their central responsibility: teaching the cultural heritage of Western civilization. Hawthorne, Thoreau, Whitman, Twain, Hemingway, Faulkner, to take just a few American examples, either are omitted completely or are inadequately represented in the high school curriculum ("The Students' Right to Read," p. 10).

The decisions on whether or not a book was a legitimate part of the cultural heritage and whether objectionable elements were indeed redeemed by context were ultimately professional decisions. Confidence in the teaching profession would have to be quite high to accept Wayne Booth's argument, for example, that "The skill required to decide whether a work is suited for a particular teaching moment is so great that only the gifted teacher, with his knowledge of how his teaching aims relate to materials chosen for students at a given stage of development, can be trusted to exercise it."[51]

Creating just such trust in the professional competence of the teacher of English was a major goal of the period of academic reform, but the pressures of the late 1960s and early 1970s insured that censorship remained a continuing professional concern. Increasing student unrest, with a concomitant assertion of student rights, liberal treatment of controversial political and sexual topics in books and popular media, and the continuing agitation for the rights of minority groups made it inevitable that the selections by teachers who wished to remain topical and current would risk offending one or another segment of the community. Claude Brown's *Manchild in the Promised Land* as well as Joan Baez's *Daybreak* have been among recent targets. Some of the most effective censorship in fact comes from within the school. The Wisconsin survey found that a high proportion of the incidents were initiated by fellow teachers, librarians, or supervisors. And even a 1969 *English Journal* article written in mild "jive" provoked a number of angry letters. Whether because they wish to protect the school from any possibility of public pressure, or because they personally object to certain political or moral viewpoints, people inside the school as well as from the community at large seem destined to continue their efforts at censorship.[52]

Other Materials

The academic approach of the early sixties also led to a redefinition of what could legitimately be considered to be literature in the first place. Lynch and Evans were not alone in their outrage at the travesties (as they saw them) committed in the name of "life adjustment." Both the adolescent novel and the anthology had come under attack by the end of the 1950s. The common objection was that these books, in attempting to serve nonliterary goals, had abandoned literature altogether; they lacked the "flesh and blood" of the classic, as Stanley Kegler put it in discussing the related genre of "simplified" works. In place of anthologies, most authors urged a curriculum based around the increasingly popular paperback books.[53]

The revival of interest in paperbacks dated to the "quarter books" of the early forties, but during the fifties and sixties their popularity among teachers rose sharply. One reason was the founding of a series of book clubs like the Weekly Reader Children's Book Club (which began in 1953) and the Teen Age Book Club, which by the 1956-57 academic year could boast sales of six million volumes. The availability of standard literary selections in paperback editions made them a natural resource for the academically oriented teacher, with a corresponding shift in emphasis from their value in outside reading to their use in the program for direct class study.[54]

Finally, the emphasis on literature as a matter of form and technique led to a redefinition of the role of the "public arts" (as they came to be called). Throughout the period of "life adjustment," studies of radio, movies, television, and journalism had followed more or less the lines of the rest of the curriculum in literature and reading. Units were offered that were to help "develop maturity," meeting the needs of youth exactly as would the units of more standard selections. Other teachers, responding to the skill emphases, would attempt to "raise standards of taste," to make students "better" or "more intelligent" consumers of the products of the popular media. Soap operas and pinup girls simply had to be suppressed.[55]

Gradually, however, as the emphasis in the teaching of standard literature shifted, so did that with the public arts. The film in particular began to be presented as a legitimate discipline, with its own rules and conventions quite distinct from other art forms. As one author protested, to apply strictly literary modes of analysis to motion pictures was like talking about the "musical qualities of a statue."[56] Though Max Herzberg and a few others had presented such arguments many years before, it was only as the academic emphases began to be apparent in other areas of the English curriculum that the study of film, radio, television, or journalism began to emerge as important in its own right.

One of the strongest proponents of the academic view of popular culture was Patrick Hazard. Radio-TV editor of *Scholastic Teacher* and a teacher himself, he initiated a column, "The Public Arts," in *English Journal* in 1956. This presented trenchant critiques of current programing, bibliographies of materials for teachers, and, always, an emphasis on the artistic successes and shortcomings of the several media. His columns kept the media firmly in perspective; at the same time, he urged their fuller consideration by teachers of English. By the mid-1960s NCTE could point to a series of publications dealing with most aspects of popular culture, each treating its subject as a legitimate field of study rather than simply as one of the utilitarian chores that English teachers had ever been willing to shoulder.[57]

The Humanities Course

Most of the changes discussed so far were the result of the work of academic scholars, with assistance from teachers only to the extent that the teachers were convinced of the value of the academic point of view. A second and quite different "academic" tradition was more directly related to the teacher's as opposed to the scholar's view. This was the so-called "humanities course."

In general, these courses emerged out of a much earlier concern with world literature as part of the "total heritage" of the American student; in the earliest forms it reflected the desire to build the friendship with which the early NCTE committee on international relations had been concerned. In 1926 the Lincoln School at Teachers College, Columbia University, introduced a world literature course that can be seen as a forerunner of present programs; in 1931 the English committee of the North Central Association recommended the teaching of some literature from other countries. Interest remained low, however, till the concern with human relations during the forties and fifties led to the introduction of such courses in a number of schools. Often, the evolution of the course of study

was strongly influenced by Mortimer Adler and the "liberal education" critics, in whose lists of Great Books translations of classical
texts figured prominently. Throughout the fifties an early form of
humanities class as world literature held its own in the schools;
Jewett reported it in 20 percent of the programs he surveyed.[58]

Two forces assisted in transforming these courses into their
present form, and in popularizing the label "humanities" in place of
the earlier course titles. One was the John Hay Fellows program,
after 1958 under the directorship of Charles Keller, chairman of the
History Department at Williams College. (Keller had also directed
the Advanced Placement program during its first two years under
College Board auspices.) The John Hay program, which provided
year-long fellowships for a carefully selected group of high school
teachers to continue their studies, produced a high proportion of
the teachers who popularized the humanities approach, experimenting with it in their classes and discussing the results in journals and
at professional meetings. The second force was the Council for a
Television Course in the Humanities for Secondary Schools, formed
in 1957 by a group of teachers from the Boston area. With Floyd
Rinker as executive director, and with funds from the Ford Fund
for the Advancement of Education, the group enlisted the aid of an
impressive series of scholars and performers to prepare a series of
television programs on the humanities. The programs that resulted
were widely distributed by Encyclopaedia Britannica Films, becoming in this form rather than their televised versions the core of many
new programs.[59]

There was little uniformity in the outward shape of the humanities programs of the sixties. Like the correlated and fused courses
that preceded them, some were organized chronologically, some
around "cultural epochs," others around themes, "Great Works,"
or—in a newer development—around elements of artistic form (with
an emphasis on a variety of media). In spite of this variety, most of
the programs had roots in the ethical tradition of English study—
with a "social conscience" rather than "scholastic competence" was
one way Keller phrased it. Almost inevitably the programs were
interdisciplinary, often involving a "team" of teachers from several
subject areas, in particular from English and the social studies.[60]
Both of these aspects have deep roots in earlier progressive programs, a parallel that has been noted by some critics.

The chief difference from the earlier programs—and it is an
important one—was the level at which the humanities courses were
pitched. Though virtually all of its proponents talked of the importance of such studies for all students, the practitioners (with a few
vocal exceptions) directed them at the college-bound classes—a
trend readily explicable by a look at the proposed content. Though
the length and organization of the list varies greatly, the titles
included would usually be quite secure on any list of "Great

Books"; sometimes it was from exactly such lists that they were originally chosen. Emphasis, as in all other parts of the academic reform, was on subject matter first, with virtually no attention to the characteristics of the student. (Such characteristics were of course being given a kind of backhanded acknowledgement by limiting the course to advanced students, usually college-bound seniors.) On the other hand, the academic emphasis insured that the courses remained very much within the humanistic tradition; they were as a whole less subject to the practices of *using* the art forms studied as vehicles for historical or sociological studies. (Whether the history teachers found their conception of historical studies being subverted is another and quite different matter.)[61]

Almost all humanities courses have relied on paperback books as the core of materials for study; there were no humanities anthologies. Very often (again on the college model) students were asked to purchase their own paperbacks, filling them with notes and marginal comments as they wished. A high proportion of the schools involved also used the humanities sequence as a means to introduce film studies into the curriculum, a trend more evident in those courses that focussed around themes or elements of art than those that chose some version of the chronological or cultural-epoch approach.

The dangers in the humanities course were exactly those of the integrated curricula of the thirties and forties: superficial coverage, "intellectual indigestion," neglect of important skills, and a broadening of the course beyond the competence of the teacher. Criticism on all these grounds was leveled against one or another of the humanities courses of the sixties, together with new charges that they used works too difficult for the high school student to discuss meaningfully—that many, indeed, provided little time for *any* discussion. Both charges were at least indirectly the result of the extent to which the humanities course took college programs as a model, offering the same works for study and using the same lecture mode of presentation. The latter trend was fostered by the enthusiasm for large group instruction and team teaching as a way to meet the multidisciplinary demands of most humanities courses; the simplest way to insure adequate treatment of history, for example, was to ask a history teacher to lecture all the students about the particular topic under study. (And similarly for art, music, religion, philosophy, or whatever.) Though such lectures were an interesting reinforcement of the image of teacher-as-scholar, some critics have questioned whether they serve any other useful function.[62]

The National Study of High School English Programs

The ferment of the early 1960s also led to the National Study of High School English Programs, directed by James R. Squire and

Roger K. Applebee. This study was designed to be an examination-in-depth of 158 schools selected because of their outstanding programs in English; the usual questionnaire data was followed up with extensive classroom observation, interviews with staff, and talks with students. Teams of observers from the University of Illinois were trained for the visits, which usually lasted two days and included observations of as many as twenty classes at a single school. School visits for the study proper were spread over two and a half years: the academic years 1963-64, 1964-65, and the first half of 1965-66. Initially designed as a means to "ascertain the ways in which stronger schools are already achieving important results in English," the study in the end became an extensive record of the initial stages of the academic approach to the teaching of English.[63]

To summarize the complex and detailed findings of the project as briefly as possible, teachers in the outstanding schools were professionally oriented. Some 72 percent had a major in English (the figure rises to 82 percent if related fields such as speech and drama are included); another 19 percent had minored in the field. Fully half had master's degrees. Compared with those in the slightly earlier National Interest surveys, the staff in the project schools were more likely to belong to professional organizations, more likely to subscribe to *English Journal*, and more likely to be provided opportunities and incentives for continuing education. Fully 20 percent of the teachers received *locally* sponsored aid to continue their studies. The organization and supervision of the English department as a whole also had a strong influence on resulting programs, so much so that the project staff called two special conferences on the role of the department chairman and published the ensuing recommendations in a separate report.[64]

The classroom visitation yielded a number of results which startled the project staff. One was the finding that an average of 52 percent of actual class time was devoted to the study of literature—rather disturbing in the age of the tripod but quite in line with the previous history of the subject. In general, literature received slightly less attention in the early years of high school, and considerably less in courses for terminal as opposed to academic students, but even with these students over 40 percent of the time observed was devoted to literature. In the traditionally more academic private schools the figure reached 83 percent. The lack of attention to other aspects of English was especially disturbing to project observers, because they found little real effort to relate the various aspects of English studies one to another.

As Dora V. Smith had found in her far less extensive visitations during the thirties and early forties, classes were overwhelmingly teacher-dominated. Though teachers professed to emphasize discussion, observations of more than 1,600 classes showed that recitation and lecture dominated; discussion and Socratic questioning together accounted for only 23 percent of class time observed. Observers also found virtually no evidence of group work or the use of audiovisual aids. A slight increase in discussion was evident between the tenth and twelfth grades, paralleling an increase in attention to literature and a shift away from formal studies of grammar and usage; classes for terminal students, however, showed higher percentages of recitation, lecture, and silent work, with corresponding decreases in discussion or other student activities. Such findings, though the staff of the National Study found them distressing, were fully in accord with the academic model for English instruction, with its glorification of the college classroom and lack of interest in most aspects of progressive methodology.

The course in literature directly reflected the academic emphases of the years immediately preceding the study. Though use of the single anthology was still the most frequently observed practice, anthologies were liberally augmented by supplementary texts, especially paperbacks. Over 50 percent of the teachers rated close textual study as of "great importance" in the teaching of literature, though observers were distressed to find that many teachers were having difficulty translating these beliefs into successful practice. The specific selections chosen for study were in general more distinctly literary than during the "life adjustment" period, but the effects of censorship—real or only threatened—were very evident; as one result, observers found evidence of a deliberate de-emphasis of major twentieth century works. Using a checklist of fifty titles that had been reported as significant high school reading experiences by gifted college students, augmented by a few others whose appropriateness had been questioned, observers used card catalogs to check whether or not they were available in 84 of the school libraries. Only two—*The Scarlet Letter* and *A Tale of Two Cities*—were available in all of the schools. *Exodus* was available in only 83 percent; *The Grapes of Wrath* and *The Ugly American* in 75 percent; *The Once and Future King* in 65 percent; and *The Sound and the Fury, A Portrait of the Artist as a Young Man, Franny and Zooey,* and *The Stranger* in less than half. Though it had been expected, the preponderance of modern fiction among the books of limited availability was nonetheless disturbing. In one of the more memorable collections an observer found six biographies of William Faulkner but not one of his works! In large part because of such limitations, nearly three-fourths of the students found the school library inadequate for their reading needs, turning instead to the public library or paperbacks.

The National Study, designed to discover the strengths of ongoing programs, also highlighted their weaknesses; foremost among these were the provisions for terminal students. Whatever criterion was chosen, the lower tracks were being shortchanged in these academically oriented schools. The teachers assigned to the slow sections were often among the least adequate in the department; the materials were of lower quality; the teaching techniques less varied; the amount of time spent on worksheets and seat-work greater. The extent of the neglect of the lower tracks, though again a natural result of the emphases of the preceding years, became clear during the course of the study in a way that had not yet really surfaced in the professional literature. Though 86 percent of the schools used one or another form of tracking which affected the composition of classes in English, very few had even begun to face the problem of what to do with their lower tracks.[65]

In general, then, the National Study of High School English Programs suggested little in the way of radical change in professional orientation, though it did make clear the need to direct attention to instruction in the lower tracks. The image of the better programs that emerged from the study was the image which the NCTE and other groups had been offering since the Basic Issues conferences in 1958: well-prepared teachers confident in their subject matter; a solid departmental organization giving scope and direction to the program as a whole; generous supplies of books and materials; reasonable teaching loads. Indeed, after expanding the study to a number of schools which had been attracting national attention for their experimental programs, the study staff felt it necessary to include a "Cautionary Note" that warned that much of what they had seen was mere administrative innovation. Though occasional programs seemed to offer the germ of an idea that would lead to useful change, the challenge to the academic ideal of the English program was not destined to develop from within these ongoing efforts.

High Points and Low Points

As has been hinted several times in the course of this chapter, the major accomplishment of the period during which the English course was remolded on the academic model was the sense of profession generated among teachers at all levels. The battle for federal funds, the attempt to provide an academic curriculum through the work of the various curriculum study centers, the summers of study in the CEEB and NDEA institutes, the renewed cooperation between NCTE and MLA—all contributed to the sense that teachers of English at all levels shared common problems.

Concurrent with the new sense of profession was a new stress by NCTE on upgrading professional standards.[66] Some of these activities have already been mentioned in the discussion of the struggle for federal funds. Others included statements on the workload of the college teacher (1966) and of the elementary teacher (1967); an

Honor Roll for schools reducing the workload of the secondary school teacher was established in 1962. Preservice training was also of concern. Agitation for improvements in state certification requirements began during the 1950s under the prompting of Eugene Slaughter, Robert Tuttle, and others, and was carried forward in the much-delayed fifth volume of the Commission on the English Curriculum series, *The Education of Teachers of English for American Schools and Colleges* (1963). This in turn was a major reference point for an English Teacher Preparation Study begun in 1965 under the joint sponsorship of NCTE, MLA, and the National Association of State Directors of Teacher Education and Certification. Before they were published in 1967, the resulting guidelines went through some twenty drafts and extensive discussions at local, regional and national levels.[67]

All of these activities contributed to the teacher's sense of self-esteem, and with it his confidence in his own competence to effect change. Here the developments in English paralleled a growing militancy within the teaching profession as a whole, highlighted most sharply by the numerous and unprecedented teachers' strikes which closed schools in many of the nation's cities. Such improvement in the caliber of the profession was desperately needed; certainly the lack of it contributed to the failure of the progressive framework for English during the 1940s. It seems likely that the teacher of English in the years to come will remain a well-trained professional, since recent changes have been institutionalized through the system of state certification requirements.

The durability and importance of the academic model for English instruction is more in doubt. In their disgust with the excesses of "life adjustment" and the isolation of the "educationists" from the rest of the academic community, the academic reformers ignored some important lessons that the progressives could have taught them. The programs that emerged were developed with little reference to the characteristics of the student or to the important issues of interest and relevance, about all of which the progressives had learned so much. As will be clear in the next chapter, the attempt to provide programs that would be viable for nonacademic students eventually posed basic questions about the curriculum for the academically talented too.

The other major lesson which the progressives could have taught the academic reformers was the need for careful and scientific evaluation of results. Subjective impressions of teachers involved in curriculum reform are almost inevitably highly positive; the excitement and stimulation inherent in the process of change itself insured that the programs of the curriculum study centers would be successful at at least this basic level. Unfortunately (and again with a few exceptions) any evaluation beyond this simplest level was ignored by most of the centers; the kind of careful documentation of long-term results that had marked the Eight-Year Study was simply beyond the ken of most of the staff involved in these efforts. The result was a mountain of essentially untested materials which no one really knew what to do with. Very few of the centers admitted to any failures, but very few carried on the kind of studies that would have told them if they had failed.[68] With federal support turning in other directions, and with leaders of the profession once again beginning to recognize the importance of the student in the educational process, it is highly unlikely that there will be any major effort to evaluate these curricula now.

It is because of these failures that the attempt to upgrade professional standards looms so large. The period of academic reform produced no curriculum materials comparable to the PSSC physics course or the UICSM math curriculum; the shape of English continues to be very much a private thing, governed by the extent to which the individual teacher responds to changing emphases in the professional journals and among his colleagues. To the extent that his professional competence and self-assurance have been strengthened, the curriculum will continue to develop at a fairly rapid rate; to the extent that the teacher remains unsure of his own professional skills, he will probably continue to cling to those methods and materials with which he is most familiar, leaving professional leaders to protest as in the past at the slow and difficult pace of change.

CHAPTER VII NOTES

1. Mortimer Adler, *How to Read a Book: The Art of Getting a Liberal Education* (New York: Simon & Schuster, 1940), p. 82.

2. Arthur E. Bestor, *Educational Wastelands* (Urbana, Ill.: University of Illinois Press, 1953), p. 11.

3. Committee on National Interest, *The National Interest and the Teaching of English: A Report on the Status of the Profession* (Urbana, Ill.: NCTE, 1961), p. 26.

4. Northrup Frye, "Elementary Teaching and Elemental Scholarship," *PMLA* 79 (May 1964): 11-18.

5. Nebraska Curriculum Development Center, *Introduction to the Elementary Program: K-6* (Lincoln: University of Nebraska, 1965).

6. Though a Great Books course was conducted by the University of Chicago extension, it was St. Johns College which came closest to embodying Hutchins's ideas in a full-scale course. The concept of Great Books is even older than this, however. See Father W. Farrar, *Great Books* (Crowell, 1898). On the courses at St. Johns and Chicago, see Daniel Bell, *The Reforming of General Education* (New York: Columbia University Press, 1966), pp. 13-26.

7. Adler, *How to Read a Book*, pp. vi-ix.

8. Mark Van Doren, *Liberal Education* (New York: Henry Holt and Co., 1943), p. 92.

9. The earlier committee specifically criticized *An Experience Curriculum, A Correlated Curriculum,* and *Conducting Experiences in English.* Joint Committee of the Faculty of Harvard College and of the Graduate School of Education, *The Training of Secondary School Teachers Especially with Reference to English* (Cambridge: Harvard University Press, 1942); *General Education in a Free Society,* Report of the Harvard Committee (Cambridge: Harvard University Press, 1945).

10. The committee on the training of teachers acknowledged its indebtedness to an earlier report from the School and College Conference on English, much of which it simply paraphrased (p. 90). School and College Conference on English, *Report of the Literature Committee,* April 1942; reprinted in *Issues, Problems, and Approaches in the Teaching of English,* ed. George Winchester Stone, Jr. (New York: Holt, Rinehart and Winston, 1964; Modern Language Association, 1961).

11. These critics provoked little reaction from secondary school teachers. Hatfield reviewed Van Doren's book when it appeared, without seeing any need to counter the arguments: W. Wilbur Hatfield, "The Debate on Liberal Education," *English Journal* 33:3 (March 1944), 167-68. A brief discussion and longer bibliography on the early criticism of progressivism is given by Lawrence A. Cremin in *The Transformation of the School: Progressivism in American Education, 1876-1957* (New York: Vintage Books, 1961), p. 325.

12. The Lynch and Evans study of English textbooks discussed in the previous chapter was among the critiques produced by this group. See Cremin, *Transformation of the School,* pp. 339-46. C. Winifred Scott and Clyde M. Hill have gathered a representative collection of the criticism and response through 1952 in *Public Education Under Criticism* (New York: Prentice-Hall, 1954).

13. Arthur E. Bestor's critique, *Educational Wastelands*, was one of the most comprehensive indictments of the "educationists." See the quote at the beginning of this chapter.

14. Sputnik was only a symbol, however; by 1957 the reform movement was already well underway. (See "English as a Discipline," later in this chapter.)

15. H. G. Rickover, *Education and Freedom* (New York: E. P. Dutton & Co., 1959), p. 15.

16. Though the profession welcomed his support for English, there was less enthusiasm for his recommendation that composition should occupy "half the time devoted to English, with an average of one theme a week." This was counter to the emphasis on the "tripod" of language, literature, and composition. James B. Conant, *The American High School Today: A First Report to Interested Citizens* (New York: Signet Books, 1964; first edition, McGraw Hill Book Co., 1959), p. 99.

17. By May 1958 there were 355 participating schools; English was the most popular subject. Similar programs developed on a state level in some areas, notably in Connecticut. The Connecticut program, proposed by the Association of Connecticut Secondary School Principals and accepted by the University Senate in 1955, involved a college-prescribed syllabus and university approval of the teachers. Daniel Bell, *Reforming of General Education* (New York: Columbia University Press, 1966), pp. 125-28; John R. Valley, "College Actions on CEEB Advanced Placement Examination Candidates," *English Journal* 48:7 (October 1959): 398-401; Helen J. Estes, "College Level English in High School," *English Journal* 48:6 (September 1959): 332-34.

18. This broader effect on the curriculum has often been recognized. See, for example, Edwin H. Sauer, "Programs for the Academically Talented in English: What Are the Gains?" *English Journal* 49:1 (January 1960): 10-15. From the late fifties till the mid-sixties, a high proportion of the new programs described in *English Journal* were directly or indirectly noted to have begun in advanced placement or college-preparatory classes.

19. Arno Jewett, "The Underprivileged in Language Arts," *English Journal* 42:3 (March 1953) 131-37. Jewett was, like Dwight Burton, a student of Dora V. Smith, but he developed her ideas in quite a different direction. For a much earlier honors program introduced in Scarsdale, New York, "to give a small group of intellectual higher-ups the opportunities they had hitherto been denied in our sometimes too democratic schools," see Lucyle Hook, "English Honors," *English Journal* 29:1 (January 1940): 10-13.

20. Arno Jewett, chairman, *English for the Academically Talented Student*, Report of the Committee on English Programs for High School Students of Superior Ability of the NCTE (Washington, D. C.: National Education Association, 1960). See also "The Talented Pupil: A Special Report," *English Journal* 47:6 (September 1958): 368-71+.

21. By the 1964-65 academic year, 1,350,000 students were using the SMSG math program alone. Bell, *Reforming of General Education*, pp. 114 ff.

22. Edward J. Gordon and Edward S. Noyes, *Essays on the Teaching of English: Reports of the Yale Conferences on the Teaching of English* (New York: Appleton-Century-Crofts, 1960).

23. The Basic Issues conferences have been widely heralded as the first recognition by professional leaders of the need to reformulate the curriculum. Shugrue dates his "decade of change" from the conferences. Of the twenty-eight teachers, only three were from high schools. The reports were published in the journals of the cooperating organizations, widely distributed in leaflet form, and reprinted in George Winchester Stone, Jr.'s *Issues, Problems and Approaches in the Teaching of English*. Michael F. Shugrue, *English in a Decade of Change* (New York: Pegasus, 1968).

24. This is virtually a paraphrase of the discussion of the fourth "basic issue," "What approaches to a literary work are possible and profitable at the various educational levels?"

25. "The Basic Issues in the Teaching of English," in Stone, *Issues, Problems and Approaches*.

26. Stone, *Issues, Problems, and Approaches*, pp. 235-38.

27. Jerome S. Bruner, *The Process of Education* (New York: Vintage Books, 1960; first edition, Harvard University Press, 1960). Teachers of English quickly realized the implications of Bruner's arguments. Ruth G. Strickland, writing as NCTE past president, asserted that the report "is as applicable to our teaching of English as it is to the teaching of science and mathematics." ("Counciletter," *English Journal* 50:4 [April 1961]: 287-88.)

28. The discussion of "Literature" began with a section titled "A Curriculum Arrived at by Consensus" (pp. 42 ff.). Only three of the sixteen members were high school teachers. Commission on English, *Freedom and Discipline in English* (New York: College Entrance Examination Board, 1965).

29. Commissioner of Education Francis Keppel credited the work of the commission with improving certification requirements in over half of the states as early as 1963, two years before the final report was published. Francis Keppel, "Who Is to Speak for English?" *PMLA* 79 (May 1964): 7-10.

30. The use of the three legs of the tripod to structure the institute course of study is one of the more direct bits of evidence of how thoroughly the commission accepted the tripod metaphor for English studies. See Commission on English, *Freedom and Discipline*, p. 14; and John C. Gerber, "The 1962 Summer Institutes of the Commission on English: Their Achievement and Promise," *PMLA* 78 (September 1963): 9-25. Gerber was chairman of the committee of twelve evaluators commissioned by the USOE.

31. Shugrue, in *English in a Decade of Change*, p. 174, commented, "The enthusiasm of the lecturers and the quality of their commentary on literature, language, and rhetoric almost redeem the painful inadequacies of the camera work and editing." The kinescopes were low-budget productions, and showed it. See also *Freedom and Discipline*, p. 162; and Commission on English, *End-of-Year Examinations in English for College-Bound Students Grades* 9-12 (Princeton: College Entrance Examination Board, 1963).

32. Hook succeeded Hatfield on October 1, 1953, giving the Council the kind of full-time leadership that Walter Barnes had urged as early as 1933. In a sense Hook's appointment marked the beginning of the Council's attempt to regain control of curriculum development in English. See "Report and Summary," *English Journal* 42:9 (December 1953): 514-16;

and J. N. Hook, "The National Council Looks Ahead," *English Journal* 44:1 (January 1955): 1-9.
33. NCTE passed a resolution on the workload of the secondary school teacher in 1957, the first since the reorganization period. A study by William J. Dusel, sponsored by the California Council of Teachers of English, was widely quoted and distributed. It paralleled the Hopkins report, also distributed by NCTE but not originating in it. William J. Dusel, "Determining an Efficient Teaching Load in English," *Illinois English Bulletin* 43 (October 1955): 1-19; and E. M. Hopkins, *Report on the Cost and Labor of English Teaching* (For MLA and NCTE. Lawrence: Journalism Press, University of Kansas, 1913).
34. Squire succeeded Hook on September 1, 1960, after spending a year as associate executive secretary. Squire provided NCTE with a dynamic and personal leadership through a period of change as significant and rapid as the first years under Hosic.
35. Committee on National Interest, *National Interest and the Teaching of English*, pp. 3, 18-21.
36. Given the general tenor of the report, one must suspect that the decimal point was used to make the number look larger, rather than for the scientific precision of the estimate.
37. The book was reprinted in full in the volume of congressional testimony on the extension of the NDEA. The Senate, in fact, included English in the revised bill, but this was deleted in the House. The funds made available came under the Cooperative Research Act of 1954. James R. Squire, "Counciletter," *English Journal* 50:6 (September 1961): 434-37; Harold B. Allen, "Counciletter," *English Journal* 50:8 (November 1961): 572-75; and J. N. Hook, "Project English: The First Year," *PMLA* 78 (September 1963): 33-35.
38. The activities suggested parallel the earlier MLA Foreign Language Program. Committee on National Interest, *The National Interest and the Continuing Education of Teachers of English: A Report on the State of the Profession, 1964* (Urbana, Ill.: NCTE, 1964). See especially pp. 16-27, 49-50, 66-69.
39. Squire commented on this aspect of the activity of these years in his final report as executive secretary, paying tribute as he did so to the efforts of John H. Fisher, his counterpart at MLA. James R. Squire, *Eight Year Report of the Executive Secretary 1960-67* (Champaign, Ill.: NCTE, 1967).
40. Project English was shaped by the leaders of MLA, NCTE, and related organizations through extensive informal contacts with USOE personnel after the enabling legislation had been passed. These contacts were formalized through the February conference.
Of the conferences, one of the most important was held at Allerton House at the University of Illinois in December 1962. It resulted in the founding of the Association of Departments of English, to which more than half of the English departments in the U.S. belong. The department chairmen present at Allerton declared their "willingness to share in the responsibility for the teaching of English," and many changes in programs at their respective colleges followed. On all these developments, see Shugrue, *English in a Decade of Change*, pp. 39 ff.; Hook, "Project English: The First Year"; James R. Squire, "English at the Crossroads: The *National Interest* Report Plus Eighteen," *English Journal* 51:6 (Sep-

tember 1962): 381-92; Ralph Flynt, "The U.S. Office of Education Looks at Project English," *PMLA* 78:6 (September 1963): 30-32; Robert W. Rogers, "Articulating High School and College Teaching of English," *English Journal* 54:5 (May 1965): 370-74 +.

41. The congressional appropriation implied primary concern with reading, composition, and other English skills, but the announcement of the program made clear that the USOE would "respect the unity of the discipline in selecting proposals to support." "Project English: An Announcement from the Office of Education," *English Journal* 51:2 (February 1962): 149-52. See Shugrue, *English in a Decade of Change*, pp. 41 ff., for a summary of important projects in other aspects of English instruction.

42. Two of the most important exceptions were the centers at Hunter College and at the University of Michigan. Both belong to the second wave of reform rather than to the initial academic emphasis and will be discussed in the next chapter.

43. On the work of the centers, see in particular Shugrue, *English in a Decade of Change*, pp. 50 ff.; and G. Robert Carlsen and James Crow, "Project English Curriculum Centers," *English Journal* 56:7 (October 1967): 986-93. Status reports prepared by the directors of each center were widely distributed: Erwin R. Steinberg, "Research on the Teaching of English," *PMLA* 79 (September 1964): 50-76; Michael F. Shugrue, "New Materials for the Teaching of English from the English Program of the USOE," *PMLA* 81 (September 1966): 1-36; and Robert Bennett, ed., *Summary Progress Report of English Curriculum Study and Demonstration Centers* (Champaign, Ill.: NCTE, 1966).

44. Northrup Frye, *Anatomy of Criticism: Four Essays* (New York: Atheneum, 1967; first edition, Princeton University Press, 1957); and Frye, "Elementary Teaching and Elemental Scholarship."

45. As they finished their work, some of the other centers arrived at the same conclusion. As Stoddard Malarkey of the Oregon center described it in a 1966 address, "Agreement as to what constitutes the 'great and simple structuring ideas' of literature seems impossible of achievement." "Sequence and Literature: Some Considerations," *English Journal* 56:3 (March 1967): 394-400 +. See Carlsen and Crow, "Project English Curriculum Centers."

46. John DeBoer introduced the topic; Lou LaBrant proposed the motion. See "Report and Summary," *English Journal* 38:6 (June 1949): 355; "The Chicago Convention," *English Journal* 38:2 (February 1949): 105-08; "Report and Summary," *English Journal* 40:4 (April 1951): 232-37; "Report and Summary," *English Journal* 40:5 (May 1951): 285-86; and "Report and Summary," *English Journal* 41:1 (January 1952): 42.

47. Hosic commented that "his conception of what constitutes wholesome reading for adolescents differs markedly from my own"; Allan Abbott suggested teachers should "move rather slowly"; A. P. Boas commented that Prescott was talking of "works of post-war disillusion and psychopathic maladjustment which already . . . are going out of fashion." Walter Barnes, however, urged "Three loud huzzas." The point is that though there has always been censorship of school materials, until recently teachers supported it. Joseph Prescott, "Sex in Literature," *English Leaflet* 35 (May 1936): 65-82.

48. The commission worried that "young people . . . will not see as unsatisfactory (both individually and socially) the pathological or sordid

behavior with which such books deal." Among the specific titles mentioned were *The Grapes of Wrath, Mr. Roberts,* and *From Here to Eternity.* Commission on the English Curriculum, *The English Language Arts in the Secondary School* (New York: Appleton-Century-Crofts, 1956), pp. 184-85.

49. Lee A. Burress, Jr., *How Censorship Affects the School,* Special Bulletin no. 8 (Wisconsin Council of Teachers of English, 1963).

50. See, for example, *Censorship and Controversy: Report of the Committee on Censorship of Teaching Materials for Classroom and Library* (Chicago: NCTE, 1953); Committee on the Right to Read, *The Students' Right to Read* (Urbana, Ill.: NCTE, 1962); John P. Frank and Robert F. Hogan, *Obscenity, the Law, and the English Teacher* (Urbana, Ill.: NCTE, 1966); and John Hove, chairman, *Meeting Censorship in the School* (Urbana, Ill.: NCTE, 1967).

51. "Censorship and the Values of Fiction," *English Journal* 53:3 (March 1964): 155-64. The NCTE Commission on Literature has recently echoed this: "No work is in itself proper or improper for the schools. Its suitability must be judged in terms of its development of the student's intelligence and critical sensitivity, and the effect on the student of the book as a whole." "This World of English," *English Journal* 57:4 (April 1968): 583-86.

52. See "Riposte," *English Journal* 58:6 (September 1969): 938-40; Judith F. Krug, "Growing Pains: Intellectual Freedom and the Child," *English Journal* 61:6 (September 1972): 805-13; and Kenneth L. Donelson, "White Walls and High Windows: Some Contemporary Censorship Problems," *English Journal* 61:8 (November 1972): 1191-98.

53. Stanley B. Kegler, "The Simplified Classic," *English Journal* 44:8 (November 1955): 475-76. One of the first attacks on the anthologies was John F. Warner, Jr., "Anthologies in the High School Classroom?—Never!" *English Journal* 48:7 (October 1959): 382-87. Many teachers vigorously defended the anthology, prompting a second article from Warner, "To the Gallows with You, Miss Zilch," *English Journal* 49:9 (December 1960): 627-29.

54. See John T. Frederick, "The Quarter Books," *English Journal* 37:5 (May 1948): 215-21; Max J. Herzberg, "Down Publishers' Row," *English Journal* 46:6 (September 1957): 362-65; and Sister M. Harriet, "Let's Use the Paperbacks," *English Journal* 46:4 (April 1957): 202-04.

55. See Helen Fox Rachford, "Developing Discrimination in Radio Listening," *English Journal* 33:6 (June 1944): 315-17; Sarah Roody, "The Effect of Radio, Television, and Motion Pictures on the Development of Maturity," *English Journal* 41:5 (May 1952): 245-50; and C. G. Hedden, "The Pin-Up Girls at School: What to Do about Movies in the Classroom," *English Journal* 35:1 (January 1946): 41-43.

56. Richard G. Lillard, "Movies Aren't Literary," *English Journal* 29:9 (November 1940): 735 ff. A brief summary of the changing attitudes from 1912 to 1960 has been provided by Henry B. Maloney, "Stepsisters of Print: The Public Arts in the High School English Class," *English Journal* 49:8 (November 1960): 570-79.

57. See Patrick D. Hazard, "The Public Arts," *English Journal* 45 (September 1956): 367-69; G. Howard Poteet, "Film as Language," *English Journal* 57:8 (November 1968): 1182-86; Robert Meadows, "Get Smart: Let TV Work for You," *English Journal* 56:1 (January 1967): 121-24; Neil Postman, *Television and the Teaching of English* (New York:

Appleton-Century-Crofts, 1961); and Marion C. Sheridan, *The Motion Picture and the Teaching of English* (New York: Appleton-Century-Crofts, 1965).

58. See "The Course of Study," in Chapter VI. For some discussion of early approaches, see H. A. Domincovich, "On Literature Considered as One of the Fine Arts," *English Journal* 30:5 (May 1941): 387-91; Lawrence P. Shehan, "Senior Humanities at Hanford High School," *English Journal* 54:9 (December 1965): 836-38; and Irving Marks, "The Great Books Course," *English Journal* 56:3 (March 1967): 447-49. Domincovich was Chairman of the NCTE Committee on International Relations and head of English at the Germantown Friends School in Philadelphia.

59. A 1964 survey found that over half of the teachers describing humanities projects were former John Hay Fellows. Robert W. Horner and Socrates A. Lagios, "An Overview of Humanities Programs throughout the Country," *English Leaflet* 63 (Fall 1964): 39-57. *English Journal* discussions of humanities programs were dominated by John Hay Fellows, dating at least to Sarah M. Bush, "A Humanities Program that Works," *English Journal* 40:4 (April 1959): 208-10. In a 1967 index to humanities programs, over 40 percent used the Encyclopaedia Britannica Films. Jonathan Corbin, comp., *Annotated Humanities Programs* (Champaign, Ill.: NCTE, 1967).

60. The rationale for team teaching is presented in James L. Stafford, *An Exploration into Team Teaching in English and the Humanities*, sponsored by the Southern California Council of Teachers of English (Champaign, Ill.: NCTE, 1963).

61. Humanities programs have been discussed in several places. *English Journal* published a series of articles, "Humanities in the High School," in March 1965; *English Leaflet*, Fall 1964, was entirely devoted to humanities, Jonathan Corbin prepared his annotations in 1967, and a similar pamphlet was prepared the following year by Richard Adler and Arthur Applebee (*Annotated Humanities Programs* [Champaign, Ill.: NCTE, 1968]). Sheila Schwartz has provided a collection of relevant readings in *Teaching the Humanities* (New York: Macmillan Co., 1970).

62. See John R. Searles, "Are Humanities Programs the Answer?" *English Journal* 54:3 (March 1965): 175-81; Fred H. Stocking, "High School Humanities Programs: Some Reservations," *English Leaflet* 63 (Fall 1964): 31-38; and Bell, *Reforming of General Education*, pp. 227-28.

63. James R. Squire and Roger K. Applebee, *A Study of English Programs in Selected High Schools Which Consistently Educate Outstanding Students in English*, Cooperative Research Project no. 1994 (Urbana, Ill.: University of Illinois, 1966). An edited and abridged edition of this report is more easily available as *High School English Instruction Today: The National Study of High School English Programs* (New York: Appleton-Century-Crofts, 1968). The study included two main samples selected on differing criteria. Because no differences emerged between the two samples of schools, for the final report results were pooled and discussed as a whole.

64. James R. Squire, Roger K. Applebee, and Robert Lacampagne, *High School Departments of English: Their Organization, Administration, and Supervision*, A Report of the Urbana and Cleveland Conferences, October-November 1964 (Champaign, Ill.: NCTE, n.d. [1965]).

65. Comments on the lower tracks were scattered throughout the report. See Squire and Applebee, *A Study of English Programs,* pp. 91, 323, 345 ff.

66. Though these activities have been discussed only as they most directly affected the teaching of literature, they represented a major NCTE effort throughout Squire's term as executive secretary. The Council's role was vigorous and effective. See Squire's *Eight Year Report* and Shugrue's *English in a Decade of Change* for a fuller account.

67. English Teacher Preparation Study, "Guidelines for the Preparation of Teachers of English," reprinted from *English Journal* 56:6 (September 1967); *Elementary English* 44:6 (October 1967); and *College English* 29:1 (October 1967). The project is discussed at length in Shugrue, *English in a Decade of Change,* and in a special issue of *English Journal* (57:4 [April 1968]).

68. See John Maxwell, "Readiness for New Curriculum Materials," *English Journal* 56:9 (December 1967): 1338-41.

Perhaps more than anything else, the disadvantaged learner needs to find his own identity and to relate himself to the larger social community. Where better than through literature can students learn to rise above themselves and to extend the range of their intellectual and emotional powers?

—Task Force on Language Programs for
the Disadvantaged, 1965[1]

Response is a word that reminds the teacher that the experience of art is a thing of our own making, an activity in which we are our own interpretive artist. The dryness of schematic imagery, symbols, myth, structural relations, et al. should be passionately avoided at school and often at college. It is literature, not literary criticism, which is the subject.

—Anglo-American Seminar on the
Teaching of English, 1966[2]

Anxious to validate our subject, we have claimed for it a place among the exacting studies presumably stabilized in a realm more secure than human. But we may have to accept the idea that the human experiences that get play in literature provide its only validation.

—NCTE Commission on Literature, 1967[3]

Educational objectives pinned to predictable, measurable student perform-ance would offer a much-needed basis for measuring program cost against program effectiveness. Such cost accounting, in turn, would promote more effective allocation of existing resources among competing educational programs.

—Leon Lessinger and Dwight Allen,
1969[4]

From these considerations we derive another concept: accountability. School administrators and school teachers alike are responsible for their perform-ance, and it is in their interest as well as in the interests of their pupils that they be held accountable.

—President Richard M. Nixon, 1970[5]

But the technology changes the values, and dictates some of its own; no technology is ever neutral. . . . Our most pressing educational problem, in short, is not how to increase the efficiency of the schools; it is how to create and maintain a humane society. A society whose schools are inhumane is not likely to be humane itself.

—Charles E. Silberman, **Crisis in the
Classroom,** 1970[6]

Chapter VIII

Winds of Change

Earlier chapters have traced the evolution of the teaching of literature in American schools from its beginnings in the reading texts of colonial days into a major subject involving some 10 percent of the nation's instructional effort. During that time professional leaders turned away from the colleges at the beginning of the twentieth century, and swung back toward them during the early 1960s. This is as far as the history of literature as a school subject can be traced with much historical perspective— with, that is, the vision of hindsight to protect our prophecies. Yet the issues which have been faced in the past continue into the present, generating during the last few years a debate which if it is not hotter in its own right, rages more fiercely for those whose interests are ultimately in the teaching of English in schools today. This chapter discusses three major challenges that have been offered to the academic model of English in the last few years, and looks briefly at the curriculum that is emerging in response. The closing chapter examines the unanswered questions which will continue to shape this history in the years ahead.

The Other Half of the Curriculum

Even as professional leaders were attempting to formulate an academic program for English, other forces were at work that would ultimately offer an instructional model more in keeping with previous progressive theory. The counter-movement began in the nation's slums, where teachers quickly found that the academic approach had little relevance. James B. Conant, whose study of *The American High School Today* (1959) was one of the more important documents in the development of the academic model, also provided an early and widely heralded perspective on the problems of urban education. His *Slums and Suburbs* (1961) drew together observations of astonishing inequities in the quality of education for urban and suburban youth. Conant worried that the problem of the cities was more than just an educational issue—in fact, "social dynamite"; he tried to convey his sense of concern:

> For without being an alarmist, I must say that when one considers the total situation that has been developing in the Negro city slums since World War II, one has reason to worry about the future. The building up of a mass of unemployed and frustrated Negro youth in congested areas of the city is a social phenomenon that may be compared to the piling up of inflammable materials in an empty building in a city block. Potentialities for trouble—indeed possibilities of disaster—are surely there.[7]

He documented his observations with details of Negro migration to the northern central cities, of unemployment, and of dropout rates and absenteeism.

Conant found that these social pressures were coupled with educational inadequacy. The schools which had money, stable staff, community interest, and relevant materials were those in the suburbs. The urban slums suffered with antiquated buildings, overcrowded classrooms, and inappropriate courses of study. His recommendations were a remarkably accurate delineation of the direction that inner-city education would move during the ensuing decade: he argued for meaningful courses, adequate financial support, involvement of parents in educational reform, and school decentralization. Battles over each of these were fought in the headlines of the sixties.

Young authors added a personal and anecdotal dimension to Conant's observations by recounting their own experiences in urban schools. Herbert Kohl, Jonathan Kozol, James Herndon, and Nat Hentoff, among others, echoed the frustration of many young teachers who had taken up urban education as part of a nationwide concern with the welfare of Black America. This frustration among a highly vocal group of teachers, coupled with a new militancy among local community groups, put great pressure on city school systems to alter their materials and approaches.[8]

National leaders in English did not respond to such problems until the middle sixties, when the forces unleashed by the 1954 Supreme Court decision on segregation began to culminate at the federal level in the Job Corps (through the Economic Opportunity Act) and the Civil Rights Act of 1964. NCTE, prompted by an eloquent address from its incoming president, Richard Corbin, took official note of the problem by using its own funds to establish a

Task Force on Teaching English to the Disadvantaged in 1964. Twenty-two experts in teaching and in the problems of the disadvantaged were charged with surveying efforts throughout the nation. In a ninety-day effort beginning in March 1965, they observed 190 programs in 115 school systems of sixty-four cities, in general following the lead of the National Study in scheduling pairs of observers for two-day visits to each program. The final report was released the following fall (1965), with extensive discussions of programs from preschool to adult levels.[9]

The Task Force attempted to dispel a number of "widespread beliefs affecting the education of the disadvantaged"; their comments implied that the educational problems of the disadvantaged differed in amount rather than in kind from those in any classroom. They found that the subculture of poverty was just as diverse and varied as the parent culture; that there was need for a variety of language experiences, not simply drill in standard English; that the children were not apathetic and did not offer unusual discipline problems; that inductive teaching could be used just as successfully with these children as with any others; and that the teacher of English needed to be just as well prepared in his own subject area to teach disadvantaged children as to teach any others.

When they looked at secondary school programs in literature, the Task Force found it resting on "a shaky foundation" (p. 109). The two most prevalent patterns were an emphasis on reading skills and workbook exercises, with a consequent neglect of literary materials, and slavish adherence to inappropriate courses of study. In one memorable class, the teacher was carefully reading *Silas Marner* aloud to a group of students who could not read it themselves, because it was "required" for all students in their grade. The Task Force's only recommendation on the teaching of literature was "that at all levels of instruction the English curriculum for disadvantaged students include appropriate imaginative literature chosen and presented with these students in mind" (p. 273), but this was a radical shift from the concerns of the period of academic reform.

Two of the Project English curriculum study centers focussed on similar problems, and ultimately produced the most successful of the new programs. One, under the direction of Marjorie Smiley at Hunter College in New York City, recognized from the beginning the progressives' lessons about the importance of student involvement and interest as first steps in English instruction. The other, led by Daniel Fader at the University of Michigan, eventually reached very similar conclusions.[10]

Gateway English, the program developed at Hunter College, focussed its units around issues of personal and social significance. Smiley was well aware of the degeneration in the quality of materials toward the end of the progressive era and took great care to choose selections which would deal maturely and in depth with the issues raised. The emphasis was on contemporary writing, including many selections by black authors, but traditional selections were also included: excerpts from the *Odyssey*, for example, and some of Aesop's *Fables*. The program was presented in a series of slim anthologies, with titles which give a good sense of the program as a whole: *A Family Is a Way of Feeling, Coping,* and *Who Am I?* were typical texts. The teacher's manuals, like the materials themselves, echoed many earlier innovators. They sought "to help these children identify the problems and to encourage them to find solutions," "to cast each of the students in a positive 'image,' " and to "enable these discouraged youth to identify with individuals, both real and fictional, who have coped with problems not unlike theirs with varying degrees of success."[11] Even when carried out with literature of acknowledged merit, such emphases had little in common with those of the academic model.

If Gateway English continued the progressive concern with personal and social problems, English in Every Classroom, the program devised at the Michigan center, focussed on extensive reading. This program was designed for the most difficult students of all: a group of delinquent boys in the W. J. Maxey Boys Training School (Michigan). Later the center expanded its work to public schools, and the program itself (popularized by Fader's 1966 presentation, *Hooked on Books*) spread to some thirty-seven states and three foreign countries.[12]

The basic principles were simple enough: students were to read as much and in as many different areas of their school experience as possible. To achieve this, the program provided a library of 1,200 paperback books and class sets of newspapers and magazines. These formed the core of the English curriculum and also provided materials to supplement the work in other subjects. In the process of implementing this approach, Fader rediscovered many educational cliches, but because of the extreme conditions under which he was working—and the obvious failure of other approaches—the cliches took on a substance and appeal that under better conditions they might have lacked. The need for every teacher to be a "teacher of English"; the importance of relevant materials; the fact that without interest nothing else would follow—these basic principles of progressive education were rediscovered in meeting the problems of education in a boys training school. There was very little that could *force* such boys to begin to read; the only hope was to make them *want* to. And this Fader did, however many cliches he discovered in the process.[13]

The British Model

At the same time that progressive methods were being reestablished in the curriculum of the inner city and the lower tracks, professional leaders were becoming aware of another model for instruction which asserted the primacy of such approaches for *all* students. Though the liberal American reformers—the same group who had originally protested against the programs in slum schools— were moving in much the same direction, it was the schools of England that offered a functioning alternative to the academic model.

Initial contacts with British educators had begun during the fifties, first through NCTE-sponsored summer tours of England and later through a series of conferences on the problems of teaching English to speakers of other languages (TESOL). As early as 1957, Harold B. Allen, who had been deeply involved in TESOL programs in Egypt, suggested that a conference on the teaching of English as a native language might be fruitful. During the following years, a number of Council leaders visited British schools, a National Association of Teachers of English (NATE) was organized in Britain, and a representative of the British Ministry of Education toured the Project English study centers. During 1964 Boris Ford, president of NATE, attended the NCTE annual convention. His remarks again led NCTE leaders to consider a joint meeting, which was arranged for the following year.[14] The 1965 meeting was followed by two other projects which brought American educators into close and stimulating contact with British approaches. The first was a month-long invitational seminar on the teaching of English, held at Dartmouth College in the summer of 1966, funded by the Carnegie Corporation, and cosponsored by NATE, MLA, and NCTE. Approximately fifty specialists in English and the teaching of English at the elementary, secondary, and college levels were brought together in an unusual attempt to gain a new perspective on their common problems. The ensuing clash of deeply rooted assumptions about the teaching of English was a cathartic experience for all involved, and sharply altered the professional emphases of NCTE leaders.[15]

At the same time plans were underway to extend the National Study of High School English Programs to include a survey of outstanding British schools. Teams of observers visited 42 schools during the spring of 1967; most of the people involved had participated in the earlier American study. As had happened at Dartmouth, the visiting Americans found their deeply rooted beliefs sharply challenged by programs in the forefront of British education, and (again as at Dartmouth) they came away feeling that the British alternative had much to recommend it.[16]

What the British offered the Americans was a model for English instruction which focussed not on the "demands" of the discipline but on the personal and linguistic growth of the child. These goals and no others justified the central place of English in the school curriculum, and this implied—as had American progressive theory—

a curriculum structured around the characteristics of the child whose growth was to be fostered. American observers were especially struck by these emphases in the lower forms in British secondary schools (roughly equivalent to American grades 7 to 10); there they found "improvised drama, imaginative writing, personal response to literature, and a large amount of informal classroom discussion. Instruction is centered on the pupil—*his* interests, *his* response, *his* view of the world" (p. 52). Subject matter (the "content" of English which had been of such concern to Americans) seemed hardly important to the British teacher; its function was to provide the experiences through which the child could experiment, testing and strengthening his linguistic and intellectual skills by using them in a variety of contexts.

Indeed, like the metaphor of "growth" itself, it was process or activity rather than content which defined the English curriculum for the British teacher. Strongly influenced by the work of the Swiss psychologist Jean Piaget, the Russian L. S. Vygotsky, and the American George Kelly, British teachers saw language as imposing a system and an order, offering (in John Dixon's words) "sets of choices from which we must choose one way or another of building our inner world."[17] Hence the teacher must accept the tentative and incomplete response as part of the process of choice, a testing out of a particular mode of thought or expression which it would be perfectly legitimate for the student to abandon in midstream. American observers found such an attitude most dramatically evident in written language instruction, where British teachers placed a much greater emphasis on the act of writing itself. They often assigned work which would never be read by the teacher, in contrast to the American pattern of write, grade, revise. In literature, a similar concern was reflected in an emphasis on "talk," a term the British used to suggest the informality and essentially unstructured nature of discussion in which responses were understood to be developing and tentative rather than complete and well formulated. Rather than the closure and summing up so often sought by the better teachers in the American study, British teachers relied on the process of discussion itself for the educative effects they were seeking.

The aspect of British programs which most surprised Americans, both at Dartmouth and during the study of British schools, was the emphasis on drama. British teachers recognized, as had American progressives, that drama was valuable both as a method for the study of literature and as a means to personal development. To act out a scene successfully—whether as improvisation or as dramatization of part of a script—implies a sophisticated level of response and understanding without requiring an explicit (or cognitive) formulation of response. In a sense the dramatic response is the antithesis of the analytic, content-oriented teaching of English against which the British were in the process of reacting. At the same time, drama is the embodiment of the role playing and experiment which are part of the British pedagogy of growth. To take a part in a drama is to take on at least for a moment new linguistic, social, and personal roles, and to do so with all the protection of self that the acknowledged "playing" in drama affords.[18]

Much of the teaching of literature observed during the study of British schools involved drama in one form or another; the remainder was undertaken in a similar spirit of fostering response and involvement rather than analysis and criticism. (The work in the last two years of secondary school, where English is a specialist rather than a general subject, was an exception to this; even it, however, seemed to observers to build on the less formal work of the earlier years.) The result was a program which alternately excited and disturbed American observers, who found it "fragmented, uncritical, antiliterary, yet often explosive, engaging, and exciting" (p. 88). Concern with a literary heritage played virtually no role, being dismissed as irrelevant or redefined as a "legacy of past satisfactions" and hence not something that could be dispensed as so many grams of knowledge.[19]

The various critical studies that had found their way into American programs were similarly of little concern: the British teachers gave comparatively little attention to close textual analysis, to the study of genres, to literary periods, or to chronology. Instead, the British teachers emphasized a thematic approach and guided individual reading. Unlike their American counterparts, the British were able to pursue these studies in virtually any direction they chose. Protected by a system of education in which schools are funded nationally rather than locally, they are virtually free from community pressures. Censorship is very rare: *Lady Chatterley's Lover* was the text in one class observed by the Americans, and similarly controversial books had a prominent role in other programs.

Perhaps the strongest tribute to the British efforts is that Americans have been willing to learn from them. Whereas the National Study of outstanding American programs had led observers to recommend that programs continue to be developed along previous lines, the visits to England led to major recommendations for change. The most important of these were concerned with the relative stress to be placed on formal and on informal, response-oriented studies; in general both study observers and Dartmouth participants were convinced that the British approach was the better alternative, with conscious formulation of critical responses deferred to the later years. "No evidence collected in this study," the directors noted, "suggests that the absence of attention to cognitive processes affects the ultimate literary reactions of British

youth" (p. 116). More stress on dramatic activities and oral approaches, greater freedom in the use of materials, less rigid curriculum guides, more attention to indirect methods of teaching, and the
search for appropriate sequence in the growth pattern of the child
are other points that followed more or less directly from acceptance
of the general approach.

The major effect of the confrontation with British programs has
been to reestablish, at least among an influential group of spokesmen for the teaching of English, some of the better parts of the
progressive vision. A concern with people rather than content has
reasserted itself; the personal and social values of literature are
once again being explored.[20] Yet the men who are leading the
movement back toward these progressive ideals are men who were
deeply involved in developing the academic model. They know its
strengths as well as its weaknesses and have insured that it, too,
continues to have its influence: they have a continuing awareness of
the need for literature which is honest and mature, literature which
will challenge rather than merely "adjust" its readers; they are
seeking to define more clearly its importance in the lives of all of us;
and they are attempting to preserve and strengthen the sense of
profession that developed in the process of building the academic
model. These emphases, of course, are also true to the original
progressive vision, but they differ greatly from the emphases that
developed after the Second World War.[21]

Industrial Models

Even as some teachers began to re-emphasize the traditional
values of English as a "humanistic" or "liberalizing" subject, a
second aspect of the early progressive movement was also gaining
new momentum. This was the concern with efficiency and utilitar-
ianism that first found expression in Franklin Bobbitt's lists of
specific objectives and later in Henry Morrison's unit method of
instruction, now reconceptualized as "behavioral objectives" and
"accountability." Reinvigorated by industrial successes with the
"systems approach" to management, as well as by a national mood
of austerity and tightening budgets, these approaches have received support from powerful segments of industry and government.

The proponents of the systems approach have taken industrial
production as their model for the educational process. At one end of
the system are the inputs, usually conceptualized as the present
achievements, attitudes, and skills of the students; at the other end
are the outputs, the skills and attitudes that it is desirable for

students to have. The discrepancy between input and output defines the educational task. Proponents have claimed a number of virtues for this system: it will be efficient instruction, in that it will be possible to eliminate activities which do not contribute to the achievement of the specified goals; it will be individualized instruction, since the discrepancy between input and output will differ from student to student; and it will provide a measure of the extent to which each district, school, or teacher achieves its stated objectives. It will also provide very direct cost accounting: the school board will be able to see which programs are working and how much they cost. Within a system conceptualized in such terms, it is a short step to considering subcontracting one or another segment of the total program, and indeed exactly such an approach has been tried on an experimental basis. In some versions, a "performance contract" has been an in-school system of incentives, with salaries of teachers tied to the extent to which their students meet or surpass prespecified performance criteria. In other versions, the contract has been made with an outside, often profit-making, corporation, again with payment contingent upon successful performance by the students. In the 1969-70 academic year, the first two experimental performance contracts went into operation; by 1970-71 there were over 100. Initial results from these projects were not encouraging. In Office of Education experiments involving six different companies, the 13,000 students in experimental classes did no better than those in conventional programs. All six companies lost money; the USOE withdrew its support for further attempts; and the number of experiments began to fall off.[22]

Still the emphasis on careful cost accounting has received very powerful support and seems likely to continue, even if experiments with performance contracts come to a halt. President Nixon, in his 1970 Education Message to Congress, emphasized that schools must be "accountable" for the results they produce, and he did so in the context of reducing expenditures. Congress has reflected similar concerns through its endorsement of the National Assessment of Educational Progress, and the USOE has sponsored large-scale demonstrations of the systems approach to educational problems. More recently, the Committee for Economic Development, an organization of 200 business leaders with considerable power to shape national policy, has endorsed similar principles in a policy statement, *Education for the Urban Disadvantaged* (1971):

> We are convinced that the financial support of the schools should be in some way tied to their actual productivity, so that a better product, when judged by competent techniques of assessment, would yield increased support. If this were achieved, we believe the schools would become more inventive, more innovative, more effective, and more productive of good education.[23]

The difficulty of providing "competent techniques of assessment" has led to a concurrent emphasis on detailed specification of
instructional objectives. Here one of the most influential publications has been a brief book by Robert F. Mager, published in 1961
as *Preparing Objectives for Programmed Instruction*. It was reissued the following year with the somewhat more general title,
Preparing Instructional Objectives. The content of the two editions
is identical even in the pagination, but the shift in title recognizes
that the specification of "behavioral objectives" has become somewhat independent of the concern with programmed instruction. The
objectives that Mager describes are distinguished from other educational objectives in that they are based on observations of the overt
behavior of the learner; to Mager, "A statement of an objective is
useful to the extent that it specifies what the learner must be able
to DO or PERFORM when he is demonstrating his mastery of the
objective." Such objectives are the necessary building blocks of a
systems approach to education. The tendency of such objectives is
toward greater and greater specificity rather than toward globally
stated or long-term goals.[24]

Programmed instruction, as suggested by the original title of
Mager's book, has been closely related to the evolution of behavioral objectives. Though it has antecedents in experiments with teaching machines dating back to the 1920s, the programming approach
gained impetus only after B. F. Skinner and his disciples began to
elaborate the pedagogical implications of his behavioral psychology. Initial experiments were carried out almost exclusively in
industrial and military training situations, where the aim was to
teach a student a particular skill as quickly and efficiently as
possible. To a large extent behavioral techniques were successful in
these contexts, whether presented by machine, through programmed texts, or with the use of instructional films or other
audiovisual aids.[25]

Since the early sixties there have been attempts to generalize the
success of these training programs into a model for reform of public
education. It was this generalization that prompted initial attempts
to specify behavioral objectives. These were to provide the necessary reduction of general goals into very specific component skills
that could be taught step by step. Each step would be assessed
individually, and progress continued only when the component had
been mastered. The great difficulties which programmers encountered in their attempts to find operational specifications of goals in
the educational literature lie at the heart of the current focus on the
objectives themselves. But the research in programmed learning
continues and seems destined to reassert itself as various subsets of
objectives become adequately specified.

The response of teachers of English to these movements has
ranged from vehement denunciations to considerable enthusiasm; a

middle group have resignedly concluded that since *someone* is going to write the objectives for English it had better be someone who understands the subject. The most notable example of this position was the Tri-University Project, which included former NCTE executive secretary J. N. Hook among its directors and Robert Mager as a "senior consultant"; many other distinguished figures in English education were involved. Supported by Office of Education funds, the project began as a two-year attempt to write and test behavioral objectives for the high school English curriculum. Somewhat skeptical about the applicability of the behavioral framework to the English program, the project as described by Hook hoped to develop a "carefully prepared, well-reasoned statement subscribed to by representative leaders in the profession" that would "guide developers of such objectives and prevent their misuse."[26]

Most criticism of behavioral objectives in English instruction centers on the measurement problems associated with the goals which teachers have long cherished, especially for the teaching of literature. What exactly does "appreciation" mean in terms of observable behaviors? How does one tell if a student has had a "confrontation," or has clarified his system of personal values as a result of what he has read? Supporters of behavioral objectives have suggested that such concepts can be operationalized if teachers of English accept a broad definition of behavior. For example, James Hoetker, then associated with the Central Midwest Regional Educational Laboratory, offered such unorthodox behavioral specifications of objectives as "the students will cut class less often" or "the students will take a walk in the woods." The Tri-University Project used a somewhat similar approach in some of the objectives in its preliminary catalog. These emphasized that "the student volunteers and participates with animation," for example, or that he "defends orally or in writing" the rights of others to read potentially offensive material. Such approaches represented an attempt to preserve within the framework of behavioral objectives the kind of behaviors which a humanistically oriented teacher is likely to favor.[27]

NCTE, through a new Commission on the English Curriculum, adopted a cautious, even slightly negative stance toward the issues posed by behavioral objectives. While granting the value of specifying more precisely the goals of the course in English, the commission offered a resolution to the 1969 annual business meeting urging in part,

> That those in the profession who do undertake to write behavioral objectives (a) make specific plans to account for the total English curriculum; (b) make an intention to preserve (and, if need be, fight for) the retention of important humanistic goals of education; and (c)

insist on these goals regardless of whether or not there exist instruments at the present time for measuring the desired changes in behavior.[28]

The papers which the commission chose to publish as a result of a special conference on behavioral objectives reflect the same cautious ambivalence, with contributions covering the full range from enthusiastic support to outright denunciation.

Toward a New Curriculum in English

The late 1960s were years in which the American high school underwent a major realignment of values. In response to the national agony over the Vietnam war, student unrest, escalating problems in the inner city, and a widespread malaise even among academically talented students, the emphasis in educational thought shifted gradually but unmistakably away from knowledge of an academic discipline toward the process of knowing and the dignity of the individual. Men who had once led the attack on the progressives shifted their ground, now attacking the dehumanization of the school that seemed to have accompanied the academic approach. Charles Silberman, an early supporter of the academic resurgence, presented one comprehensive critique (1970) on behalf of the Carnegie Corporation, turning to Britain for a constructive alternative. The progressives and John Dewey—the archenemies of the late fifties—became once again leaders behind whom teachers and their spokesmen were proud to march.[29]

This shift in values has led to its own period of experiment in the teaching of English. "Relevance" is one focus of concern; this is the contemporary version of the progressive educator's emphasis on the needs and interests of his students. In this context it is not surprising to find that many of the experiments being offered are variations upon methods that were central to progressive pedagogy. Drama and oral expression, contracts, the project method, unit instruction, student-directed seminars, popular media, contemporary literature and social commentary, minimum essentials, interdisciplinary study—all have reemerged in the past few years.[30] There have also been new approaches: simulation techniques ("gaming") and sensitivity training are the more prominent examples.[31] How these proposals will evolve is still uncertain. Rather than a new and fully formulated curriculum, they represent the attempts of the present generation of teachers to explore their own version of the progressive vision. As yet these explorations are open minded; they have not coalesced around a new metaphor of the educational process nor produced their own articulated body of theory. But it is out of them, and out of the many different theorists from whom the suggestions stem, that that metaphor and that theory will eventually emerge.

Yet if the new pedagogy remains uncertain, the pressures on the English course have already begun to break down the traditional five-day-a-week, four-year institutional framework within which that pedagogy will be implemented. The erosion of the institutional form of the course is highly significant, for it marks the end of a long tradition of high school organization and opens the way for even more radical experiments than have yet been proposed.

The first attacks on the institutional pattern of the high school were sponsored by the Ford Fund for the Advancement of Education during the 1950s. Early admissions and advanced placement have already been discussed, but they are clearly relevant here too; both implied that the four-year high school course was not inviolable. Team teaching was another approach which received some support from the Ford Fund; it was especially popular in humanities programs where the breadth of content required the talents of teachers trained in several different subject areas. Experiments with instructional groups of different sizes often evolved out of these teaching teams: large-group lectures one day, for example, followed by seminar discussions the next.[32] The "Rutgers Plan" was another early experiment that advocated variable class size. This emerged from a six-week workshop, held at Rutgers under Ford Fund sponsorship during the summer of 1959. This workshop sought ways to allow teachers to work with students individually or in small discussion groups, without forcing schools to enlarge their faculties. Their proposal, quite radical for its time, involved a complete restructuring of the time schedule and the use of "paraprofessionals" as nonteaching monitors. English classes would spend two days a week doing free reading, in groups as large as 200; one day a week doing diagnostic tests and self-correcting homework; one day a week in group discussions of student papers; and one day a week in group discussions of literature. Though the Rutgers Plan was not widely adopted, it is important as another early suggestion that class size and class groupings might be varied for different instructional purposes.[33]

The approach which is now becoming widespread is the elective curriculum in English, but this is a blanket label for a wide variety of different approaches to curriculum reform. Electives themselves are of course not new: a four-year English course as a graduation requirement has never been fully established. Even where students must take four years of English, the senior course has often offered electives which could be taken either to supplement or to replace the standard course. Most of the humanities courses discussed in the previous chapter were offered as electives; so were the world literature courses out of which they grew. This form of elective never posed a challenge to the traditional course, however; the choice was usually as much a matter of "tracking" as it was of "electing," with certain courses clearly regarded as the prerogative of the college-bound and others clearly appropriate for the terminal student. During the late 1960s, however, this changed radically, with the elective curriculum in its various manifestations being suggested as a replacement for the junior and senior high school course in English.[34]

One source of this shift has been the failure of the academic model for the curriculum to find any widely accepted structuring principles. If there is no structure, the argument has gone, then there is no reason to impose one artificially through a four-year, required course of study. Let the teacher teach what he knows best, and the students study the subjects in which they are most interested. Courses which have emerged from this point of view have often been constructed on a loose analogy with the college curriculum, with highly academic offerings like "Eighteenth Century Poetry," "Communications," or "The Modern Novel." In spite of such traditionalism, however, a major argument in support of the elective curriculum has been that it is more responsive to the demands of the students, more "relevant," than the traditional course. The hope is that if students are allowed to choose what they will study, their interest and enthusiasm will increase. In many schools this has been coupled with an attempt to discover the courses which students would like to have offered, rather than simply giving them a choice among the particular interests of the teachers.

In some of the more interesting experiments, interest groups resulting from a completely elective program of study have been used to replace the traditional age-grade organization of the high school. Teaching groups may contain the whole secondary school age range, though more usually this is restricted through a "phase elective" system roughly comparable to the system of introductory, intermediate, and advanced courses of the college curriculum. The nongraded curriculum was popularized by experiments at the Melbourne (Florida) High School during the early sixties, but it was only later combined with the elective approach.[35] Where electives have been carried furthest, they have been combined with radical restructuring of the curriculum as a whole into "short-courses" or "mini-courses" of anywhere from a few weeks to a semester in length; these provide students with new sets of options at regular intervals. Class periods of variable length, courses which meet only a few times a week instead of every day, and independent study have been natural results of the attempt to fit the institutional structure to the course content, instead of the courses to the existing institutional frame. Computer-compiled timetables have been crucial in some of these programs, overcoming the otherwise overwhelming complexities inherent in frequent readjustment of complex schedules.[36]

Finally, proponents of behavioral objectives and programmed instruction have also found that a program of electives is one of the more convenient ways to introduce their approaches, often pairing them with some form of minimum essentials examination. In some versions of such programs, students enter the elective phase only after successfully completing an introductory "basic skills" course or proficiency examination. In others, the two proceed in concert, with programmed (or "self-paced") instructional units forming part of the work and elected courses forming the remainder. There is usually no choice about the skills program; all students must work their way to a certain level of competence, though instruction is "individualized" in that they can proceed at their own pace. Even this is not universal, however; in some programs a wide variety of self-paced units are offered as electives.[37]

At present, elective English is an administrative convenience; it represents no particular pedagogical theory though it has usefully served the ends of several. Because it has no structuring principles of its own, the elective program is volatile. All kinds of new studies and new approaches can find a place in the curriculum, and older studies that have usually taken second place can emerge on an equal footing. Film has become a full-fledged part of the English program in many schools; drama has emerged from its long doldrums; literatures from other countries are receiving new and more focussed attention. On the other hand, the very openness of the elective approach leaves it vulnerable to charges of frivolousness, triviality, and lack of coherence[38]—charges which emphasize the need for the elective curriculum to be treated as a way to implement a broader pedagogical theory, rather than as an end in itself. Until it is placed within such a larger framework, the elective curriculum totters between the Scylla of the academic, subject-centered approach and the Charybdis of meeting trivial and temporary "needs and interests."

CHAPTER VIII NOTES

1. Richard Corbin and Muriel Crosby, cochairmen, *Language Programs for the Disadvantaged*, The Report of the NCTE Task Force on Teaching English to the Disadvantaged (Urbana, Ill.: NCTE, 1965), pp. 273-74.

2. D. W. Harding, "Response to Literature: The Report of the Study Group," in *Response to Literature*, Papers Relating to the Anglo-American Seminar on the Teaching of English, ed. James R. Squire (Urbana, Ill.: NCTE, 1968), p. 26.

3. William Stafford, *Friends to This Ground*, A Statement for Readers, Teachers, and Writers of Literature from the NCTE Commission on Literature (Urbana, Ill.: NCTE, 1967), p. 19.

4. Leon M. Lessinger and Dwight H. Allen, "Performance Proposals for Educational Funding: A New Approach to Federal Resource Allocation," *Phi Delta Kappan* 51 (November 1969): 136-37.

5. President Richard M. Nixon, Education Message of 1970. Cited by Leon Lessinger in "Robbing Peter to Pay Paul: Accounting for Our Stewardship of Public Education," *Educational Technology* (January 1971), p. 14.

6. Charles E. Silberman, *Crisis in the Classroom: The Remaking of American Education* (New York: Random House, 1970), pp. 201-03.

7. James B. Conant, *Slums and Suburbs* (New York: Signet Books, 1961), p. 24. On the earlier book, see "A Crisis of Confidence" in Chapter VII.

8. Shugrue calls the education of the disadvantaged "the major educational issue in the United States." Michael F. Shugrue, *English in a Decade of Change* (New York: Pegasus, 1968), p. 142.

9. Corbin and Crosby, *Language Programs for the Disadvantaged*. There had been sporadic attention to such problems earlier. Morris Finder, "Teaching English to Slum-Dwelling Pupils," *English Journal* 44:4 (April 1955): 199-204+; Herbert F. Ostrach, "English and the Lower-Class Student," *English Journal* 52:3 (March 1963): 196-99; and "Riposte," *English Journal* 52:7 (October 1963): 542-46.

10. For further discussion of these programs, see Shugrue, *English in a Decade of Change*, and Corbin and Crosby, *Language Programs for the Disadvantaged*. Progress reports were also included in the curriculum study center reports. See footnote 43 in Chapter VII.

11. Corbin and Crosby, *Language Programs for the Disadvantaged*, pp. 112-13. These texts were eventually published by the Macmillan Co.

12. There have been three reports on the program. The first presented it as it had developed at the W. J. Maxey Boys Training School. The second presented a slightly fuller discussion together with the results of studies of its effectiveness. The third recounts the evolution of the program after it was introduced into the Garnet-Patterson Junior High School in Washington, D.C. The reports are, respectively, Daniel N. Fader and Morton H. Shaevitz, *Hooked on Books* (New York: Berkley Publishing Co., 1966); Daniel N. Fader and Elton B. McNeil, *Hooked on Books: Program and Proof* (New York: Berkley Publishing Co., 1968); and Daniel N. Fader, *The Naked Children* (New York: Macmillan Co., 1971. The figures on the spread of the program are from Fader and McNeil, p. 21.

13. Fader's program resembles most of the other products of the curriculum study centers, in that it is impossible to untangle its various portions to decide which were most important. The "proof" of success offered in the second volume is weak; most of the results can be explained in terms of the excitement and dedication of the teachers involved.

14. The conference was reported by James R. Squire as *A Common Purpose: The Teaching of English in Great Britain, Canada, and the United States* (Urbana, Ill.: NCTE, 1966). The background is recounted in the introduction, pp. i-iii.

15. The seminar has been widely discussed and written about. Two official reports were prepared: John Dixon, *Growth through English* (Reading: National Association for the Teaching of English, 1967); Herbert J. Muller, *The Uses of English* (New York: Holt, Rinehart, and Winston, 1967). In addition, a series of NCTE pamphlet publications reprinted selections from seminar discussion papers.

16. James R. Squire and Roger K. Applebee, *Teaching English in the United Kingdom* (Urbana, Ill.: NCTE, 1969). Jerry Walker of the University of Illinois summed up his reactions in a convention address the following November. He had gone to England confident that the British approaches were wrong; he came back to say, "Maybe they are right." His conversion was typical. "Bach, Rembrandt, Milton, and Those Other Cats," *English Journal* 57:5 (May 1968): 631-36.

17. Dixon, *Growth through English*, p. 9. The fullest statement of this point of view is James Britton's *Language and Learning* (London: Allen Lane, The Penguin Press, 1970).

18. Over 30 percent of the class time observed was devoted to speech or dramatic activities, compared to at most 12 percent in American schools. On drama, see Dixon, *Growth through English*, pp. 37 ff.; Muller, *Uses of English*, pp. 129 ff.; Squire and Applebee, *Teaching English in the United Kingdom*, pp. 197 ff.; and Douglas Barnes, ed., *Drama in the English Classroom*, Papers Relating to the Anglo-American Seminar on the Teaching of English (Urbana, Ill.: NCTE, 1968).

19. James Britton, "Response to Literature," in Squire, *Response to Literature.*

20. There is much evidence of this shift within the teaching of English and within the teaching profession as a whole. The NCTE Commission on Literature issued a statement in 1967 which directly challenged the conception of English as a discipline and once again talked of its importance as a "generator of values and insights" and as a part of a process of discovery (see the quotation at the opening of this chapter). More generally, Charles E. Silberman (*Crisis in the Classroom*) has urged a return to more humane values for American education as a whole.

21. Personally as well as historically, the British experience led many to a reassertion of concerns important earlier in their careers. Squire for one had begun with an emphasis on response. In his first *English Journal* article he had recommended finger-painting and charcoal sketching as legitimate approaches in teaching poetry, though such activities fell out of favor during the period of academic concern. James R. Squire and Merritt Beckerman, "The Release of Expression," *English Journal* 39:3 (March 1950): 145-49.

22. See Daniel J. Dieterich, "Performance Contracts," *English Journal* 61:4 (April 1972): 606-14; "For the Members," *English Journal* 61:4 (April 1972): unpaginated insert.

23. Committee for Economic Development, *Education for the Urban Disadvantaged*, A Statement on National Policy by the Research and Policy Committee (New York: CED, March 1971), p. 60; Sue M. Brett, "The Federal View of Behavioral Objectives," in *On Writing Behavioral Objectives for English*, ed. John Maxwell and Anthony Tovatt (Urbana, Ill.: NCTE, 1970). See the quotation introducing this chapter.

24. Robert F. Mager, *Preparing Objectives for Programmed Instruction* (San Francisco: Fearon Publishers, 1961); *Preparing Instructional Objectives* (San Francisco: Fearon Publishers, 1962). See especially pp. xii, 13.

25. For a brief, lucid, and sympathetic discussion of the evolution of programming approach, see W. Lee Garner, *Programmed Instruction* (New York: Center for Applied Research in Education, 1966).

26. J. N. Hook, "The Tri-University BOE Project: A Progress Report," in *On Writing Behavioral Objectives*, ed. Maxwell and Tovatt. See p. 76.

27. James Hoetker, "Limitations and Advantages of Behavioral Objectives in the Arts and Humanities," in *On Writing Behavioral Objectives*, ed. Maxwell and Tovatt. For a preliminary list of objectives from the Tri-University Project, see Arnold Lazarus, "Performance Objectives in Reading and Responding to Literature," *English Journal* 61:1 (January 1972): 52-58. For a thorough attempt to repudiate objections to behavioral objectives, see W. James Popham, "Probing the Validity of Arguments Against Behavioral Goals," in *Behavioral Objectives and Instruction*, Robert J. Kibler, Larry L. Barker, and David T. Miles (Boston: Allyn and Bacon, 1970).

28. Maxwell and Tovatt, *On Writing Behavioral Objectives*, p. ix. In the spring of 1971, the commission adopted a "Statement on Accountability" which similarly urged a broad perspective on goals for English instruction, while at the same time accepting "the broad principle of accountability." Both sides of the debate are presented in further detail in *Accountability and the Teaching of English*, ed. Henry B. Maloney (Urbana, Ill.: NCTE, 1972); and *Goal Making for English Teaching*, ed. Henry B. Maloney (Urbana, Ill.: NCTE, 1973).

29. Silberman, *Crisis in the Classroom*.

30. For examples of some of these innovations, see Saralee Amsden, "Have You Ever Tried Contracting for Grades?" *English Journal* 59:9 (December 1970): 1279-82; Kenneth R. McCormic and C. Louis Kaupp, "An Elective English Program for the Non-College Bound," *English Journal* 61:2 (February 1972): 277-80; Gary Cavanaugh, "Sanity and Balance in a High School English Program," *English Journal* 61:2 (February 1972): 270-276 +; and Deborah W. Manaster, "An Experiment in Student-Run Seminars," *English Journal* 61:1 (January 1972): 113-16. For a comprehensive review of recent interest in drama and dramatics, see James Hoetker, *Dramatics and the Teaching of English* (Urbana, Ill.: NCTE, 1969).

31. T-groups, deriving from the methods of Carl Rogers, are advocated by Thomas D. Klein in "Personal Growth in the Classroom," *English*

Journal 59:2 (February 1970): 235-43. On gaming, see James M. Brewbaker, "Simulation Games and the English Teacher," *English Journal* 61:1 (January 1972): 104-09+; Sarane S. Boocock, *Simulation Games in Learning* (Beverly Hills: Sage Publications, 1968); and Elliott Carlson, "Games in the Classroom," *Saturday Review*, April 15, 1967.

32. These and other early experiments with the form of the English curriculum are discussed by James R. Squire and Roger K. Applebee, *High School English Instruction Today* (New York: Appleton-Century-Crofts, 1968), pp. 204-36. On team teaching, see James L. Stafford, *An Exploration into Team Teaching in English and the Humanities*, Sponsored by the Southern California Council of Teachers of English (Champaign, Ill.: NCTE, 1963).

33. The plan was presented by Paul B. Diederich, "The Rutgers Plan for Cutting Class Size in Two," *English Journal* 49:4 (April 1960): 229-36 +. For a negative reaction, see Lawrence Niblett, "The Rutgers Plan: Not Enough or the Right Kind of Help," *English Journal* 49:7 (October 1960): 481-82. For a recent review of the use of paraprofessionals, see Howard G. Getz, *Paraprofessionals in the English Department* (Urbana, Ill.: NCTE/ERIC, 1972).

34. George Hillocks, Jr., has presented a lengthy appraisal of the elective movement, including details of many different courses. *Alternatives in English: A Critical Appraisal of Elective Programs* (Urbana, Ill.: NCTE, 1972).

35. G. Robert Carlsen defends the nongraded elective system—pioneered at the University of Iowa laboratory school in 1960—as providing "alternatives for students who are different minded." "Some Random Observations—About the English Curriculum," *English Journal* 61:7 (October 1972): 1004-09. See also B. Frank Brown, *The Non-Graded High School* (Englewood Cliffs, New Jersey: Prentice-Hall, 1964); Donald Weise, "Nongrading, Electing, and Phasing: Basics of Revolution for Relevance," *English Journal* 59:1 (January 1970): 122-36; and Ann M. Jaekle, "Spontaneity with a Purpose: Elective English Programs," *English Journal* 61:4 (April 1972): 529-35.

36. See for example Adele H. Stern, "Sorry, Dr. Silberman! Mini-Courses in the High School," *English Journal* 61:4 (April 1972): 550-54; and Sister Mary Sylvia, "Individualized Education and/or the Mod Squad," *English Journal* 61:1 (January 1972): 78-80.

37. See John Rishen, "The Changing Face of English—One School's New Program," *English Journal* 59:3 (March 1970): 524-27; and Vivian Geddes, "Individualized Self-Paced English," *English Journal* 61:3 (March 1972): 413 ff.

38. See the criticisms offered by Robert J. Fitzgerald after visiting a number of popular programs. Fitzgerald was an early supporter of electives but became disillusioned by what he found. "The New Supermarket: A 'Dystopian' View of English Electives," *English Journal* 61:4 (April 1972): 536-49.

This chapter is a summary of a number of continuing problems in the teaching of English. It is a personal statement, not an historical one, but it arises out of the long immersion in historical questions that preparing this book required. In a sense, it is a statement of the lessons of history, as one person learned them.

Chapter IX

Afterword:
The Problems Remaining

Teachers of literature have never successfully resisted the pressure to formulate their subject as a body of knowledge to be imparted.

The teaching of literature has from the beginning been under considerable pressure to formulate itself as a body of knowledge, a recognized content to be acquired by the student. In the deliberations of the Committee of Ten and its Vassar Conference such a conceptualization was overt, a necessary precondition if the subject were to take its place beside the other subjects as a true disciplinary study. In later years it was more often covert, emerging not in the philosophy of the subject matter, but in the way in which that philosophy was operationalized in the classroom. Thus the progressives of the late thirties, who provided the most complete rationale for English as a series of experiences rather than a specific set of content, in the end structured their curriculum around a series of "enabling objectives" which continued to stress knowledge; the "primary objectives" derived from the experience approach had little direct influence on the classroom.

This stress on content has been in part responsible for the uneasiness which teachers of English have traditionally felt about the definition of their subject matter. The Committee of Ten in effect brought together a number of disparate subjects, each with its own body of rules and formal subject matter, and called them "English." Beyond the cliché that each of these studies deals with language, they have no real unity *as subject matter;* attempts to interrelate them have been artificial and, for the most part, short-lived. Whether the model for the educational process has been growth in language, the four basic skills (reading, writing, listening, speaking), or the three basic disciplines (language, literature, and composition), some aspect of what teachers considered to be important has been lost, reemerging to assert its own values and undercut the basis of the reconciliation. Inevitably, the edges of the subject have blurred and wavered, creating for the teacher of English a perpetual crisis of identity.

The acknowledged goals of the teaching of literature are in conflict with the emphasis on specific knowledge or content.

Part of the uneasiness which teachers have felt with attempts to define their subject matter as a body of knowledge results from an awareness, often unarticulated, that the goals which they seek to accomplish through the teaching of literature are ultimately not defined by such knowledge, but rather are questions of values and perspective—the kinds of goals usually summed up as those of a "liberal" or "humanistic" education. At all stages of our history, including those in which the primary goals of education would seem most antithetical to such emphases, teachers have paid at least passing tribute to the broadening aspects of literature. Only rarely have they considered, however, the implications of such an emphasis for the way their subject should be taught, being for the most part content to assume that the humanistic benefits would follow naturally from exposure to the proper content; the repeated observation that the teaching of literature was failing to achieve those broader ends with any significant number of students has usually been mustered during the course of an attempt to substitute one body of content for another, rather than to suggest that it is the stress on content itself that is at fault.

Teachers of English need to make the distinction between knowledge which informs their teaching, and that which should be imparted to the student.

Virtually every development in scholarship in English studies has been seen as offering the inevitably proper definition of the content of the secondary school class. Grammar and rhetoric in the eighteenth century, philology in the nineteenth, sociology during the thirties, semantics in the forties, and the New Criticism in the sixties have been taken up and transplanted by enthusiastic teachers; and each has been supplanted in its turn by equally enthusiastic proponents of a newer critical perspective, or, in periods of extreme disorientation, by those who claim that *everything* is valid (and necessary) if we are to give students a full experience of literature.

Yet without questioning the value of scholarship, it is legitimate to ask whether such developments in critical theory should be so directly generalized to the presumably less sophisticated studies of the secondary school classroom. There must be some level of response to (or knowledge about) literature that intervenes between that of the novice and that of the scholar, and it is presumably with those intervening levels that a secondary school teacher should be concerned. The generalizations of scholarship and criticism will certainly be of importance in providing teachers with a frame of reference to order and direct their teaching, but a frame of reference for the teacher and a body of knowledge for the student are different things.

This over-responsiveness to scholarly emphases has led proponents of virtually all points of view to ask that the secondary program in literature achieve a goal or series of goals which in fact have not been realized at any level of scholarship. The attempts at defining a curriculum which fall into this category are endless: the survey course designed to give an historical view of literature, when a comprehensive history of literature has yet to be written; the core curriculum designed to unify the various fields of knowledge, when philosophers and scholars alike have struggled to achieve such a synthesis even for themselves; the spiral curriculum which seeks to build a sequence and scope on the basis of the structure of the discipline, when scholarly views of the "discipline" of English are themselves only beginning to emerge and are often in conflict; the attempt to prescribe critical standards for motion pictures before the medium had evolved or critical theory had built up around it. The quarrel in all of these cases is not with the vision of the teacher as coequal in the struggle to solve complex professional and scholarly problems; it is with the parochial presupposition (so evident in many discussions) that the solutions are ready at hand, waiting only for the teacher to have the courage to abandon his outmoded ways and, finally, bring the light and power of knowledge to his students.

There is a need to reconceptualize the "literary heritage" and its implications for patterns of teaching.

The proposition that a meaningful literary heritage may be something other than knowledge of the Great Books has too rarely been entertained. The teaching of literature began as an attempt to introduce students to the best authors and writings of the English tradition, with instruction at times concentrating wholly on biographical and historical data. Such studies were thought to have several justifications: they would provide a common set of reference points for the culture at large; they would teach the student to respect that culture by giving him a sense of his "heritage"; and they would improve his personal system of values. Only gradually did the implicit faith in the power of these books begin to be replaced by an awareness that they do not automatically exert their benevolent influence.

Any definition of a literary heritage in terms of specific books or authors distorts the cultural significance of a literary tradition by failing to recognize that what the Great Books offer is a continuing dialogue on the moral and philosophical questions central to the culture itself. The usefulness of the heritage lies in the confrontation with these issues which it provides; any acquaintanceship which avoids the confrontation is both trivial and irrelevant, an observation often subsumed in the comment that each generation takes from the past what it needs, reconstructing the literary hierarchy on contemporary terms.

Yet even accepting such a need for engagement, there remain difficult questions about what exactly is necessary to achieve the desired goals. Does a sense of heritage require that all readers have experience with the same books? the same authors? some writings from the same centuries? Or can it, as the authors of the Harvard report on general education asserted, arise simply from contemporary reinterpretations of the central philosophical issues? One could argue from this point of view that the teacher should turn to contemporary voices not as bridges to works of the past, but because they are themselves the living embodiment of that part of the literary heritage which is of most concern. This is not to deny that the perspective of the past offers important insights into the present, nor that it can deepen and enrich contemporary thought; it is simply to assert that it is the contemporary thought which is of foremost importance.

The teaching of literature is a political act.

From the time of its use in colonial primers, the power of literature to shape values and beliefs has been recognized and put to use. How it has been used has been to some extent responsive to cultural and political forces, during the nineteenth century shifting from religious doctrine to secularizations of the Protestant ethic, and later still toward the social and political reform of the progressive era. The progressive educators recognized perhaps most fully that literature is fundamentally a progressive force in society. Not only do contemporary authors tend to challenge and redefine conventional beliefs, but the much vaunted "broadening" of experience that literature offers implies that it is valuable to broaden the personal and social perspectives of the peer culture. To transcend boundaries—geographical, social, ethnic, historical, or moral— through literature is a first step toward transcending them in other aspects of one's life.

Of all of the approaches to the teaching of literature, that associated with providing students with a sense of their literary heritage is most often associated with a conservative point of view, yet even it is ultimately a disruptive rather than a stabilizing element. It would be very difficult to argue that the values which give continuity and stability to a society such as ours are in fact those to be found in the literature of the past. Though we may find continuing attention to certain moral (and political) dilemmas, the resolutions offered by Shakespeare certainly differ radically from those of Plato or Sartre, just as the conception of democracy which one can find in the writings of the founding fathers differs in certain basic ways from that which guides our country today. If our cultural traditions were those of stability rather than change, and if our great literature arose out of and reflected those values, we might be able to offer the literary heritage as the stabilizing force it is often thought to be. Instead, the Great Works offer the same challenges to the parochial point of view as do contemporary writers, though they do not deal with them in contemporary terms. The moral dilemmas, the shifting perspective, the catholicity of views are implicitly offered to anyone who studies literature at all.

These progressive goals of improving the individual (and through him, society) may be in direct opposition to the goals of a body politic concerned primarily with stability. An implicit recognition of this tension between literature and convention may be a contributing factor in the teacher's continuing search for ways to define a circumscribed and thus safer body of knowledge. Because the school is locally controlled and vulnerable to community pressure, because the teacher is often a product of that community and that culture, it has simply been more convenient to teach *about* literature and thus to limit its progressive impulses.

Language skills have been narrowly conceptualized as an independent and functional aspect of the English program.

Language skills have played a central role in justifications for the role of English in the school curriculum. Whether educating immigrants at the turn of the century or defending the importance of English to national defense during the sixties, teachers have been quick to cite the importance of speaking, listening, reading, and writing in day-to-day life. More often than not, such defenses have provided the screen behind which the teaching of literature could continue to flourish.

Yet in spite of the continuing importance of skills to the defense cf the curriculum as a whole, there has been precious little consideration of the relationship between the skills of English and the "higher" goals of expression or response to literature. Almost without exception, skills have been treated as subjects for direct teaching, sometimes within a framework of lessons, sometimes as "incidental" or "functional" instruction opportunistically inserted in the course of other work. In language the tenacity of direct teaching is especially clear because of the old and well-documented

evidence that grammatical knowledge has no demonstrable relationship to writing ability; but grammar has held its place in the
curriculum, protected by the desire of teachers to have something
concrete and "useful" to do in their classes. In the teaching of
literature, the focus on skills has meant attention to reading, with
any special skills involved in the reading of literature lumped
together as "higher" reading skills.

Yet consider the implications of asserting that the humanistic
aspects of English *build on* skills. It is then legitimate—even
wise—to assert that there is no point in teaching literature when
the students have not "mastered" all of the skills of reading. One
of the sad results of exactly such a conceptualization of literature
as the culmination of the reading program has been the nearly
complete elimination of literary materials from elementary school
readers, a trend that has begun to reverse itself somewhat in
response to widespread criticism of the Dick and Jane stories, as
well as the more positive examples offered by such children's
authors as Dr. Seuss. At the high school level, similar assumptions
have led to the rather pedestrian selections that fill the anthologies
for the lower tracks.

Considerable evidence has accumulated to suggest—if common
sense is not enough—that literary response is not the last part of
the hierarchy of reading skills but is indeed primal and immediate.
Children's love of word games and nursery rhymes is well known
and has often been cited as the first stage of literary development—
surely preceding the development of reading skills—and the professional literature is full of anecdotal accounts of non-readers who,
like Fader's delinquent boys, responded immediately and with
considerable depth to literary selections far above their "reading
level," as well as to artistic presentations through media such as
stage or film. Few indeed would assert that it is good pedagogy to
provide a tenth grader reading at a second grade level with a second
grade reading text; yet that is the logical conclusion to draw if one
accepts literature as representing a set of "higher reading skills."
More progress might be expected in the teaching of literature if
teachers recognized that it involves a response to patterns of
experience not necessarily dependent upon reading skills at all.

*A focus on correcting taste has obscured the need for fostering
response.*

The notion of "taste" in literature is another term which, like
"heritage," has suffered from the attempt to define the subject as a
body of content. Concentrating on adult standards of mature (or
"good") literature, teachers have conceptualized children's preferences negatively, as something to be exposed in their shallowness
and eliminated. This has been most evident in attitudes toward

journalism and motion pictures; these were confronted at least initially as evils lurking just over the horizon, ready to lure the unsuspecting pupil away from his six-foot shelf. Similar attitudes, however, have led teachers of literature to spend many class hours deriding Zane Grey, O. Henry, or (more recently) James Bond. It is a curiously negative stance for a profession that prides itself on the broadening and humanistic values of its subject matter, a stance that condemns without providing a real alternative; the ready and easy path for the student to follow is to discover the teacher's preferences, a body of knowledge about acceptable responses to be learned and used during English class, and promptly set aside thereafter.

It is exactly because it produces this result that the stress on taste is antithetical to the underlying goals of instruction. The way to build taste—as has been recognized by some teachers in all of our historical periods—is to open new vistas rather than to shut off old ones. Everyone reads with pleasure at many different levels; even the sophisticated literary scholar has been known to admit that in (daily) moments of weakness he picks up the comic strips. It is a natural and perfectly wholesome response, and the base on which any more sophisticated response must build.

The stress on developing "good taste" through their classes in literature has made teachers overly sensitive to the less distinguished products of contemporary culture. Somehow students always read less than they "used to"; poetry is always "neglected completely"; teaching has obviously "failed" when the second-rate movie draws the largest crowds, and *Forever Amber* or *Love Story* tops the best seller lists. Few realize the extent to which each generation has had its formula authors; we are simply more aware of our own because time has dimmed the memory of those that came before.

If the teacher has failed, it has been a failure to recognize that the appeal of the second rate involves a legitimate *literary* response upon which he should seek to build. The greatest art is structured from the same elements; it differs from the lesser only in the subtlety and complexity with which those elements are put to use. It is this very structural complexity and subtlety, if we accept the one lesson the New Critics should have driven home to us all, which gives the "great" literature its depth of meaning and significance, and which allows us to return again and again for fresh insights and new perspectives.

The educative effects of the act of reading need to be defined.

Because skills have been viewed as a separate dimension of work in English, often undertaken as a "service" to other areas of the school, there has been little attention to the extent to which they are a natural result of other aspects of English studies. Though teachers have exhibited an implicit faith that the act of reading is itself educative when they have encouraged wide reading as an adjunct of their regular program of instruction, there have been virtually no attempts to formulate what exactly those effects are. Proponents of extensive study have been content with the vague supposition that such work in some sense "broadens" the student; supporters of intensive work have just as assuredly asserted that response follows understanding.

Yet this surely is an oversimplification; a reader begins with *some* sense of meaning, however incomplete, and it is this original response which is refined and guided by the process of close analysis and explicit interpretation. But if reading does begin with some sense of meaning, the very structural features which close reading emphasizes must exert a certain discipline over the reader's response, shaping and controlling his experience perhaps to a greater extent than teachers have recognized or been willing to admit. The patterned nature of a work of literature will bring a reader up short if his own interpretation begins to wander too far from that which the author intended, though it may still remain at quite a distance from the scholar's perception of the work, or even from a response that a scholar would accept as "correct" (in the sense of fully consistent, parsimonious, and nontrivial). Even granting that the response of the novice will miss much of the complexity and subtlety of the "great works," it does not necessarily follow that the educative power of well-written passages is not strong enough to develop in the student who is reading widely exactly the same sensitivity that the advocates of close reading have been concerned with. Since the effects of extensive reading are more personal and less explicitly formulated, they may provoke a response less subject to the "distancing" and loss of involvement that can result from the imposition of a cognitive, content-centered frame of reference.

Goals for the study of English depend upon prior assumptions about the nature and purpose of education.

Much attention has always been given to the specification of adequate goals for instruction in English. It has been taught as a way to exercise the faculties of memory and reason, to teach basic language skills, to provide guidance and adjustment, to introduce the student to the conceptual structure of an academic discipline. Such goals are often in conflict and can be ordered only on the basis of principles which derive from assumptions about education as a whole. If academic subject matter is to be at the top of the educational hierarchy, goals for instruction must logically be based in the discipline itself. Any discovery that the discipline is ill defined and somewhat unstable does not alter this, though it may make the problem more difficult during the interim period of attempting to reformulate what Frye has called the "elementary teaching principles." Conversely, if the purpose of education is personal and linguistic growth, then the goals for instruction must be formulated in terms of that growth rather than in the structuring principles of the discipline of English—even if those principles have been agreed upon.

It has always been possible to provide an "inventory" of goals (behavioral or otherwise) for English, but such an inventory confuses rather than clarifies the instructional issues: an inventory in itself provides no way to determine which goals are central and which peripheral and derivative. This is the importance of the perennial question, "What is English?" To answer it is to specify implicitly which goals are central and which of lesser importance. If, for example, English is defined as a set of mechanical skills in language use, a goal such as "good spelling" may emerge near the top of the hierarchy. It becomes important in itself and instruction can be focussed directly upon it. This has in fact sometimes happened because spelling has been defined as a mark of a good education; students have been tested and drilled in spelling for its own sake. If, however, English is defined as a way to order and understand the world through language, then spelling becomes a secondary goal. The focus of instruction will be on using language in a significant exploration of the world, with spelling simply a skill which is useful but not central in that process. Though spelling may still be taught directly, such teaching will have to be assessed in terms of its effect on the larger goal rather than simply in terms of improvement in spelling ability.

Sequence in the study of English must derive from psychological rather than logical principles.

Nineteenth century pedagogy derived from mental discipline and faculty psychology represented the extreme opposite of this point of view: at that time the educational value of a subject was held to stem from its logical principles, and these were taught directly. In the teaching of English the rules of grammar, rhetoric, and composition were originally important for these reasons. Dewey and the progressives emphasized that this was improper, that education must be based on the psychology of the child rather than the logic of the discipline; but their admonitions were never widely observed at the secondary school level. The problem was and is that psychological patterns are far more complex and less fully understood than logical ones; anything more than a metaphorical use of terms like "growth" and "experience" is extremely difficult.

This is one of the problems with behavioral objectives: they carry with them pedagogical principles which assume that desired goals can be reached through the acquisition of component behaviors. Though this approach may seem reasonable, it represents a quantum leap in our knowledge about the psychological processes underlying the teaching and learning of English. We can attempt, as the Tri-University Project has done, to list the end points of the program; and given the end points we can define a beginning as "where the student is." The territory between these two extremes is vast and uncharted; there is no reason to assume that the best way from one to another will be a straight line—or even that there is one "best" route that students should follow.

The most evident examples come from the teaching of composition. For many years the classroom emphasis in this aspect of English has been on exactly the sorts of skills that can be most easily formulated in terms of behavioral objectives: correct spelling, good grammar, paragraph form, and the like. All of these are seen as very direct antecedents of what has been viewed as good adult writing. Yet when the mechanics of good writing have been successfully taught, good expression has not necessarily followed; the one does not grow steadily into the other. In a similar way, within the study of literature the emphasis on the skills of reading has not led, as some have hoped, into the "higher" skills involved in response to literature. Whether formulated in the pedagogical terms of W. S. Gray and the reading specialists or in the literary terms of the New Critics, the attempt to provide the "missing elements" of the mature response has not been successful—presumably because the relationship between the mature response and the elements which make it up has a different psychological nature than those attempts have assumed.

The proponents of behavioral objectives quite rightly assert that if we are going to teach a lesson, we had better know why we are teaching it. Yet to be able to formulate objectives for a course, and in finer grain for any given lesson, does not mean that we can specify a sequence of component behaviors that contribute to those goals. Behavioral objectives are the wrong sort of objectives for the teaching of English not because they emphasize behavior, and not because they ask us to be precise about what we are doing, but because they divert attention from the central problem of establishing and maintaining instructional priorities. They assume that there are clear and precise "steps along the way" to the goals we desire, and that the best way to those goals is to concentrate upon those "steps." But the teaching of literature is a more tentative enterprise than this implies; we know too little about fostering the kind of development we seem to cherish. The very materials with which we are working are so complex, touching upon such different aspects of the child's linguistic and moral development, that they may *always* resist formulation in the short-term stages that behavioral objectives imply. What we seek to do in English is not to add discrete components of skill or knowledge, but gradually to elaborate the linguistic and intellectual repertoire of our students, a process that is more fluid than linear, more fortuitous than predictable.

The defenders of behavioral objectives argue that such complex and humanistic objectives need not be abused but in fact can be clarified and illuminated; but this is naive. The pressures for a hard content in English are strong, and the balance of instructional effort easily tipped in their favor. On the other hand, there is a clear need for a well-formulated set of goals within a conceptual frame from which the sequence and direction of instruction can be specified. One of the failures of the progressive program in the late thirties was its inability to specify precisely its structuring principles, leaving the "experience curriculum" subject to a continuing loss of focus and gradual erosion. When the principles on which the scope and sequence of instruction are to be based are not clearly specified, it is inevitable that irrelevant activities will claim a place; and it is just as inevitable that, if this second stratum of the curriculum has an internal logic of its own, that logic will seek to fill the gap in curriculum theory and establish itself in a central rather than a secondary role. Certainly such a filling-of-the-void had much to do with the replacement of experience by adjustment during the forties and fifties, for adjustment had at least a clearly defined end point.

The Next Chapters

English as a school subject is relatively young; its history stretches back barely a hundred years, its place of prominence much less than that. During that time English has responded openly to changing pedagogical and social concerns, assimilating and redefining them as necessary. Though its very openness has led to many false starts and temporary diversions—even a propensity for fads and gimmicks—over the long term it has shed the distortions of one point of view after another. Here, too, we may be dealing with the educative effects of the subject matter: the scope of English is too broad, its influence on those who teach it too consuming, for it to long remain confined within a narrow framework. Today's teachers of English are better trained than their predecessors, with a stronger national organization and a more professionally oriented body of colleagues than at any previous time. Though the shape of the "new English" may be unclear from the perspective of the present, the next chapters of this history, when they are written, will surely describe a curriculum better than any we have seen in the past.

This section gathers together important secondary sources and surveys of the teaching of English; those which figured prominently in the present study are briefly annotated. The many contemporary books, articles, and monographs out of which the history grew are not listed here; representative examples are referenced in the appropriate places in the text. Dissertations dealing with any aspect of the history of English instruction are included in the bibliography, even when not directly relevant to the teaching of literature.

Selected Bibliography

Achtert, Walter Scott. *A History of English Studies to 1883 Based on the Research of William Riley Parker*. Dissertation, New York University, 1972. University Microfilms No. 72-31,057.

Adler, Richard, and Applebee, Arthur N. *Annotated Humanities Programs*. Urbana, Ill.: NCTE, 1968. Descriptive annotations of programs in all parts of the nation. No summary or evaluation provided in this report.

Aikin, Wilford M. *The Story of the Eight-Year Study*. New York: Harper and Bros., 1942. Summary of the Eight-Year Study of the Progressive Education Association by its director. Discusses background and aims.

Allen, Don Cameron. *The Ph.D. in English and American Literature*. New York: Holt, Rinehart & Winston, 1968. First chapter discusses development of English studies in American colleges and universities.

Anderson, Scarvia. *Between the Grimms and 'The Group': Literature in American High Schools*. Princeton, N.J.: Educational Testing Service, 1964. Random survey of course requirements.

Beesley, Patricia. *The Revival of the Humanities in American Education*. New York: Columbia University Press, 1940. Summarizes changes in college programs as part of general education movement.

Bell, Daniel. *The Reforming of General Education*. New York: Columbia University Press, 1966. Includes good discussion of history and current trends.

Bennett, Robert, ed. *Summary Progress Report of English Curriculum Study and Demonstration Centers*. Champaign, Ill.: NCTE, 1966. Reports from the directors of the study centers.

Berberi, Edel Ann Winje. *A Descriptive Analysis of Anthologies for the Tenth Grade as the Texts Are Related to the Objectives for the Study of Literature as Expressed by National Professional Groups*. Dissertation, Indiana University, 1965. University Microfilms No. 65-14031. Traces attitudes of MLA, NCTE, CEEB, NSSE, NEA, and NASSP toward "modern" philosophy of instruction in literature. Concludes texts follow major trends.

Bernd, John Muth. *Approaches to the Teaching of Literature in Secondary School, 1900-1956.* Dissertation, University of Wisconsin, 1957. University Microfilms No. 24,264. Good discussion of justifications for the various approaches in successive periods: classics, historical/chronological, types, themes, problems, individual reading, correlation.

Bernhardt, Norma Woosley. *Trends in the Teaching of English Written Composition in the Secondary Schools of the United States: 1900-1960.* Dissertation, University of North Carolina (Chapel Hill), 1963. University Microfilms No. 64-1834.

Bessy, Mabel A. *Report of a Committee of the NCTE on the Use of the Magazine in the High School English Classroom.* Chicago: NCTE, 1935. 1934 survey of magazine use in classrooms of 600 teachers.

Bibb, Evelyn Rezek. *Anthologies of American Literature, 1787-1964.* Dissertation, Columbia University, 1965. University Microfilms No. 66-1728. Traces evolution of commerical as well as school anthology. Best available discussion of early forms of these books.

Billett, Ray O. *Provisions for Individual Differences, Marking, and Promotion.* USOE Bulletin 1932, no. 17 (National Survey of Secondary Education Report no. 13). Washington, D.C.: Government Printing Office, 1933. Survey of practice in 8,594 secondary schools; discusses Dalton, Morrison, project, problem, contract, and other methods.

Boring, Edwin G. *A History of Experimental Psychology.* New York: Appleton-Century-Crofts, 1929. Discusses changes in psychology during early twentieth century.

Botts, Roderic Chellis. *Influences on the Teaching of English, 1917-35: An Illusion of Progress.* Dissertation, Northwestern University, 1970. University Microfilms No. 71-1799.

Bowers, C. A. *The Progressive Educator and the Depression.* New York: Random House, 1969. Background on social movements and educational reform during the 1930s, especially on the social reconstructionists.

Braddock, Richard, et al. *Research in Written Composition.* Urbana, Ill.: NCTE, 1963. Critical review and summary of research.

Broome, Edwin C. *A Historical and Critical Discussion of College Admission Requirements.* Contributions to Philosophy, Psychology, and Education, nos. 3-4. New York: Columbia University Press, 1903. Traces requirements from their origin in colonial colleges.

Burd, Henry A. "English Literature Courses in the Small College," *English Journal* 3:2 (February 1914), 99-108. Report of an NCTE survey.

Bureau of the Census. *Historical Statistics of the United States.* Washington, D.C.: Government Printing Office, 1960. Summarizes census and Bureau of Education statistics on the growth of the schools; includes estimates of students enrolled in English after 1900.

Burress, Lee A., Jr. *How Censorship Affects the School.* Special Bulletin no. 8. Wisconsin Council of Teachers of English, 1963. Survey of censorship in Wisconsin schools.

Butler, Donna, and O'Donnell, Bernard. *A Guide to Available Project English Materials.* Urbana, Ill.: NCTE, 1969. Abstracts and bibliographical information for available materials.

Callahan, Raymond E. *Education and the Cult of Efficiency.* Chicago: University of Chicago Press, 1962. Major source on the efficiency movement in education in early twentieth century.

Carpenter, George R.; Baker, Franklin T.; and Scott, Fred N. *The Teaching of English in the Elementary and the Secondary School.* New York: Longmans, Green, and Co., 1903. Extensive discussions of trends in the teaching of English up to 1900. Thorough bibliographies on all aspects of instruction.

Clapp, John Mantle. *The Place of English in American Life.* Report of an Investigation by a Committee of the National Council of Teachers of English. Chicago: NCTE, 1926. Survey of the uses of English in various occupations and social classes.

Clapp, John Mantle. "Report of Committee on Place and Function of English in American Life," *English Journal* 15:2 (February 1926), 110-34. Summary of committee report.

Commager, Henry Steele, ed. *McGuffey's Fifth Eclectic Reader.* New York: New American Library, 1962. Commager's introduction to this reprint edition outlines the history and influence of the series of readers.

Commission on English. *Examining the Examination in English.* Harvard Studies in English, vol. 17. Cambridge, Mass.: Harvard University Press, 1931. Reviews the history and form of the examinations set by the College Board.

Commission on English. *Freedom and Discipline in English.* New York: College Entrance Examination Board, 1965. Reviews the work of the Commission on English established in 1959.

Committee of the Faculty of Harvard College and of the Graduate School of Education. *The Training of Secondary School Teachers Especially with Reference to English.* Cambridge, Mass.: Harvard University Press, 1942. Reviews effect of the expansion of public education upon teacher education; comments on the influence of NCTE.

Committee of the Massachusetts Teachers Association. "English in Secondary Schools," *The Academy* 3 (January 1889), 593-609. Survey of Massachusetts schools and of 50 "important" high schools in other states; spread and characteristics of course, methods of study.

Committee of the Northern Illinois High School Teachers' Association. "English in the High School," *The Academy* 4 (May 1889), 179-200. Report of 1888 survey of national sample of 135 schools.

Committee of Ten of the NEA. *Report of the Committee of Ten on Secondary School Studies, with the Reports of the Conferences Arranged by the Committee.* New York: American Book Co. for the NEA, 1894. Contains the report of the Vassar Conference on English held in 1893.

Committee on College Entrance Requirements in English. "The Influence of the Uniform Entrance Requirements in English," *English Journal* 1:2 (February 1912), 95-121. Survey carried out by NEA committee chaired by Hosic.

Committee on English Equipment. "Report of the Committee," *English Journal* 2:3 (March 1913), 178-84. Early NCTE survey.

Committee on General Education. *General Education in a Free Society.* Cambridge, Mass.: Harvard University Press, 1945. Reviews changes in the high schools in relation to general education.

Committee on the High School Course in English. "Types of Organization of High-School English," *English Journal* 2:8 (November 1913), 575-96. Questionnaire survey of national sample of 307 schools; class size, organization, emphases, and titles.

Committee on National Interest. *The National Interest and the Continuing Education of Teachers of English: A Report on the State of the Profession, 1964.* Urbana, Ill.: NCTE, 1964. Second survey on teaching conditions and teacher preparation.

Committee on National Interest. *The National Interest and the Teaching of English: A Report on the Status of the Profession.* Urbana, Ill.: NCTE, 1961. Extensive description of professional conditions, including some new data from questionnaire surveys.

Committee on Plays in Schools and Colleges. "Report of the Committee," *English Journal* 4:1 (January 1915), 34-40. NCTE survey.

Committee on Preparation of High School Teachers of English. "Report of the Committee," *English Journal* 4:5 (May 1915), 323-32. NCTE questionnaire survey; summarizes 450 responses from 1,500 forms distributed.

Conant, James B. *The American High School Today: A First Report to Interested Citizens.* New York: Signet Books, 1964. First edition by McGraw Hill Book Co., 1959. Report of school visits with recommendations on the comprehensive high school.

Conant, James B. *Slums and Suburbs.* New York: Signet Books, 1961. Second report, contrasting urban and suburban education.

Conrad, Erna B., and Hickok, Katherine. "Placement of Literary Selections for Junior and Senior High Schools," *English Journal* 19:5 (May 1930), 377-84. Summarizes grade placement of literary works in 44 courses of study published since 1920; 22 of these were state courses.

Cook, Albert S. *A Brief Summary of the Proceedings of the Conference on Uniform Entrance Requirements in English.* New York: The Conference, 1899. Official account of the background and early history of the conference.

Corbin, Jonathan. *Annotated Humanities Programs.* Champaign, Ill.: NCTE, 1967. Descriptive summaries of programs from all parts of the nation. No summary or evaluation provided in this report.

Corbin, Richard, and Crosby, Muriel. *Language Programs for the Disadvantaged.* The Report of the NCTE Task Force on Teaching English to the Disadvantaged. Urbana, Ill.: NCTE, 1965. Summary of observations of programs at all age levels by a team of 22 observers; descriptive rather than statistical report.

Counts, George S. "Approved High Schools of the North Central Association of Colleges and Secondary Schools," in *A Study of the Colleges and High Schools in the North Central Area.* Bureau of Education Bulletin 1915, no. 6. Washington, D.C.: Government Printing Office, 1915. Reports enrollments and subjects offered.

Counts, George S. *The Senior High School Curriculum.* Supplementary Educational Monographs no. 29. Chicago: University of Chicago Press, 1926. Discusses English programs in 15 "progressive" cities.

Cremin, Lawrence A. *The Transformation of the School: Progressivism in American Education.* New York: Vintage Books, 1961. Essential background on all aspects of the progressive movement.

Davis, Calvin O. *A History of the North Central Association.* Ann Arbor, Mich.: NCA, 1945.

Dexter, Edwin C. "Ten Years' Influence of the Report of the Committee of Ten," *School Review* 14 (April 1906), 254-69. Contrasts courses of study in 1905 and 1895, nationwide.

Donlan, Daniel Mahaney. *Dilemma of Choice: Revolution in English Curricula, 1958-1968.* Dissertation, Stanford University, 1972. University Microfilms No. 72-16,712.

Douglas, Harl R. and Filk, Anna M. "The Classroom Practices of Minnesota Teachers of High-School English," *English Journal* 27:3 (March 1938), 252-57. Briefly reported checklist study of methods.

Ehrenpreis, Irvin. *The "Types Approach" to Literature.* New York: King's Crown Press, 1945. Most thorough discussion of the evolution of the types approach and its emergence in the high school curriculum.

Elson, Ruth Miller. *Guardians of Tradition: American Schoolbooks of the Nineteenth Century.* Lincoln: University of Nebraska Press, 1964. Extensive discussion of school readers.

Emerson, Oliver Farrar. "English in Preparatory Schools," *The Academy* 5 (February 1890), 104-08. Survey report.

Evans, Mae J. "How Much Work Is Done in American Literature in the High Schools?" *School Review* 11 (October 1903), 647-54. Survey report.

Fay, Robert Sargent. *The Reorganization Movement in English Teaching, 1910-1917.* Dissertation, Harvard University, 1968. University Microfilms No. 68-12,068. Traces goals and influence of the movement, as a case study in educational reform.

Finch, Hardy R. "Film Production in the School—A Survey," *English Journal* 28:5 (May 1939), 365-71.

Ford, Paul Leicester, ed. *The New England Primer.* New York: Teachers College, Columbia University, 1962. Reprint edition with Ford's classic introduction.

Garner, W. Lee. *Programmed Instruction.* New York: Center for Applied Research in Education, 1966. Sympathetic description of the evolution of this approach.

Gerber, John C. "The 1962 Summer Institutes of the Commission on English, *PMLA* 78 (September 1963), 9-25. Report from the chairman of the team of evaluators.

Getz, Howard G. *Paraprofessionals in the English Department.* Urbana, Ill.: NCTE/ERIC, 1972. Review and questionnaire survey of schools in Illinois, Indiana, and Michigan.

Gibson, James Chester. *An Examination of Speech Teaching in Selected Georgia Educational Institutions, 1732-1900.* Dissertation, University of Georgia, 1971. University Microfilms No. 72-2485.

Giles, H. H.; McCutchen, S. P.; and Zechiel, A. N. *Exploring the Curriculum: The Work of the Thirty Schools from the Viewpoint of the Curriculum Consultants.* New York: Harper and Bros., 1942. Describes the evolution of the core curriculum.

Graham, Patricia A. *Progressive Education: From Arcady to Academe.* New York: Teachers College, Columbia University, 1967. History of the PEA.

Grandgent, Charles H. "The Modern Languages," in *The Development of Harvard University Since the Inauguration of President Eliot, 1869-1929,* edited by Samuel Eliot Morison. Cambridge, Mass.: Harvard University Press, 1930. Briefly describes the beginnings of English instruction at Harvard.

Grimes, Mildred L. "These Latter Years," *English Leaflet* 50 (Whole number 442: February 1951), 17-36. Recent history of New England Association of Teachers of English.

Grommon, Alfred H. "A History of the Preparation of Teachers of English," *English Journal* 57:4 (April 1968), 484-527. Detailed and useful.

Gruen, Ferdinand B. *English Grammar in American High Schools Since 1900.* Washington, D.C.: Catholic University of America, 1934.

Guder, Darrell L. *The History of Belles-Lettres at Princeton: An Investigation of the Expansion and Secularization of Curricula at the College of New Jersey with Special Reference to the Curricula of English Language and Letters.* Unpublished dissertation, University of Hamburg, 1965.

Hanson, Charles Lane. "The Early Years of Our Association," *English Leaflet* 48 (Whole number 427: March 1949): 33-47. History of first years of New England Association of Teachers of English.

Harvard University. *Twenty Years of School and College English.* Cambridge, Mass.: Harvard University Press, 1896. Details the changing entrance requirements.

Hatfield, W. Wilbur. "Farewell!" *English Journal* 44:5 (May 1955), 288-89. Brief reflections on retiring from the editorship.

Hatfield, W. Wilbur. "General and Specialized Literary Clubs," *English Journal* 15:6 (June 1926), 450-56. Survey report; descriptive rather than statistical.

Hays, Edna. *College Entrance Requirements in English: Their Effects on the High Schools.* Contributions to Education, no. 675. New York: Teachers College, Columbia University, 1936. Detailed history of the requirements and their effects.

Hickman, Lucian G. "The Teaching of Composition and Literature in the High Schools of Indiana," *English Journal* 10:3 (March 1921), 142-59. Useful survey report.

Hillocks, George, Jr. *Alternatives in English: A Critical Appraisal of Elective Programs.* Urbana, Ill.: NCTE, 1972. Review of movement and analysis of 76 program guides.

Hoetker, James. *Dramatics and the Teaching of Literature.* Urbana, Ill.: NCTE, 1969. Critical review of current approaches and historical background.

Holman, Alfred, Jr. *The Teaching of Literature in American Secondary Schools: An Historical Study of the Theories of Literature Instruction Since 1900.* Unpublished dissertation, University of Cincinnati, 1945.

Hook, J. N. "Characteristics of Award-Winning High Schools," *English Journal* 50:1 (January 1961), 9-15. Survey of schools producing NCTE Achievement Award winners.

Hooper, Cyrus L. "Existing Conditions in the Teaching of English," *School Review* 15 (April 1907), 261-74. Survey report on 70 schools.

Hopkins, E. M. *Report on the Cost and Labor of English Teaching.* For MLA and NCTE. Lawrence, Kansas: Journalism Press, University of Kansas, 1913. Focusses on composition.

Horner, Robert W., and Lagios, Socrates A. "An Overview of Humanities Programs throughout the Country," *English Leaflet* 63 (Fall 1964), 39-57. Survey report.

Hosic, James Fleming. "The National Council of Teachers of English," *English Journal* 10:1 (January 1921), 1-10. Reviews early history.

Hosic, James Fleming. "The National Council after Twenty Years," *English Journal* 21:2 (February 1932), 107-13. Reviews early history.

Hosic, James Fleming, comp. *Reorganization of English in Secondary Schools.* Bureau of Education Bulletin 1917, no. 2. Washington, D.C.: Government Printing Office, 1917. Report of the Joint Committee on English; reviews history and present status of the teaching of English.

Hotopf, W. H. N. *Language, Thought and Comprehension: A Case Study of the Writings of I. A. Richards.* London: Routledge and Kegan Paul, 1965. Background on Richards's thought and influence.

Hudelson, Earl. "English Composition, Its Aims, Methods, and Measurement," in National Society for the Study of Education, *Twenty-Second Yearbook.* Bloomington, Ill.: Public School Publishing Co., 1923. Surveys aims and methods in 240 high schools.

Hudelson, Earl. "Our Course of Study in Literature," *English Journal* 12:7 (September 1923), 481-87. Summarizes required and recommended reading in 38 state courses of study.

Huston, Jon Reckard. *An Analysis of English Grammar Textbooks Used in American Schools Before 1850.* Dissertation, University of Pittsburgh, 1954. University Microfilms No. 8896.

Jewett, Arno. *English Language Arts in American High Schools.* U.S. Office of Education Bulletin 1958, no. 13. Washington, D.C.: Government Printing Office, 1959. Survey of 258 courses of study in current use; examines organization, goals, content.

Jewett, Ida A. *English in State Teachers Colleges: A Catalogue Study.* Contributions to Education no. 286. New York: Teachers College, Columbia University, 1927. Studies offerings in all phases of English in 1900 and 1925.

Johnson, Clifton. *Old-Time Schools and School-Books.* New York: Dover Publications, 1963. First edition 1904. Antiquarian view of early texts, copiously illustrated.

Katz, Michael. *The Irony of Early School Reform: Educational Innovation in Mid-Nineteenth Century Massachusetts.* Cambridge, Mass.: Harvard University Press, 1968. Discusses motivation behind mid-century extension of education; high school as instrument of social control.

Kelly, Louis G. *25 Centuries of Language Teaching.* Rowley, Mass.: Newbury House, 1969. Traces methods and approaches in language teaching to their origins in classical civilizations.

Krouse, Harry B. *History and Evaluation of the Critical Trends, Exclusive of Fiction, in the* Atlantic Monthly, *1857 to 1898.* Dissertation, University of Wisconsin, 1972. University Microfilms No. 72-22,101. Attitudes toward literature in later nineteenth century; not directly concerned with educational issues.

Krug, Edward A. *Charles W. Eliot and Popular Education.* New York: Teachers College, Columbia University, 1961. Good introduction to the struggle between the "ancient" and "modern" subjects; reprints some of Eliot's discussions of the teaching of English.

Krug, Edward A. *The Shaping of the American High School.* New York: Harper & Row, 1964. Background on the expansion of the school after 1880, through the reorganization period.

Leonard, Sterling Andrus. *The Doctrine of Correctness in English Usage 1700-1800.* University of Wisconsin Studies in Language and Literature no. 25. Madison: University of Wisconsin Press, 1929. Thorough history of the prescriptive tradition in grammar and rhetoric.

Lewis, John Smith, Jr. *The History of Instruction in American Literature in Colleges and Universities of the United States.* Dissertation, New York University, 1941. University Microfilms No. 431. Includes discussion of instruction in nineteenth century colleges.

Lull, Herbert Galen. *Inherited Tendencies of Secondary Instruction in the United States.* University of California Publications in Education vol. 3, no. 3 (April 1913), 155-281. Useful illustrations of eighteenth and nineteenth century instruction, especially as it related to faculty psychology and mental discipline.

Lynch, James J., and Evans, Bertrand. *High School English Textbooks: A Critical Examination.* Boston: Little, Brown and Company, 1963. Exhaustive analysis and critique of language and literature texts.

Lyon, Leverett S. "The Business-English Situation in the Secondary School," *English Journal* 7:9 (November 1918), 576-87. Status survey.

McCrosky, Cecile B. "The Administration of English in the High-School Curriculum," *English Journal* 7:2 (February 1918), 108-17. Summarizes replies from 33 Ohio schools on conditions and equipment.

McDavid, Raven I., Jr. *An Examination of the Attitudes of the NCTE toward Language.* Research Report no. 4. Urbana, Ill.: NCTE, 1965. Chronicles changing attitudes in journal discussions; little analysis.

Macgowan, Kenneth. *Footlights Across America.* New York: Harcourt, Brace and Co., 1929. Discusses background of the little theater movement.

Madsen, Harold Stanley. *An Historical Study of the Forces That Have Shaped English Instruction in Utah's Secondary Schools.* Dissertation, University of Colorado, 1965. University Microfilms No. 66-3256.

Malone, Kemp. "The Rise of Modern Philology," *Bulletin of the Modern Humanities Research Association* 30 (November 1958), 19-31. Traces roots of modern philology back to ancient Greece; useful background.

Maloney, Henry B., ed. *Accountability and the Teaching of English.* Urbana, Ill.: NCTE, 1972. Continues in further detail the arguments pro and con presented in *On Writing Behavioral Objectives for English.*

Maloney, Henry B., ed. *Goal Making for English Teaching.* Urbana, Ill.: NCTE, 1973. A collection of varied personal opinion on uses and limitations of performance objectives for English.

Maloney, Henry B. "Stepsisters to Print: The Public Arts in the High School English Class," *English Journal* 49:8 (November 1960), 570-79. Includes brief chronicle of changing journal attitudes.

Mason, James Hocker. *The National Council of Teachers of English— 1911-1926.* Unpublished dissertation, George Peabody College for Teachers, 1962. University Microfilms No. 62-5681. Detailed chronicle of first years of NCTE; based on interviews with early leaders and on materials later destroyed by a fire at Council headquarters.

Maxwell, John, and Tovatt, Anthony, eds. *On Writing Behavioral Objectives for English.* Urbana, Ill.: NCTE, 1970. Spectrum of opinion prevailing during the height of this controversy.

Meade, Richard A. "Organization of Literature for Juniors and Seniors," *English Journal* 36:7 (September 1947), 366-70. Summarizes organization and aims of 15 state courses of study published between 1936 and 1946; very brief.

Meikle, Henry W. "The Chair of Rhetoric and Belles Lettres," *University of Edinburgh Journal* 13 (Autumn 1945), 89-103. Prime source on the Scottish rhetoricians and the events at Edinburgh: Stevenson, Smith, and Blair.

Mersand, Joseph. "The Teaching of Literature in American High Schools: 1865-1900," in *Perspectives on English*, edited by Robert C. Pooley. New York: Appleton-Century-Crofts, 1960. Useful discussion of early developments.

Michael, Ian. *English Grammatical Categories and the Tradition to 1800.* Cambridge: Cambridge University Press, 1970. Thorough analysis of the content of early grammars, in relation to those of the classical languages.

Morris, Charles R. "From the Age of Confidence to Roosevelt's First Term," *English Leaflet* 50 (Whole Number 441: January 1951), 1-14. History of New England Association from 1910 onward.

Mott, John H. *Reading Interests of Adolescents: A Critical Study of Fifty Years of Research.* Dissertation, University of Northern Colorado, 1971. University Microfilms No. 71-4203.

Moulton, Dorothy Evelyn. *The Teaching of Literature in the Senior High School: An Historical and Critical Study of Recent Trends Based upon an Analysis of Selected Professional Publications, 1911-55.* Dissertation, University of Michigan, 1959. University Microfilms No. 59-4966.

"The National Council, 1911-36," *English Journal* 25:10 (December 1936), 805-36. Lengthy review of early history; useful for perspective but inaccurate in its detail.

Neel, Helen McDonnell. *An Analysis of History of English Literature Textbooks Used in American Secondary Schools Before 1900.* Dissertation, University of Pittsburgh, 1954. University Microfilms No. 8907.

Nelson, Jack, and Roberts, Gene, Jr. *The Censors and the Schools.* Boston: Little, Brown and Co., 1963. Good discussion and historical overview.

Olson, James Warren. *The Nature of Literature Anthologies Used in the Teaching of High School English 1917-1957.* Dissertation, University of Wisconsin, 1969. University Microfilms No. 69-22,454. Excellent discussion of general trends in the teaching of literature as well as detailed analysis of the anthologies.

O'Neal, Robert. "World Literature in the High School," *English Journal* 52:2 (February 1963), 94-96. Chain letter survey by NCTE committee, with responses from 167 schools; lists titles used in these courses.

Palmer, D. J. *The Rise of English Studies.* London: Oxford University Press, 1965. Describes the evolution of English studies in Britain, especially at the university level.

Parker, William Riley. "Where Do English Departments Come From?" *College English* 28:5 (February 1967), 339-51. Fascinating but loosely documented account of early teaching of English in American colleges.

Payne, William Morton. *English in American Universities.* Boston: D.C. Heath and Co., 1895. Reprint of 1894 series in *The Dial.* Describes programs, emphases at 20 institutions.

Piché, Gene Laurence. *Revision and Reform in the Secondary School English Curriculum, 1870-1900*. Dissertation, University of Minnesota, 1967. University Microfilms No. 68-1559.

Pierson, George Wilson. *Yale College: An Educational History 1871-1921*. New Haven: Yale University Press, 1952. Includes brief account of early teaching of English at Yale.

Purves, Alan C., and Beach, Richard. *Literature and the Reader: Research in Response to Literature, Reading Interests, and the Teaching of Literature*. Urbana, Ill.: NCTE, 1972. Summary of research.

Quinn, Arthur Hobson. *A History of the American Drama from the Civil War to the Present*. New York: Appleton-Century-Crofts, 1936. Focusses on plays and playwrights.

Radner, Sanford. *Fifty Years of English Teaching: A Historical Analysis of the Presidential Addresses of NCTE*. Champaign, Ill.: NCTE, 1960. Brief summaries of all the presidential addresses.

Reeder, Rudolph R. *The Historical Development of School Readers and of Methods in Teaching Reading*. New York: Macmillan Co., 1900. Useful account of early readers.

Rogers, Rose Marie. *The Development of American Textbooks in Business English and Correspondence in the Secondary Schools*. Dissertation, University of Pittsburgh, 1958. University Microfilms No. 58-2035. 1900-1950.

Rosewell, Paul Truman. *A Historical Survey of Recommendations and Proposals for the Literature Curricula of American Secondary Schools since 1892*. Dissertation, University of Nebraska Teachers College, 1965. University Microfilms No. 66-2081. Useful summaries of the major curriculum statements and proposals; extensive quotations.

Rudolph, Frederick. *The American College and University: A History*. New York: Vintage Books, 1962. Background on all aspects of college education from colonial times; includes full discussion of the extra-curriculum.

Rugg, Harold. "Three Decades of Mental Discipline: Curriculum Making Via National Committees," in *Curriculum Making Past and Present*. Twenty-Sixth Yearbook of the National Society for the Study of Education, Part One. Bloomington, Ill.: Public School Publishing Co., 1926. Reviews the work of the major committees, including those of the reorganization period.

Rusk, Elizabeth Hartley. *The Treatment of 167 English Usages in Twelfth-Grade Language Textbooks, 1931-1951*. Dissertation, University of Illinois, 1953. University Microfilms No. 6007.

Ryan, Thomas Kevin. *Mass media and the Secondary School: An Examination of the Attitudes of the National Council of Teachers of English, 1911-1960, Toward Five Selected Mass Media as Expressed in The English Journal*. Dissertation, Ball State University, 1971. University Microfilms No. 72-7517.

Salter, Thomas I. *A Study of the Trends in the Teaching of English in Texas High Schools Since 1884*. Dissertation, University of Houston, 1955. University Microfilms No. 13,824.

Searles, John Rexford. *Some Trends in the Teaching of Literature Since 1900 in American High Schools*. Unpublished dissertation, University of Wisconsin, 1942. Contains the most thorough discussion of early texts on English and the teaching of English.

Shayer, David. *The Teaching of English in Schools: 1900-1970.* London and Boston: Routledge and Kegan Paul, 1972. History of English instruction in British schools; very little of relevance to American pattern.

Sherwin, J. Stephen. *Four Problems in Teaching English: A Critique of Research.* Scranton, Pennsylvania: International Textbook Co. for the NCTE, 1969. Definitive summary of research, with some historical perspective, in spelling, writing, diagramming, and the relationship between English and Latin instruction.

Shugrue, Michael F. *English in a Decade of Change.* New York: Pegasus, 1968. Useful account of developments since 1958.

Shugrue, Michael F. "New Materials for the Teaching of English from the English Program of the USOE," *PMLA* 81 (September 1966), 1-36. Summaries from the curriculum study centers of work in progress.

Silberman, Charles E. *Crisis in the Classroom: The Remaking of American Education.* New York: Random House, 1970. Critique and survey of current trends, for Carnegie Corporation.

Sizer, Theodore R., ed. *The Age of the Academies.* New York: Teachers College, Columbia University, 1964. Good background on patterns preceding high school movement; reprints a number of interesting early documents.

Sizer, Theodore R. *Secondary Schools at the Turn of the Century.* New Haven: Yale University Press, 1964. Committee of Ten, its background and influence.

Smith, Adam. *Lectures on Rhetoric and Belles Lettres.* Edited with an introduction and notes by John M. Lothian. Camden, N.J.: Thomas Nelson Sons, 1963. An expanded version of the original Edinburgh lectures, from a student's notes. Includes useful background on the transition from formal rhetoric to the Belles Lettres, and the general cultural shift of which it was a part.

Smith, Dora V. *Evaluating Instruction in Secondary School English.* A Report of a Division of the New York Regents' Inquiry into the Character and Cost of Public Education in New York State. Chicago: NCTE, 1941. Thorough study of New York schools, based on questionnaires, testing, and school visits.

Smith, Dora V. *Instruction in English.* Bureau of Education Bulletin 1932, no. 17. National Survey of Secondary Education Monograph no. 20. Washington, D.C.: Government Printing Office, 1933. Based on survey of 156 courses of study issued since 1925, and visits to 90 schools selected for interesting features of their programs. Detailed analyses of goals, methods, content in all areas of English nationally.

Smith, Nila Banton. *American Reading Instruction.* New York: Silver, Burdett and Co., 1934. Explores early history: texts, methods, philosophy.

Squire, James R., ed. *A Common Purpose: The Teaching of English in Great Britain, Canada, and the United States.* Urbana, Ill.: NCTE, 1966. Report of special conference in 1965; contains brief review of initial contacts with British programs.

Squire, James R. *Eight Year Report of the Executive Secretary 1960-1967.* Champaign, Ill.: NCTE, 1967. Retrospective review of developments in English and the NCTE during Squire's term of office.

Squire, James R. "English Literature," in *Encyclopedia of Educational Research*. Edited by Robert L. Ebel. New York: Macmillian Co., 1969. Review of research.

Squire, James R., ed. *A New Look at Progressive Education*. 1972 Yearbook of the ASCD. Washington, D.C,: ASCD, 1972. Reviews major aspects of progressivism in relation to current thought.

Squire, James R. and Applebee, Roger K. *High School English Instruction Today: The National Study of High School English Programs*. New York: Appleton-Century-Crofts, 1968. Study-in-depth of English instruction in 158 leading high schools of the early 1960s.

Squire, James R., and Applebee, Roger K. *Teaching English in the United Kingdom*. Urbana, Ill.: NCTE, 1969. Extension of the National Study to 42 British schools offering alternatives to typical American patterns of instruction.

Stahl, Donald E. *The Development of the English Curriculum in Chicago Public Schools from 1856 to 1958*. Dissertation, Northwestern University, 1960. University Microfilms No. 60-4798.

Stahl, Donald E. *A History of the English Curriculum in American High Schools*. Chicago: Lyceum Press, 1965. Published version of his thesis.

Steinberg, Erwin R. "Research on the Teaching of English," *PMLA* 79 (September 1964), 50-76. Project English status reports.

Stoddard, Francis H. "Conference on Uniform Entrance Requirements in English," *Educational Review* (1905), 375-83. History of the early years of the conference.

Stone, George Winchester, Jr. *Issues, Problems, and Approaches in the Teaching of English*. New York: Holt, Rinehart & Winston, 1964. (Copyright 1961 by the MLA.) Reprints a number of early statements on the teaching of English, including reports of the School and College Conference on English.

Stout, John Elbert. *The Development of High-School Curricula in the North Central States from 1860 to 1918*. Supplementary Educational Monographs vol. 3, no. 3. Chicago: University of Chicago Press, 1921. Extensive summary of course offerings in North Central schools. Considerable background on trends in English.

Tanner, George W. "Report of the Committee Appointed by the English Conference to Inquire Into the Teaching of English in the High Schools of the Middle West," *School Review* 15 (January 1907), 37-45. Surveys 67 schools, with special attention to influence of Uniform Lists.

Thirty Schools Tell Their Story. New York: Harper and Bros., 1942. Descriptions by the thirty schools of the Eight-Year Study, of the evolution of their courses of study. Much attention to English as part of core curriculum.

Thwaite, M. F. *From Primer to Pleasure*. London: The Library Association, 1963. Recounts history of children's literature as well as of school texts.

Veilh, Donald P. *An Historical Analysis of the Relations Between "English" and "Speech" Since 1910*. Unpublished dissertation, Teachers College, Columbia University, 1952. Concentrates on relations between Speech Association of America and NCTE.

Wellek, Rene. "Literary Scholarship," in *American Scholarship in the Twentieth Century*, edited by Merle Curti. Cambridge, Mass.: Harvard University Press, 1953. Good discussion of trends in scholarship, including nineteenth century background.

White, Helen C. *Changing Styles in Literary Studies.* Presidential Address of the Modern Humanities Research Association. London: Cambridge University Press for the MHRA, 1963. Interesting retrospective account of trends during twentieth century.

Williams, Raymond. *Culture and Society 1780-1950.* London: Chatto and Windus, 1958. Background on changing definitions of culture and the arts during the Romantic period.

Witt, Peter D. *The Beginnings of the Teaching of the Vernacular Literature in the Secondary Schools of Massachusetts.* Dissertation, Harvard University, 1968. University Microfilms No. 69-11,507. Fullest account of instruction in the early years; concentrates on limited geographic region, but one that was central in shaping patterns of instruction.

Wright, Grace S. *Core Curriculum in Public High Schools: An Inquiry into Practice, 1949.* U.S. Office of Education Bulletin 1950, no. 5. Washington, D.C.: Government Printing Office, 1950. Results from questionnaire to 13,816 high schools; discusses patterns and geographic distribution.

Zielonka, Alfred Walter. *The Modern Language Association of America 1883-1960: An Historical Account of Selected Activities.* Dissertation, State University of New York at Buffalo, 1964. University Microfilms no. 64-13,673.

Appendices

c. 1690   *The New England Primer* issued by Benjamin Harris.

1755   Ebenezer Kinnersley appointed professor of the English tongue and oratory, College of Pennsylvania.

1759-84   Hugh Blair lectures at Edinburgh, continuing an earlier series by Adam Smith; publishes *Lectures on Rhetoric and Belles Lettres* (1783).

1783-95   Noah Webster publishes his *Grammatical Institute of the English Language.*

1819   The College of New Jersey sets an entrance requirement in English grammar.

1836   The first volume of McGuffey's *Readers* appears.

1848   Thomas Budge Shaw's *Outlines of English Literature* published in London; American edition follows in 1849.

1857   Francis Andrew March appointed professor of English language and comparative philology, Lafayette College.

1867   Matthew Arnold publishes *Culture and Anarchy.*

1867   William James Rolfe, principal at Cambridge High School, Massachusetts, publishes an annotated *Julius Caesar.*

1874   Harvard requires the reading of standard authors as part of its entrance requirement in English composition.

1876   Francis James Child appointed professor of English at Harvard; his student, Robert Grant, earns the first American Ph.D. in English literature.

1893-94   Vassar Conference on English called by the Committee of Ten; Yale sets an entrance requirement in English literature separate from composition; National Conference on Uniform Entrance Requirements in English organized.

1895   Hiram Corson publishes his *Aims of Literary Study.*

1899   John Dewey's *School and Society* published; NEA Committee on College Entrance Requirements makes its report.

1901   First regional association of teachers of English organized, in New England.

1902-03   Textbooks on the teaching of English published by Percival Chubb and by George R. Carpenter, Franklin T. Baker, and Fred N. Scott.

1910-11   New York State protests about the entrance requirements in English lead to the founding of the National Council of Teachers of English, in Chicago, December 1, 1911.

1916   College Board decides to offer two examinations in English, one of which will not require the study of a set list of books.

1917   National Joint Committee on English, cosponsored by NCTE and NEA, publishes its report, *Reorganization of English in Secondary Schools.*

1918   William H. Kilpatrick describes the project method; *Cardinal Principles of Secondary Education* published.

1922-24   Scott, Foresman *Literature and Life* series sets the pattern for school anthologies.

1926   NCTE committee report on "The Place and Function of English in American Life" justifies English as a functional study, but ignores literature.

1927   Nancy Coryell completes the first major experimental study in the teaching of literature.

1929   I. A. Richards publishes *Practical Criticism.*

1931   College Board Commission on English recommends abolishing of entrance examination based on list of texts; the recommendation is accepted and leads to the dissolution of the National Conference on Uniform Entrance Requirements in English.

1932   Eight-Year Study of the Progressive Education Association begins.

1935   NCTE Curriculum Commission presents its major report, *An Experience Curriculum in English.*

1938   Louise Rosenblatt publishes *Literature as Exploration* for the PEA; Cleanth Brooks and Robert Penn Warren publish *Understanding Poetry.*

1940   Mortiner Adler attacks the progressives in *How to Read a Book.*

1945   NCTE Commission on the English Curriculum organized; its report on the secondary school not published till 1956.

1950-52   National Science Foundation established; Ford Fund for the Advancement of Education begins experiments with early admissions and advanced placement.

1957   Sputnik launched; educators focus on the academically talented.

1958   National Defense Education Act omits funds for English; NCTE cosponsors a series of Basic Issues Conferences with MLA and other interested organizations.

1959   Woods Hole Conference held, leading to Bruner's report, *The Process of Education* (1960). College Board Commission on English begins formulation of an academic curriculum in English.

1962   First summer institutes in the teaching of English, under College Board sponsorship; Project English and curriculum study centers begin.

1963   National Study of High School English Programs begins.

1966   Anglo-American Seminar on the Teaching of English held at Dartmouth.

1967   National Study extended to British schools.

1968-70 Disillusionment with academic reform leads to reassertion of progressive principles in the teaching of English; reports from Dartmouth and the study of British schools suggest new models; electives adopted by many secondary schools.

Appendix II: Offerings in English in the North Central Area, 1860-1900.

Percent of Schools Offering*

Course Title	1860-65	1866-70	1871-75	1876-80	1881-85	1886-90	1891-95	1896-1900
First Year English	—	—	—	—	—	26	32.5	42.5
Second Year English	—	—	—	—	—	26	22.5	35.0
Third Year English	—	—	—	—	—	23	15.0	27.5
Fourth Year English	—	—	—	—	—	3	7.5	15.0
English	—	—	—	—	4	—	—	—
English Literature	30	65	90	70	72	70	52.5	37.5
American Literature	—	10	10	15	12	20	22.5	15.0
Literature	5	—	—	—	16	20	32.5	35.0
History of English Literature	5	5	5	10	4	—	—	—
Classics	5	—	—	—	32	3	25.0	15.0
Elements of Criticism	20	—	—	5	—	—	—	—
Reading	30	35	5	10	24	30	2.5	10.0
English Language	—	5	5	10	—	—	—	—
Composition	55	40	60	60	36	42	52.5	42.0
Rhetoric	90	75	85	85	84	83	67.5	62.5
Grammar	60	45	40	30	52	66	35.0	35.0
Analysis	55	40	35	25	24	25	2.5	2.5
Word Analysis	20	—	—	5	12	17	10.0	12.0
Orthography	—	—	—	—	—	3	—	5.0
Elocution	5	10	10	5	16	6	—	—
(Latin	80	85	90	75	92	83	95	97.5)

*The schools for the various periods overlap but are not strictly identical. After 1900, "literature" and "composition" were offered in 100 percent of the schools. This is an excerpt from John E. Stout, *The Development of High School Curricula in the North Central States from 1860-1918*, Supplementary Educational Monographs vol. 3, no. 3. (Chicago: University of Chicago Press, June 1921), Table X, pp. 71-74.

Appendix III: College Entrance Requirements in English Literature, 1874-1900

Authors and Titles in Order of Their First Appearance on the Entrance Lists.*

Shakespeare	1874:	*The Tempest*
		Julius Caesar
		The Merchant of Venice
	1878:	*Macbeth*
		Coriolanus
		As You Like It
	1879:	*Richard II*
		A Midsummer Night's Dream
	1880:	*King Lear*
		Much Ado about Nothing
	1881:	*Romeo and Juliet*
		Hamlet
	1882:	*Othello*
		King John
	1893:	*Twelfth Night*
Goldsmith	1874:	*The Vicar of Wakefield*
	1881:	*She Stoops to Conquer*
	1882:	*The Deserted Village*
Scott	1874:	*Ivanhoe*
		The Lay of the Last Minstrel
	1877:	*Waverley*
		Marmion
	1878:	*Kenilworth*
		The Lady of the Lake
	1879:	*Guy Mannering*
	1880:	*Quentin Durward*
	1881:	*The Abbot*
	1882:	*The Bride of Lammermoor*
	1889:	*Rob Roy*
	1891:	*Old Mortality*
	1892:	*The Talisman*
	1896:	*Woodstock*
Irving	1878:	*The Sketch Book*
	1881:	*Life of Goldsmith*

*This is a rearrangement of an appendix provided by Edna Hays, *College Entrance Requirements in English: Their Effects on the High Schools* (New York: Teachers College, Columbia University, 1936), pp. 133-35.

	1887:	*Bracebridge Hall*
	1891:	*The Alhambra*
	1896:	*Tales of a Traveler*
Byron	1879:	*The Prisoner of Chillon*
Thackeray	1879:	*Henry Esmond*
	1888:	*The English Humorists*
Macaulay	1879:	*Essay on Addison*
	1880:	*Life of Johnson*
	1887:	*Essays on Milton and Dryden*
	1888:	*The Lays of Ancient Rome*
	1890:	*Essays on Lord Clive*
	1892:	*Second Essay on the Earl of Chatham*
Southey	1898:	*Life of Nelson*
DeQuincey	1898:	*The Flight of a Tartar Tribe*
Cooper	1899:	*The Last of the Mohicans*
Addison	1879:	*Sir Roger de Coverley Papers*
Gray	1880:	*An Elegy Written in a Country Churchyard*
Johnson	1880:	*Six Chief Lives of the Poets*
	1887:	*Lives of Milton and Addison*
	1888:	*Lives of Addison and Pope*
	1889:	*Lives of Swift and Gray*
Dickens	1880:	*A Tale of Two Cities*
	1893:	*David Copperfield*
Carlyle	1880:	*Essay on Johnson*
	1882:	*Essay on Scott*
	1884:	*Essay on Burns*
Milton	1881:	*Paradise Lost* (Books I and II)
	1895:	*L'Allegro*
		Il Penseroso
		Comus
		Lycidas
Hawthorne	1881:	*Our Old Home*
	1890:	*The House of the Seven Gables*
	1897:	*Twice-Told Tales*
Eliot	1881:	*Silas Marner*
	1882:	*The Mill on the Floss*
	1892:	*Scenes of Clerical Life*
Burns	1884:	*The Cotter's Saturday Night*
Emerson	1885:	*Essay on Eloquence*
	1893:	*The American Scholar*
Pope	1886:	*The Rape of the Lock*
	1888:	*An Essay on Criticism*
	1898:	*Iliad* (Books I and XXII)
Lowell	1886:	*The Vision of Sir Launfal*

Dryden	1887:	*Alexander's Feast*
	1899:	*Palamon and Arcite*
Dobson	1888:	*Eighteenth Century Essays*
Austen	1888:	*Pride and Prejudice*
Swift	1889:	*Gulliver's Travels*
Coleridge	1890:	*The Rime of the Ancient Mariner*
Longfellow	1890:	*Evangeline*
	1892:	*The Courtship of Miles Standish*
Webster	1890:	*First Bunker Hill Oration*
Arnold	1894:	*Sohrab and Rustum*
Defoe	1896:	*A Journal of the Plague Year*
Burke	1897:	*Speech on Conciliation with the Colonies*
Tennyson	1898:	*The Princess*

Appendix IV: Most Frequently Anthologized Works, 1917-1957

Twenty most popular selections in each period, ranked by order of frequency.*

1917-34

Childe Harold's Pilgrimage (excerpts)	Byron
The Princess (excerpts)	Tennyson
Home Thoughts, from Abroad	Browning
In Memoriam (excerpts)	Tennyson
The Vision of Sir Launfal	Lowell
History of England (excerpts)	Macaulay
Walden (excerpts)	Thoreau
Idylls of the King (excerpts)	Tennyson
How They Brought the Good News from Ghent to Aix	Browning
To a Waterfowl	Bryant
The Rime of the Ancient Mariner	Coleridge
Each and All	Emerson
The Last Leaf	Holmes
The Chambered Nautilus	Holmes
The Autocrat of the Breakfast Table (excerpts)	Holmes
Gettysburg Address	Lincoln
Annabel Lee	Poe
The World Is Too Much With Us	Wordsworth
Sohrab and Rustum	Arnold
Life of Johnson (excerpts)	Boswell

1935-45

The Princess (excerpts)	Tennyson
Autobiography (excerpts)	Franklin
Idylls of the King (excerpts)	Tennyson
Walden (excerpts)	Thoreau
Invictus	Henley
Ode on a Grecian Urn	Keats
Annabel Lee	Poe
Beowulf (excerpts)	Anon.
On His Blindness	Milton

*Excerpted from Tables VIII, IX, and X, James Warren Olson, *The Nature of Literature Anthologies Used in the Teaching of High School English 1917-1957* (Dissertation, University of Wisconsin, 1969; University Microfilm No. 69-22,454), pp. 316-18.

Home Thoughts, from Abroad	Browning
The Rime of the Ancient Mariner	Coleridge
Life of Johnson (excerpts)	Boswell
Kubla Khan	Coleridge
Ode to the West Wind	Shelley
Diary (excerpts)	Pepys
Il Penseroso	Milton
L'Allegro	Milton
The Man with the Hoe	Markham
History of England (excerpts)	Macaulay
On First Looking into Chapman's Homer	Keats

1946-57

She Dwelt among Untrodden Ways	Wordsworth
The People, Yes (excerpts)	Sandburg
Walden (excerpts)	Thoreau
Home Thoughts, from Abroad	Browning
The Soldier	Brooke
My Last Duchess	Browning
Autobiography (excerpts)	Franklin
An Elegy Written in a Country Churchyard	Gray
Loveliest of Trees	Houseman
Annabel Lee	Poe
Macbeth	Shakespeare
In Memoriam (excerpts)	Tennyson
The Princess (excerpts)	Tennyson
Mending Wall	Frost
To the Virgins, to Make Much of Time	Herrick
Speech in the Virginia Convention	Henry
On First Looking into Chapman's Homer	Keats
I Hear America Singing	Whitman
To a Waterfowl	Bryant
John Anderson, My Jo	Burns

Appendix V: The Growth of English, 1900-1949

Year	Number of High School Students	Percent of Students Enrolled in* English	Latin
1900	519,251	38.5	50.6
1910	739,143	57.1	49.0
1915	1,165,495	58.4	37.3
1922	2,155,460	76.7	27.5
1928	2,896,630	93.1	22.0
1934	4,496,514	90.5	16.0
1949	5,399,452	92.9	7.8

*Estimates and percentages based on enrollments in the four senior high school years. The data derive from surveys carried out for the U.S. Commissioner of Education; summarized in Bureau of the Census, *Historical Statistics of the United States* (Washington, D.C.: Government Printing Office, 1960), p. 210.

Appendix VI: Major Officers of the National Council of Teachers of English, 1912-1974

NCTE Presidents

Year	Name	Affiliation While Holding Office
1912	Fred Newton Scott	University of Michigan
1913	Fred Newton Scott	University of Michigan
1914	Franklin T. Baker	Teachers College Columbia University
1915	E. H. Kemper McComb	Manual Training High School Indianapolis, Indiana
1916	Edwin M. Hopkins	University of Kansas
1917	Allan Abbott	Teachers College Columbia University
1918	Edwin L. Miller	Northwestern High School Detroit, Michigan
1919	Joseph M. Thomas	University of Minnesota
1920	James Fleming Hosic	Chicago Normal College
1921	H. G. Paul	University of Illinois
1922	Charles Robert Gaston	Richmond Hill High School New York City
1923	J. W. Searson	University of Nebraska
1924	Thomas C. Blaisdell	Slippery Rock State Normal College, Pennsylvania
1925	T. W. Gosling	Madison Public Schools Wisconsin
1926	Sterling Andrus Leonard	University of Wisconsin
1927	Dudley Miles	Evander Childs High School New York City
1928	Charles Carpenter Fries	University of Michigan
1929	Rewey Belle Inglis	University of Minnesota
1930	Ruth Mary Weeks	Paseo High School Kansas City, Missouri
1931	R. L. Lyman	University of Chicago

1932	Stella S. Center	John Adams High School New York City
1933	Walter Barnes	New York University
1934	Oscar J. Campbell	University of Michigan
1935	Charles Swain Thomas	Harvard University
1936	Dora V. Smith	University of Minnesota
1937	Holland D. Roberts	Stanford University
1938	Marquis E. Shattuck	Detroit Public Schools
1939	Essie Chamberlain	Oak Park High School, Illinois
1940	E. A. Cross	Colorado State College of Education Greeley
1941	Robert C. Pooley	University of Wisconsin
1942	John J. DeBoer	Chicago Teachers College
1943	Max J. Herzberg	Weequahic High School, Newark, New Jersey
1944	Angela M. Broening	Baltimore Public Schools
1945	Harold A. Anderson	University of Chicago
1946	Helene W. Hartley	Syracuse University
1947	Porter G. Perrin	University of Washington
1948	Thomas Clark Pollock	New York University
1949	Marion C. Sheridan	New Haven High School Connecticut
1950	Mark Neville	John Burroughs School St. Louis, Missouri
1951	Paul Farmer	Henry W. Grady High School Atlanta, Georgia
1952	Lennox Grey	Teachers College Columbia University
1953	Harlen M. Adams	Chicago State College
1954	Lou L. LaBrant	Atlanta University
1955	John C. Gerber	State University of Iowa Iowa City
1956	Luella B. Cook	Minneapolis Public Schools
1957	Helen K. Mackintosh	U.S. Office of Education
1958	Brice Harris	Pennsylvania State University University Park
1959	Joseph Mersand	Jamaica High School Jamaica, New York
1960	Ruth G. Strickland	School of Education Indiana University

1961	Harold B. Allen	University of Minnesota Minneapolis
1962	George Robert Carlsen	State University of Iowa Iowa City
1963	David H. Russell	University of California
1964	Albert R. Kitzhaber	University of Oregon
1965	Richard Corbin	Hunter College High School New York City
1966	Muriel Crosby	Wilmington Public Schools Delaware
1967	Albert H. Marckwardt	Princeton University
1968	Alfred H. Grommon	Stanford University
1969	William A. Jenkins	University of Wisconsin—Milwaukee
1970	James E. Miller, Jr.	University of Chicago
1971	Robert A. Bennett	San Diego Unified School District
1972	Virginia M. Reid	Oakland Public Schools
1973	Walker Gibson	University of Massachusetts
1974	Margaret J. Early	Syracuse University

NCTE Secretary-Treasurer

1912-1919	James Fleming Hosic	Chicago Normal College
1920-1953	W. Wilbur Hatfield	Chicago Normal College

NCTE Executive Secretary

1954-1959	J. N. Hook
1960-1967	James R. Squire
1968-	Robert F. Hogan

Editor of English Journal

1912-1921	James Fleming Hosic	Chicago Normal College
1922-1955	W. Wilbur Hatfield	Chicago Normal College
1956-1964	Dwight E. Burton	Florida State University
1965-1973	Richard S. Alm	University of Hawaii
1973-	Stephen N. Judy	Michigan State University

Index

284